Cloud Architecture and Engineering

Cloud Architecture and Engineering

Edited by **Conor Suarez**

New York

Published by Willford Press,
118-35 Queens Blvd., Suite 400,
Forest Hills, NY 11375, USA
www.willfordpress.com

Cloud Architecture and Engineering
Edited by Conor Suarez

International Standard Book Number: 978-1-68285-099-2 (Hardback)

The publisher's policy is to use permanent paper from mills that operate a sustainable forestry policy. Furthermore, the publisher ensures that the text paper and cover boards used have met acceptable environmental accreditation standards.

Printed in the United States of America.

Contents

Preface

Over the recent decade, advancements and applications have progressed exponentially. This has led to the increased interest in this field and projects are being conducted to enhance knowledge. The main objective of this book is to present some of the critical challenges and provide insights into possible solutions. This book will answer the varied questions that arise in the field and also provide an increased scope for furthering studies.

This book provides a comprehensive overview of the emerging field of cloud architecture and engineering. The chapters included herein are an assimilation of concepts such as cloud storage, framework and algorithms for cloud structures, cloud database systems, etc. It attempts to understand the multiple branches that fall under this discipline as well as elucidate the prominent concepts and applications of cloud computing. The aim of this book is to serve as a resource guide for students and experts alike and contribute to the growth of the field.

I hope that this book, with its visionary approach, will be a valuable addition and will promote interest among readers. Each of the authors has provided their extraordinary competence in their specific fields by providing different perspectives as they come from diverse nations and regions. I thank them for their contributions.

Editor

Flood modelling for cities using Cloud computing

Vassilis Glenis[1], Andrew Stephen McGough[2]*, Vedrana Kutija[1], Chris Kilsby[1] and Simon Woodman[2]

Abstract

Urban flood risk modelling is a highly topical example of intensive computational processing. Such processing is increasingly required by a range of organisations including local government, engineering consultancies and the insurance industry to fulfil statutory requirements and provide professional services. As the demands for this type of work become more common, then ownership of high-end computational resources is warranted but if use is more sporadic and with tight deadlines then the use of Cloud computing could provide a cost-effective alternative. However, uptake of the Cloud by such organisations is often thwarted by the perceived technical barriers to entry. In this paper we present an architecture that helps to simplify the process of performing parameter sweep work on an Infrastructure as a Service Cloud. A parameter sweep version of the urban flood modelling, analysis and visualisation software "CityCat" was developed and deployed to estimate spatial and temporal flood risk at a whole city scale – far larger than had previously been possible. Performing this work on the Cloud allowed us access to more computing power than we would have been able to purchase locally for such a short time-frame (~21 months of processing in a single calendar month). We go further to illustrate the considerations, both functional and non-functional, which need to be addressed if such an endeavour is to be successfully achieved.

Keywords: Cloud computing, Task execution, Flood modelling, Parameter sweep execution

Introduction

We are now able to collect vast quantities of data about the physical world but this has little significance until we are able to process it, through analysis or simulation, to extract understanding and meaning. The so called fourth paradigm [1] of data-intensive discovery often requires significant computational power. All sectors of society (commercial, public and academic) have a need to exploit this new approach.

For large organisations (companies, governments or large research projects) access to appropriate levels of computational resources is easily within their reach. However, for smaller organisations this can often be beyond their means – especially if the organisation is not expecting to make significant use of the resources. Traditionally these organisations have relied on access to shared resources managed by others or making do with the resources available – which may preclude them from

meeting tight deadlines or require them to make compromises in order to achieve these deadlines. These compromises may be through reduced complexity models (simpler or less realistic) or the processing of smaller data sets than desired.

The problem outlined above is no more prevalent than in cases where an organisation is required to complete a task within pre-defined budget and time-limit constraints. The use of the Cloud [2] offers a potential solution by allowing the organisation to gain access to vast quantities of computing power almost instantaneously, often far greater quantities of computing power than the budget would allow them to purchase and use within the defined time-constraints and without the associated lead-time required to acquire and install resources. The use of the Cloud does, however, lead to a situation where after completion of the task the organisation lacks any collateral which could be used for future tasks. However, if such task requirements are rare these extra resources would have little if any value for the organisation. Thus the choice to use the Cloud or not rests on an analysis of the cost-time benefits of performing the work on the Cloud as

*Correspondence: stephen.mcgough@newcastle.ac.uk
[2]School of Computing Science, Newcastle University, Newcastle upon Tyne, UK
Full list of author information is available at the end of the article

opposed to a comparison with upfront purchasing of the appropriate hardware resource(s).

The Cloud allows scaling of resource to meet current needs with payment being only for the time that the organisation 'rents' the resources. This allows organisations access to a wide variety of computational resource types either not normally available to them or which would not gain enough utilisation to warrant purchasing.

Many organisations are required to run the same software (often developed by themselves or adapted to their own needs) multiple times with different starting conditions in order to determine characteristics about a problem space or identify an "optimal" solution. This process, referred to as parameter sweep, can be performed in parallel over a large number of computers and would seem to match nicely with the Cloud model of (apparently) infinite resources available on demand. If the same software is required by many different users then the process of performing the parameter sweep and this software can be made available to the end user in a Software as a Service (SaaS) manner in which the user interacts with the Cloud through an external interface with all work being performed for them. However, if the user wishes to run his/her own software then such a SaaS offering could be too restrictive. Instead tooling could be provided to an Infrastructure as a Service (IaaS) simplifying the process of performing parameter sweep executions. However, adding an external user interface to these tools would allow them to be exposed as a SaaS.

Once a decision is made to run large parameter sweeps on the Cloud, then the development of a parameter sweep-ready task is needed. This often requires making the jobs which make up the task parameter sweep-ready-removing the need to interact directly with each job thus allowing many jobs to be invoked quickly, and providing the correct environment in which to run the job [3]. Tasks then need to be enacted on the Cloud-provisioning appropriate resources on the Cloud, uploading of executables to the Cloud along with any associated dependencies and data, the execution of the jobs and finally the staging of data back to the organisation. This process is clearly nontrivial to perform and not unique to the Cloud–similar problems exist in Grid and other distributed computing environments.

Although the financial barrier to using the Cloud is (relatively) low, the technical aspect of actually using the Cloud is still a barrier to entry. Many organisations lack the technical expertise to deploy work to the Cloud and make efficient use of it, reducing uptake. Also if digital technologies are not the core activities of the organisation neither should we expect them to be proficient in using Cloud infrastructure.

In this paper we propose a generic architecture which automates many of the stages in using the Cloud for parameter sweep based batch-processing type problems, thus reducing the barrier to entry for organisations. We exemplify the use of this architecture for an application in pluvial flood risk assessment using the CityCat flood modelling simulation tool to identify areas of high flood risk during rare-event storms (once every one to 200 years). We further exemplify the cost-time implications by having a limited budget of £20,000 (~$32,500) and a project deadline of one month. Assessing both the perceived 'best' Cloud provider to use a priori along with an assessment of the performance achieved from running these simulations. We present preliminary results for the Pluvial flood modelling before considering the non-functional issues encountered during this work.

Background and related work
Flood risk assessment using CityCat

Pluvial flood risk analysis, where intense direct rainfall overwhelms urban drainage systems, is complex and time-consuming as it is sensitive to the spatial-temporal characteristics of rainfall, topography of the terrain and surface flow processes influenced by buildings and other man-made features. Assessment of urban flood risk is based on the results of flood models which provide the depth and velocity of surface water generated by intense rainfall. Surface water flow is well described by the two dimensional, depth averaged, hydrodynamic shallow water equations which are partial differential equations of time dependent conservation of mass and momentum [4]. These equations can only be solved using a numerical method which requires discretisation of the domain into small cells and discretisation of the period of simulation into small time steps.

The method of finite volumes with higher order accurate shock capturing schemes provides the most accurate solution for propagation of flood wave over initially dry surfaces and for flows with discontinuities [5]. However, it requires significant computation at each cell at each time step. Additionally, in order to ensure stability of the numerical solution, adaptive time steps based on the Courant-Friedrichs-Lewy (CFL) condition are used [6]. This results in variable time steps ranging from 0.01 s to 10 s due to the size of the cells and the changeable flow conditions. Smaller time steps increase the execution time of the simulation. Therefore accurate and stable solutions require the modelling of large domains at high resolution. This leads to high memory requirements (~40GB) and execution times (~weeks). However, a meaningful flood risk assessment requires modelling of multiple rainfall events, covering different durations and probabilities of occurrence. This increases significantly the computational requirements and it becomes exacerbated when future climate scenarios are considered.

Due to these computational complexities the assessment of pluvial flood risk is usually carried out at relatively small scales using a restricted number of design storms [7]. Alternatively, for large city-scale assessments, simplified models are used [8]. The use of fully detailed numerical models for larger areas is in its infancy for two reasons. Firstly, most of the models in this field are compiled as 32-bit applications and this limits the addressable memory and constrains the size of the computational domain. Secondly, detailed modelling of larger areas results in high computational requirements which are best resolved using High Performance Computing (HPC) or cluster based facilities. However, such facilities might not be easily accessible to water consulting and engineering companies and local authorities that have to carry out flood risk assessment studies.

Cloud for computationally intense applications

Using the Cloud for computationally intense tasks has been seen in recent years as a convenient way to process data quickly. Deelman [9] evaluated the cost of using Amazon's Elastic Compute Cloud (EC2) [10] and Amazon's Simple Storage Service (S3) [11] to service the requirements of a single scientific application. Here we add the constraints of memory dominant executions under fixed time limits.

De Assuncao [12] proposed the use of Cloud computing to extend existing clusters to deal with unexpectedly high load – greater than that which can be handled locally. This work was further extended by Mattess [13] by proposing the use of Amazon spot instances, supply-and-demand driven pricing of instances, to further reduce the cost of Cloud Bursting. Our approach differs to these in that we seek to optimise the execution of a single set of simulations rather than the general capacity of an organisation. However, we see that the use of spot instances could be a mechanism to increase the number of hours available for a given budget.

Palankar [14] showed the criticality of data locality in the Cloud. In our work we take into account the effects of uploading and downloading data from the Cloud by making use of Cloud storage facilities such as S3. This minimises external data transfers and allows instances to terminate sooner.

Evangelinos [15] evaluated the use of Cloud resources for running High Performance Computing applications, showing a decrease in performance in comparison with dedicated supercomputing facilities and more akin to low-cost clusters. However, as our application is processing parameter sweeps of jobs in a batch-processing manner (often referred to as High Throughput Computing) we do not expect to see the same degradation in performance.

Lu [16] presents an application for processing gene sequences on the Cloud. Although this work is similar, in batch-processing, to our own we present a more generic architecture.

Cloud execution architecture

Staff in many organisations do not possess the skills to perform parameter sweep executions on the Cloud – starting up Cloud instances, deploying and managing jobs on these instances along with transferring data to and from the Cloud. Nor should they be expected to perform such tasks-especially if their need to use the Cloud is intermittent and not part of their main function. In this section we present an architecture which abstracts the user away from the complexities of using the Cloud to perform parameter sweep executions presenting them instead with a command line interface that captures the information required to run these executions on the Cloud.

Figure 1 shows the architecture for our system which interacts with an Infrastructure as a Service Cloud offering. The user interacts with the system through the user interface – currently this is a command line interface though this could easily be replaced by a GUI or web portal. The user interface sends information to the Cloud Enactor which is responsible for deploying new cloud instances when required and terminating those that are no longer required. The Cloud enactor is also responsible for simple task deployment to the Cloud (starting a task off on a Cloud instance) along with monitoring these running tasks. We exploit the load-balancing facilities of existing batch queuing technologies such as HTCondor [17] in the situation where the number of Cloud instances is less than the number of parameter sweep jobs we wish to perform. DeltaCloud [18] is used to abstract us away from the underlying Cloud infrastructure allowing our architecture to run over multiple Clouds.

The user interface collects information about the maximum number of instances to use and the location of a compressed file containing the executable (or script to run) including any settings, dependencies or data required by the executable [3], other compressed files (which are assumed to be further data used by the executable), the number of runs which are to be processed, along with the name of the executable.

The first compressed archive is inspected to see if the named executable appears within the root directory of the archive. In such cases it is assumed that the particular parameter sweep task is enacted by the cloud enactor passing an index value when invoking the executable. Otherwise it is assumed that there will be n sub-directories within the archive each containing a copy of the executable. Where n is the number of runs to perform. It should be noted that these directories need not contain the actual executable but may contain a script that calls a single executable stored in a different location.

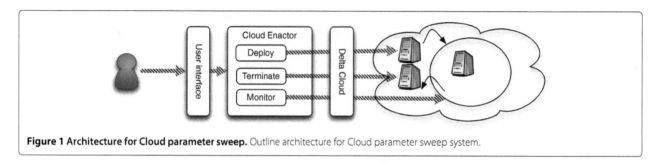

Figure 1 Architecture for Cloud parameter sweep. Outline architecture for Cloud parameter sweep system.

Cloud interaction is handled through the Cloud enactor module. The archives are first uploaded to the Cloud data store (such as Amazon S3 [11]) before Cloud instances are deployed. Once deployed the Cloud enactor gives each instance the locations of the archive(s) in Cloud storage. The instance can then download and decompress these before executing them. The system provides two execution models. If the maximum number of Cloud instances is smaller than the number of parameter sweep jobs then the tasks will be deployed through a HTCondor [17] cluster, provisioned by the Cloud enactor, formed from the deployed instances. We use HTCondor here as our own deployment mechanism does not support load-balancing of work across resources. However, if the number of Cloud instances matches the parameter sweep count then the jobs will just be deployed on the Cloud instances. This removes the overheads of deploying and using HTCondor on the Cloud just to execute a single job per instance.

Once a task has completed then the files which remain will be compressed before uploading to the Cloud storage. Due to data transfer costs the application developer is encouraged to delete any superfluous files as part of his/her executable (or script) before the job terminates.

Once all tasks are completed on a given instance then the instance will be terminated. All result data are uploaded to the user's own storage space on the Cloud for later retrieval through the (command line) interface.

Parameter sweep enabling the CityCat application

"CityCat" is an urban flood modelling, analysis and visualisation tool. It is based on the solution of the shallow water equations using the method of finite volume with shock-capturing schemes. Originally, CityCat was developed and compiled as a 32-bit application using Borland Delphi [19], under the Windows operating system with an integrated Graphical User Interface (GUI) for data preparation and visualisation of results. Figure 2 shows the

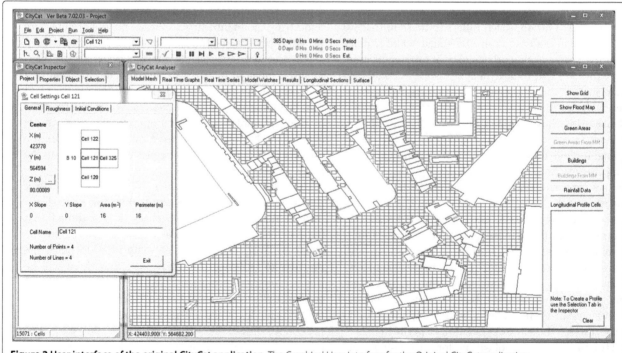

Figure 2 User interface of the original CityCat application. The Graphical User Interface for the Original CityCat application.

original GUI. Note that, as well as dividing the landscape up into a regular grid of cells, buildings are 'stamped' out of this grid. However, this configuration of CityCat is not easily usable in a parameter sweep consisting of many invocations as it requires the interaction of the user through the GUI in each invocation. In order to overcome this limitation a new version was developed by separating the computational engine from the GUI. The computational engine can be controlled through the use of configuration scripts which contain the initial parameters and the input/output file names.

The maximum addressable memory of 4GB for the 32-bit CityCat application limited the number of computational cells to less than one million. To overcome this limitation a 64-bit version of the application was developed and this enabled simulations of much larger domains using the high memory instances on the Cloud.

Deployment of a Windows application on the Cloud requires the installation of the Windows OS at each Cloud instance and this incurs additional costs. In order to avoid unnecessary expenditure and allow for 64-bit compilation (increasing the size of models that could be run), the model was ported and compiled under Linux using the Lazarus Linux IDE [20] and the Free Pascal compiler [21]. This had an impact on the performance of the code, increasing the execution time by approximately 10% – assumed to be a consequence of moving from 32-bit to 64-bit code and the Free Pascal compiler not optimising the code as well as the Delphi compiler. However, as the saving in cost for using Linux based instances was at least 20% this increase in execution time was considered acceptable as it was felt that the increase in the number of instances which could be run offset the increased execution time.

Scientific experimental environment

We have been able to apply the computational engine of CityCat to much larger domains and for more extensive event durations (through the ability to run multiple long-running simulations on the Cloud). Three different domains, ranging in size from one million to 16 million cells were tested, much larger than the domains used in current engineering practice – normally of the order of 5,000 to 50,000 cells. Additionally, for one of the domains, four different grid sizes were used which resulted in very different model sizes. Table 1 shows the different areas used within this work. All of the pluvial flood models were then run using a set of 36 rainfall events, containing a combination of six different return periods and six different storm durations. See Table 2 for the storm details. Rainfall events were generated following the standard FEH procedure [22]. All these simulations required different memory and computational effort leading to differing run times. Table 3 presents the system requirements, in terms of memory, for these simulations. Note that the

index for these simulations (column 1) matches with the index (column 1) of Table 1.

Cost-time analysis for the CityCat simulations

Here we investigate the cost-time analysis of using different Cloud options along with the relative cost for performing the same work on locally provisioned resources. The CityCat application is a single threaded simulation model which is memory dominant – we use the memory requirements which were presented in Table 3.

As it is not possible to tell a priori the exact amount of time that these simulations will take to perform we instead define two metrics by which to compare the cost of using each offering: cost per simulation hour and maximum number of hours available within a single month. The cost per simulation hour for Cloud offerings is computed as p/c where p is defined as the unit cost per hour, for the Cloud instance, and c is the number of concurrent runs of CityCat that the instance can handle without each run affecting the others. For locally provisioned resources we can define the cost per unit hour as $p = E/M$, where E is the cost of purchasing the resource and M is the number of hours during which the work we are conducting must be completed – in our case one month. We appreciate that this artificially gives higher values for purchasing resources locally and hence do not use this as justification for using Cloud resources over local resources, only including it here for comparison.

Although (in theory) the number of Cloud hours available per month is infinite there are practical limitations on this, cost and vendor capping being the most significant. Each vendor provides a capping limit on the maximum number of instances which can be running concurrently – Amazon for example limits this to 20 per region – though this limit can be overcome through prior arrangement with the vendor. We therefore provide a figure for the number of hours available as $c \times i \times h$, where c is the number of concurrent runs of CityCat on the resource, i is the number of resources that can be run (the lower of 36 or the maximum number of resources which keeps us within budget) and h is the number of hours per month. The same equation is used for locally provisioned resources with i limited to the number of resources which can be purchased.

Note that a selection of Cloud providers have been evaluated here, though not all. All evaluations were conducted in November 2011. Note that although each offering will exhibit different run-times – a consequence of variations in processor speed and memory bandwidth – these considerations are not being taken into account here as we expect these to be marginal. We present below only the cost-time analysis for the small data problem (simulation sets 1 and 4) – i.e. 3GB memory requirement, and the very

Table 1 The different areas and scales used for the simulations

	Domain	Area	Cell size	Boundary conditions	Event duration	Number of runs
1	Newcastle city centre	4 km²	2 m	Rainfall events 1-36	See rainfall events	36
2	Newcastle city centre	4 km²	1 m	Rainfall events 1-36	See rainfall events	36
3	Newcastle city centre	4 km²	0.5 m	Rainfall events 1-36	See rainfall events	36
4	Newcastle city centre	4 km²	2 m	Hypothetical flood wave	2 hrs	1
5	Whole Newcastle City Council area	120 km²	4 m	Rainfall events 1-36	See rainfall events	36
6	Thames estuary	~1100 km²	15 m	Tidal surge water level	33 hrs and 21 hrs	2

large data problem (simulation set 3) – 40GB memory requirement.

Locally provisioned resources

A large server machine purchased by the School of Computing in November 2011 cost ∼ £3,182 (∼$5,142), this had 12 CPUs and 128GB RAM. Table 4 shows the cost-time analysis for this resource. Given our initial budget we could have purchased six such servers. Note that the cost of installing managing and energy for these servers is not factored in here. We assume that the remaining money would cover these costs. We also do not factor in the time for delivery and commissioning of such systems – which would often take longer than our one month deadline – and appreciate that this cannot be fairly compared with

the Cloud. Hence, we do not use this as a justification for or against the use of the Cloud, rather just a comparison of the cost for performing work on locally provisioned resources.

Amazon EC2 instances

Amazon Elastic Cloud Compute (EC2) [10] offers computational power as an Infrastructure as a Service (IaaS). Amazon has a large range of computational offerings. Table 5 shows the cost-time analysis for EC2 for the 3GB simulation runs and Table 6 for the 40GB simulation runs. Note that in all cases only resource types capable of running the simulation are provided. Also note that the number of concurrent instances of the software is computed from the number of concurrent runs which can fit

Table 2 Frequency and duration of the different rainfall events

Rainfall event	Return period years	Duration mins	Rainfall event	Return period years	Duration mins	Rainfall event	Return period years	Duration mins
1	2	15	13	20	15	25	100	15
2	2	30	14	20	30	26	100	30
3	2	60	15	20	60	27	100	60
4	2	120	16	20	120	28	100	120
5	2	180	17	20	180	29	100	180
6	2	360	18	20	360	30	100	360
7	10	15	19	50	15	31	200	15
8	10	30	20	50	30	32	200	30
9	10	60	21	50	60	33	200	60
10	10	120	22	50	120	34	200	120
11	10	180	23	50	180	35	200	180
12	10	360	24	50	360	36	200	360

Table 3 Computational requirements (size and memory) for the six simulation areas

	Number of cells	Cell size	Required memory
1	1,000,000	2 m	3 GB
2	4,000,000	1 m	11 GB
3	16,000,000	0.5 m	40 GB
4	1,000,000	2 m	3 GB
5	7,500,000	4 m	20 GB
6	~5,000,000	15 m	13 GB

into memory at the same time. As the code was unable to exploit more than one core the processor load was not considered.

In the case for the small simulation runs (3 GB) the Quad XL and Double XL instances show the best cost-time values. Thus going for the larger instances and running multiple simulations concurrently would appear to give better cost-time performance. Only one resource type is capable of running the large (40 GB) jobs–Quad XL.

Microsoft Azure instances

Microsoft Azure [23] offers a Platform as a Service (PaaS) option on which users are given a modified Windows 2008 server instance. At the time of analysis Azure was unable to offer instances capable of running the 40GB simulation. Table 7 shows the cost-time analysis for the Azure instance types running the 3 GB jobs.

Azure provides a very level offering in which the simulation cost per hour is the same for all instance types along with the number of hours which could be used within a month.

GoGrid instances

GoGrid [24] offers IaaS instances in which each offering is effectively double, in core count, memory and disk space, the previous instance. GoGrid had instance types which support the 3 GB simulation jobs and the cost-time analysis is presented in Table 8.

GoGrid provides a slight advantage for their largest instance type (16/16/800) though this is more due to the ability to pack simulations more efficiently into memory than due to their costing model.

Table 4 Cost-time analysis for locally provisioned resources

Simulation memory	Cost per simulation hour	Max hours
3GB	$0.576	53,568
40GB	$2.304	13,392

RackSpace instances

RackSpace [25] is a UK based IaaS provider. It offers only one instance type suitable for the 3GB simulation runs – see Table 9. Being UK-based could be beneficial if restrictions require that work is performed within the UK although that was not a constraint in this case.

Summary

If we were to just take the raw cost for performing the work on the Cloud into account this would seem to make a compelling reason for choosing this option, with most providers managing to undercut the localy purchased hourly cost. However, if we factor in the ownership of the resources and the fact that they could be re-used for future projects the story is not so clear. Given a three year life-expectancy for a server this would require six months' worth of use over the three year life for the 3 GB simulation jobs to be more cost-effective on the local resources than even the best Cloud offering whilst only around 1.15 months of the 40 GB simulations would be required over this time scale.

The biggest advantage in using the Cloud, however, comes from the number of hours of compute time which can be obtained within the one month available, providing up to 563% more hours for the 3GB simulations and 20% for the 40 GB simulations. When you factor in the number of simulations that can be provisioned concurrently (40 large (40 GB) simulations on Amazon EC2 as opposed to 18 large simulations on local resources) and the time to provision the resources (within minutes for the Cloud as opposed to the purchasing, delivery, installation, and configuration cycle for local resources) this makes the Cloud more appealing. The Cloud hours can be consumed within 16 days as opposed to the full 31 days for the locally provisioned resources.

Cloud simulation results

We present here the results from running the City-Cat computational engine on the Cloud. The simulations were all performed between the 20th November 2011 and the 20th December 2011. All Cloud costs are based on those in force at that time. For computation resources these have been presented in Section 'Amazon EC2 instances', whilst for data transfer ingress was free and egress was $0.12 per GB. It should be noted that the cost for using the Cloud changes. In general the cost for using the Cloud has come down since these simulations were run which would allow for more work to be performed. To aid readers, the number of hours of computation and data egress volumes are presented allowing the cost to be recomputed based on the current charging model.

Table 5 Cost-time analysis for 3GB simulations on EC2

Name	Cores	Memory	Concurrent	Unit Cost	Hours	Cost per simulation hour
Large	4	7.5	2	$0.34	190,000	$0.17
Extra Large	8	15	4	$0.68	190,000	$0.17
High Memory XL	6.5	17.1	5	$0.50	323,000	$0.10
Double XL	13	34.2	11	$1.00	355,300	$0.091
Quad XL	26	68.4	22	$2.00	355,300	$0.091
High CPU XL	20	7	2	$0.68	95,000	$0.34
Cluster Compute	33.5	23	7	$1.60	141,312	$0.229

Newcastle city centre – simulation set 1

For these simulations an estimated runtime of 30 minutes to one hour was predicted. Four large Cloud instances were used (m1.large on Amazon), each with 7GB of RAM and four compute units. Although each resource was capable of running two CityCat simulations concurrently only one was run per Cloud instance. As the problem size was relatively small it was decided to run this as a parameter sweep using fewer resources than the number of simulation runs. Thus HTCondor was used to perform job coordination. Figure 3 shows the execution timelines of the 36 simulations where each horizontal line represents the execution of a single simulation on Cloud computers C1 to C4. All Cloud computers were started between 08:50 and 09:30 and terminated by C1 – 06:30, C2 – 06:00 and C3 – 07:00 the following morning. Note that Computer C4 was terminated manually at 18:20 to determine if the system could cope with such a loss. This represents some 76 hours of Cloud chargeable time at a total of $25.84 – large instances were $0.34 per hour in December 2011.

The total amount of simulation run-time for this was 29 hours and 21 minutes, giving an effective charge of $0.88 per hour of simulation. It should be noted that this does not take into account the time for transferring data files to and from the Cloud instances.

Data ingress to the Cloud was free whilst egress was charged at $0.12 per GB over the first GB. As the compressed data egress was 11GB this incurred a charge of $1.20 for data transfer.

Newcastle city centre – simulation set 2

Figure 4 shows the execution timelines for the Newcastle City Centre simulations – simulation set 2. The Amazon Quad XL instances used for this simulation set were

capable of running six simulations per instance, requiring a total of six instances. Simulations were allocated to instances in order – hence simulations 1 to 6 were run on instance 1. Note that simulation 36 was started manually later as there was a bug in the original code which failed to launch it.

The total simulation time for all 36 runs was 4,589 hours and four minutes. However, due to the order in which simulations were allocated to instances the longest of each set of six jobs kept the instance alive even though the other simulations had finished. Thus the number of Cloud instance hours was 2,361 costing a total of $4,722. This equates to a real simulation cost per hour of $1.03. If jobs had been grouped by expected execution time then this could have brought the execution time down substantially. Manually re-ordering the jobs would bring the number of cloud hours down to 906 and the cost per simulation hour down to $0.395.

Data egress for this simulation set was 10GB resulting in a charge of $1.08. Note that all simulation sets apart from set 1 required downloading of their data during December. The one free GB of data transfer has been arbitrarily discounted from this set.

Newcastle city centre – simulation set 3

These simulations each required 40GB of RAM and were run individually on Amazon Quad XL instances. Figure 5 shows the timelines for these simulation executions. Note that only simulations 1 to 4 of each set of six were executed as it was decided that the runtime for simulations 5 and 6 would take us beyond our month deadline. The red timelines indicate those simulations which failed to complete before the month deadline was reached. These simulations were manually terminated, although the results up till the point of termination are still valid.

Table 6 Cost-time analysis for 40GB simulations on EC2

Name	Cores	Memory	Concurrent	Unit cost	Hours	Cost per simulation hour
Quad XL	26	68.4	1	$2.00	16,150	$2.00

Table 7 Cost-time analysis for 3GB simulations on Azure

Name	Cores	Memory	Concurrent	Unit cost	Hours	Cost per simulation hour
Medium	2	3.5	1	$0.24	134,583	$0.24
Large	4	7	2	$0.48	134,583	$0.24
Extra Large	8	14	4	$0.96	134,583	$0.24

The simulations consumed a total of 6,856 hours and 50 minutes. However, with an average of three minutes to deploy the instance and decompress the files, along with an average of 30 minutes to compress the data and upload it to Cloud storage this brings the number of Cloud chargeable hours up to 6,929, costing $13,858. This equates to a real simulation cost per hour of $2.02. Thus the overhead for running this work on the Cloud is marginal. A total of 18GB of data egress was required for this simulation set at a cost of $2.16.

Newcastle city centre – simulation set 4

This single simulation was run on an Amazon High Memory XL instance taking 33 hours and 54 minutes. This consumed 35 hours of Cloud time at a cost of $17.50. The data transfer for this single job was just 195M – less than $0.12. This single run produced a cost per simulation hour of $0.51. However, an extra simulation of the 36 rain pattern from set 6 was also run on this computer, thus giving greater utilisation of the hardware.

Whole Newcastle city council area – simulation set 5

These simulations each required 20GB of RAM allowing three simulations per Amazon Quad XL instance. Figure 6 depicts the timelines for these simulations. Note that the blue timelines indicate runs which were restarted due to an error in the system. The total simulation time is 3,623 hours and 21 minutes. With additional time for Cloud initiation, file decompression, file re-compression and file transfer this brings the number of Cloud chargeable hours up to 2,212 costing $4,424, thus giving a real simulation cost per hour of $1.22. This value is roughly twice the expected value due to the late starting of some of the jobs and the arbitrary ordering of jobs. Re-ordering of these jobs could have brought the number of Cloud hours down to 1,413 ($2,826) and a simulation hour cost of $0.780. A total of 12GB of data egress was required for this simulation set at a cost of $1.44.

Thames estuary – simulation set 6

Only two 13GB simulations were run for this case, those for simulations 24 and 36. These simulations took a total of 322 hours and 42 minutes. This was achieved through a total of 162 chargeable Cloud hours totalling $324. This gives a real simulation cost per hour of $1.006 – very close to optimal. Data transfer of 4GB added an additional cost of $0.48.

Preliminary result of the CityCat simulations

We present preliminary results for two of the simulations presented in Section 'Scientific Experimental Environment'. The use of Cloud computing in performing these simulations has generated a large amount of output which now requires significant effort to process.

Newcastle city council area – simulation 5

The whole area of Newcastle City Council which covers approximately 120 km^2, depicted in Figure 7, was used to demonstrate that by using Cloud Computing and CityCat, organisations would be able to model areas of such scale for Surface Water Management Planning. Running the model at such a scale (cell count) allows more accurate predictions to be made. In urban catchments, water pathways are quite complex because they are influenced by the topography and man-made features. The conventional approach of detailed modelling of small domains is dangerous, however, because delineation of catchments can be difficult in complex and dynamic situations. Larger domains are therefore required to ensure inclusion of upstream sources which may not be obvious a priori.

Thames estuary – simulation 6

The largest domain we simulated was the Thames estuary with an area of approximately 1,100 km^2. In order to keep the cell count within bounds we used a cell size of 15 m – resulting in five million cells. The propagation of the tidal surge upstream along the Thames was modelled to see if CityCat could also be used in coastal and fluvial

Table 8 Cost-time analysis for 3GB simulations on GoGrid

Name	Cores	Memory	Concurrent	Unit cost	Hours	Cost per simulation hour
Server 4/4/200	4	4	1	$0.76	42,500	$0.76
Server 8/8/400	8	8	2	$1.52	42,500	$0.76
Server 16/16/800	16	16	5	$3.04	53,125	$0.608

Table 9 Cost-time analysis for 3GB simulations on RackSpace

Name	Cores	Memory	Concurrent	Unit cost	Hours	Cost per simulation hour
4096/160	1	4	1	$0.252	128,174	$0.252

flood risk studies. The boundary condition for this simulation was the tidal water level given as a function of time and placed at the east boundary of the domain. Figures 8 and 9 illustrate the Thames tidal surge at 27 and 31 hours after onset. The use of high-end Cloud instances allows us to model the effects of a tidal surge at an unprecedented level of detail and scale. This development could have significant impact on modelling of such phenomena around the world in the future.

Non-functional issues with Cloud deployment
Local alternatives
As discussed in the section 'Cost-time analysis for the CityCat simulations' the main benefits of using the Cloud come more from the rapid provisioning of resources to meet immediate deadlines rather than the cost-effectiveness of resources, especially over the whole lifetime of a resource. Large organisations, such as universities, are constantly looking at the long term benefit of the purchases they make. Hence, given the scenario where money is to be spent on a short-term benefit of Cloud computing as opposed to purchasing of local resources which could be used by others over a longer period of time the university naturally favours the latter.

However, given a situation where strict deadlines prevent the purchasing of enough resources in a timely enough manner to meet requirements, this long-term view can often be too restrictive. A careful balance needs to be drawn between short-term benefits and long-term goals. In an ideal environment all would favour the long-term goals and contribute their resources to a global pool allowing others to obtain their short-term requirements from this. However, if people instead favour the short-term benefits then none can benefit from the global pool. Persuading management that a short-term benefit is more important can often be a challenge and requires management to fully appreciate the need for rapid turn-around.

Credit cards
The (apparent) democratic process for access to Cloud resources is achieved by a credit card purchasing model. It is assumed that anyone in a position to purchase time on the cloud will be in possession of a credit card and that this is the Cloud providers' only requirement for any user. Although this simplifies the process – if you have money (or credit) then you can use the resources – it has knock-on effects when purchasing significant amounts of computational time on the Cloud. A credit limit of say $10,000 is easy enough to obtain, though a limit of $32,500 which was needed for this project was much harder to obtain.

This problem was compounded by the fact that many large institutional organisations, including Newcastle University, have tight regulations on credit card spends. These include not only low credit limits but also maximum values for individual purchases. Also as the exact cost of using the Cloud could not be determined a priori it was difficult to convince the finance department that this purchase was not going to spiral out of control.

Eventually a compromise was reached in which a lower credit limit could be used by splitting the Cloud usage over two billing periods along with tight monitoring of monies spent.

Conclusions
Cloud computing has enabled higher resolution larger scale modelling of pluvial flooding on a much larger scale than usually performed. Additionally, the use of the Cloud has provided access to enough resources to allow simultaneous simulations of different rainfall events required in studies of flood risk.

Results of the city-wide pluvial flood risk simulations for Newcastle upon Tyne obtained using Cloud computing show excellent correlation with the flooding observed during the recent pluvial flood event in Newcastle. On 28th June 2012, over a period of two hours, 45 mm of rain fell over the whole city. A more detailed verification

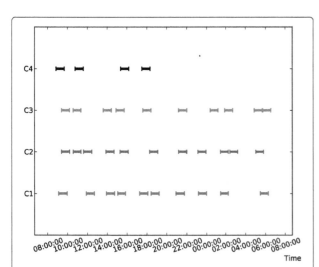

Figure 3 Simulation run times for Newcastle city centre (simulation 1). Time profile for the one million cell simulation of Newcastle City Centre at 2m by 2m resolution – simulation set 1.

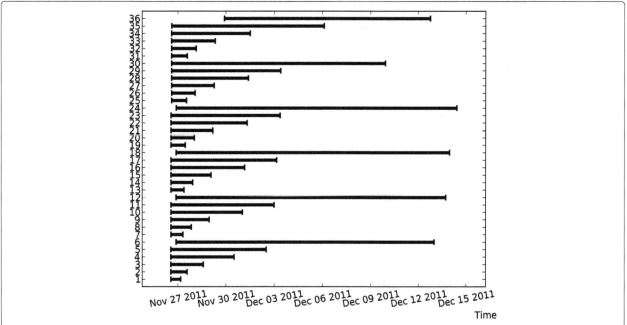

Figure 4 Simulation run times for Newcastle city centre (simulation 2). Time profile for the four million cell simulation of Newcastle City Centre at 1 m by 1 m resolution – simulation set 2.

study, which is currently being undertaken using crowed sourced images of the flooding over the whole Tyne urban area, will show the full potential for using Cloud computing in urban flood risk management and will be reported elsewhere.

The city-wide application demonstrated here can be replicated for other cities in the United Kingdom using readily available data sets from the Ordnance Survey (MasterMap building information) and airborne lidar available from various providers. Similar data are available in many parts of the world and there is considerable demand for such detailed urban flood risk assessments in the insurance industry, government authorities and other hazard management and civil protection agencies.

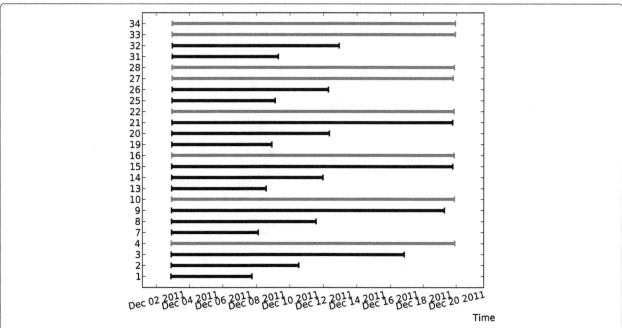

Figure 5 Simulation run times for Newcastle city centre (simulation 3). Time profile for the 16,000,000 cell simulation of Newcastle City Centre at 0.5 m by 0.5 m resolution – simulation set 3.

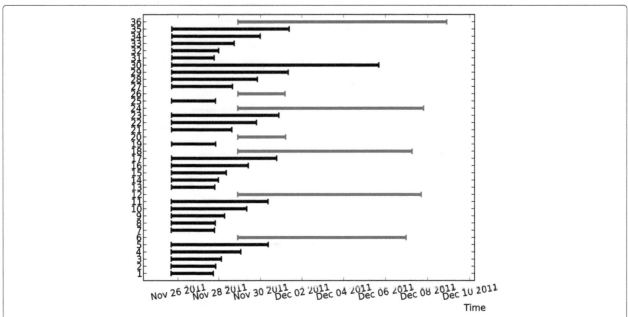

Figure 6 Simulation run times for whole Newcastle city council area (simulation 5). Time profile for the 7,500,000 cell simulation of Newcastle City Centre at 4 m by 4 m resolution – simulation set 5.

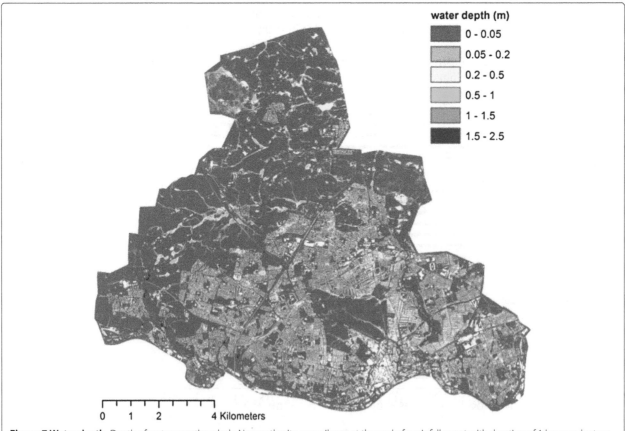

Figure 7 Water depth. Depth of water over the whole Newcastle city council area at the end of a rainfall event with duration of 1 hour and return period of 100 years.

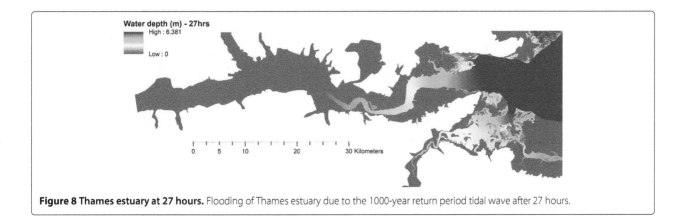

Figure 8 Thames estuary at 27 hours. Flooding of Thames estuary due to the 1000-year return period tidal wave after 27 hours.

These simulations produced a huge amount of detailed results which, in order to become meaningful to end users, need to be combined and presented in the form of maps and video animations. The automatic visualisation and analysis of flood risk was lost when the numerical engine and the GUI of "CityCat" were separated in order to be deployed on the Cloud for parameter sweeps. Therefore, a potential area for further development is automatic creation of flood risk maps and animations based on the CityCat results generated on the Cloud.

Although this work does not present a motivational case for using the Cloud based on financial concerns it does support the notion that Cloud computing can provide rapid access to computational resources as and when needed without the need for significant financial outlay and continued expenses for maintaining the resources. This can be of particular benefit to organisations for whom performing such computational work is an infrequent process.

Significant care needs to be taken to ensure high utilisation of Cloud resources to ensure that they are cost-effective. This is no different to the utilisation issues for existing HPC facilities. As each individually 'rented' resource is now charged for independently this can quickly lower the utilisation and hence increase the cost per simulation hour. Adaptation of the Cloud deployment tool to take into account the expected execution time of the different runs could help alleviate much of this problem. However, the additional costs for using the Cloud – data transfer and (de)compression – are relatively small in these cases and have little impact on the overall cost of using the Cloud.

The adaptation of an application to run as a parameter sweep is often a non-trivial task – as in this case. However, this process only needs to be performed once and would still have been needed if the application were to have been run on locally provisioned resources. The benefits of adaptation of the code are easily apparent – the ability to run parameter sweeps of simulations concurrently and the ability to script multiple scenarios quickly. This is an example of where closer inter-relationships between those experienced in using parameter sweep executions and the Cloud and those who are experts in the science is essential to ensure the transfer of appropriate skills. Although this process consumed a significant amount of effort, the ability to process more than 15,450 hours (~21 months) of simulation time within one calendar month is significant and can be re-used easily in the future.

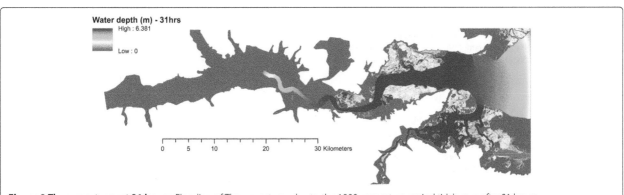

Figure 9 Thames estuary at 31 hours. Flooding of Thames estuary due to the 1000-year return period tidal wave after 31 hours.

Competing interests

The authors declare that they have no competing interests.

Authors' contributions

VG decomposed the CityCat execution engine from the GUI and produced the simulation run requirements. ASM and SW proposed and developed the architecture for performing parameter sweep applications on the Cloud and conducted the simulation runs on the Cloud. VK, VG and CK drafted the Abstract; Background (Flood Risk Assessment using CityCat); Parameter sweep enabling the CityCat application; Scientific Experimental Environment; Preliminary result of the CityCat simulations and parts of the Conclusions. ASM drafted the Introduction; Cloud for computationally intense applications; Cloud execution architecture; Cost-time analysis for the CityCat simulations; Cloud simulation results and Non-functional Issues with Cloud deployment. ASM and SW drafted parts of the Conclusions. All authors read and approved the final manuscript.

Acknowledgements

The authors are grateful to the EPSRC/JISC grant EP/I034351/1 which allowed this work to be conducted. The authors are grateful to the reviewers for their constructive comments.

Author details

[1]School of Civil Engineering and Geosciences, Newcastle University, Newcastle upon Tyne, UK. [2]School of Computing Science, Newcastle University, Newcastle upon Tyne, UK.

References

1. Hey T, Tansley S, Tolle K (Eds) (2009) The Fourth Paradigm. Data-Intensive Scientific Discovery. Redmond, Washington. Microsoft Research. http://research.microsoft.com/en-us/collaboration/fourthparadigm/
2. Armbrust M, Fox A, Griffith R, Joseph AD, Katz R, Konwinski A, Lee G, Patterson D, Rabkin A, Stoica I, Zaharia M (2010) A view of Cloud computing. Commun ACM 53(4): 50–58
3. McGough AS, Lee W, Das S (2008) A standards based approach to enabling legacy applications on the Grid. Future Generation Comput Syst 24(7): 731–743. http://www.sciencedirect.com/science/article/pii/S0167739X08000095
4. Wei Yan T (1992) Shallow water hydrodynamics. Elsevier Oceanography Series, vol 55. Elsevier, Amsterdam, p 434
5. Toro EF (2001) Shock-capturing methods for free-surface shallow flows. John Wiley & Sons, Chichester, p 309
6. Toro E (2009) Riemann solvers and numerical methods for fluid dynamics, third edition. Springer-Verlag, Berlin Heidelberg, p 724
7. Hunter N, Bates P, Neelz S, Pender G, Villanueva I, Wright N, Liang D, Falconer R, Lin B, Waller S, Crossley A, Mason D (2008) Benchmarking 2D hydraulic models for urban flooding. In: Proceedings of the ICE - Water Management, vol 161. pp 13–30. http://centaur.reading.ac.uk/1180/
8. Neal JC, Bates PD, Fewtrell TJ, Hunter NM, Wilson MD, Horritt MS (2009) Distributed whole city water level measurements from the Carlisle 2005 urban flood event and comparison with hydraulic model simulations. J Hydrol 368(1-4): 42–55. http://www.sciencedirect.com/science/article/pii/S002216940900047X
9. Deelman E, Singh G, Livny M, Berriman B, Good J (2008) The cost of doing science on the Cloud: the Montage example. In: Proceedings of the 2008 ACM/IEEE conference on Supercomputing, SC '08. IEEE Press, Piscataway, 50:1–50:12
10. Amazon Web Services. Elastic Compute Cloud. http://aws.amazon.com/ec2/
11. Amazon Web Services. Simple Storage Service. http://aws.amazon.com/s3/
12. de Assuncao MD, di Costanzo A, Buyya R (2009) Evaluating the cost-benefit of using Cloud computing to extend the capacity of clusters. In: Proceedings of the 18th ACM international symposium on High performance distributed computing, HPDC '09. ACM, New York, pp 141–150
13. Mattess M, Vecchiola C, Buyya R (2010) Managing peak loads by leasing cloud infrastructure services from a spot market. In: Proceedings of the 2010 IEEE 12th International Conference on High Performance Computing and Communications, HPCC '10. IEEE Computer Society, Washington, pp 180–188
14. Palankar MR, Iamnitchi A, Ripeanu M, Garfinkel S (2008) Amazon S3 for science grids: a viable solution? In: Proceedings of the 2008 international workshop on Data-aware distributed computing, DADC '08. ACM, New York, pp 55–64
15. Evangelinos C, Hill CN (2008) Cloud computing for parallel scientific HPC applications: Feasibility of running coupled atmosphere-ocean climate models on Amazon's EC2. In: Cloud Computing and its applications. https://my.cloudme.com/seadog5339/webshare/CloudComputing/Cloud%20Computing/Applications/Cloud%20Computing%20and%20its%20Applications%20-%202008/Paper34-Chris-Hill.pdf
16. Lu W, Jackson J, Barga R (2010) AzureBlast: a case study of developing science applications on the Cloud. In: Proceedings of the 19th ACM International Symposium on High Performance Distributed Computing, HPDC '10. ACM, New York, pp 413–420. http://doi.acm.org/10.1145/1851476.1851537
17. Litzkow M, Livney M, Mutka MW (1998) Condor-a hunter of idle workstations. In: 8th International Conference on Distributed Computing Systems. IEEE Computer Society, Washington, pp 104–111
18. Apache Software Foundation. Deltacloud. http://deltacloud.apache.org/
19. Borland. Delphi. http://www.embarcadero.com/products/delphi
20. The Lazarus Team. Lazarus. http://www.lazarus.freepascal.org/
21. Free Pascal Team. Free Pascal: Free Pascal Compiler. http://www.freepascal.org/
22. Institute of Hydrology (1999) Flood estimation handbook, vol 3: Statistical procedures for flood frequency estimation. Institute of Hydrology, Wallingford, UK
23. Microsoft. Windows Azure Platform, Microsoft Cloud Services. http://www.microsoft.com/windowsazure/
24. GoGrid. Cloud Hosting. http://www.gogrid.com/
25. RackSpace. Cloud Servers. http://www.rackspace.co.uk/cloud-servers/

## 2

Handling compromised components in an IaaS cloud installation

Aryan TaheriMonfared[1][*] and Martin Gilje Jaatun[2]

Abstract

This article presents an approach to handle compromised components in the OpenStack Infrastructure-as-a-Service cloud environment. We present two specific use cases; a compromised service process and the introduction of a bogus component, and we describe several approaches for containment, eradication and recovery after an incident. Our experiments show that traditional incident handling procedures are applicable for cloud computing, but need some modification to function optimally.

Introduction

Although Cloud Computing has been heralded as a new computing model, it is fundamentally an old idea of providing computing resources as a utility [1]. This computing model will reduce the upfront cost for developing and deploying new services in the Internet. Moreover, it can provide efficient services for special use-cases which require on-demand access to scalable resources.

Cloud Computing has a variety of service models and deployment models which have been in use in various combinations for some time [2]. The chosen service and deployment model of a cloud environment will determine what kind of vulnerabilities might threaten it. One of the main obstacles in the movement toward Cloud Computing is the perceived insufficiency of Cloud security. Although it has been argued [3] that most of the security issues in Cloud Computing are not fundamentally novel, a new computing model invariably brings its own security doubts and issues to the market.

In a distributed environment with several stakeholders, there will always be numerous ways of attacking and compromising a component, and it is not possible to stop all attacks or ensure that the system is secure against all threats. Thus, instead of studying attack methods, a better approach is to assess the risk and try to understand the impact of a compromised component. To do this, the exact functionalities of each component must be determined, after which efficient approaches to tolerate such

an attack can be identified. The first step of this process is to detect, and then analyze the incident, something which is subject to a set of best practice procedures which are dependent on knowledge about the normal behavior and operation of the system. The next step is about containing the incident. There are currently several public cloud providers; however, none of them disclose their security mechanisms. This highlights the need to study applicable mechanisms and introduce new ones to fulfill security requirements of a given cloud environment; in this article, we describe our work on an open-source deployment of a cloud environment based on the OpenStack cloud platform. When we talk about a compromised component in this document, we mean those components in a cloud environment that are disclosed (i.e., private contents revealed), modified, destroyed or even lost [4]. Finding compromised components and identifying their impacts on a cloud environment is crucial.

A brief primer on OpenStack

We have found the OpenStack cloud platform to be the best choice for a real case study in our research. In our laboratory configuration, we used the simple flat deployment structure. This will avoid further complexity which would be caused by a hierarchical or peer-to-peer architecture. We have four physical machines; one of them will be the cloud controller, and other three are compute worker nodes. The abstract diagram of our lab setup is depicted in Figure 1. It should be noted that although we focus on the OpenStack as a specific cloud software in our study, more or less the same components and processes can be found in other cloud platform implementations.

---
*Correspondence: aryan@uninett.no
[1] UNINETT, Trondheim, Norway
Full list of author information is available at the end of the article

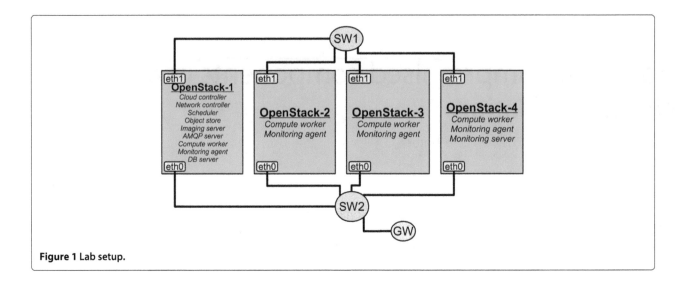

Figure 1 Lab setup.

OpenStack consists of a set of open-source projects which provide a variety of services for an Infrastructure as a Service (IaaS) model. Its five main projects deliver basic functionalities that are required for a cloud infrastructure, comprising: Nova (compute), Swift (storage), Glance (VM image), Keystone (identity), and Horizon (dashboard). The OpenStack community is fairly big, with a lot of leading companies involved. A big community for an open-source project has its own advantages and disadvantages, but further discussion on this topic is out of the scope of this article.

The Compute project (Nova) provides fundamental services for hosting virtual machines in a distributed yet connected environment. It handles provisioning and maintenance of virtual machines, as well as exposing appropriate APIs for cloud management. The object storage project (Swift) is responsible for delivering a scalable, redundant, and permanent object storage. It does not facilitate a regular file system in the cloud. Virtual machine disk images are handled by the Image Service project (Glance). Discovery, uploading, and delivery of images are exposed using a REST[a] interface. The image service does not store the actual images, but utilizes other storage services for that purpose, such as OpenStack Object Storage. The identity project (Keystone) unifies authentication for the deployed cloud infrastructure. Cloud services are accessible through a portal provided by the dashboard project (Horizon) [5].

The OpenStack architecture is based on a Shared Nothing (SN) and Message Oriented architecture. Thus, most of the components can run on multiple nodes and their internal communication functions in a synchronous fashion via a messaging system. In this deployment (and in the default installation of OpenStack), RabbitMQ is used as the messaging system. RabbitMQ is based on the Advanced Messaging Queue Protocol (AMQP) standard.

These architectures are used to avoid common challenges in a distributed environment, such as deadlock, live lock, etc.

We have decided to focus on the Compute project of OpenStack, which has enabled us to dive deeply into the details, and exercise different modules in the Compute project. However, the same results are applicable to the rest of the OpenStack projects. All projects follow the same architectural concepts and design patterns, so despite their functionalities, their behavior in a distributed and highly scalable environment would be similar.

OpenStack Compute has 5 interacting modules, comprising: compute controller, network controller, volume controller, scheduler, and API server. These modules are depicted in Figure 2. They provide basic functionalities for hosting, provisioning and maintaining virtual machine instances. The compute controller interacts with the underlying hypervisor and allocates required resources for each virtual machine. The network controller provides networking resources (e.g. IP addresses, VLAN specification, etc.) for VM instances. The volume controller handles block storages devices for each VM instance, and the scheduler distributes tasks among worker nodes (i.e. compute controllers). The API server exposes all these functionalities to the outside world.

Article structure

We will continue to discuss general aspects of incident handling in a specific cloud environment, and our case studies for possible attack scenario to such a model.

The rest of the paper is structured as follows: First, we will explain the adapted form of the NIST incident handling guideline for the cloud model (Section "Incident handling"). Then two incidents will be processed by the adapted guideline (Section "Case studies"). Applying the guideline leads us to a set of new challenges that have

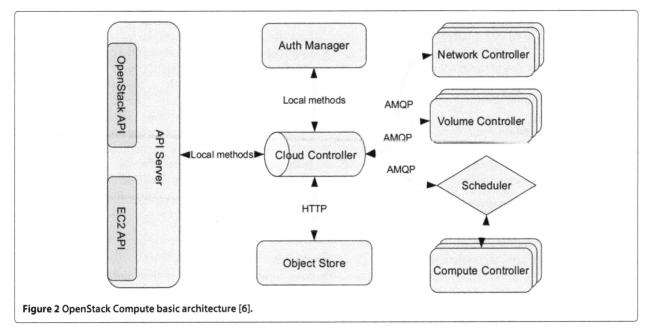

Figure 2 OpenStack Compute basic architecture [6].

not been addressed previously or require a careful re-analysis. Finally, by analyzing these challenges, a group of security mechanisms are proposed which address existing deficiencies (Section "Approaches for containment and recovery"). A brief comparison of mechanisms are provided as well (Section "Comparison").

Incident handling

We will focus on cloud platform components, specifically on their functionalities, access methods, interacting components and the impacts in case of being compromised. The symptoms of a compromised component are useful in detecting security breaches and must be considered when performing further analysis. Studying the detection and analysis phase of the incident handling procedure, and applying new characteristics of the Cloud Computing model, we identified several requirements for a cloud provider and a cloud consumer. Additionally, some influential challenges which will hinder implementation of these requirements or adaptation of existing mechanisms will be explained.

Detection and analysis of the compromised component

Studying the detection and analysis phase of the NIST incident handling guideline [7], and applying new characteristics of the Cloud Computing model, we identified several requirements for a cloud provider and a cloud consumer.

Cloud provider requirements

The cloud provider should develop the following items to play its role in the incident handling process. Most of these items are orthogonal. In other words, a cloud consumer may request several items (i.e. security functionalities,

services) together. Also, different consumers may not have similar demands. Thus, it may be beneficial for the provider to develop most (if not all) of the following items if it wishes to cover a larger set of consumers.

- **Security APIs:** The cloud provider should develop a set of APIs that deliver event monitoring functionalities and also provide forensic services for authorities. Event monitoring APIs ease systematic incident detection for cloud consumers and even third parties. Forensic services at virtualization level can be implemented by means of virtual machine introspection libraries. An example of an introspection library is XenAccess that allows a privileged domain to access live states of other virtual machines. A cross-layer security approach seems to be the best approach in a distributed environment [8].
- **Precursor or Indication Sources:** The cloud provider deploys, maintains and manages the cloud infrastructure. The provider also develops required security sensors, logging and monitoring mechanisms to gather enough data for incident detection and analysis at the infrastructure level. As an example, security agents, intrusion monitoring sensors, application log files, report repository, firewall statistics and logs are all part of security relevant indication sources. In case of a security incident, the cloud provider should provide raw data from these sources to affected customers and stakeholders. Thus they will be capable of analyzing raw data and characterizing incident properties.
- **External reports:** The cloud provider should provide a framework to capture external incident reports. These incidents can be reported by cloud consumers,

end users or even third parties. This is not a new approach in handling an incident, however finding the responsible stakeholders for that specific incident and ensuring correctness of the incident[b] requires extensive research. E.g., Amazon has developed a "Vulnerability Reporting Process" [9] which delivers these functionalities.

- **Stakeholder interaction:** A timely response to an incident requires heavy interaction with stakeholders. In order to ease this interaction at the time of crisis, the responsibilities of each stakeholder should be described in detail.
- **Security services:** Cloud consumers may not be interested in developing security mechanisms. The cloud provider can deliver a security service to overcome this issue. Security services which are delivered by the provider can be more reliable in case of an incident and less challenging in the deployment and the incident detection/analysis phases.
- **Infrastructure information:** When the cloud consumer or another third party wants to develop incident detection and analysis mechanisms, they will need to understand the underlying infrastructure and its architecture. However, without cloud provider cooperation that will not be feasible. So, the cloud provider should disclose enough information to responsible players to detect the incident in a timely fashion and study it to propose the containment strategy.

Cloud consumer requirements

A cloud consumer must fulfill requirements to ensure effectiveness of the incident detection and analysis process.

- **Consumer's security mechanisms:** The cloud consumer might prefer to develop its own security mechanisms (e.g. incident detection and analysis mechanisms). The customer's security mechanisms can be based on either the cloud provider's APIs or reports from a variety of sources, including: provider's incident reports, end-users' vulnerability reports, third parties' reports.
- **Provider's agents in customer's resources:** By implementing provider's agents, the cloud consumer will facilitate approaching a cross-layer security solution. In this method, the cloud consumer will know the exact amount and type of information that has been disclosed. Moreover, neither the cloud consumer nor the provider needs to know about each others' architecture or infrastructure design.
- **Standard communication protocol:** In order to have systematic incident detection and analysis mechanisms, it is required to agree on a standard communication protocol that will be used by all

stakeholders. This protocol should be independent of a specific provider/customer.

- **Report to other stakeholders:** If the customer cannot implement the provider's agent in its own instances, another approach to informing stakeholders about an incident is by means of traditional reporting mechanisms. These reports should not be limited to an incident only, customers may also use this mechanism to announce a suspicious behavior for more analysis.
- **Cloud consumer's responsibilities:** Roles and responsibilities of a cloud consumer in case of an incident should be defined ahead of time, facilitating immediate reaction in a crisis.

Case studies

We now present two examples that illustrate handling a compromised node and an introduced bogus node, respectively.

Case One: a compromised compute worker

In the first case only one component, the nova-compute service in the compute worker, is compromised, as shown in Figure 3. Two incidents have happened simultaneously in this scenario: malicious code and unauthorized access. The malicious code is injected to the nova-compute service and introduces some misbehavior in it, such as malfunctions in the hosting service of virtual machine instances.

A malfunction can be provoked, e.g., through nefarious use of granted privileges to request more IP addresses, causing IP address exhaustion. The incident description for this scenario is given in Table 1.

The malicious code is injected after another incident, unauthorized access. The attacker gains access to resources on the OpenStack-4 host, that he/she was not intended to have. Using those escalated privileges, the attacker changed the python code of the nova-compute and restarted the service, causing it to behave maliciously.

Recommended actions by NIST and their corresponding realization in an OpenStack deployment are explained next. They will fulfill requirements, implied by the containment, eradication, and recovery phase. As explained before, the described scenario consists of two incidents, *unauthorized access* and *malicious code*. Thus, we will in the following briefly discuss recommended responses for both types of incident; an extended discussion can be found in [10].

The following discussion is given in two parts. In each part, actions proposed by the NIST guideline are adapted to the cloud model. First, containment actions from Table 2 will be adapted. Then, adapted forms of eradication and recovery actions are explained. A major effort has been put into adapting containment actions:

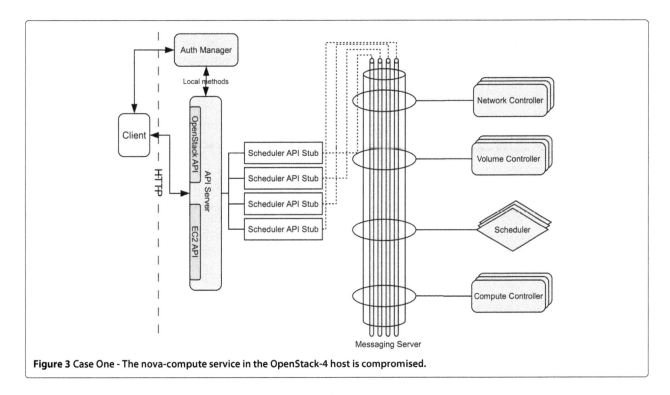

Figure 3 Case One - The nova-compute service in the OpenStack-4 host is compromised.

- **"Identifying and Isolating Other Infected Hosts"**
  Study the profile of the infected host and compare it to other worker nodes' profiles, in order to identify compromised hosts. Comparing profiles of components is simple, using provided monitoring facilities in our experimental environment.
- **"Blocking Particular Hosts"**
  The strategy should be analyzed in depth before its application. In a cloud environment when the consumer's instance is running in an infected worker

node, it is not reasonable to disconnect the node without prior notice/negotiation to affected consumers (This constraint can be relaxed by providing the proper Service-level Agreement (SLA)). In addition, blocking the compromised host can be done with different levels of restrictions. Initially the communication with the outside of the organization should be blocked[c] assuming that the attacker is located outside of the organization infrastructure. Also, any further attack to the outside of the organization using compromised hosts will be mitigated.

In the second step, communication of the compromised host with other components in the infrastructure is also restricted and the host is marked as compromised/infected/suspicious. Thus, other nodes will avoid non-critical communication with the compromised node. It will help the infrastructure to communicate with the compromised node for containment, eradication, and recovery procedures; and at the same time the risk of spreading the infection is reduced.

The last step can be blocking the host completely. In this approach staff should access the host directly for analyzing the attack as well as assessing possible mitigation and handling strategies.

However, blocking infected hosts will not contain the incident. Each host has several consumers' instances (VM instances) and volumes running on and attached to it. Blocking hosts will only avoid spreading the

Table 1 Case One - A compromised compute worker scenario specifications

	Incident description
Incident type	Malicious code and Unauthorized access
Current status	Ongoing attack, the malicious code is not patched nor contained yet
Compromised component(s)	One compute worker host
Physical Location	OpenStack-4
Affected Layers	Cloud platform layer, the OpenStack nova-compute service
General Information	Malicious code is injected into the nova-compute service of the OpenStack-4 host
Resources at risk	Running instances on OpenStack-4, Stakeholders and resources interacting with running instances on OpenStack-4 or the infected nova-compute service

Table 2 Containment strategies

NIST recommended action	Brief description
"Identifying and Isolating Other Infected Hosts"	Extract incident symptoms to detect other infected hosts.
"Blocking Particular Hosts"	After identifying the compromised component and its corresponding host (i.e. the compromised worker/compute host), that host should be blocked.
"Soliciting User Participation"	Interaction among cloud stakeholders (e.g. cloud providers, cloud consumers, third parties, end users, etc.) is a mandatory step toward fulfilling incident containment requirements.
"Disabling Services"	Disabling the infected service (nova-compute in our scenario) may reduce impacts of the compromised host. Disabling a service can disrupt other services and cause deviation from promised SLA by the provider

incident to other hosts but instances are still in danger. An approach in a cloud environment is to disconnect instances and volumes from the underlying compromised layer. Signaling the cloud software running on the compromised host to release/terminate/shutdown/migrate instances and detach volumes are our proposed approaches. This approach is illustrated in Figure 4. We should use a quarantine compute worker node as the container for migrated instances. After ensuring the integrity and healthiness of instances, they can be moved to a regular worker node. This quarantine compute worker will be explained more in the following section. These approaches can be implemented at the cloud infrastructure layer for simplicity (Blocking by means of nodes firewall, routers, etc.)

- **"Soliciting User Participation"**
  The interaction can be implemented using different methods. Distributing security bulletins maintained by cloud or service providers is an example of notifying other stakeholders about an incident. Incident or vulnerability reporting mechanisms are also useful when an outsider detects an incident or identifies a vulnerability. These two methods can be developed and deployed independently of the cloud platform. Security bulletins are provided by the security team who handles security related tasks. Also, reporting mechanisms are delivered by means of ticketing and reporting tools. Direct and real-time communication among stakeholders is a complement to the above mentioned methods.
- **"Disabling Services"**
  In order to disable a particular service, we should first check the service dependencies diagram. An example of such a diagram is depicted in Figure 5. Disabling a service can take place in two ways.

It is possible to stop the service at the compromised host (Figure 6). In our scenario we can stop the nova-compute service to disable the compute service. It will instantly disconnect the cloud platform from running VM instances. *In the OpenStack platform stopping the nova-compute service will not terminate running instances on that host.* Thus, although the compute service is not working anymore, already running instances will continue to work even after nova-compute is terminated. Additionally, it is not possible to terminate an instance after stopping its corresponding compute service, because the

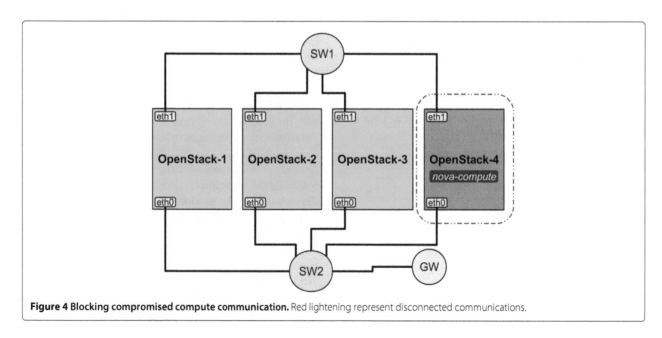

Figure 4 Blocking compromised compute communication. Red lightening represent disconnected communications.

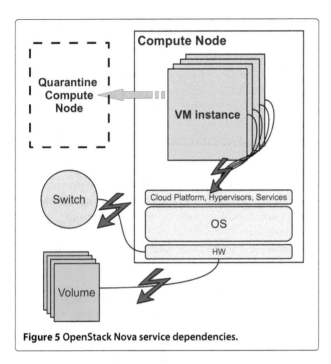

Figure 5 OpenStack Nova service dependencies.

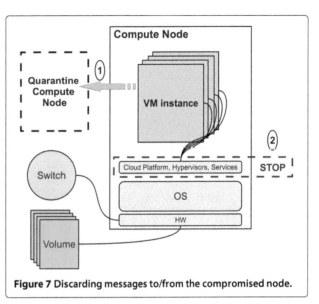

Figure 7 Discarding messages to/from the compromised node.

administration gateway (i.e. nova-compute) is not listening to published messages. In order to maintain control over running instances we should migrate instances from the compromised node to a quarantine node before we terminate the compute service.

Another approach is discarding messages published by the compromised component or those destined to it (Figure 7). This is a centralized method and the cloud controller or the messaging server should filter out messages with the source/destination of the infected host[d]

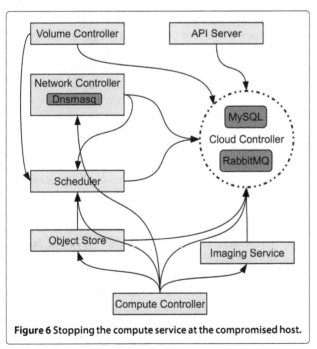

Figure 6 Stopping the compute service at the compromised host.

We continue by explaining four other actions which are recommended responses to an unauthorized access incident:

- **"Isolate the affected systems"**
  The same procedures as those which have been explained for "Identifying and Isolating Other Infected Hosts" (Section "Case One: a compromised compute worker") and "Blocking Particular Hosts" (Section "Case One: a compromised compute worker") can be applied here.
- **"Disable the affected service"**
  The same procedure as the one which has been explained for "Disabling Services" (Section "Case One: a compromised compute worker") can be applied here.
- **"Eliminate the attacker's route into the environment"**
  Access methods which have been used by the attacker to access cloud components should be blocked. Implementing filtering mechanisms in the messaging server is a crucial requirement which is highlighted in different strategies. The cloud provider should be capable of blocking messages which are related to the attack and blocks the attacker's route into the cloud environment. It should be noted that the mechanisms which we have used to meet requirements imposed by "Blocking Particular Hosts", "Identifying and Isolating Other Infected Hosts", "Disabling Services" (Section "Case One: a compromised compute worker") are appropriate actions for eliminating attackers' routes.
- **"Disable user accounts that may have been used in the attack"**
  A compromised user account may reside in multiple layers, such as the system, cloud platform, or VM

instance layer[e]. Based on the membership layer, the disabling and containment procedure will differ. Additionally, in each layer a variety of user types exist. As an example, in the cloud platform layer, the cloud provider's staff and cloud consumers have a different set of user types.

As it was explained, three phases are adapted. Containment phase was discussed, and eradication phase is the next one to be studied:

- **"Disinfect, quarantine, delete, and replace infected files"**
  These strategies are applicable in two layers depending on the container of the injected malicious code. The malicious code can be injected into either the cloud platform services (i.e. nova-compute) or the OS modules/services. If the injected malicious code is in OS modules/services, utilizing existing techniques is effective. By existing techniques, we refer to anti virus software and traditional malware handling mechanisms. In this case nothing new has happened, although side effects of the incident may vary a lot. However, if the malicious code is injected into a cloud platform service (in our case nova-compute), existing anti virus products are not useful, as they are not aware of the new context. Cleaning a cloud platform service can be very hard, so other approaches are more plausible. In general, we can propose several approaches for eradicating a malicious code incident in a cloud platform:

  - Updating the code to the latest stable version and apply appropriate patches to fix the vulnerability.
  - Purging the infected service on the compromised node
  - Replacing the infected service with another one that uses a different set of application layer resources (e.g. configuration files, repositories, etc.)

  It should be noted that in a highly distributed system such as a cloud environment, doing complicated tasks such as fixing a single infected node in real time fashion does not support the cost effectiveness policy. Thus, terminating the infected service or even the compromised node and postponing the eradication phase can be an appropriate strategy.
- **"Mitigate the exploited vulnerabilities for other hosts within the organization"**
  In order to complete the task, we should also update the cloud platform software on other nodes and patch identified vulnerabilities.

The last phase is about recovery of the system which was under attack:

- **"Confirm that the affected systems are functioning normally"**
  Profiling the system is useful in the recovery phase as well as in the detection and analysis phase. After containment and eradication of the compromised component, the component profile should be the same as a healthy component or be the same as its own profile before being infected. Using the provided tools in our deployment (i.e. Cacti) we can specify the exact period and components which we want to compare.
- **"If necessary, implement additional monitoring to look for future related activity"**
  After identifying attack patterns and the compromised node profile, we should add proper monitoring alarms to cover those patterns and profiles. As an example, if the compromised compute worker starts to request a large number of IP addresses after its infection, this pattern should be saved and monitored on other compute workers. So, if we experience a compute worker with the same profile and behavior, that worker node will flagged as possibly infected. In our monitoring tools, the administrator can define a threshold for different parameters; if the current profile of the system violates the threshold, graphs will be drawn with a different color to notify the user. We can also add other monitoring tools to generate the ticket in case of a matching profile.

Case Two: a bogus component

A bogus service is a threat to OpenStack is an open source software, an attacker can access the source code or its binaries and start a cloud component that delivers a specific service. When the attacker is managing a service, he/she can manipulate the service in a way that threatens the integrity and confidentiality of the environment. This section will discuss such an incident, where a bogus nova-compute service is added to the cloud environment. The incident description for this case is given in Table 3.

A bogus nova-compute service (or, in general, any cloud platform component) can run on a physical machine or a virtual instance. It is unlikely that an attacker will be capable of adding a physical node to the cloud infrastructure; however, for the sake of completeness we study both the case that the bogus service is running on a new physical machine and the one where it is running on a virtual instance. Both cases are depicted in Figures 8 and 9.

When the bogus service is running on top of an instance, the network connectivity may be more limited than compared to the other case (i.e., the bogus service is running

Table 3 Case Two - A bogus component scenario specifications

	Incident description
Incident type	Inappropriate Usage
Current status	Ongoing attack, the bogus compute worker is still up and serving a part of requests
Physical Location	OpenStack-5
Affected Layers	Cloud platform layer, the OpenStack nova-compute service, consumers' instances
General Information	A bogus compute worker node is added to the platform, it is a threat to the provider's and consumers' data confidentiality and integrity. Also a threat for the system availability.
Resources at risk	Running instances on OpenStack-5, Stakeholders and resources interacting with running instance on OpenStack-5

on a physical node). Initially, any given instance is only connected to the second interface (*eth1*). This connectivity is provided by means of the bridge connection (*br100*) that connects virtual interfaces (*vnetX*) to the rest of the environment. Thus, a running instance has no connectivity to the switch *SW2* by default. However, connectivity to the outside world can be requested by any consumer

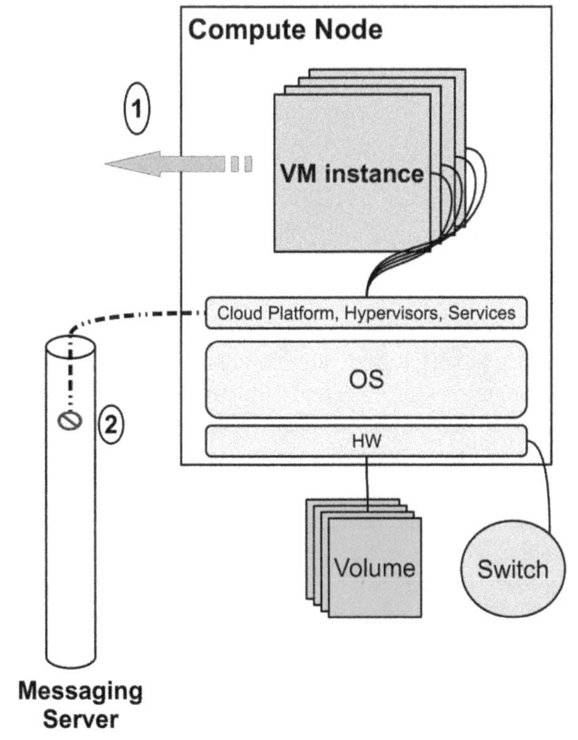

Figure 8 Case Two - A physical bogus compute worker node is added to the infrastructure.

(e.g., an attacker) through a legitimate procedure. Thus, in Figure 9, we also connect the instance to *SW2*.

We simulated the virtual bogus compute worker by deploying the nova-compute service on a running instance. There were multiple obstacles for simulating this scenario, including: the running instance, which turns out to be also a bogus worker, must have hosting capabilities; the bogus worker must respond to cloud controller requests to be recognized as a working node.

Detecting a bogus worker node or instance is a complex task if the infrastructure has not previously employed a proper set of mechanisms. However, a few parameters can be monitored as an indication of a bogus worker. Generally, a bogus worker is not working as well as a real one, because its main goal is not providing a regular service. A bogus worker aims to steal consumers' data, intrude on the cloud infrastructure, disrupt the cloud environment Quality of Service (QoS), and so forth. Without any prior preparation, a suspicious worker can be identified by monitoring the service availability and QoS parameters on each worker. Moreover, a suspicious virtual worker can also be recognized because of its high traffic towards the cloud infrastructure messaging servers.

Containing a bogus worker consists of both proactive and reactive techniques. When a bogus worker is detected, the containment procedure is fairly simple (i.e., applying reactive techniques). However, deploying a set of proactive techniques is more challenging. These techniques can be implemented as a group of security mechanisms and policies, such as *node authentication, manual confirmation, trust levels and timeouts*, and *no new worker policy*. They will be discussed further in Section "Policies".

Approaches for containment and recovery

This section introduces our proposed approaches for containment of intruders, eradication of malicious processes and recovery from attack. The proposed strategies can be grouped based on two criteria: The responsible stakeholder for developing and deploying the strategy, and the target layer for that strategy. Based on the first criterion we may have either the cloud provider or the cloud consumer as the responsible stakeholder; based on the second criterion, the target layer can be either the infrastructure/hardware layer or the service/application layer. We have devised a set of approaches which will be explained in detail in the following.

Restriction, disinfection, and replication of infected cloud platform components

A general technique for containing an incident is restricting the infected component. The restriction can be applied in different layers, with a variety of approaches,

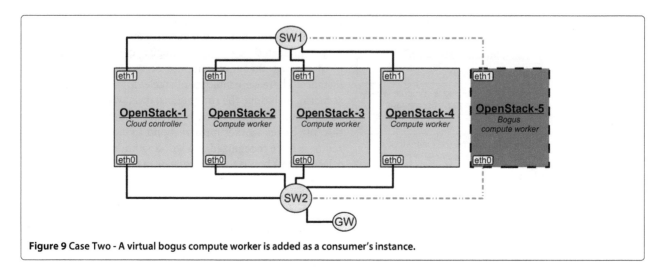

Figure 9 Case Two - A virtual bogus compute worker is added as a consumer's instance.

such as: filtering in the AMQP server, filtering in other components, disabling the infected service or disabling the communicator service. Additional measures can also be employed to support the restriction, like: removing infected instances from the project VLAN, disabling live migration, or quarantining infected instances. We explain each of these approaches in the following sections.

Filtering in the messaging server (cloud controller)

We will propose several filtering mechanisms in the messaging server in order to contain and eradicate an incident in a cloud environment. The OpenStack platform has been used to build our experimental cloud environment. This approach is a responsibility of the cloud provider and the target layer in the cloud platform application layer.

Advantages

- The filtering task at the messaging server level can be done without implementation of new functionality. We can use existing management interfaces of the RabbitMQ (either command line or web interface) to filter the compromised component.
- The filtering task can be done in a centralized fashion by means of the management plug-in, although we may have multiple instances of the messaging server.
- Implementing this approach is completely transparent for other stakeholders, such as cloud consumers.
- We can scale out[f] the messaging capability by running multiple instances of the RabbitMQ on different nodes. Scaling out the messaging server will also scale out the filtering mechanism[g].
- This approach is at the application layer, and it is independent of network architecture and employed hardware.

- The implementation at the messaging server level helps in having a fine-grained filtering, based on the message content.

Disadvantages

- A centralized approach implies the risk of a single point of failure or becoming the system bottleneck.
- Implementing the filtering mechanism at the messaging server and/or the cloud controller adds an extra complexity to these components.
- When messages are filtered at the application layer in the RabbitMQ server, the network bandwidth is already wasted for the message that has an infected source, destination, or even context. Thus, this approach is less efficient than one that may filter the message sooner (e.g. at its source host, or in the source cluster).
- Most of the time application layer approaches are not as fast as those in the hardware layer. In a large scale and distributed environment the operation speed plays a vital role in the system availability and QoS. It is possible to use the zFilter technique [11] as a more efficient implementation of the message delivery technique. It can be implemented on either software or hardware. The zFilter is based on the bloom-filter [12] data structure. Each message contains its state; thus this technique is stateless [11]. It also utilizes source routing. zFilter implementations are available for the BSD family operating systems and the NetFPGA boards at the following address, *http://www.psirp.org*.
- Filtering a message without notifying upper layers may lead to triggered timeouts and resend requests from waiting entities. It can also cause more wasted bandwidth.

Realization A variety of filtering mechanisms can be utilized in the messaging server; each of these mechanisms focuses on a specific component/concept in the RabbitMQ messaging server. We can enforce the filtering in the messaging server *connection*, *exchange*, and *queue* as will be discussed next.

- **Connection:** A connection is created to connect a client to an AMQP broker [13]. A connection is a long-lasting communication capability and may contain multiple channels [14]. By closing the connection, all of its channels will be closed as well. A snapshot of connections in our OpenStack deployment is available in Figure 10.

- **Exchange:** An exchange is a message routing agent which can be durable, temporary, or auto-deleted. Messages are routed to qualified queues by the exchange. A Binding is a link between an exchange and a queue. An exchange type can be one of *direct*, *topic*, *headers*, or *fanout* [15]. An exchange can be manipulated in different ways in order to provide a filter mechanisms for our cloud environment:

  - **Unbinding a queue from the exchange:** The compromised component queue won't receive messages from the unbound exchange. As an example, we assume that the compute service of the OpenStack-4 host is compromised. Now, we want to block nova traffic to and from the compromised compute service; so, we unbind the NOVA topic exchange from the queue COMPUTE.OPENSTACK-4. The RabbitMQ management interface is used to unbind the exchange, as shown in Figure 11.

  - **Publishing a warning message:** Publishing an alert message to that exchange, so all clients using that exchange will be informed about the compromised component. Thus, by specifying the compromised component, other clients can avoid communicating with it. The main obstacle in this technique is the requirement for implementing new functionalities in clients.

  - **Deleting the exchange:** Deleting an exchange will stop routing of messages related to it. It may have multiple side effects, such as memory overflow and queue exhaustion.

- **Queue:** The queue is called a "weak FIFO" buffer; each message in it can be delivered only to a single client unless re-queuing the message [15].

  - **Unbinding** a queue from an exchange avoids further routing of messages from that exchange to the unbound queue. We can unbind the queue which is connected to the compromised component and stop receiving messages by the infected client.

  - **Deleting** a queue not only removes the queue itself, but also remove all messages in the queue and cancel all consumers on that queue.

  - **Purging** a queue removes all messages in the queue that do not need acknowledgment. Although it may be useful in some cases, it may not be as effective as required during an incident.

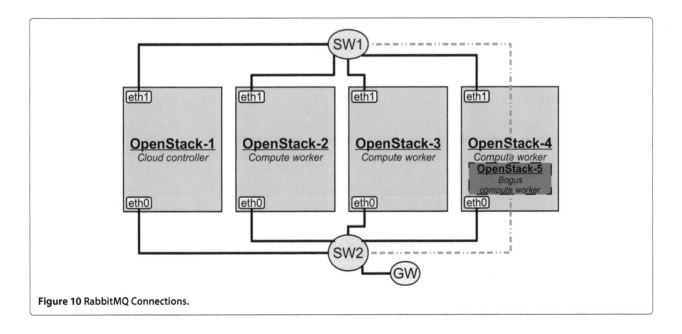

Figure 10 RabbitMQ Connections.

Connections

Network			Overview		
Peer address	From client	To client	Channels	User name	State
129.241.252.116:41057	604B/s (32.4MB total)	125B/s (6.7MB total)	1	guest	running
129.241.252.116:41058	220B/s (11.8MB total)	125B/s (6.7MB total)	1	guest	running
129.241.252.116:41059	330B/s (18.0MB total)	122B/s (6.7MB total)	1	guest	running
129.241.252.117:33649	227B/s (12.1MB total)	128B/s (6.9MB total)	1	guest	running
129.241.252.117:33650	347B/s (18.5MB total)	129B/s (6.9MB total)	1	guest	running
129.241.252.117:33651	623B/s (33.3MB total)	128B/s (6.9MB total)	1	guest	running
129.241.252.118:49885	585B/s (32.0MB total)	121B/s (6.6MB total)	1	guest	running
129.241.252.118:49886	325B/s (17.8MB total)	121B/s (6.6MB total)	1	guest	running
129.241.252.118:49887	214B/s (11.7MB total)	121B/s (6.6MB total)	1	guest	running
129.241.252.119:48262	229B/s (12.2MB total)	129B/s (6.9MB total)	1	guest	running
129.241.252.119:48263	347B/s (18.5MB total)	129B/s (6.9MB total)	1	guest	running
129.241.252.119:48264	626B/s (33.3MB total)	129B/s (6.9MB total)	1	guest	running
129.241.252.119:49251	249B/s (13.5MB total)	129B/s (7.0MB total)	1	guest	running
129.241.252.119:49252	367B/s (20.0MB total)	129B/s (7.0MB total)	1	guest	running
129.241.252.119:49253	646B/s (35.1MB total)	129B/s (7.0MB total)	1	guest	running
129.241.252.119:49254	229B/s (12.4MB total)	129B/s (7.0MB total)	1	guest	running
129.241.252.119:49255	348B/s (19.1MB total)	129B/s (10.8MB total)	1	guest	running
129.241.252.119:49256	626B/s (34.0MB total)	129B/s (7.0MB total)	1	guest	running

Figure 11 Unbinding a queue from an exchange using the Queues Management page of RabbitMQ.

Figure 12 depicts a simplified overview of messaging server internal entities and the application points of our approaches.

Filtering in each component

Applicable filtering mechanisms in the messaging server have been studied in the previous section. This section discusses mechanisms that are appropriate for other components. These components are not essentially aware of messaging technique details and specifications.

Advantages

- The implementation of the filtering mechanism in each component avoids added complexity to the messaging server and cloud controller.

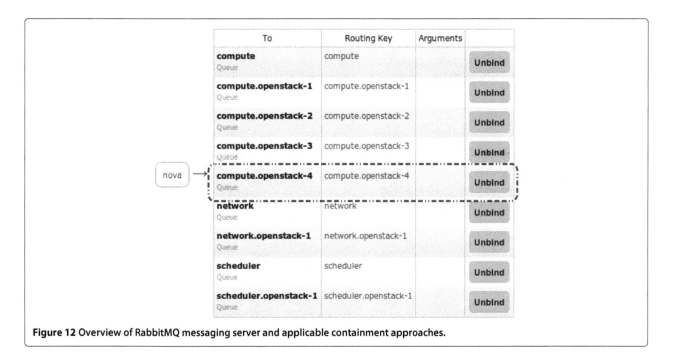

Figure 12 Overview of RabbitMQ messaging server and applicable containment approaches.

- This approach is a distributed solution without a single point of failure, in contrast to the previous one with a centralized filtering mechanism.
- Assuming the locality principle in the cloud, wasted bandwidth is limited to a cluster/rack which hosts the infected components. Network connections have much higher speed in a rack or cluster.
- This approach does not require a correlation/coordination entity for filtering messages. Each component behaves independently and autonomously upon receiving an alarm message which announces a compromised node. Traditionally, most security mechanisms have been employed at the organization/system boundaries. However, as there is no boundary in the cloud, performing security enforcement at each component is a more reliable approach.

Disadvantages

- When the filtering must be performed in each component, all interacting components must be modified to support the filtering mechanism. However, this issue can be relaxed by using a unified version of the messaging client (e.g., pika python client) and modifying the client in case of new requirements.
- The message which should be discarded traverses all the way down to the destination, and wastes the link bandwidth on its route.
- Dropping a message without notifying upper layers, may lead to triggered timeouts and resend requests

from waiting entities. It can also cause more wasted bandwidth.

Realization This approach can be implemented at two different levels: blocking at either the messaging client level (e.g. AMQP messaging client) or the OpenStack component/service level.

First, the responsible client can be modified to drop messages with specific properties (e.g. infected source/destination). As an example, the responsible client for AMQP messaging in OpenStack is amqplib/pika; we must implement the mechanism in this AMQP client (or its wrapper in OpenStack) to filter malicious AMQP messages. Using this method, more interaction between OpenStack and clients may be required to avoid resend requests. Because of using the same AMQP client in all components, the implementation is easier and the modification process requires less effort. The second method is to develop filtering in each of the OpenStack components, such as nova-compute, nova-network, nova-scheduler, etc. This method adds more complexity to those components and it may not be part of their responsibilities.

We propose a combination of these methods. Implementing the filtering mechanism in the carrot/amqplib wrapper of OpenStack has advantages of both methods, and avoids unnecessary complexity. The OpenStack wrapper for managing AMQP messaging is implemented in *src/nova/rpc.py*. In order to identify the malicious message, we use the message address which is part of its context. Then, the actual dropping happens in the *AdapterConsumer* method. Assuming that the source address is set in the context variable, filtering is straightforward. By checking the message address and avoiding the method call, most of the task is done. The only remaining part is to inform the sender about the problem, this can be implemented by means of the existing message reply functionality.

Disabling services

Disabling services is a strategy for containing the incident. The disabled service can be either the infected service itself or the communicator service. The latter handles task distribution and delegation. This method can be used only by the cloud provider, and is at the application layer.

Disabling an infected service An incident can be contained by disabling the infected service. It has several advantages, including:

- After the nova-compute service is stopped, running instances will continue to work. Thus, as a result consumers' instances will not be terminated nor disrupted.
- All communications to and from the compromised node will be stopped. So, the wasted bandwidth will be significantly reduced.
- Shutting down a service gracefully avoids an extra set of failures. When the service is stopped by the Nova interfaces, all other components will be notified and the compromised node will be removed from the list of available compute workers.

Like any other solution, it has multiple drawbacks as well, including:

- Keeping instances in a running state can threaten other cloud consumers. The attacker may gain access to running instances on the compromised node.
- The live migration feature will not work anymore. Thus, the threatened consumers cannot migrate running instances to a safe or quarantine compute worker node.
- Neither the cloud provider nor consumers can manage running instances through the OpenStack platform.

This approach requires no further implementation, although we may like to add a mechanism to turn services on and off remotely.

Disabling a communicator service An incident can be contained by disabling or modifying its corresponding communicator service. An example of a communicator

service in an OpenStack deployment is the nova-scheduler service. The nova-scheduler decides which worker should handle a newly arrived request, such as running an instance. By adding new features to the scheduler service, the platform can avoid forwarding requests to the compromised node. Advantages of this approach are:

- No more requests will be forwarded to the compromised node.
- Consumers' instances remain in the running status on the compromised node. So, consumers will have enough time to migrate their instances to a quarantine worker node or dispose of their critical data.
- This approach can be used to identify the attackers, hidden system vulnerabilities, and the set of employed exploits. In other words, it can be used for forensic purposes.

Disadvantages of disabling communication include:

- New features must be implemented.
  These new features are more focused on the decision algorithm of the scheduler service.
- This approach will not secure the rest of our cloud environment, but it avoids forwarding new requests to the compromised node. However, this drawback can be seen as an opportunity. We can apply this approach and also move the compromised node to a **HoneyCloud**. In the HoneyCloud we don't restrict the compromised node, but instead analyze the attack and the attacker's behavior. But even by moving the compromised node to a HoneyCloud, hosted instances on that node are still in danger. It is possible that consumers' instances are all interconnected. Thus, those running instances on the compromised node in the HoneyCloud could threaten the rest of the consumers' instances. The rest of the instances may even be hosted on a secure worker node.
  The next proposed approach is a solution for this issue.

Replicating services

An approach to overcome the implications of an incident is replicating services. A service in this context is a service which is delivered and maintained by the cloud provider. It can be a cloud platform service (e.g nova-compute) or any other services that concern other stakeholders. The replication can be done passively or actively, and that is due to new characteristics of the cloud model. The replication of a cloud service can be done either at the physical or virtual machine layer.

Replicating a service on physical machines is already done in platforms such as OpenStack. The provider can replicate cloud services either passively or actively when facing an issue in the environment.

Replication of a service on virtual machines has multiple benefits, including:

- Virtual machines can be migrated while running (i.e. live migration), this is a practical mechanism for stateful services that use memory.
- Replication at the instance layer is helpful for forensic purposes. It is also possible to move the compromised service in conjunction with the underlying instance to a HoneyCloud. This is done instead of moving the physical node, ceasing all services on it, and changing the network configuration in order to restrict the compromised node communication.
- By using virtual machines in a cloud environment we can also benefit from the cloud model elasticity and on demand access to computing resources.

This approach is also the main idea behind the *Virtualization Intrusion Tolerance Based on Cloud Computing* (CC-VIT) [16]. By applying the CC-VIT to our environment, the preferred hybrid fault model will be Redundant Execution on Multiple Hosts (REMH), and the group communication is handle using the AMQP messaging. We can use physical-to-virtual converters to have the advantages of both approaches. These tools convert a physical machine to a virtual machine image/instance that can be run on top of a hypervisor. Moreover, each of these replicas can be either active or passive. This will have a great impact on the system availability.

Disinfecting infected components

Disinfecting an infected component is a crucial task in handling an incident and securing the system. It can be accomplished with multiple methods having a variety of specifications. None of the following approaches will be used for cleaning the infected binary files, instead less complex techniques are employed that can be applied in a highly distributed environment. Cleaning a binary file can be offered by a third party security service provider, but that will not be discussed further here.

1. **Updating the code**
   The service code can be updated to the latest, patched version. This process should be done in a smooth way so that all components will be either updated or remain compatible with each other after a partial component update. Several tools has been developed for this purpose; one of the best examples is the Puppet project [17].

2. **Purging the infected service**
   Assuming that the attacker has stopped at the cloud platform layer, we can ensure containment of the incident by removing the service completely.

3. **Replacing the service**
   Another method which is not as strong as the others is achieved by replacing the infected service with another one that uses a different set of application layer resources, such as configuration files, binaries, etc. Thus, we can be sure that the infected resources have no effect on the new service.

Isolation, disinfection, and migration of instances

In the following part, techniques which are handling virtual machine instances are discussed. Three major approaches can be chosen for handling an attacked instance: isolating, disinfecting, and migrating a given one. Each of them will be explained next.

Removing instances from the project VLAN

This approach does not contain the compromised node, instead it focuses on containing instances hosted by the compromised worker node. This is important because those instances may have been compromised as well. The first step toward securing the consumer's service is to disconnect potentially infected instances. The main usecase of this approach is when the attacker disrupts other solutions (e.g., disabling nova-compute management functionalities through escalated privileges at the OS layer), or when instances and the consumer's service security is very important (e.g., eGovernment services). It has several advantages specifically for cloud consumers, including:

- It can disconnect potentially infected instances from the rest of the consumer's instance.
- It does not require implementation of new features.
- The attacker cannot disrupt this method.

The disadvantages are as follows:

- This method only works in a specific OpenStack networking mode (i.e., the VLANManager networking mode).
- The consumer completely loses control over isolated instances, this may lead to data loss or disclosure, service unavailability, etc.

Disabling live migration

Live migration can cause widespread infection, or can be a mechanism for further intrusion to a cloud environment. It may take place intentionally or unintentionally (e.g., an affected consumer may migrate instances to resolve the attack side effects, or the attacker with consumer privileges migrates instances to use a hypervisor vulnerability and gain control over more nodes). Disabling this feature helps the cloud provider to contain the incident more easily, and keep the rest of the environment safer.

Quarantining instances

When we migrate instances from a compromised node, we cannot accept the risk of spreading infection along instance migration. Thus, we should move them to a quarantine worker node first. The quarantine worker node has specific functionalities and tasks, including:

- This worker node limits instances' connectivity with the rest of cloud environment. As an example, only cloud management requests/responses are delivered by the quarantine host.
- It has a set of mechanisms to check instances' integrity and healthiness. These mechanisms can be provided by the underlying hypervisor, cloud platform, or third parties' services

In order to deploy a quarantine node, a set of mechanisms should be studied and employed. Tools that implement such mechanisms will be presented below.

1. **Virtual Machine Introspection**
   This mechanism simplifies inspecting the memory space of a virtual machine from another virtual machine. The task is fairly complex because of the semantic gap between the memory space of those two virtual machines. XenAccess [18] is an example of an introspection library. Using XenAccess the privileged domain can monitor another Xen domain.

2. **Domain Monitoring**
   One of the basic methods to identify a compromised instance is by means of profiling and monitoring the instance behavior. Domain monitoring techniques provide an abstract set of data, compared to the detailed, low level output of a VM introspection tool. For a virtual machine running over a Linux box we can use the libvirt [19] library to access the suspicious instance and study its behavior.

3. **Intrusion Detection**
   Having an intrusion detection system in the hypervisor or cloud platform layer not only provide better visibility for security mechanisms but is also more resistant against a targeted attack from an unauthorized access to an instance. Livewire [20] is a prototype implementation of an intrusion detection system in a hypervisor. Another way to benefit from an intrusion detection system is Amazon's approach, which offers you a standalone Amazon Machine Image (AMI) that contains Snort and Sourcefire Vulnerability Research Team rules. The consumer can then forward its instances' traffic to the virtual machine with intrusion detection capabilities. The

same approach can be utilized in our deployment. The main issue is the approach's performance and utilization.

4. **Utilizing trusted computing concepts**
   Trusted computing is a technology for ensuring the confidentiality and integrity of a computation. It is also useful for remote attestation. Thus, we can use the technology not only for securing our deployment but also to build a better quarantine and infection analysis mechanism. Approaches that have used this concept include vTPM: Virtualizing the Trusted Platform Module [21], TCCP: Trusted Cloud Computing Platform [22], and TVDc: IBM Trusted Virtual Datacenter [23].

It should be noted that although cloud providers or third-party service providers can offer an IDS agent service inside each instance, they cannot force the consumer into accepting it. It is a reasonable argument due to the consumer's organization internal security policies and resource overhead because of the security agent. Thus, applying security services to the underlying layer (i.e. hypervisor, cloud platform) is a preferred solution. Detailed specifications of such a compute worker node is a great opportunity for future work.

Recovering an instance

Recovering an infected or malfunctioning instance can be performed using different techniques. An instance can either be disinfected internally or rebooted from a clean image. However, a tight collaboration between provider and consumer is required for any of these techniques.

Obviously, disinfection of an instance cannot be performed solely by the provider, because it should not access the instance internally, but can only provide a disinfection service (e.g. instance anti-virus) to be used by the consumer at its own will. On the other hand, rebooting an instance from a clean image can be done by the provider or the consumer. Nevertheless, there are several issues in performing the reboot action. First, one must make sure that the instance termination will be done gracefully, so no data will be lost. Second, the VM image must be analyzed for any flaws or security vulnerabilities. Third, before attaching the storage to the rebooted instance, the volume must be disinfected.

Migrating instances

The affected consumer can migrate a specific instance or a set of instances to another compute worker or even another cloud environment. The migration among different providers is currently an open challenge, because of the weak interoperability of cloud systems and lack of standard interfaces for cloud services. In our deployment, both Amazon EC2 APIs and Rackspace APIs are supported. Thus, in theory a consumer can move between any cloud environment provided by the Amazon EC2, RackSpace, and any open deployment of OpenStack without any problem.

Policies

In addition to all techniques that have been studied, a group of security policies should be developed and exercised. These policies can be implemented and enforced inside those techniques, as additional measures.

Component authentication

The component authentication policy enforces that each worker must have a certificate signed by a trusted authority. This authority can be either an external one or the cloud controller/authentication manager itself. Having a signed certificate, the worker can communicate with other components securely. The secure communication can bring us any of the following: confidentiality, integrity, authentication, and non-repudiation.

In this case, the worker's communication confidentiality and authenticity is important for us. For this purpose we can use two different schemes: message encryption or a signature scheme. Each of these schemes can be used for the whole communication or the handshake phase only. When any of those schemes are applied only to the handshake phase, any disconnection or timeout in the communication is a threat to the trust relation. As an authenticated worker is disconnected and reconnected, we cannot only rely on the worker's ID or host-name to presume it as the trusted one. Thus, the handshake phase should be repeated to ensure the authenticity of the worker. Although applying each scheme to all messages among cloud components is tolerant against disruption and disconnection, its overhead for the system and the demand for it should be studied case by case. By applying each of those schemes to all messages, we can tolerate disconnection and disruption. However, using cryptographic techniques for all messages introduce an overhead for the system which may not be efficient or acceptable.

Implementing this method in our environment is simple. The RabbitMQ has features that facilitate communication encryption and client authentication. The *RabbitMQ SSL support* offers encrypted communication [24]. Moreover, an authentication mechanism using the client SSL certificate is offered by the *rabbitmq-auth-mechanism-ssl* plugin [25].

No new worker policy

In addition to the previously discussed technical approaches, a set of management policies can also relax the issue. As an example, no new worker should be added

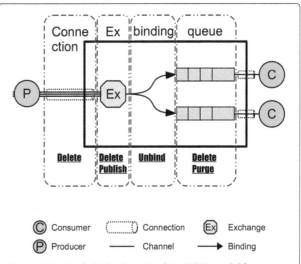

unless there is a demand for it. The demand for a new worker can be determined when the resource utilization for each zone is above a given threshold.

Trust levels and timeouts

Introducing a set of trust levels, a new worker can be labeled as a not trusted worker. Workers which are not trusted yet, can be used for hosting non-critical instances, or can offer a cheaper service to consumers. In order to ensure the system trustworthiness in a long run, a not-trusted worker will be disabled after a timeout. A simple Finite State Machine (FSM) model of those transitions is depicted in Figure 13.

Assuming we have only two trust levels, Figure 14 depicts transitions between them. As an example, *T0* can be achieved by human intervention; and the second level of trust *T1* is gained by cryptographic techniques or trusted computing mechanisms.

This policy can be implemented in the cloud platform scheduler (e.g. nova-scheduler is the responsible component in the OpenStack platform). Implementing

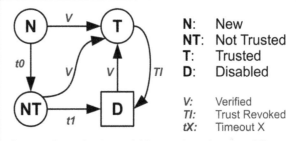

Figure 14 A simple FSM model for transitions between different trust levels of a component.

Table 4 Comparison (RS: Responsible stakeholder, CP: Cloud Provider, CC: Cloud Consumer, P: Proactive, R: Reactive)

Approach	RS	P/R	Service impact	Implementation/Enforcement difficulties	Dependencies
Filtering in the messaging server	CP	R	Platform components may never receive an expected message.	Unless deployed in distributed mode, can become a bottleneck.	Messaging server
Filtering in each component	CP	R	Platform components may never receive an expected message.	All components should be modified to support it.	Platform components
Disabling services	CP	R	Healthy components can become inaccessible. Losing control over instances managed by disabled components.	-	Platform interfaces
Replicating services	CP	P	Services should be replicated based on requirement and performance analysis of the environment.	-	Platform components
Disinfecting infected components	CP	R	Healthy components can become inaccessible. Losing control over instances managed by disabled components.	Configuration management tools and cloud platform interfaces should be deployed and configured.	Configuration management tools, Platform interfaces
Removing instances from the project VLAN	CP CC	R	The instance won't be accessible for the consumer and its services.	Highly dependent on the OpenStack VLAN-Manager networking mode.	Platform components
Disabling live migration	CP	R	Consumer experiences lower QoS.	-	Platform interfaces
Quarantining instances	CP CC	R	Quarantined instances won't be accessible for the consumer.	Implementing this solution requires a lot of effort as discussed briefly in [10].	-
Disinfecting an instance	CP CC	R	-	A framework for analyzing VM images and disinfecting running instances must be developed	Platform interfaces
Migrating instances	CP CC	R	Consumer may experience lower QoS.	The cloud environment should consist of distributed and independent zones.	Platform interfaces
Component authentication	CP	P	Small overhead for all communications.	Developing a system for managing components certificates and identity.	Messaging server and identity services
No new worker policy	CP	P	-	Developing a policy manager component	Messaging server and policy manager
Trust levels and timeouts	CP CC	P	Lower QoS for non-critical use-cases Lower resource volume for critical use-cases	High complexity	Platform interfaces, and scheduler component

this policy will allow the cloud provider to offer more resources for non-critical use-cases. However, the offered QoS might not be as good as before. The effectiveness of this approach is highly dependent on a few parameters, such as the ratio of adding new workers, trust mechanisms and their performance, and consumers' use-cases and requested QoS.

A major challenge in this approach is about trust mechanisms. The simplest mechanisms will be manual determination and confirmation of authenticity and trust level. A recently added worker won't be used for serving consumers' requests until its authenticity is confirmed by the relevant authority (e.g. cloud provider). However, this does not scale: The human intervention can simply become a bottleneck in the system.

Comparison

A list of security mechanisms have been discussed. Although most of them are orthogonal to each other, they can be compared in terms of their common criteria (Table 4). A few criteria are extracted and explained in the following part.

- **Responsible stakeholder**: Each mechanism must be delivered by a single stakeholder or a group of stakeholders. Identifying those responsibilities and assigning them to the right bodies is a crucial step toward building a secure environment.
- **Proactive/Reactive**: Both proactive and reactive mechanisms have been discussed above. Knowing mechanisms' behavior is useful in their enforcement and comparison.
- **Service impact (Affected entities)**: Inevitably, enforcing each mechanism will introduce a set of side effects to delivered services and working entities. Identifying these side effects makes the enforcement process much more predictable.
- **Implementation/Enforcement difficulties**: Finding out implementation challenges of security mechanisms is important. These challenges are meaningful measures in comparing mechanisms with each other.
- **Dependencies**: Dependencies of approaches make them bounded to a specific platform and libraries. Having less or looser dependencies makes the solution more portable. Portable approaches can be developed as generic services that can be applied to a variety of platforms. Thus, we can see the importance of having common and standard interfaces among different platforms, such as Open Cloud Computing Interface (OCCI) and Cloud Data Management Interface (CDMI).

Conclusion

Cloud computing is a new computing model, whose definitions and realizations have new characteristics compared to other computing models. New characteristics hinder the application of existing mechanisms. In some cases, existing approaches are not applicable, and in other cases adaptation is required. Initially, we studied different aspects of a real cloud environment, working on a deployed environment instead of focusing on an imaginary computing model. Experimenting on a deployed environment is helpful in reducing the gap between academic research and industrial deployment/requirements. Many questions that are discussed in an academic environment are already solved in industry, or are not the right questions at all. A good blog post on this issue can be found in [26].

Although our lab setup was not big enough to be industry realistic, it was useful for understanding the ecosystem of the cloud model, and observing possible weaknesses in it. Obviously, deploying a larger infrastructure reveals more information about the exact behavior of the environment, and the result will be more accurate. However, that may not be feasible as a university project unless big players in the cloud are willing to contribute, as can be seen in efforts such as OpenCirrus [27] (supported by HP, Intel, and Yahoo!), the Google Exacycle [28] program, and Amazon grants for educators, researchers and students [29].

In our study we have decided to use the OpenStack cloud software. There were multiple reasons behind this decision, such as:

- Working on an open source project helps the community, and pushes the open source paradigm forward.
- Analysis of the platform and experimenting with different approaches is easier and more efficient when we can access the source code.
- Big companies are involved in the OpenStack project, and many of them are using the platform in their own infrastructure. Thus, OpenStack can become a leading open source cloud platform in the near future.

This study was started only 4 months after the first release of OpenStack, and much of the required documentation was either not available or not good enough. We studied the OpenStack components and identified their functionalities and other specifications. Moreover, working with a platform which is under heavy development, has its own challenges.

In order to secure the environment against a compromised component, we have to handle the corresponding incident. The NIST incident handling guideline has been studied and applied to our experimental cloud environment. During the application process we did not limit ourselves to the lab setup, because it was not large/distributed enough. So, in the proposed approaches we considered a large scale, highly distributed target environment; and made those approaches compatible with such an environment. Moreover, the NIST guideline recommends a set of actions for each handling phase. These actions can be realized using a variety of mechanisms. We have studied several mechanisms and discussed their compatibilities with the cloud model. Additionally, we have proposed new approaches that are helpful in fulfilling incident handling requirements. Furthermore, in this process multiple questions and challenges were raised that can be interesting topics for future work in cloud incident handling and in general security of a cloud environment. We itemize a few of them in the following:

- Statistical measurement and analysis of each approach and study of the exact performance overhead.
- Large scale deployment of OpenStack with its latest release.
- Implementation of proposed approaches as a set of security services, and study their effectiveness for a cloud consumer and the cloud environment in general.
- Study the compatibility of approaches and guidelines to other cloud environments, specifically with those operated by industry or commercial cloud providers (e.g. Amazon, Rackspace, Google App Engine, Azure).

Endnotes

[a] REpresentational State Transfer

[b] Avoiding false positive alarms

[c] By the term *organization*, we mean all entities who are responsible for managing the cloud infrastructure, which can be referred to as the cloud provider

[d] In a publisher/subscriber paradigm the destination may be eliminated or masked by other parameters. So, we may filter messages that contain any evidence of being related to the infected host

[e] It should be noted, although we may use directory and federation services to unify users among services and layers, this may not be a feasible approach in a cloud environment. However, federation is applicable at each layer (e.g. system, cloud platform, VM instances)

[f] Scaling out or horizontal scaling is referred to the application deployment on multiple servers [30]

[g] But it may require a correlation entity to handle the filtering tasks among all messaging servers

Competing interests
The authors declare that they have no competing interests.

Author's contributions
ATM performed the configuration and testing of the OpenStack lab environment, and drafted the paper. MGJ supervised the practical work, and contributed to the writing to improve the quality of the text. All authors read and approved the final document.

Acknowledgements
This article is based on results from MSc Thesis work performed at Norwegian University of Science and Technology (NTNU).

Author details
[1]UNINETT, Trondheim, Norway. [2]SINTEF ICT, Trondheim, Norway.

References
1. McCarthy J (1999) MIT Centennial Speech of 1961 cited in Architects of the Information Society: Thirty-five Years of the Laboratory for Computer Science at MIT. S.L. Garfinkel Ed. MIT Press, Cambridge MA
2. Mell P, Grance T (2011) The NIST Definition of Cloud Computing, Technical Report SP 800-145. National Institute of Standards and Technology, Information Technology Laboratory
3. Chen Y, Paxson V, Katz RH What's New About Cloud Computing Security? Technical Report UCB/EECS-2010-5, EECS Department, University of California, Berkeley 2010. http://www.eecs.berkeley.edu/Pubs/TechRpts/2010/EECS-2010-5.html
4. TaheriMonfared A, Jaatun MG (2011) As Strong as the Weakest Link: Handling compromised compoeents in OpenStack. In: Proceedings of the third IEEE International Conference on Cloud Computing Technology and Science (CloudCom)
5. OpenStack Community (2011) OpenStack Projects page. http://openstack.org/projects/
6. Walsh S (2011) Multiple Cluster Zones. http://wiki.openstack.org/MultiClusterZones
7. Scarfone K, Grance T, Masone K (2008) Computer Security Incident Handling Guide. Special Publications SP 800-61 Rev. 1, NIST. http://csrc.nist.gov/publications/nistpubs/800-61-rev1/SP800-61rev1.pdf
8. TaheriMonfared A, Jaatun MG (2011) Monitoring Intrusions and Security Breaches in Highly Distributed Cloud Environments. In: Proceedings of CloudCom 2011
9. AWS Security Team (2011) Vulnerability Reporting. http://aws.amazon.com/security/vulnerability-reporting/
10. TaheriMonfared A (2011) Securing the IaaS Service Model of Cloud Computing Against Compromised Components. MSc thesis, Norwegian University of Science and Technology (NTNU)
11. Jokela P, Zahemszky A, Esteve Rothenberg C, Arianfar S, Nikander P (2009) LIPSIN: line speed publish/subscribe inter-networking. In: Proceedings of the ACM SIGCOMM 2009 conference on Data communication, SIGCOMM '09. ACM, New York, pp 195–206. http://doi.acm.org/10.1145/1592568.1592592
12. Broder A, Mitzenmacher M (2002) Network Applications of Bloom Filters: A Survey. In: Internet Mathematics. pp 636–646
13. RabbitMQ Core API Guide (2011) http://www.rabbitmq.com/api-guide.html
14. Trieloff C, McHale C, Sim G, Piskiel H, O'Hara J, Brome J, van der Riet K, Atwell M, Lucina M, Hintjens P, Greig R, Joyce S, Shrivastava S (2006) Advanced Message Queuing Protocol Protocol Specification. amq-spec, AMQP.org. [Version 0.8]
15. Samovskiy D (2008) Introduction to AMQP Messaging with RabbitMQ
16. Tan Y, Luo D, Wang J (2010) CC-VIT: Virtualization Intrusion Tolerance Based on Cloud Computing. In: Information Engineering and Computer Science (ICIECS), 2010 2nd International Conference on. pp 1–6
17. Puppet Labs (2011) http://www.puppetlabs.com/
18. XenAccess (2009) http://www.xenaccess.org/
19. libvirt Wiki (2011) http://wiki.libvirt.org/page/Main_Page#libvirt_Wiki
20. Garfinkel T, Rosenblum M (2003) A Virtual Machine Introspection Based Architecture for Intrusion Detection. In: Proc. Network and Distributed Systems Security Symposium

21. Berger S, Cáceres R, Goldman KA, Perez R, Sailer R, van Doorn L (2006) vTPM: Virtualizing the Trusted Platform Module. Research Report RC23879, IBM Research Division
22. Santos N, Gummadi KP, Rodrigues R (2009) Towards Trusted Cloud Computing. In: HOTCLOUD, USENIX
23. Berger S, Cáceres R, Pendarakis D, Sailer R, Valdez E, Perez R, Schildhauer W, Srinivasan D (2007) TVDc: Managing Security in the Trusted Virtual Datacenter. Research Report RC24441, IBM Research Division
24. RabbitMQ SSL (2011) http://www.rabbitmq.com/ssl.html
25. MacMullen S (2011) Who are you? Authentication and authorisation in RabbitMQ. http://www.rabbitmq.com/blog/2011/02/07/who-are-you-authentication-and-authorisation-in-rabbitmq-231/
26. Welsh M (2011) How can academics do research on cloud computing? http://matt-welsh.blogspot.com/2011/05/how-can-academics-do-research-on-cloud.html
27. Open Cirrus (2011) https://opencirrus.org/
28. Belov D (2011) 1 billion core-hours of computational capacity for researchers. http://googleresearch.blogspot.com/2011/04/1-billion-core-hours-of-computational.html
29. AWS in Education (2011) http://aws.amazon.com/education/
30. Michael M, Moreira J, Shiloach D, Wisniewski R (2007) Scale-up x Scale-out: A Case Study using Nutch/Lucene. In: Parallel and Distributed Processing Symposium, 2007. IPDPS 2007. IEEE International. pp 1–8

## 3

Discrete control for ensuring consistency between multiple autonomic managers

Soguy Mak karé Gueye[1]*, Noël De Palma[1], Eric Rutten[2], Alain Tchana[1] and Daniel Hagimont[3]

Abstract

The increasing complexity of computer systems has led to the automation of administration functions, in the form of autonomic managers. Today many autonomic managers are available but they mostly address a specific administration aspect which makes necessary their coexistence for a complete autonomic system management. However, coordinating them is necessary for proper and effective global administration. Such coordination can be considered as a problem of synchronization and logical control of managers actions. We therefore investigate the use of reactive models with events and states, and discrete control techniques to solve this problem. This paper presents an application of the latter approach for coordinating autonomic managers addressing resource optimization, in the perspective of green computing. The managers control server provisioning (self-sizing manager) and CPU frequency (Dvfs manager), and the coordination controller controls the managers actions so as to avoid incoherent management decisions. The coordination controller is designed using synchronous programming and Discrete controller synthesis (DCS) which are well-suited for the design of reactive systems. Experimental results are presented to evaluate the efficacy of the approach.

Introduction

Computing systems have become more and more complex and harder to manage manually. Their architecture is mostly distributed involving several hardware and software components operating in a dynamic heterogeneous environment. Manual management of such systems can be time-consuming, expensive and error-prone. Autonomic computing [1] proposes a solution for the management issues consisting in automating the management functions in the form of an autonomic manager. An autonomic manager continuously monitors the managed system so as to detect any change in the system state that is in contrast to its objectives. When it detects such a change, it applies administration operations to lead the system to a state in which its objectives are satisfied. An autonomic manager is generally implemented in a closed loop, which can be inspired by techniques from control theory, continuous as well as discrete. Today many autonomic managers are available but they mostly address a specific administration aspect which makes necessary their coexistence

for a complete autonomic system management. However the coexistence of several managers has to be coordinated to avoid incoherent and conflicting management decisions. Implementing manually such a coordination can be tedious, difficult to test and validate, and maintain.

This paper proposes an approach for coordinating multiple autonomic managers based on the discrete control approach. This provides high level programming languages for formal specification of a control system, and tools for automating the verification and validation of properties, and Discrete Controller Synthesis (DCS) for the synthesis of the control logic allowing to guarantee the properties, and code generation. Formal descriptions and proofs of correction of the techniques and tools used are presented in [2] and the theories and mathematical models in [3]. The benefit of this approach is the automatic generation of the coordination controller instead of manually programming it in which case it could be complex, tedious and error-prone.

To put our approach into practice, we consider the coordination of two autonomic managers addressing the resource optimization of a system. One addresses the resource optimization within a machine (e.g., *Dynamic Voltage/Frequency Scaling (DVFS)*) while the other

*Correspondence: soguy-mak-kare.gueye@inria.fr
[1] ERODS Team - Bât. IMAG C, 220 rue de la Chimie, 38 400 St Martin d'Hères, France
Full list of author information is available at the end of the article

addresses the resource optimization within a replication-based system (e.g., *server provisioning (self-sizing)*). These managers act on different management levels, but their actions are complementary to improve resource optimization when coordinated, hence reducing the energy consumption of the managed system.

In the following, we present in section 'Autonomic managers for resource optimization' two autonomic managers, self-sizing and Dvfs. We details in section 'Synchronous programming and discrete controller synthesis' the principles of BZR, a synchronous programming language allowing modelling a system through automata and integrating *DCS* within its compiler. We detail in section 'Discrete control for coordinating self-sizing and Dvfs managers' the design of a coordination controller for the two managers and show how it is integrated within a management system in section 'Implementation'. We show evaluation of the coordinated execution with our approach in section 'Experimentation' and discuss related work in section 'Related work'. Finally, in section 'Conclusion and future work', we conclude the paper and outline directions for future work.

Autonomic managers for resource optimization

This section presents two autonomic managers dealing with resource optimization. Their management decisions consist to reduce the resource allocated to the managed system while preserving good performance. They act at different management levels but their management actions are complementary to improve energy optimization through resource optimization when coordinated.

Server provisioning manager: Self-Sizing

This manager, inspired from [4], addresses the management of the degree of replication of a replicated-based system where each replicated server handles a part of the workload. It dynamically adapts the number of active replicated servers depending on the load of the machines hosting the replicated servers. The load of the machines is measured through the load of their CPU.

As shown in Figure 1, the management decisions of the manager rely on thresholds (maximum threshold and minimum threshold) delimiting the optimal CPU load range. The manager collects the CPU load of the machines hosting the active replicated servers and computes a moving average (**Avg_CPU**). When **Avg CPU** is higher than the maximum threshold, it considers that the servers (hosts) are overloaded and it adds a new replicated server. When **Avg_CPU** is less than the minimum threshold, it considers that the servers are underloaded, removes a replicated server and turns off the machine that hosts the server.

CPU-frequency manager: Dvfs

This manager, inspired from [5], targets a single machine management. Its role is to dynamically adapt the CPU-frequency of the machine depending on its CPU load.

As shown in Figure 2, the management decisions rely also on thresholds (maximum threshold and minimum threshold) delimiting the optimal CPU load range. When the CPU load of the machine is higher than the maximum threshold, the manager increases the CPU-frequency if the maximum frequency is not reached. It decreases the CPU-frequency when the CPU load of the machine is less than the minimum threshold if the minimum CPU frequency is not reached. This manager runs on the machine it manages. It is implemented either in hardware or software. The one we use is a software implementation and follows the on-demand policy.

Coexistence problem

The coexistence of both self-sizing and Dvfs managers can improve resource optimization. While using the self-sizing manager to optimize the number of active machines allocated to a replication-based system, Dvfs managers can be deployed on each active machine to perform local optimization by adjusting the CPU frequency. However their coexistence has to be coordinated to avoid incoherent management decisions. Indeed when each machine hosting a replicated server is equipped with a Dvfs manager, their CPU-frequency might not be maximal all the time. The Dvfs managers can lower the frequency of the CPU of the machines which makes the latter work slower. In higher frequency a CPU can handle more instructions per time unit than in lower Frequency. A workload which can overload a CPU in lower frequency can possibly be supported by the CPU in higher frequency. So when self-sizing detects an overload in lower CPU frequency, the adding operation it performs can be unnecessary if increasing the CPU frequency of the active machines before the adding operation is sufficient to support the workload. More when an overload occurs in lower frequency and is detected by self-sizing and Dvfs, the adding operation and the CPU increase operations performed by the managers can cause a decrease of the CPU utilization under the minimum threshold leading to removal and CPU decrease operations. When an underload occurs in higher frequency, the removal operations and CPU decrease operations performed by the managers can cause an increase of the CPU utilization over the maximum threshold leading to adding and CPU increase operations.

Coordination strategy

A strategy to achieve an efficient resource optimization and avoid incoherent operations could be to delay as long as possible adding a new replicated server when the machines hosting the active servers are not in their

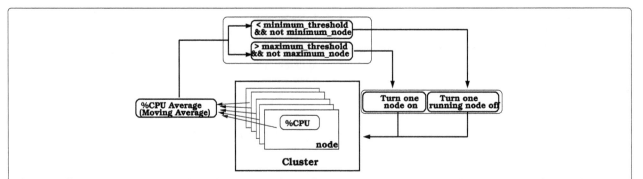

Figure 1 Self-sizing manager. Figure 1 shows the execution scheme of the server provisioning manager. The CPU utilization of the machines hosting the replicated servers are measured and a moving average is computed. If this moving average is higher than the fixed maximum threshold, the manager adds a new server on one unused machine. If the moving average is less than the fixed minimum threshold, the manager removes a server and turns the machine running the stopped server off.

maximum CPU frequency. Indeed the evaluation of an overload by self-sizing is relevant only in higher CPU frequency in which case the CPU frequency can no more be increased. This can be stated as follows:

- **Ignoring overload of the machines hosting the replicated servers** — if these machines are not in their maximum CPU frequency.

This allows to add a new replicated server only when the active ones are in maximum CPU frequency and become overloaded.

Synchronous programming and discrete controller synthesis

Synchronous programming allows to model the dynamics (functional and/or non-functional aspects) of a system as an automaton. A system composed of several sub-systems can be modelled via a composition of automata, where each single automaton models the dynamics of each specific sub-system. Hence, the composition models the state of the system as a whole.

With some controllable transitions in the automata, Discrete Controller Synthesis (DCS) tools [6] can compute a controller that restrains the set of reachable states (i.e., all possible behaviours) to those satisfying a *control objective* (e.g., a coordination policy).

In this Section, we first briefly introduce the basics of the synchronous language Heptagon. We then describe the main features of BZR, that extends Heptagon with a new construct for expressing behavioural contracts [3]. BZR is the language we use for the synthesis of a coordination controller.

Automata and data-flow nodes

The Heptagon language allows the programming of reactive systems by means of mixed synchronous data-flow equations and automata with parallel and hierarchical composition [7]. The basic behaviour is that of the synchronous data-flow languages family [8]: at each reaction step, values of the input flows are used, as well as local and memory values, in order to compute the values of the output flows for that step, and memories for the next step. Inside *nodes* (i.e., block of codes defining an automaton or

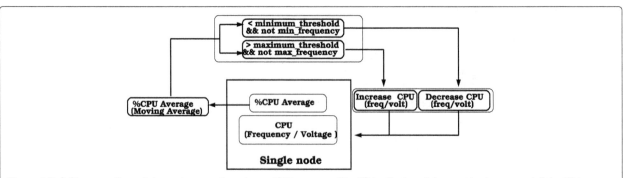

Figure 2 Dvfs Manager. Figure 2 shows the execution scheme of this manager. The CPU utilization of the machine is measured. If the CPU utilization is higher than the fixed maximum threshold, the manager increases the CPU frequency of the machine. If the CPU utilization is less than the fixed minimum threshold, the manager decreases the CPU frequency of the machine.

a composition of automata), these computations are specified as a system of equations defining, for each output and local, the value of the flow in terms of an expression on other flows and memories.

Figure 3 shows a small program in Heptagon. It expresses the control of a `delayable` task that can either be idle, waiting or active. When it is in the initial Idle state, the occurrence of the **true** value on input r *requests* the start of the task. Another input c (which will be controlled by an external controller) can either allow the activation, or temporarily block the request and make the automaton go to a waiting state (Wait). When in Active, the task can end and go back to the Idle state, upon the notification input e. The `delayable` node has two outputs, a representing activity of the task, and s being emitted on the instant when it becomes active : this latter triggers the concrete start operation in the system's API.

Such automata and data-flow reactive nodes can be composed in parallel and in a hierarchical way. They can be defined and re-used by instantiations of the nodes (see Figure 4 bellow for an illustration, with two instances of Figure 3's node). They run in parallel, defined by synchronous composition (noted " ; "): one global step corresponds to one local step for every equation, i.e., here, for every instance of the `delayable` node.

The compilation of an Heptagon program produces executable code in target languages such as C or Java, in the form of an initialization procedure *reset*, and a *step* procedure implementing the transition function of the resulting automaton. *step* takes incoming values of input flows gathered in the environment, computes the next state on internal variables, and returns values of the output flows. It is called at relevant instants from the infrastructure where the program is used.

Contracts and control in BZR

[3] propose BZR[a] that extends Heptagon with a new construct for expressing behavioural contracts. Its com-

$$twotasks(r_1, e_1, r_2, e_2) = a_1, s_1, a_2, s_2$$

enforce not $(a_1$ **and** $a_2)$

with c_1, c_2

$$(a_1, s_1) = delayable(r_1, c_1, e_1)$$
$$(a_2, s_2) = delayable(r_2, c_2, e_2)$$

Figure 4 Mutual exclusion enforced by DCS in BZR. Figure 4 shows the design of a controller in BZR programming language. In this example we compose two instances of the program shown in Figure 3 and enforce a mutual exclusion between two instances.

pilation involves discrete controller synthesis [6]. DCS can be described as a formal operation on automata [9]: given an automaton representing all possible behaviours of a system, its variables are partitioned into controllable and uncontrollable variables. For a given control objective (e.g., staying permanently inside a subset of states, considered "good"), the DCS algorithm automatically computes, for each state and value of the uncontrollables, the constraint on controllable variables so that all remaining behaviours satisfy the objective. This constraint is the least necessary, inhibiting the minimum possible behaviours, therefore it is called *maximally permissive*. Formalisms and algorithms are related to model-checking techniques for state space exploration. They are described elsewhere by [6] and [10].

Concretely, the BZR language permits the declaration, using the **with** statement, of controllable variables, the value of which being not defined by the programmer. These free variables can be used in the program to describe choices between several transitions. They are then defined, in the final executable program, by the controller computed by DCS, according to the expression given in the **enforce** statement. A possibility exists, not

```
node delayable(r,c,e:bool) returns (a,s:bool)
  let
    automaton
      state Idle
        do a = false ; s = r and c
        until r and c then Active
          | r and not c then Wait
      state Wait
        do a = false ; s = c
        until c then Active
      state Active
        do a = true ; s=false
        until e then Idle
    end
  tel
```

Figure 3 Delayable task in textual and graphical syntax. Figure 3 shows an example of a program with the BZR programming language. In the left hand side, we show the syntax of the language. In the right hand side, we depict the corresponding automaton.

used here, to take into account some knowledge about the environment in an **assume** statement; observers can be used to have objective like: always having a task t_1 between t_2 and t_3". BZR compilation invokes a DCS tool, and inserts the synthesized controller in the generated executable code. The latter has the same structure as above: *reset* and *step* procedures.

Figure 4 shows an example of contract coordinating two instances of the delayable node of Figure 3. The twotasks node has a **with** part declaring controllable variables c_1 and c_2. The **enforce** part asserts the property to be enforced by DCS. Here, we want to ensure that the two tasks running in parallel will not be both active at the same time: **not** (a_1 **and** a_2). The controllable variables c_1 and c_2 will be used by the computed controller to block some requests, leading automata of tasks to the Wait state whenever the other task is in its Active state. Observe that the constraint produced by DCS can have several solutions: the BZR compiler generates deterministic executable code by favouring, for each controllable variable, value **true** over **false**, in the order of declaration in the **with** statement.

Discrete control for coordinating self-sizing and Dvfs managers

This section presents the design of a coordination controller for the self-sizing and Dvfs managers. We first describe the automata modelling the self-sizing and Dvfs managers, then we describe how the coordination controller is designed from these models. The self-sizing is modelled with some control point allowing the control of its operations. In this work, the Dvfs actions are not controlled, we model the global states of the set of Dvfs which are necessary for controlling the self-sizing operations. Indeed the management actions of each Dvfs depend mainly on the load its managed machine receives, which affects the CPU utilization.

Modelling the self-sizing manager

This section presents the automata modelling the self-sizing manager. They represent both the behaviours of the manager (Figure 5) and the control of its operations (Figure 6). The automaton in Figure 5 shows the behaviours of the manager. Initially in the **UpDown** state, When an overload occurs and the upsizing operations are allowed, the manager requests a new node, and goes to the **Adding** state. It awaits in this state until the requested server is available and active. During this period it can no longer perform operations. When **node_added** occurs, the manager returns back to the **UpDown** state or goes the **Down** state if the maximum number of active servers is reached. The **Down** state is left once one node is removed upon an **Underload** event. The **Up** state represents the state in which the degree of replication is minimum and

can no longer be decreased. In this case the manager will not perform a downsizing operation regardless the workload (i.e., only upsizing operations can be performed). Table 1 describes the input and output variables of the automaton. The automaton in Figure 6 models the control of the adding operations. Initially in the **Idle** state where adding operations are inhibited, when **c** becomes **true** the automaton goes to the **Active** state allowing to perform adding operations. It stays in this state until **c** becomes **false** and returns back to the **Idle** state. As shown in Table 2, this automaton has one output, i.e., **delay**, which allows upsizing operations when it is **false**. This output feeds the input **delay** in Figure 5. The input and output variables of the automaton are described in Table 2.

Modelling the global states of the set of Dvfs

This section presents the automaton modelling the global states of the set of Dvfs managers presented in Figure 7. Initially in the **Normal** state, the automaton goes to the **Max** state when all Dvfs managers are in their maximum CPU-frequency or to the **Min** state when all Dvfs managers are in their minimum CPU-frequency. It returns back to the **Normal** state when all Dvfs are neither in their maximal frequency nor in the minimal frequency. As shown in Table 3, this automaton has two outputs, **max_freq** being **true** when all local Dvfs reach their maximum frequency and **min_freq** being **true** when all local Dvfs reach their minimum frequency. The input and output variables of the automaton are described in Table 3.

Designing the coordination controller for self-sizing and Dvfs

This section presents the design of the coordination controller for self-sizing and the set of active Dvfs. As shown in Figure 8, the automata modelling the self-sizing and the Dvfs are composed in parallel. The composition of the automata models the uncoordinated coexistence of the managers. The coordination policy is expressed as a contract to be enforced on the latter composition. At compilation DCS automatically generates the control logic capable to attribute value to the controllable variable so as to enforce the coordination policy and restrain the composition to the states satisfying the coordination policy. The composition of the automata and the generated control logic model the coordinated coexistence of the managers.

Contract

To achieve the coordination strategy, we formally define an invariant. The invariant is expressed via the outputs of the automata. It is specified as a contract to be enforced at compilation time.

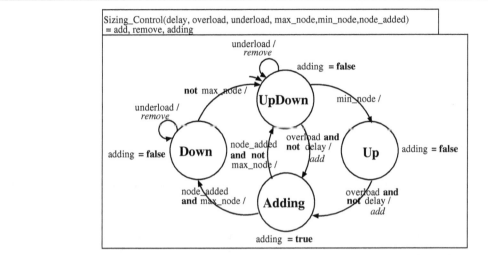

Figure 5 Modelling self-Sizing behaviours. Figure 5 shows the automaton modelling the behaviours of the self-sizing manager.

Coordination policy The strategy consists in preventing the self-sizing manager from adding a new replicated server when the machines hosting the current active servers are not in maximum CPU frequency. This means that the adding operations are inhibited when the Dvfs managers can increase the CPU frequency of their managed machines. To this end, the invariant is defined as follows:

- $invariant = (\text{max\_freq and not } \texttt{delay}) \text{ or } (\textbf{not } \text{max\_freq and } \texttt{delay})$

Enforcement

At compilation, the BZR compiler will synthesize a control logic capable of enforcing the coordination policy in the composition by acting on the controllable variable **c** which is an input of the automaton in Figure 6. The composition of the automata and the computed control logic is

generated in a target language (i.e., in Java for this work), which will constitute the coordination controller for the managers within the managed system. This coordination policy is very simple but allows to perform the complete experiment including implementation as shown in next section.

Implementation

This section shows how the generated program from BZR compiler is integrated into the management system. This consists in connecting the inputs of the automata to the corresponding events and the outputs of the automata to the corresponding commands or operations.

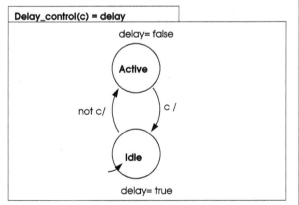

Figure 6 Modelling the control of self-Sizing. Figure 6 models the control of the self-sizing adding operations.

Table 1 Variables of the automaton modelling the self-sizing behaviours

Variable	Type	Description
delay	Input	Upsizing operations are suspended.
overload	Input	An overload occurs in the system.
underload	Input	An underload occurs in the system.
min_node	Input	The minimum number of replicas is reached
max_node	Input	The maximum number of replicas is reached.
node_added	Input	The completion of an upsizing operation.
adding	Output	The manager is waiting for the completion of an upsizing operation.
add	Output	The manager is launching an upsizing operation. Its value depends on the value of delay and overload.
remove	Output	The manager is launching the downsizing operation. Its value depends on the value of underload.

Table gives a description of the input and output variables of the automaton modelling the self-sizing behaviours.

Table 2 Variables of the automaton modelling the control of self-sizing

Variable	Type	Description.
c	Input	The upsizing operations must be suspended.
delay	Output	The manager has suspended the launch of upsizing operations.

Table gives a description of the input and output variables of the automaton modelling the control of the self-sizing.

Connecting the automata

The automata model an aspect of the dynamics of the self-sizing and Dvfs. Their inputs correspond to the events that trigger transitions between the states in the dynamics (e.g., overload for self-sizing and maximum CPU frequency reached for Dvfs). Their outputs reflect the current state in which the automata are and possibly the operations which should be processed (e.g., add server).

The automaton shown in Figure 7 takes the state of the sef of Dvfs represented by the inputs **maximum** and **minimum**. The input **maximum** (respectively **minimum**) being **true** corresponds to the state where the set of Dvfs reaches the maximum CPU frequency (respectively the minimum CPU frequency). The automaton in Figure 5 models the dynamics of the decision making module of the self-sizing and its control. The input **overload** (resp. **underload**) is the event that triggers **upsizing** (resp. **downsizing**) if **max_node** (resp. **min_node**) is false.**overload** and **underload** are the result of the evaluation of the **CPU_Avg** while **max_node** and **min_node** are the result of the execution of the management operations **upsizing** and **downwsizing**. The triggering of **upsizing** (resp. **downsizing**) is represented by the output **add_node** (resp. **remove_node**) being **true**. The automaton in Figure 6 models the control of the decision making module. It has one input (**i.e., c**) which is controllable. The latter is managed by the synthesized control logic through DCS and the output (**delay**) of the automaton is used

Table 3 Variables of the automaton modelling the global states of the set of Dvfs

Variable	Type	Description
maximum	Input	Corresponds to the conjunction of all *max*.
minimum	Input	Corresponds to the conjunction of all *min*.
max_freq	Output	All Dvfs manager are in the maximum CPU-frequency.
min_freq	Output	All Dvfs manager are in the minimum CPU-frequency.

Table gives a description of the input and output variables of the automaton modelling the global states of the set of Dvfs managers.

to control the value of the input delay in the automaton in Figure 5 in order to control transitions leading to the adding state when necessary.

Integration of the generated code for coordinating managers

The compilation of the BZR program returns a set of Java classes corresponding to the composition of the automata presented above with the computed control logic. A main Java class allows to interact with the program. This class has two methods: *reset* and *step*. The *reset* method allows to initialize the program (i.e., initialize all automata and the generated controller) and the *step* method allows to compute transitions (i.e., transition in the automata). The *step* method takes arguments corresponding to the inputs of the automata and returns outputs corresponding to outputs of the automata. A loop has to be defined to call the *step* with the appropriate inputs and to manage the outputs referring to commands such as preventing upsizing operations of the Self-sizing manager. We implement a loop that receives events from sensors, calls the *step* method with required inputs and transmits the outputs of the *step* method to managers.

Figure 9 represents the architecture of a system in which the coordination controller is integrated. Since the role of this coordination controller is to control which manager should react or not to events, all detected events are first transmitted to the coordination controller. The outputs of the latter are forwarded to the controlled managers i.e in this case the self-Sizing manager. The interface allows interaction between the synchronous program, the sensors and the managers.

Experimentation

In this paper we only focus on the integration of a controller obtained through the Discrete control techniques for the coordination of autonomic managers. The purpose is to show that the latter controller react properly regarding the coordination policy although the system considered is small.

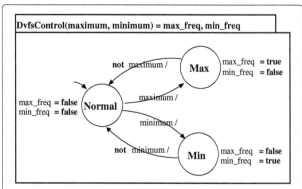

Figure 7 Modelling the global states of the set of Dvfs. Figure 7 models the global states of the set of Dvfs managers.

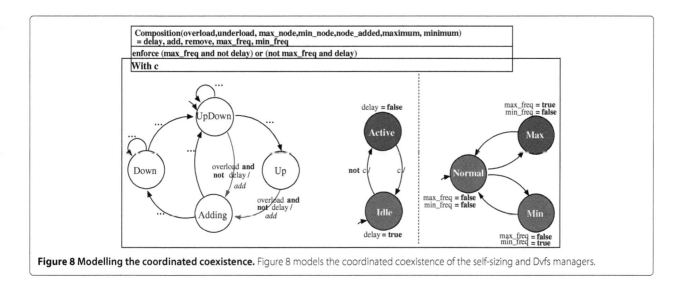

Figure 8 Modelling the coordinated coexistence. Figure 8 models the coordinated coexistence of the self-sizing and Dvfs managers.

The experimental platform, as shown in Figures 10 and 11, consists of a network of three nodes with the same characteristics (CPU, memory, etc.). node 0 hosts the Apache server, the coordination controller and self-sizing. node 1 and node 2 host a Tomcat server. The Apache server acts as a load balancer, it receives all clients requests and distributes the requests to active Tomcat servers for treatment. The self-sizing manager controls the number of active Tomcat servers. Initially, only node 1 is on, self-sizing either turns node 2 on when node 1 is not able to handle all clients requests or off when clients requests can be treated by node 1. node 1 and node 2 have two CPU frequency levels which are 800MHz being their minimum CPU frequency and 1.20GHz being their maximum CPU frequency. The experimental application is CPU bound. We use jmeter[b] to simulate clients sending HTTP requests to the managed system.

In the following we calibrate the thresholds of the managers in order for them to react properly individually at runtime. Then we present executions, to evaluate the behaviours of the synthesized controller.

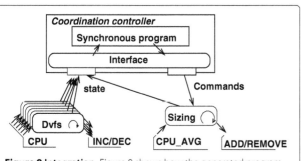

Figure 9 Integration. Figure 9 shows how the generated program can be integrated within a management system.

Calibrating the managers thresholds

This section details how the *Maximum Threshold* and the *Minimum Threshold* for both self-sizing and Dvfs managers are determined. We perform heuristic experimentations to determine these thresholds. For both managers, the *Maximum Threshold* can be statically fixed while the *Minimum Threshold* can be dynamically adapted.

Determining the maximum threshold (T^{max}) for self-sizing and Dvfs

The CPU load is 100 percent means that the CPU is fully utilized. This causes delay on the execution of instructions and the degradation of the performance of the machine. So it is better to consider a maximum threshold less than 100. We choose arbitrary *90 as T^{max}*. At 90 percent, a machine becomes overloaded but it executes instructions in an optimal period of time. This allows to perform operations for monitoring (i.e., CPU load) and reconfiguring (i.e., increase of the CPU frequency) sufficiently fast to avoid performance degradation. The Maximum Threshold (T^{max}) for self-sizing as well as for Dvfs is fixed to 90 percent.

Determining the minimum threshold (T^{min}) for self-Sizing and Dvfs

We use different workloads following the same profile (a ramp-up phase followed by a constant phase), to observe the impact of the management operations of the managers on the CPU utilization. The management operations are performed manually once the workload is constant and stable to evaluate the factor by which the CPU utilization varies. The difference between the workload is the amount of requests injected. This allows to determine if the factor is the same for each workload. This allows to deduct an equation for calculating the *Minimum*

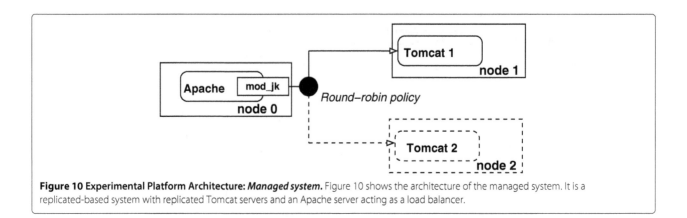

Figure 10 Experimental Platform Architecture: _Managed system._ Figure 10 shows the architecture of the managed system. It is a replicated-based system with replicated Tomcat servers and an Apache server acting as a load balancer.

Threshold based on the _Maximum Threshold,_ and the number of active replicated servers for self-sizing.

Minimum threshold (T^{max}) for self sizing Figure 12 shows experimentations in which adding operations are performed. We start each experimentation with one server. Once the load becomes stable, we add a new replicated server. Since the workload is fairly distributed between the active servers, we expect a decrease of the CPU utilization by half. However the average load measured is always higher than the expected average. Figures 13 shows experimentations in which we perform removal operations. We start each experimentation with two servers. Once the load becomes stable, we remove a replicated server. The load of the remaining server increases but not by factor of two compared to the load before the removal. This means that, for a replicated-based system that can run at most two replicated servers, $T^{min} = T^{max}/2$.

However, in a replicated server-based system there are possibly more than two replicated servers and we want to

remove a machine as soon as possible. Removing a server as soon as possible when its workload can be distributed to the remaining servers without overloading them leads to a dynamic estimation of T^{min} depending on the current active servers. This can be expressed as follows:

$$T^{min} + \frac{T^{min}}{(n-1)} < T^{max},$$

where n is the current number of servers.

$$T^{min} < T^{max} * \frac{(n-1)}{n} \implies T^{min} = [T^{max} * \frac{(n-1)}{n}] - C$$

C is a margin. It denotes the difference between the maximum value of T^{min} and the acceptable value of T^{min} sufficiently high for detecting underload and sufficiently far from T^{max} to avoid oscillations of the CPU utilization between the maximum threshold and the minimum threshold which possibly trigger unnecessary reconfiguration operations. In our experimentations, we consider $C = 0$. In case of two machines, we have: $T^{min} = [\frac{T^{max}}{2}] - C$.

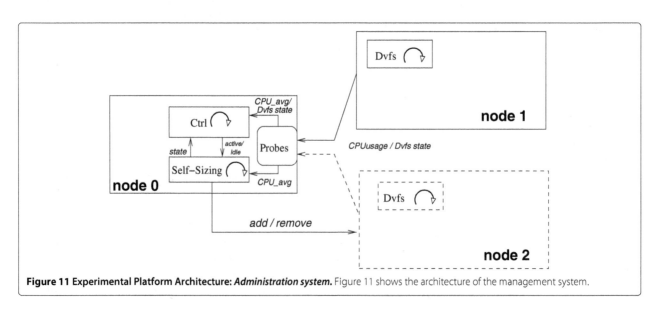

Figure 11 Experimental Platform Architecture: _Administration system._ Figure 11 shows the architecture of the management system.

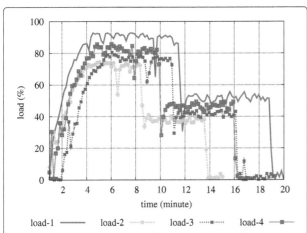

Figure 12 Calibrating self-sizing minimal threshold. Figures 12 shows executions, with different workloads. During these executions, we add a replicated server in order to observe the impact of these operations on the CPU utilization.

As shown in Figures 12, the CPU load does not decrease by half when one server was added and Figures 13, the CPU load does not double when one server was removed. This equation, $T^{min} = [fracT^{max}2]$, is enough to avoid side effects. So there is no risk of oscillations.

Determining the value of C – To avoid oscillation when the number of servers becomes large a maximum value for T^{min} can be fixed. This avoid T^{min} to be close to T^{max}. In this case the maximum value of T^{min} is used whenever the computed value of T^{min} is higher than the latter.

Minimum threshold (T^{min}) for Dvfs In our platform, the machines hosting replicated server have two CPU frequency levels, 800Mhz and 1.2Ghz. A workload that overloads the machine in frequency 800Mhz could possibly be supported when increasing the frequency up to 1.2Ghz. Theoretically, in frequency 1.2Ghz, the machine performs 1.5 times more instructions than in frequency 800Mhz. This corresponds to the theoretical factor of decrease of the CPU utilization.

Figure 14 shows that the ratio of the maximum frequency to the minimum frequency for different workload profiles. For each workload, the ratio is constant and is less than 1.5. This allows to define the *Minimum Threshold* depending on the *Maximum Threshold* and the ratio of two consecutive frequencies. Indeed, when we put the CPU frequency of machine to a higher frequency than the previous, if the load before the operation was higher or equal to the *Maximum Threshold*, once the operation is done, the load obtained will be higher than (*Maximum Threshold* over 1.5) in our platform. The decrease of the load is higher than the "theoretical" decrease, hence this latter could be used as *Minimum Threshold* since it is reached only if the workload decreases. We can consider the dynamic estimation of the *Minimum Threshold* expressed as follows:

$$T^{min} = T^{max} * \frac{next\ lower\ frequency}{current\ frequency}$$

Coordination controller evaluation

This section presents the evaluation of our approach. We apply our approach for coordinating the self-sizing and Dvfs managers for the management of a replicated-based system. We inject different workload profiles. Each workload profile is defined by two phases, a first phase that consists of a ramp-up load about three minutes then a second phase that consists of a constant the load after the

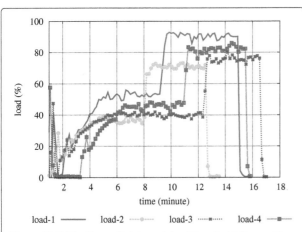

Figure 13 Calibrating self-sizing minimal threshold. Figures 13 shows executions, with different workloads. During these executions, we remove a replicated server in order to observe the impact of these operations on the CPU utilization.

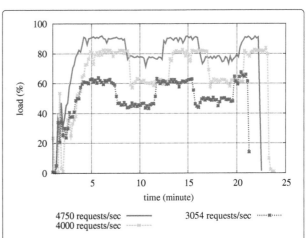

Figure 14 Calibrating Dvfs thresholds. Figures 14 shows executions, with different workloads. During these executions, we changed the CPU frequency on the fly in order to observe the impact of these operations on the CPU utilization.

ramp-up phase. For each workload profile, we performed two executions, one without coordinating managers and another one by coordinating managers execution. At each experimentation, each machine hosting an active Tomcat server starts with its minimum CPU frequency, the local Dvfs adjusts it on the fly. Initially, one Tomcat server is started. The second Tomcat server was either added or removed automatically by the self-sizing manager depending on the workload. The executions takes 20 minutes. After this duration, we stopped sending requests. In this paper, we present three workload profiles *Workload1 (4750 requests/sec), Workload2 (5000 requests/sec)* and *Workload3 (5542 requests/sec)*. *Workload1* and *Workload2* are supportable by one Tomcat server at max CPU frequency. *Workload3* necessitates two Tomcat servers for treatment.

Without coordination, for *Workload1* (Figures 15) as well as for *Workload2* (Figures 16), the overload detection triggers adding operation and CPU frequency increase operation because the machine hosting the Tomcat server is at minimum CPU capacity. In Figure 15, the overload is detected by self-sizing (*Avg_load*) about 8 minutes after starting sending requests, hence a new server is requested. One minute later Dvfs detects the overload and increase the CPU frequency (*CPUFreq_node1 at 9 min*). Once the new Tomcat server becomes active on node 2 (*about 11 min*), the CPU utilization for both machines hosting the Tomcat servers are around 60% after the Dvfs on node 1 decreases its CPU frequency. We observe the same behaviour in Figure 16. Unlike to uncoordinated executions, in the coordinated executions for *Workload1* (Figures 17) as well as for *Workload2* (Figures 18), only CPU frequency increase is observed. No adding operation is performed when the overload is detected. Once the CPU frequency is executed, the CPU utilization decreases.

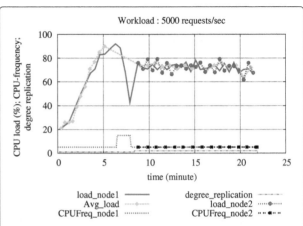

Figure 16 Uncoordinated execution: *Workload2 (5000 requests/sec)*. This figure shows an execution in which self-sizing and Dvfs managers are not coordinated.

For *Workload3*, in the uncoordinated execution (Figure 19) as well as in the coordinated execution (Figure 20), a new Tomcat server is added. In contrast to the executions in Figures 19, In Figures 20 the adding operation (*about 6 min*) is performed later after the increase of the CPU frequency on node 1 (*about 4 min*). After increasing the CPU frequency, the overload is not persists (*6 min*) and a new Tomcat server is added since no more CPU-frequency increase operation was possible. The generated coordination controller does not prevent from adding new replicated Tomcat server when it is necessary. The coordination controller is able to ensure the respect of coordination policy. Unlike to the execution without coordination, where undesired behaviours have been observed, we observe that the coordination execution follows the defined policy. Adding operations are

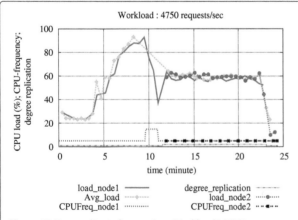

Figure 15 Uncoordinated execution: *Workload1 (4750 requests/sec)*. This figure shows an execution in which self-sizing and Dvfs managers are not coordinated.

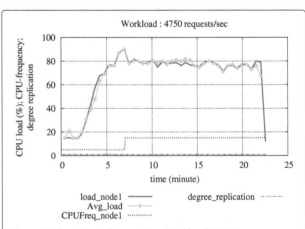

Figure 17 Coordinated execution: *Workload1 (4750 requests/sec)*. This figure shows an execution in which self-sizing and Dvfs managers are coordinated.

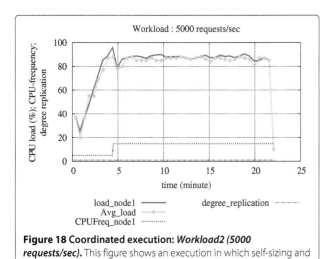

Figure 18 Coordinated execution: *Workload2 (5000 requests/sec).* This figure shows an execution in which self-sizing and Dvfs managers are coordinated.

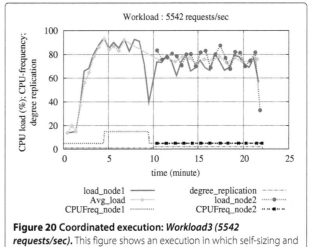

Figure 20 Coordinated execution: *Workload3 (5542 requests/sec).* This figure shows an execution in which self-sizing and Dvfs managers are coordinated.

performed only when all active nodes hosting a Tomcat server are in their maximum CPU frequency.

Related work

Concerning energy control, many works addressed energy management on datacenters. Some of these researches are based on (i) hardware with voltage and frequency control (e.g., DVFS [11]), (ii) resource allocation: Reducing power consumption by reducing the clock frequency of the processor has been widely studied [5,12], Flautner et al. [13] explored a software managed dynamic voltage scaling policy that sets CPU speed on a task basis rather than by time intervals. [14] proposes a power budget guided job scheduling policy that maximizes overall job performance for a given power budget. Many works such as [4,15-18] focused on dynamic resource provisioning in response to dynamic workload changes. These techniques monitor

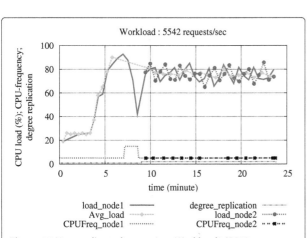

Figure 19 Uncoordinated execution: *Workload3 (5542 requests/sec).* This figure shows an execution in which self-sizing and Dvfs managers are not coordinated.

workloads or other SLA (Service Level Agreement) metrics experienced by a server and adjust the instantaneous resources available to the server. Depending on the granularity of the server (single or replicated), the dynamically provisioned resources can be a whole machine in the case of replicated servers. Energy efficiency is achieved using a workload-aware, just-right dynamic provisioning mechanism and the ability to power down subsystems of a host system that are not required.

While these works are relevant, they did not address the problem of coordinating multiple energy managers. Our work is complementary since it can be used to build a system that includes more that one of the previous approaches. Few works have also investigated manager coordination for energy efficiency. Kumar [19] proposes vManage, a coordination approach that loosely couples platform and virtualization management to improve energy savings and QoS while reducing VM migrations. Kephart [20] addresses the coordination of multiple autonomic managers for power/performance trade-offs based on a utility function in a non-virtualized environment. Nathuji [21] proposes VirtualPower to control the coordination among virtual machines to reduce the power consumption. These works involve coordination between control loops, but these loops are applied to the managed applications. However, these work propose adhoc specific solutions that have to be implemented by hand. If new managers have to be added in the system the whole coordination manager need to be redesigned. Also, the design of the coordination infrastructure becomes complex if the number of co-existing autonomic managers grows. Instead, we propose an approach for coordinating several managers based on control techniques. The latter provide high level programming languages and discrete controller synthesis techniques for the automated synthesis of the controller capable to ensure the coordination. [22] propose an approach for synchronizing multiple Control-Loops to ensure stability of their behaviours based on a binary linear program. It introduces an Actions Synchronization Module (ASM) that selects, whenever a set of actions needs to be synchronized, the best subset allowed to execute which maximizes a set of QoS metrics. Our approach is similar to the latters since it allows, among a set of actions, a subset to execute. However, contrary to a binary linear program, in our approach the decision is based on the invariants on Control-Loops behaviours. [23] address stability in autonomic networking. It identifies three issues that must be considered to ensure stability which are interactions, conflicts resolution and Time scaling of control-loops. The Game theory approach which provides analytical tools is proposed for studying the efficient collaboration of control-loops. An architectural design is proposed based on the GANA architecture which provides features for structuring control-loops and ensuring their synchronization to achieve stability through Action Synchronization Functions presented in [22]. This approach is based on optimization, typically of QoS metrics, by means of Game theory, whereas our approach proposes an enforcement of logical properties upon states or sequences of actions.

In contrast with [24], which relies on formal specification to derive a formal model that is guaranteed to be equivalent to the requirements, our work can be related to the applications of control theory to autonomic or adaptive computing systems [25]. In particular, Discrete Event Systems in the form of Petri nets models and control have been used for deadlock avoidance problems [26]. Compared to these works, we rely on synchronous programming and discrete controller synthesis. Once an autonomic manager is modelled as automata, inserting this autonomic manager with other pre-existing just require to update the coordination invariants. The new coordination manager is automatically generated from the managers models and the coordination invariants.

In contrast with [27], which addresses the management of datacenters based on thermal awareness with external sensing infrastructure for energy and cooling efficiency, the work, presented in this paper, focuses on coordinating multiple workload-aware managers to ensure an energy efficiency.

Conclusion and future work
One major challenge in system administration is coordinating multiple autonomic managers for correct and coherent system management. In this paper we presented an approach for coordinating multiple autonomic managers in a consistent manner. This approach, based on synchronous programming and Discrete Controller Synthesis, has the advantage of generating by construction

the correct controller to enable the coordination of managers.

The advantages of this approach are following: (1) High-level of programming, (2) Automated generation/synthesis of the controller and (3) correctness of the controller, (4) that is maximally permissive. The resulting controlled automaton is correct in the sense that the formal technique of DCS has been applied to guarantee, in a form of verification, that it can have only behaviours that satisfy the property to be enforced. It is also maximally permissive in the sense that all behaviours that satisfy the property are kept possible by the controller.

We tested this approach for coordinating two autonomic managers addressing resource optimization: self-Sizing, which manages the degree of replication for a system based on a load balancer scheme, and Dvfs, which manages the level of CPU frequency for a single node. In this case, the coordination policy was to allow self-Sizing to add new node only when all Dvfs modules cannot apply increase operations at all in response to the increasing load the system receives. The experimentations shows that the generated controller ensures a correct coordination with respect of our coordination policy. However, we used thresholds as base for managers decision. These thresholds are not sufficient to capture only overload and underload since there is a probability for a peak of load not to correspond to an overload.

For future work, we plan to improve the model with the use of continuous control to take into account quantitative aspects and avoid oscillations and reduce decision errors. We will improve our use of discrete control by considering more advanced control techniques with cost functions and optimal control. We plan to evaluate this approach for large scale coordination with more complex coordination policies and several managers, combining both self-optimization and self-regulation frequency managers with self-repair manager that heal fail-stop clustered multi-tiers system.

Endnotes
a available at http://bzr.inria.fr/
b http://jmeter.apache.org/

Competing interests
The authors declare that they have no competing interests.

Authors' contributions
The contributions of the paper are threefold: The use of **synchronous programming** to model the autonomic managers coexistence; The use of **discrete controller synthesis** for the automatic computation of a controller capable to enforce the coordination policy expressed in a declarative way; The **evaluation** of the coordination controller for self-sizing and set of Dvfs for the management of a replication-based system. All authors read and approved the final manuscript.

Acknowledgements
This research is supported by ANR INFRA (ANR-11-INFR 012 11) under a grant for the project ctrl-Green.

Author details
[1]ERODS Team - Bât. IMAG C, 220 rue de la Chimie, 38 400 St Martin d'Hères, France. [2]INRIA Grenoble - Rhône-Alpes, 655, avenue de l'Europe, Montbonnot 38334 St-Ismier cedex, France. [3]IRIT/ENSEEIHT, 2 rue Charles Camichel - BP 7122, 31071 Toulouse cedex 7, France.

References
1. Kephart JO, Chess DM (2003) The vision of autonomic computing. Computer 36: 41–50. http://dx.doi.org/10.1109/MC.2003.1160055
2. Marchand H, Gaudin B (2002) Supervisory Control Problems of Hierarchical Finite State Machines In: 41th IEEE Conference on Decision and Control, Las Vegas, USA, pp 1199–1204
3. Delaval G, Marchand H, Rutten É (2010) Contracts for modular discrete controller synthesis In: Proceedings of the ACM SIGPLAN/SIGBED 2010 Conference on Languages, Compilers, and Tools for Embedded Systems. LCTES '10, ACM, New York, NY, USA, pp 57–66
4. Chase JS, Anderson DC, Thakar PN, Vahdat AM, Doyle RP (2001) Managing energy and server resources in hosting centers In: Proceedings of the eighteenth ACM symposium on Operating systems principles. SOSP '01, ACM, New York, NY, USA, pp 103–116. http://doi.acm.org/10.1145/502034.502045
5. Weiser M, Welch B, Demers A, Shenker S (1994) Scheduling for reduced CPU energy In: Proceedings of the 1st USENIX conference on Operating Systems Design and Implementation, OSDI '94. USENIX Association, Berkeley, CA, USA. http://dl.acm.org/citation.cfm?id=1267638.1267640
6. Besnard L, Marchand H, Rutten E (2006) The Sigali tool box environment. Workshop on Discrete Event Systems, WODES'06 (Tool Paper). Ann-Arbor, (MI, USA). http://www.irisa.fr/vertecs/Logiciels/sigali.html
7. Colaço JL, Pagano B, Pouzet M (2005) A conservative extension of synchronous data-flow with state machines In: Proceedings of the 5th ACM International Conference on, Conference on Embedded Software. EMSOFT '05, ACM, New York, NY, USA, pp 173–182
8. Benveniste A, Caspi P, Edwards S, Halbwachs N, Le Guernic P, de Simone R (2003) The synchronous languages 12 years later. Proc IEEE 91: 64–83
9. Ramadge P, Wonham W (1987) Supervisory control of a class of discrete event processes. SIAM J. on Control Optimization 25: 206–230
10. Cassandras CG, Lafortune S (2006) Introduction to discrete event systems. Springer-Verlag New, York, Inc., Secaucus, NJ, USA
11. Fox A, Gribble SD, Chawathe Y, Brewer EA, Gauthier P (1997) Cluster-based scalable network services In: Proceedings of the sixteenth ACM symposium on Operating systems principles. SOSP '97, ACM, New York, NY, USA, pp 78–91. http://doi.acm.org/10.1145/268998.266662
12. Govil K, Chan E, Wasserman H (1995) Comparing algorithm for dynamic speed-setting of a low-power CPU In: Proceedings of the 1st annual international conference on Mobile computing and networking. MobiCom '95, ACM, New York, NY, USA, pp 13–25. http://doi.acm.org/10.1145/215530.215546
13. Flautner K, Reinhardt S, Mudge T (2002) Automatic performance setting for dynamic voltage scaling. Wirel Netw 8: 507–520. http://dx.doi.org/10.1023/A:1016546330128
14. Etinski M, Corbalan J, Labarta J, Valero M (2010) Optimizing job performance under a given power constraint in HPC centers In: Proceedings of the International Conference on Green Computing. GREENCOMP '10, IEEE Computer Society, Washington, DC, USA, pp 257–267. http://dx.doi.org/10.1109/GREENCOMP.2010.5598303
15. Lin M, Wierman A, Andrew LLH, Thereska E (2011) Dynamic right-sizing for power-proportional data centers In: Proc. IEEE INFOCOM, Shanghai, China, pp 1098–1106. http://www.caia.swin.edu.au/cv/landrew/pubs/RightSizing.pdf
16. Bouchenak S, De Palma N, Hagimont D, Taton C (2006) Autonomic Management of Clustered Applications In: Cluster Computing, 2006 IEEE International Conference on, pp 1–11
17. Pinheiro E, Bianchini R, Carrera EV, Heath T (2001) Load balancing and unbalancing for power and performance in cluster-based Systems In: Proceedings of the Workshop on Compilers and Operating Systems for Low Power (COLP'01). http://research.ac.upc.es/pact01/colp/paper04.pdf
18. Rodero I, Jaramillo J, Quiroz A, Parashar M, Guim F, Poole S (2010) Energy-efficient application-aware online provisioning for virtualized clouds and data centers In: Proceedings of the International Conference on Green Computing. GREENCOMP '10, IEEE Computer Society, Washington, DC, USA, pp 31–45. http://dx.doi.org/10.1109/GREENCOMP.2010.5598283
19. Kumar S, Talwar V, Kumar V, Ranganathan P, Schwan K (2009) vManage: loosely coupled platform and virtualization management in data centers In: Proceedings of the 6th international conference on Autonomic computing. ICAC '09,ACM, New York, NY, USA, pp 127–136. http://doi.acm.org/10.1145/1555228.1555262
20. Das R, Kephart JO, Lefurgy C, Tesauro G, Levine DW, Chan H (2008) Autonomic multi-agent management of power and performance in data centers In: Proceedings of the 7th international joint conference on Autonomous agents and multiagent systems: industrial track. AAMAS '08, Richland SC, pp 107–114. http://dl.acm.org/citation.cfm?id=1402795.1402816
21. Nathuji R, Schwan K (2007) VirtualPower: coordinated power management in virtualized enterprise systems In: Proceedings of twenty-first ACM SIGOPS symposium on Operating systems principles. SOSP '07, ACM, New York, NY, USA, pp 265–278. http://doi.acm.org/10.1145/1294261.1294287
22. Tcholtchev N, Chaparadza R, Prakash A (2009) Addressing Stability of Control-Loops in the Context of the GANA Architecture: Synchronization of Actions and Policies In: Proceedings of the 4th IFIP TC 6 International Workshop on Self-Organizing Systems, IWSOS '09. Springer-Verlag, Berlin, Heidelberg, pp 262–268. http://dx.doi.org/10.1007/978-3-642-10865-5_28
23. Kastrinogiannis T, Tcholtchev N, Prakash A, Chaparadza R, Kaldanis V, Coskun H, Papavassiliou S (2010) Addressing stability in future autonomic networking. In: Pentikousis K, Calvo RA, García-Arranz M, Papavassiliou S (eds) MONAMI, Lecture Notes of the Institute for Computer Sciences, Social Informatics and Telecommunications Engineering. Springer, pp 50–61. http://dblp.uni-trier.de/db/conf/monami/monami2010.html#KastrinogiannisTPCKCP10
24. Sterritt R, Hinchey M, Rash J, Truszkowski W, Rouff C, Gracanin D (2005) Towards Formal Specification and Generation of Autonomic Policies In: Embedded and Ubiquitous Computing, pp 1245–1254. http://dx.doi.org/10.1007/11596042_126
25. Hellerstein JL, Diao Y, Parekh S, Tilbury DM (2004) Feedback Control of Computing Systems. John Wiley & Sons
26. Wang Y, Kelly T, Lafortune S (2007) Discrete control for safe execution of IT automation workflows In: Proceedings of the 2nd ACM SIGOPS/EuroSys European Conference on Computer Systems 2007. EuroSys '07, ACM, New, York, NY, USA, pp 305–314. http://doi.acm.org/10.1145/1272996.1273028
27. Viswanathan H, Lee E, Pompili D (2011) Self-organizing sensing infrastructure for autonomic management of green datacenters. Ieee Netw 25(4): 34–40. http://ieeexplore.ieee.org/lpdocs/epic03/wrapper.htm?arnumber=5958006

## 4

Cloud-Based Code Execution Framework for scientific problem solving environments

Thomas Ludescher[1]*, Thomas Feilhauer[1] and Peter Brezany[2]

Abstract

In this paper we present a novel Code Execution Framework that can execute code of different problem solving environments (PSE), such as MATLAB, R and Octave, in parallel. In many e-Science domains different specialists are working together and need to share data or even execute calculations using programs created by other persons. Each specialist may use a different problem solving environment and therefore the collaboration can become quite difficult. Our framework supports different cloud platforms, such as Amazon Elastic Compute Cloud (EC2) and Eucalyptus. Therefore it is possible to use hybrid cloud infrastructures, e.g. a private cloud based on Eucalyptus for general base-level computations using the available local resources and additionally a public Amazon EC2 for peaks and time-dependent calculations. Our approach is to provide a secure platform that supports multiple problem solving environments, execute code in parallel with different parameter sets using multiple cores or machines in a cloud environment, and support researchers in executing code, even if the required problem solving environment is not installed locally. Additionally, existing parallel resources can easily be utilized for ongoing scientific calculations. The framework has been validated by and used in our real project addressing large-scale breath analysis research. Its research-prototype version is available as a PaaS cloud service model. In the future researchers will be able to install this framework on their own cloud infrastructures.

Introduction

The project we are working on is driven by the breath research domain [1,2] but can be used for similar structured research area as well. In many scientific domains several different specialists (e.g. physician, mathematicians, chemists, computer scientists, etc.) are working together and executing long running CPU-intensive computations.

Figure 1 shows the common workflow of a scientific study with probands. Proband is a term used most often in medical fields to denote a particular subject (person or animal) being studied or reported on. Several different specialists, such as physician, medical researchers, technician, chemists and mathematicians could be involved in a single study. In this example, sample data of a proband are collected and used for further analysis (e.g. breath

sample, electrocardiogram data). At step (1), a physician takes the sample of a proband and collects additional information (e.g. smoker/non smoker). At step (2), the chemist measures the sample with several different sensors; each sensor device type generates its own raw data format. The chemist mostly uses a problem-solving environment, such as MATLAB, to pre-process the raw data (3). The mathematician uses the pre-processed data to create/adapt/improve/maintain new mathematical algorithms (4). Depending on the goal of the study, different mathematical algorithms are performed (e.g. classification, pattern recognition, clustering, generate mathematical models). The mathematician must be able to recalculate the pre-processed data if required, even if the specific PSE is not installed locally. In our test example his/her results are the output of one single study.

The proposed *Code Execution Framework (CEF)* will support scientists to work together on the same study during all data preparation and data analysis steps, which could be executed recursively.

The following list outlines some challenges that we handle within this effort.

*Correspondence: thomas.ludescher@fhv.at
[1] Fachhochschule Vorarlberg, University of Applied Sciences, Hochschulstrasse 1, 6850 Dornbirn, Austria
Full list of author information is available at the end of the article

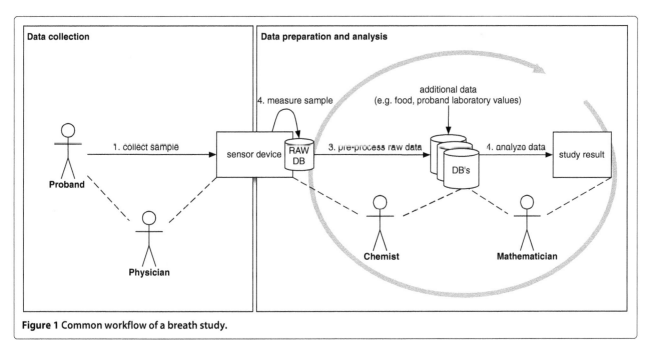

Figure 1 Common workflow of a breath study.

- All involved specialists will iteratively improve this workflow during the development phase. To increase these iterative steps, each researcher should be able to use his/her favorite problem solving environment. At the moment MATLAB [3], Octave [4] and R [5] are supported. The CEF has been implemented in an ongoing project with the breath analysis community. In this domain the researcher mostly uses MATLAB for pre-processing the data and R or MATLAB for all further mathematical analysis.

- Different specialists use different PSEs for their calculations and provide their results to other scientists for further analysis, probably with another PSE. For example a chemist uses MATLAB to prepare the input data of a mass-spectrometry to identify the required substances and a statistician uses this data to generate statistical analysis in R. That means that two different PSEs must work together within a single study.

- Each scientist must be able to execute different problem solving environment source files out of his/her favorite PSE, without having the other PSE installed. This is especially important for non open source or free PSEs, such as MATLAB. The CEF provides a solution to execute MATLAB code without having MATLAB installed.

- Long running calculations block the computer of the scientists and in terms of a failure (e.g. no disk space) the whole calculation may fail. If the scientist uses the CEF it will manage the failure recovery and invoke the calculation at a new machine again. Additionally, the client computer is free for other uses.

- Nowadays most desktop computers have multiple cores or even multiple processors. MATLAB already supports multi-threaded computation for a number of functions [6]. Some problem solving environments (e.g. Octave and R) are generally single-thread applications. However, these PSEs use existing numeric libraries that can take advantage of parallel execution. R and Octave provide different toolboxes to support multiple cores or the scientist must start the PSE several times for different calculations. Within the CEF, the user specifies the specific method that should be executed in the cloud with different parameter sets in parallel. The results will be merged together and returned back to the client.

The goal of the proposed CEF is to support multiple different problem solving environments and to execute long running CPU-intensive calculations in parallel in a cloud infrastructure. Depending on the requirements of the user, specific calculations must be finished within a certain amount of time. The system can be configured to use a local Eucalyptus installation meeting the demand for base level computations; if required, Amazon EC2 instances can be connected to speed up (bursting) the calculations (hybrid cloud). This can have advantages in terms of time and costs.

The main contributions of this paper include: (a) executing PSE code (R, Octave and MATLAB) in parallel in a cloud platform (preliminary, for Amazon EC2 and Eucalytpus), (b) supporting researchers in PSE code execution, even if the required problem solving environment is not installed locally, (c) allowing the CEF-clients to use the research prototype as a Platform as a Service (PaaS) solution, and (d) in the future, the whole CEF will be offered for a local installation using an own cloud platform.

The rest of the paper is organized as follows. Section 'Background and related work' gives some background information about problem solving environments, parallel execution services, cloud environments, and workflow management systems. The usage of the CEF can be seen in Section 'Usage of the Code Execution Framework within different PSEs'. In Section 'Code Exe- cution Framework (CEF) concept' the CEF is specified and all involved components are defined. Section 'Implementation' describes the the prototype implementation. Section 'Performance tests' contains the performance results. At the end the open problems and our future work are described in Section 'Open problems and future work'.

Background and related work

Cloud computing [7] provides computation, software, data access, and storage resources without requiring cloud users to know the location and other details of the computing infrastructure. In general, the amount of data is growing rapidly and the systems processing this data must deal with several data management challenges. Moshe Rappoport [8] outlines the challenges as the four V's: the Volume, Variety, Velocity and Veracity. This big amount of data must be analyzed with innovated technologies to discover new knowledge. The book [9] presents the most up-to-date opportunities and challenges emerging in knowledge discovery in big data, helping readers develop the technical skills to design and develop data-intensive methods and processes.

According to the applied deployment model, the cloud infrastructure can be divided into public clouds, community clouds, private clouds, and hybrid clouds [10]. The difference between these groups are the location, owner, payment, and user. Several different cloud platforms exist, such as Amazon Web Service (AWS) [11], Eucalyptus [12], and so on. Each cloud infrastructure uses its own storage resources. At AWS it is called S3 [13], at Eucalyptus they use Walrus. Walrus is an open source implementation of S3 and provides the same interface. Different types of service models can be accessed on a cloud computing platform - the most favorite types include Infrastructure as a service (IaaS), Platform as a Service (PaaS) and Software as a Service (SaaS).

A Problem Solving Environment (PSE) is a specialized computer application for solving mathematical or statistical problems, mostly with a graphical user interface [14].

Many scientific research groups use PSEs, such as MATLAB [3], Octave [4] and R [5] for their calculations. For example, in [15] several different applications of MATLAB in science and engineering are shown.

Considering parallel execution services, there are several frameworks described in the literature, such as ParallelR [16], NetWorkSpace for R [17], RevoDeployR [18], and Elastic-R [19] for executing R code in parallel. There are packages and extensions for MATLAB and Octave including Parallel-Octave [20], Multicore [21], and MatlabMPI [22].

There exists already some Web/cloud based tools to remotely communicate with PSEs. There are two different approaches to use MATLAB within the Cloud. The first approach was developed by MathWorks and uses concrete licenses (e.g. MATLAB Distributed Computing Server license). The latter one uses the Component Runtime (MCR) of MATLAB, which does not require licenses for each node. The white paper [23] describes the MathWorks approach in detail. This white paper walks you through the steps of installation, configuration, and setting up clustered environments using these licensed products from MathWorks on Amazon EC2. This license based approach is very expensive, depending on the number of nodes. The advantage of using the Parallel Toolbox is to be able to execute even a for-loop in parallel on different nodes. It is possible to use Red Cloud [24] as a Cloud Service (IaaS) to execute MATLAB code with the MATLAB Distributed Computing Server. With the MCR-approach it is possible to develop a WebService without any costs for licenses. In the paper [25] exactly this approach was addressed within the Grid infrastructure. As further work, the author mentioned that they would like to find out how GridMate behaves on Cloud resources.

With Octave and R, which are developed under the GNU license, all license problems are solved. There already exists a possibility to use Octave as a Cloud Service [26]. With the R-Cloud workbench [27] it is possible to execute R code in parallel in a provided cloud infrastructure (R-Cloud). For R there are solutions to execute R in the Amazon EC2 Cloud [28].

The above mentioned parallel or cloud based execution frameworks have great potential allowing to manage parallel/cloud based code execution for a single PSE. However, the challenge the scientists are facing, e.g. in our ABA-project [29], is dealing with code of different PSEs, sometimes within a single study. Therefore, an infrastructure is needed that provides services to execute own PSE code in the cloud independent from the PSE type or without the need to have a particular PSE installed. Most existing parallel execution services support homogeneous parallelization (execute code in parallel within one PSE type), while our CEF can be used in a heterogeneous environment, as well. For example, it is possible to execute R code within an Octave code execution.

Workflow engines, such as Taverna [30], Kepler [31], ClowdFlows [32], and ADAMS [33], can be used to orchestrate analysis tasks in a workflow. A user of a workflow management system is able to define its own workflows and execute it. A workflow can consist of data services, calculation services, and other services. Our system does not directly include any workflow engine. However, with our CEF it is possible to execute arbitrary R/Octave and MATLAB code in the cloud. The framework provides a Web service interface that can be used within a complex workflow to execute PSE code in parallel. We have already implemented a Taverna activity that is based on these CEF Web services.

In many domains, personal data (e.g. patient data) is involved and therefore privacy and security are very important. The proposed CEF uses a Kerberos based security concept. In [34] we discussed several challenges and their solution, including how to (a) use client authentication through all levels of the system, (b) guarantee secured execution of time consuming cloud based analysis, and (c) inject security credentials into dynamically created virtual machine instances.

Usage of the Code Execution Framework within different PSEs

In this section, we will demonstrate how the CEF can be used to execute MATLAB or R code in parallel in the cloud. The corresponding Octave code can be implemented in a similar way. To illustrate the usage of the framework, we calculate PI with a Monte-Carlo method [35] as an example for a compute intensive job that can easily be parallelized. This example will be used in Section 'Performance tests' for the performance evaluation.

To execute the Monte-Carlo method in parallel, we put a grid over the unit circle (Figure 2) and calculate the number of points in the circle and the total number. PI can be calculated with the following formula

$$\Pi = 4 \cdot \frac{\sum \text{number\_of\_points\_in\_circle}}{\sum \text{total\_number}}$$

First of all the provided MATLAB or R Code Execution Library must be installed. Secondly we must implement the MATLAB function that should be executed in parallel, as described above. This function uses one array as parameter with 3 values. The first value contains y_{min}, the second value y_{max}, and the last value is the step size. The code iterates from y_{min} to y_{max} and from 0 to 1 (x-coordinate) with the given step size and calculates the number of values inside the unit circle (numCircle) and the total number (numAll).

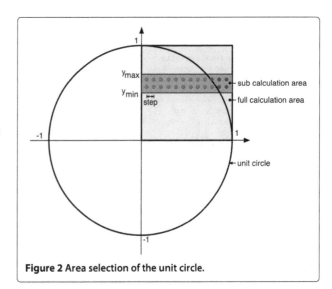

Figure 2 Area selection of the unit circle.

The y_{min} and y_{max} parameters are used to select a specific area of the unit circle. Figure 3 shows the calcPi code that calculates the numbers of points inside the unit circle (numCircle) and the total number (numAll).

Figure 4 shows the codes (MATLAB and R) to (a) generate the parameter sets, (b) make a connection to the Code Execution Controller (CEC), (c) execute the calcPi function, and (d) load the calculated result from the CEC. With the three parameters of the CodeExecution constructor you are able to specify whether you would like to execute the calculation in the cloud or locally (1st parameter), the domain name and the port of the used CEC, and whether you would like to use the GUI login or the console login. During the development phase the scientist is able to test her/his method at her/his local machine (the required PSE must be installed). By adopting the first parameter, the whole code will be executed at the cloud based Code Execution Infrastructure.

At the *executeCalculation* method the scientist must provide the different parameter sets, the method name that should be executed in parallel, and whether this method should be blocked (synchronous) until the parallel execution in the cloud is finished.

To execute PSE code within another PSE (e.g. execute Octave code within R) the scientist can (a) download an existing one by using our PSE, (b) download an existing code by using the Web portal [36], or (c) create a zip file with the new code and a specific property (codeExecution.properties) file. The property file must contain the methodName and the PSE type (e.g. methodName=calcPi, PSE=R). Figure 5 shows how to download PSE code from an already executed calculation and execute the existing code with your favorite PSE and a new parameter set. This can be done even within a remotely executing calculation (recursive). All other methods (described in Section 'Code

MATLAB code	R code

<pre>function [result] = calcPi(param)
  y_min = param(1);
  y_max = param(2);
  step = param(3);
 	
  numCircle = 0;
  numAll   = 0;
 	
  % iterates from y_min to y_max
  % and from 0 to 1 (x-coordinate) with
  % the given step size
  nSteps = round((y_max-y_min)/step+1);
  for y = linspace(y_min,y_max,nSteps)
    for x = linspace(0,1,1/step+1)
      numAll = numAll+1;
      if ((y^2 + x^2) <=1)
        numCircle = numCircle+1;
      end
    end
  end
 	
  % create and return result
  result = [numCircle, numAll];
end</pre>
	<pre>calcPi <- function(y_min,y_max,step) {
	
	  numCircle <- 0
	  numAll <- 0;
	
	  # iterates from y_min to y_max
	  # and from 0 to 1 (x-coordinate) with
	  # the given step size
	  for(y in seq(y_min,y_max,step)) {
	    for(x in seq(0,1,step)) {
	      numAll <- numAll+1
	      if((y^2 + x^2) <=1) {
	        numCircle <- numCircle+1
	      }
	    }
	  }
	
	  # create and return result
	  return(
	    data.frame(
	      'numCircle' = numCircle,
	      'numAll' = numAll
	    )
	  )
	}</pre>

Figure 3 R and MATLAB codes of the calcPi method, that will be executed in parallel.

MATLAB code	R code

<pre>% max num of sub-calculations
numCalc = 20
 	
% step width
step   = 0.00005;
 	
% create params (first quadrant)
tmp   = linspace(0, 1, numCalc+1);
params = [];
for num = 1:numCalc
  params(num,:) = [
                   tmp(num)+step,
                   tmp(num+1),
                   tmp
                  ];
end
params(1,1) = 0;
 	
% initialize Code Execution Controller
ce   = CodeExecution(
        true,   % use CEF
        'DNS:PORT'   % URL of Controller
        true   % use login GUI
       );
 	
% execute calculation
calc = ce.executeCalculation(
        params,   % parameters
        'calcPi',   % method name
        true   % block calculation
       );
 	
% load results
results = ce.getCalculationResults(calc);</pre>
	<pre># max num of sub-calculations
	numCalc <- 20
	
	# step width
	step <- 0.00005
	
	#create param (first quadrant)
	tmpArray <- seq(0,1,1/numCalc)
	params <- rbind()
	for(num in 1:numCalc) {
	  params <- rbind(params,
	                  c(tmpArray[num]+step,
	                    tmpArray[num+1],step
	                   )
	                 )
	}
	params[1,1] <- 0
	
	# initialize Code Execution Controller
	ce <- initCodeExecution(
	        TRUE, # use CEF
	        DNS:PORT" # URL of Controller
	        TRUE # use login GUI
	       )
	
	# execute calculation
	calc <- executeCalculation(
	        ce, # CE connection
	        params, # parameters
	        'calcPi', # method name
	        TRUE # block calculation
	       )
	
	# load results
	result <- getCalculationResults(ce,calc)</pre>

Figure 4 How the CEF can be used with R and MATLAB codes.

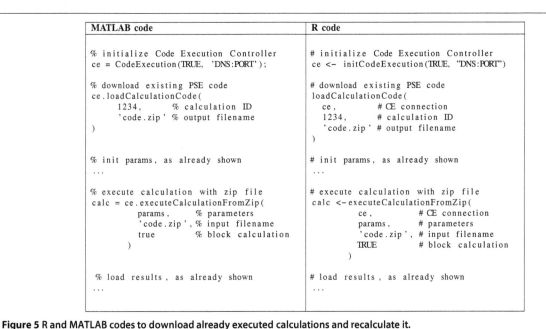

MATLAB code	R code
| ```
% initialize Code Execution Controller
ce = CodeExecution(TRUE, 'DNS:PORT');

% download existing PSE code
ce.loadCalculationCode(
      1234,       % calculation ID
      'code.zip' % output filename
)


% init params, as already shown
...


% execute calculation with zip file
calc = ce.executeCalculationFromZip(
      params,     % parameters
      'code.zip', % input filename
      true        % block calculation
      )


% load results, as already shown
...
``` | ```
# initialize Code Execution Controller
ce <- initCodeExecution(TRUE, "DNS:PORT")

# download existing PSE code
loadCalculationCode(
   ce,           # CE connection
   1234,         # calculation ID
   'code.zip' # output filename
)


# init params, as already shown
...


# execute calculation with zip file
calc <- executeCalculationFromZip(
      ce,           # CE connection
      params,       # parameters
      'code.zip', # input filename
      TRUE          # block calculation
      )


# load results, as already shown
...
``` |

Figure 5 R and MATLAB codes to download already executed calculations and recalculate it.

Execution Framework (CEF) concept'), can be used in the same way as *executeCalculation* or *getCalculationResults*.

Code Execution Framework (CEF) concept

In the following sections, the concept of the CEF will be described. We start with describing how the CEF access activation is selected by the specific system parameter *useCEF* accepting the values FALSE and TRUE. If the value *useCEF* is FALSE, the whole calculation will be executed in the PSE on the local machine separately. The scientist is able to use all features of the PSE, such as debugging, printing, but must wait until the calculation is completely finished. Without parallel extensions a PSE uses only one core. Depending on the power of the computer used, long running calculations can take a while. If the scientist sets *useCEF* to TRUE, the CEF will be used. The Code Execution Controller starts the required amount of VMs, transmits the calculation to VMs, executes the calculations, and generates the combined result. The administrator of the CEF must define which cloud platforms (e.g. Amazon EC2, Eucalyptus) are used. For each cloud platform he/she must set (a) what machines types should be used (e.g. m1.small, m1.xlarge), (b) how many instances can be started simultaneously, (c) the shut down behavior (e.g. shut down immediately after all waiting calculations are finished or just before the researcher has to pay for another hour for this idle machine), and (d) the total available daily/monthly budget for this cloud platform. The Code Execution Controller (CEC) is able to call the WorkerNodeStatus Web service from each VM to request the number of available cores, core usage, total and available memory. At the

moment the CEC starts the maximum available amount of virtual machines if required, the maximum cost boundary is not yet implemented. The CEC stores all started VMs in a queue. If a calculation is waiting, the first free VM will be used for this execution. In terms of security, the worker node (VM) only accepts requests of the CEC that started the VM. When the calculation at a worker node is finished or failed, the result and log information will be sent to the CEC and afterwards all files from this calculation will be deleted immediately. In the future, the CEC will send sub-calculations from one user to a worker node at the same time, even if multiple cores are available. Therefore it is impossible to spy out data of other users by executing dangerous PSE code.

The advantages for the scientists are (a) the result will be available much faster than running locally, (b) the scientists can use the client computer for other purposes, (c) the scientist can look up the status of the calculation at the CEF-Portal, (d) the scientist is able to download the result to another computer, and (e) the scientist is able to execute other PSE code, even if the required PSE is not installed locally.

Figure 6 shows an overview of the whole CEF. It provides a framework for executing code from different PSEs, including MATLAB, R, and Octave. The system consists of four main parts. That is (a) the Code Execution Controller (CEC) Web application, (b) the different client libraries, (c) the Cloud infrastructure, and (d) the required Code Execution Framework virtual machine. Components depicted in color represent third party libraries that are being reused.

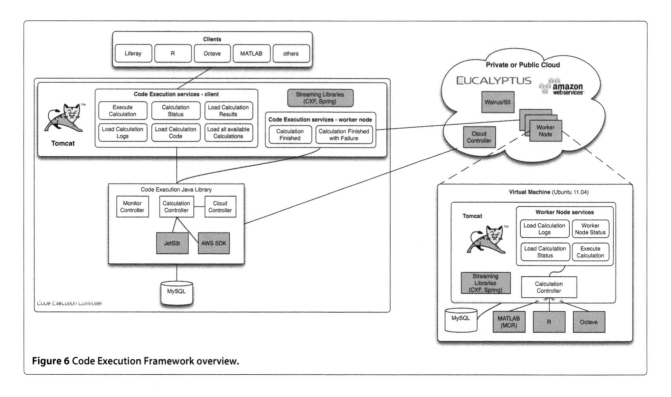

Figure 6 Code Execution Framework overview.

Components description

In the section we describe the components in detail.

Code Execution Controller (CEC)

The CEC consists of the Code Execution Java Library, two different Web service groups (client and worker node services), and a MySQL database to store all calculations and sub-calculations. The Java library is at the heart of the CEF. It provides methods to produce sub-calculations, start and stop virtual machines, to copy the code to be executed into S3 (AWS) or Walrus (Eucalyptus), as well as to monitor running calculations and virtual machines. The CEF supports parallel code execution on the level of executing methods in parallel with different parameter sets.

The client Web services support online execution of functions, methods, and scripts written in different PSEs (e.g. MATLAB, R, Octave, etc.). The user of the system communicates with the client Web services while worker node services are used only internally. In the following these two groups of services are described.

- Client services - These services must be invoked by one of the clients (e.g. Octave, MATLAB, R, Liferay and Taverna). They include

  - Execute Calculation - this service can be used to start a new calculation. In order to execute a new calculation, all parameters for parallelization needed in the code are passed as comma-separated values to the service. At the beginning, this service generates parallel executable sub-calculations (same method with different parameters). Afterwards the PSE code will be stored at S3/Walrus to reduce time and data transfer for parallel execution. Finally, the sub-calculations will be transmitted to a free worker node virtual machine (VM) to be executed.

  - Calculation Status - this service allows for the monitoring of the code execution by requesting the current status, which can either be *compiling, waiting, running, finished,* or *error.* The status can be requested either for the entire calculation or for each sub-calculation.

  - Load Calculation Results - this service loads the results from either the entire calculation or from each sub-calculation.

  - Load Calculation Logs - this service loads the logs from sub-calculations. This includes all output on the console from the used PSE.

  - Load Calculation Code - this service can be used to download already executed code from the CEC. This code contains the source code and, in case of MATLAB code, the compiled code as well. This compressed zip file can be used as code for additional code executions with different parameter sets. If the code contains an already compiled MATLAB code

the execution with the same parameter set will be faster than without the compiled code. The CEC recognizes the compiled code and skips the compilation step, depending on the amount of code this can last from some seconds up to a couple of minutes.
- Load All Available Calculations - this service returns all accessible calculations of the authenticated user. The Code Execution Liferay [37] portlet uses this method to show an overview on the calculations.

- Worker Node services - These services will be invoked by the worker node VM. They include

  - Calculation Finished - this service informs about successfully finished sub-calculations and receives the calculation results and logs from the VM.
  - Calculation Finished with Failure - in case the calculation finished with errors, then this service receives the calculation logs from the VM.

Supported clients
The CEF will be easily accessible from different clients. Each user is able to communicate with the CEF from within R/Octave/MATLAB, the workflow engine Taverna, or even from the Web without needing to install any specific environment. To support Taverna we implemented a Taverna activity, that is able to use the Web services of the CEF. We provide several different R/Octave/Matlab code examples (e.g. PI calculation, recursive CEF invocation, download code and re-execute the downloaded code). All Web services described above can be used with these client libraries, and have been tested on Windows, Linux, and OS X. Additionally, a researcher is able to start new calculations or monitor running calculations within our Web portal (Liferay). Each client/toolbox communicates with the client CEC Web services.

Cloud infrastructure
The CEF uses the EC2 API to communicate with the cloud infrastructure. The controller needs to start/stop instances on the cloud and store data within the data storage (Walrus/S3). All these steps can be done with the AWS SDK for Java and the Jets3t library.

Code Execution Framework virtual machine
We provide a specific worker node virtual machine (Amazon EC2 and Eucalyptus) for the execution of the different PSE code. On this VM all three PSEs (R, Octave, MATLAB

Component Runtime) are installed and a Tomcat application server is running, hosting Code Execution Services of the CEF.

The worker node Web application provides several different Web services for the CEC. They include:

- Execute Calculation - this service can be used to start a new calculation at the specific worker node. In order to execute a new calculation all parameters needed in the code are passed as comma-separated values to the service. The worker node downloads the required PSE code from the Walrus/S3. All information or error outputs will be stored in files during the whole calculation. After the calculation is finished or failed the result and log information will be sent back to the CEC and all files will be deleted.
- Worker Node status - this service returns information about the worker node, such as total and used memory, number of available cores, used cores, etc. The worker node uses the SIGAR (System Information Gatherer And Reporter) Java library to request the required values from the machine.
- Load Calculation status - this service returns information about one specific sub-calculation, such as used memory, used CPU, etc.
- Load Calculation Logs - this service returns the log of a running calculation.

Execution sketches
In this section we walk through a complete execution sketch.

Figure 7 shows more details of the whole calculation process. The arrows show the direction of the communication between the involved systems. At the moment, the CEF can exchange CSV data. To be more generically usable in the future, we are planning to support HDF5 [38] as well. The whole code execution workflow can be started within a supported PSE, Taverna or the Web. Each client has to prepare the code and parameter data. At the first step the client converts the parameter set (e.g. in MATLAB cells or arrays) to a CSV string and zips the required code files (step 1). The maximum number of parallel executable sub-calculations is the number of rows of the parameter set. At the moment, the CEC starts one sub-calculation per row on idle VMs. In the future, the CEC is able to execute several sub-calculations with one Web service invocation at one worker node VM to reduce the transfer and Web service overhead. The number of starting VMs depends on (a) the number of available worker nodes, and (b) the duration of one single sub-calculation. The zip file contains the PSE code and a text file (java properties file) that includes information about the PSE used, compilation status, function name, and their input/output parameters. After

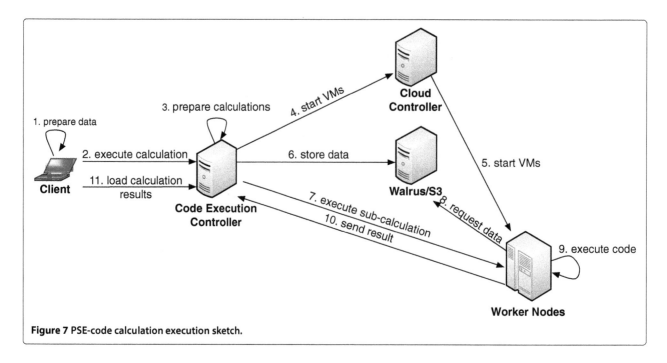

Figure 7 PSE-code calculation execution sketch.

the data preparation the client invokes the *executeCalculation* Web service at the CEC (step 2). The Code Execution Controller (a) stores the received data on the disk, (b) compiles the MATLAB source code, if required (for further information have a look at Section 'MATLAB Component Runtime approach'), (c) generates the sub-calculations, (d) adds all sub-calculations to the calculation queue (step 3), and (e) starts additional Code Execution VMs, if required (step 4, step 5). A specific thread processes the calculation queue. For each calculation the code will be sent once to the Walrus or S3, depending on the cloud infrastructure used (step 6). This reduces the amount of transmitted data and the required time and costs. Afterwards the sub-calculation will be executed at an idle Code Execution VM(step 7). The worker node (a) requests the Code from Walrus/S3 (step 8), (b) executes the code in the shell (step 9), (c) generates the result CSV, (d) sends the result back to the CEC (step 10), and (e) deletes all generated files. Step (e) is important to keep a minimal amount of free disk space, otherwise we have to start a new instance if the Worker Node has not enough free disk space for further calculations. Additionally this must be done because of security reasons. At the end of the execution, the CEC checks the received data and updates the status information of the calculation. The researcher is able to request the status of the calculation (e.g., running, finished) and the results. Therefore the client invokes the *loadCalculationResult* Web service method with the id to download the result (step 11). The CEC (a) authorizes the user, (b) checks if the calculation is finished, and (c) generates the result CSV. At the end, the client converts the

received CSV result set to the internal data structure of the corresponding PSE.

MATLAB Component Runtime approach

The MATLAB Component Runtime (MCR) enables a cloud node to execute compiled MATLAB methods without the need of any costly MATLAB license. In [39] MathWorks writes *"All deployed components and applications can be distributed free of charge. The deployment products support the MATLAB language, most MATLAB toolboxes, and user-developed GUIs."* In order to use the MCR, the MATLAB method needs to be compiled into a standalone application, which can then run without the MATLAB interpreter. The following text segment is taken from the MATLAB Compile toolbox documentation, showing clearly the drawback of this approach: *"... the components generated by the MATLAB Compiler product cannot be moved from platform to platform as is."* In order to deploy a MATLAB method to a machine with an operating system different from the machine used to develop the method, it is necessary to rebuild the program on the desired targeted platform. To solve this problem we generated and deployed a MATLAB compiler Web service on another machine with the same operating system as our worker node VM (Ubuntu 11.04). For this compile service we need a MATLAB license with all required toolboxes and additionally the MATLAB compiler toolbox. The administrator of the MATLAB compiler Web service must determine which toolboxes must be installed. If, nevertheless, a user would like to use a MATLAB toolbox, that is not installed, the compile step (first step) will fail and a corresponding error will be reported to the user.

At our online test installation no additional toolboxes are installed. With this step, every user of the CEF is able to execute MATLAB source files without having to buy a MATLAB license.

MathWorks products license example

To calculate the license cost with and without CEF, the following six assumptions are made: (1) the company is allowed to use the academic price list (2013); (2) five researchers of the company are using Matlab at their computers (individual licenses); (3) all researchers must have all six Computational Finance toolboxes (financial toolbox, econometrics toolbox, datafeed toolbox, database toolbox, spreadsheet Link EX, and financial instruments toolbox); (4) the license for MATLAB itself costs €500 (single named user or single computer); (5) all Computational Finance toolboxes cost €200 each; (6) the MATLAB Compiler toolbox costs €500.

With these assumptions without CEF the total license costs are €8500 (for each user the MATLAB license costs and additionally all six Computational Finance toolboxes). In the best case with CEF the total license costs are €2200 (one MATLAB license costs for a single machine, all six Computational Finance toolboxes, and additionally the MATLAB Compiler toolbox). You must take into account, that without having a valid MATLAB license for each user the development process is more complicating (e.g. no debugging, no GUI, no auto completion).

Implementation

In this section, detailed information about the implementation is given. Each component provides different Web services as described in Section 'Code Execution Framework (CEF) concept'. All Web services are implemented with CXF [40]. The data (PSE source code and CSV parameters) are streamed with MTOM [41]. In our project personal related data is involved and we must implement a fitting security concept. The whole CEF is implemented with a Kerberos based security concept which has been described earlier by us in [34].

Figure 8 gives an overview on our prototype. The figure depicts all involved components. Server 1 (S1, Ubuntu 11.04) is connected to the Internet with a public IP address, located at the university of applied sciences in Dornbirn; this is necessary to be able to use the system outside of the private institute network. This machine is used for several different services. The Key Distribution Center (KDC) and the DNS-Service are used for our Kerberos based security framework. The CEC manages and monitors all calculations. The Web-Portal (Liferay) can be used to monitor calculations without having any PSE installed. Server 2 (S2, Ubuntu 11.04) has a MATLAB with the Compiler toolbox installed. Additionally the own-implemented Web Service to compile MATLAB code is running in the Tomcat on this machine. As Cloud infrastructure, we tested our own Eucalyptus (2.0) and Amazon EC2. Theoretically, all other EC2 compatible cloud infrastructures should work with our system, however we have not tested it so far. Most likely, the VM image must be created for each cloud infrastructure separately. There exist discrepancies how the assignment of internal IP addresses of the VM must be done. At the moment, we provide an image for Amazon EC2 and Eucalyptus. All different cloud infrastructures can be combined to a hybrid system. This can have advantages in terms of speed and costs. The Code Execution Framework can be used in several different ways. The scientist at the client side has to use one of the provided interfaces.

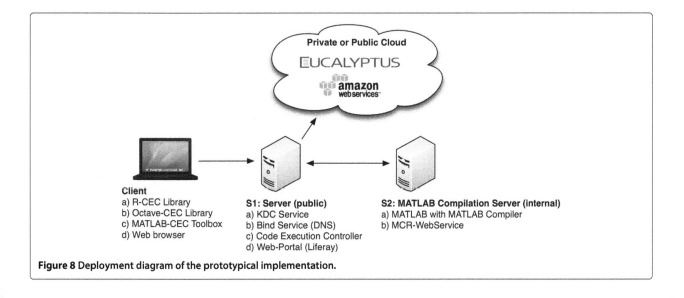

Figure 8 Deployment diagram of the prototypical implementation.

The VM (Ubuntu 11.04) that is used to execute jobs from the CEC contains:

- Startup Tool - This tool will be executed after booting the VM. It (a) requests the required security information from the CEC, (b) downloads a zip file from the storage controller that contains additional files and scripts, (c) downloads the Web application for the Worker Node from the storage control, and (d) starts the Web application within the Tomcat (7.0) application server. Step (b) is used to be able to change the VM (e.g., install libraries, execute shell scripts, etc.) without creating a new VM. We use this feature during our framework development phase.
- Worker Node Web Services - This Web application only accepts requests from the corresponding CEC and manages and monitors all running calculations.
- PSEs - To be able to execute R and Octave code, these libraries with all required toolboxes must be installed. To execute compiled MATLAB code, the VM needs to have the MATLAB Compiler Runtime (MCR) installed.

At the moment, it is possible to test the CEF with your Web portal [36], the R-Client. You are allowed to use our test CEF infrastructure with two worker nodes to execute R, Octave, or already compiled MATLAB code. For more information have a look to the Online-Demo page at our Web portal.

Performance tests

The Code Execution VM is provided for both, AWS and Eucalyptus Cloud platforms. The key performance characteristics are compute, memory, I/O bound. At the moment, the breath analysis community uses mostly CPU intensive calculations and we decided to evaluate the overhead for these criteria. Therefore most relevant performance measures for our application are number of CPUs, size of memory, and data transfer rates (while using a hybrid infrastructure). Therefore we have defined performance evaluations based on these criteria.

The results of the evaluation represent important information aiming to predict the overhead of different infrastructures, which is required to generate the best possible execution plan if multiple cloud platforms are available. To predict the required execution time, we need to execute at least one sub-calculation.

During the following performance tests we found several important results:

- The execution time for our test calculation mainly depends on the cloud infrastructure used and the problem solving environment used.

- MATLAB is the fastest PSE for executing our time consuming PI calculation, even if we need to compile the PSE code.
- The boot procedure of a VM depends not only on the used virtual machine type: The VM must be transmitted from the S3/Walrus to the host node, if it is not already in the cache.
- The transfer speed between CEC and VM cannot be neglected, especially if the internet connection is slower and large data sets must be transmitted (e.g., input data, code, parameter).

In the following paragraphs we provide the detailed results of our performance tests.

In order to evaluate the first prototype of our Code Execution Services, we have conducted three different experiments. In the first experiment we tested the execution time with CPU intensive MATLAB, Octave, and R examples in order to measure the VM overhead and the performance of the whole framework; in the second test we tried to retrieve the rate for the data transfer, and in the last experiment we measured the boot time of the Code Execution VM. A small Eucalyptus private cloud has been installed at our lab at the University of Applied Sciences.

We have implemented Monte-Carlo methods [35] calculating PI in MATLAB, R, and Octave as shown in Section 'Usage of the Code Execution Framework within different PSEs'. This PI calculation is CPU intensive and can easily be parallelized. Calculating PI is one of the major cloud (MapReduce) evaluation use cases [42,43]. The calculations were executed in different code execution scenarios: (a) local (1 thread), (b) on a private Eucalyptus cloud, (c) on Amazon Elastic Compute Cloud (EC2), and (d) on a hybrid cloud (Eucalyptus and Amazon Elastic Compute Cloud). All tests have been executed 50 times and the results are arranged in the following tables showing the arithmetic means and standard deviation of the measured values.

Evaluation of the VM overhead

To measure the virtual machine overhead we tested the same calculation at (a) Intel core i7 16 GB RAM, Ubuntu 11.04 locally (not in a VM), (b) two different Eucalyptus machines (m1.small = 1 GB RAM, m1.xlarge = 2 GB RAM, worker node has an I7 CPU and 16 GB RAM), Ubuntu 11.04, and (c) two different Amazon EC2 machines (m1.large, c1.xlarge), Ubuntu 11.04. The PI example is CPU intensive and does not need much data or RAM, therefore it depends mainly on the processor used. Table 1 shows the results of the R, Octave, and MATLAB tests. All MATLAB tests have used already compiled MATLAB code. For the same calculation, MATLAB (269.6 s) needs less than half the time required by R (794.7 s)

Table 1 Evaluation of the VM overhead

	Cores	R	Octave	MATLAB
Local (16GB RAM, I7)	1	794.7 s ± 9.7	868.1 s ± 15.2	269.6 s ± 1.8
Direct Eucalyptus (m1.small)	1	808.4 s ± 9.6	852.4 s ± 1.6	270.8 s ± 2.2
Direct Eucalyptus (m1.xlarge)	1	788.1 s ± 3.0	851.7 s ± 1.4	257.4 s ± 2.7
Direct EC2 (m1.large)	1	2099.9 s ± 22.6	2171.0 s ± 7.5	710.7 s ± 0.9
Direct EC2 (c1.xlarge)	1	1562.1 s ± 6.7	1612.9 s ± 3.3	537.5 s ± 0.8

The values are given as mean ± standard deviation.

or Octave (868.1 s). This should be taken into account for choosing the appropriate PSE for a specific calculation.

The overhead of the local machine (i7) and the Eucalyptus VM (m1.small) is minimal (for R about 1.5%, for MATLAB about 0.5%). Therefore the VM overhead can be ignored for our further performance analysis. It is interesting to see that the Amazon calculation (m1.large) takes up to 2.6 times longer than the Eucalyptus or even the local execution (compute intensive and non-memory bound). To verify this overhead we decided to use another CPU intensive test example as shown in [44]. For this test we used the command *time for i in 0..10000; do for j in 0..1000; do :; done; done* in the terminal. At the local machine, the execution takes 19 seconds, in EC2 with the m1.large 47 sec and with c1.xlarge 37 seconds. With this test, the EC2 (m1.large) takes about 2.5 times longer than the local execution, which means approximately the same performance overhead as with the CEF. In [45] Amazon describes EC2 compute units: *"In order to make it easy for developers to directly compare CPU capacity between different instance types, we have defined an Amazon EC2 Compute Unit. The amount of CPU that is allocated to a particular instance is expressed in terms of these EC2 Compute Units. We use several benchmarks and tests to manage the consistency and predictability of the performance of an EC2 Compute Unit. One EC2 Compute Unit provides the equivalent CPU capacity of a 1.0–1.2 GHz 2007 Opteron or 2007 Xeon processor."* That is the reason why it is not possible to compare one EC2 instance with a local machine with a specific CPU.

Code Execution Framework performance analysis

Table 2 shows the R performance evaluation, Table 3 the Octave performance evaluation, and Table 4 the MATLAB performance evaluation. In the last column we show the speed-up of the CEF execution in comparison to the local usage. With R and Octave, the theoretically optimal values can almost be reached. With three Eucalyptus VMs (3x m1.small - 3 cores), the theoretical speed-up is 3, while our measured values are 2.64 (R) and 2.71 (Octave). The overhead of the CEF, including the necessary data transfer, is therefore approx. 10%. With two Eucalytpus VMs (2x m1.xlarge - 4 cores), the speed-up is 3.27 (R) and 3.37 (Octave). At Amazon Elastic Compute Cloud, the speed-up of the CEF execution in comparison to the local usage is not able to reach the theoretical value (e.g. 2.32 instead of 6). You must take in account, that, for example, using R, the single execution in EC2 (m1.large: 2099.9 s) takes much longer than the local one (794.7 s).

The reasons why we could never reach exactly the theoretically optimal value are (a) different CPU types in EC2 and AWS, (b) overhead for splitting calculations into sub-calculations, (c) overhead for distributing sub-calculations to free worker nodes, (d) overhead for converting the transmitted CSV-parameters to internal data structures of the used PSE, (e) data transfer time for the parameter and the code, and (f) number of sub-calculations cannot be divided by the number of cores without there being a remainder of tasks. Issue (f) is especially important for tests with several cores (e.g. 6, 8, or 12).

Table 2 R performance evaluation

	Cores	Seconds	Speed-up
3 × Eucalyptus (m1.small)	3	301.1 s ± 3.2	2.64
2 × Eucalyptus (m1.xlarge)	4	242.8 s ± 5.3	3.27
3 × AWS (m1.large)	6	342.2 s ± 4.7	2.32
1 × AWS (c1.xlarge)	8	285.3 s ± 4.6	2.79
2 × Eucalyptus (m1.xlarge) and 1 × AWS (c1.xlarge)	12	140.5 s ± 15.8	5.66

The values are given as mean ± standard deviation.

Table 3 Octave performance evaluation

	Cores	Seconds	Speed-up
3 × Eucalyptus (m1.small)	3	320.2 s ± 4.1	2.71
2 × Eucalyptus (m1.xlarge)	4	257.6 s ± 9.6	3.37
3 × AWS (m1.large)	6	449.7 s ± 6.5	1.93
1 × AWS (c1.xlarge)	8	265.0 s ± 3.0	3.28
2 × Eucalyptus (m1.xlarge) and 1 × AWS (c1.xlarge)	12	177.1 s ± 2.0	4.90

The values are given as mean ± standard deviation.

Table 4 MATLAB performance evaluation

	Cores	Seconds	Speed-up
3 × Eucalyptus (m1.small)	3	144.3 s ± 3.1	1.87
2 × Eucalyptus (m1.xlarge)	4	124.1 s ± 4.8	2.17
3 × AWS (m1.large)	6	168.4 s ± 4.8	1.60
1 × AWS (c1.xlarge)	8	131.8 s ± 5.5	2.05
2 × Eucalyptus (m1.xlarge) and 1 × AWS (c1.xlarge)	12	74.0 s ± 4.5	3.64

The values are given as mean ± standard deviation.

Table 4 shows the measured results of the execution of the compiled MATLAB code. By increasing the number of cores, the calculation time is reduced, but the theoretical speed-up value cannot be reached (e.g. 1.87 instead of 3). The reason for this is that the worker node needs a certain amount of time to start the MATLAB Component Runtime Environment (MCR). To reduce the MCR overhead and the Web service, overhead each sub-calculation should be a long running calculation. If a sub-calculation is completed fast enough, it is possible to send multiple sub-calculations within one Web service call.

The compilation of our test MATLAB code takes in average 39.1 seconds. This contains (a) the Web service invocation, (b) transfer of source code to the MATLAB compiler Web service, (c) compilation of the source code, and (e) transfer of the compiled code back to the CEC. These approx. 40 seconds must be taken into account if we need to compile the MATLAB code. Additionally we tested the same code execution within the MATLAB environment (304.3 seconds) and as a Compiled MATLAB Code with the MCR (293.3 seconds). In our case the improvement while using the MCR is eleven seconds (almost 4% of the complete time). Depending on the calculation, this could be an important speed-up.

When using Amazon EC2, the type of VM (m1.large or c1.xlarge) is very important. It is most likely that the c1.xlarge instance ($0.744 per hour) is the better choice than a corresponding amount of m1.large instances ($0.360 per hour). For example: One VM of type c1.xlarge (eight cores) costs in total $0.744 per hour. The execution of the test example with R takes 285.3 seconds. If you are using three machines of type m1.large (sum 6 cores) instead, the total costs are higher ($1.08 per hour) but the same R code execution takes longer (342.2 seconds). At all other PSE types (Octave and MATLAB) you can see the same result.

Evaluation of transfer constants

Additionally, we have conducted some data transfer tests which are important to consider with the Code Execution Services presented in this paper. The different data transfer rates must be taken into account while choosing a cloud infrastructure (Eucalyptus or EC2) for execution or predicting the calculation time. The data transfer rate evaluation consists of (a) client to CEC, (b) CEC to Walrus/S3, and (c) Walrus/S3 to worker node VM. We implemented a tool that evaluates all different transfer rates of the involved components ten times with multiple different file sizes (10 MB up to 1 GB) and calculate the mean value. The transfer rate from the client to the CEC does not have any influence on the CEC and therefore will not be further investigated. The only influence between the client and the CEC is the Internet connection of these two participants. The transfer rate from the CEC to our local Walrus is about 10.5 MB/s, independent of the file size. The transfer rate from our institute to Amazon S3 (Ireland) varied from 4 MB/s to 10 MB/s. The transfer rate from our local Walrus to the Worker Node VM varied from 10 MB/s to 60 MB/s. The transfer speed from Amazon S3 to the EC2 Worker Node VM is maximal 40 MB/s. For test purposes we installed the CEC at a place with a slower Internet connection (approx. 4 Mbit/s). In this case the transfer rate from the CEC to the Amazon S3 was much lower (250 KB/s) than within our institute. Especially for places with a slower Internet connection the transfer speed must be considered.

In our model for predicting the calculation we must consider the transfer rate of the different cloud infrastructures and locations. The transfer rates depend mostly on the Internet connection of the CEC and from the connection between the controller and the different cloud infrastructures (e.g., Amazon EC2, Eucalyptus).

Booting time

For this performance evaluation it is important to know that the VM-images are already in the cache of the host system. Eucalyptus and EC2 need approx. 20 seconds to copy the image (8 GB) from the cache to the temporary directory. The boot-time depends on the number of cores of the VM and takes between 45 and 55 seconds. These numbers must be considered when new instances must be started. If the host system does not have the required VM in the cache, it takes more than 2 minutes to copy the image from Walrus/S3/EBS to the host system. For development reasons we added the possibility to inject code (download from Walrus/S3) to be able to change the VM without generating a new instance. At the moment we installed (a) all R and Octave Code Execution Client libraries, and (b) the worker node Web application. Depending on this overhead, the boot time can increase several seconds. Tomcat needs from a minimal of about 50 seconds up to a maximum of 450 seconds for the whole startup process. At the moment we are not sure where this time difference results from. This will be investigated as part of our ongoing work.

Open problems and future work

At the moment the CEF supports only parameters specified in the CSV format. Because of that constraint only CSV compatible data structures can be transmitted between the CEC and the worker nodes. We plan to support HDF5 [38] for parameter exchange in the future, as well. It is very important to enable transfer of all different kinds of parameters. Load balancing is another feature which is not yet implemented. We currently simply start one calculation at each available core. In the future we will use CPU- and RAM-usage to enable monitoring virtual machines and start additional calculations if possible. Additionally, it is possible to reduce the transfer or Web service overhead by sending multiple sub-calculations to a worker node VM, depending on the available VMs or the execution time of a single sub-calculation. We plan to use this information to generate an execution plan that matches the required boundary conditions (e.g. costs, time) as good as possible. To be able to use the CEF with different prioritized users, we need to add a priority to each calculation/user. The administrator must be able to set a maximum boundary for the costs. This is very important, especially for Amazon usage (VM per hour, data transfer, etc.). In the future we will test the CEF not only with CPU-intensive calculations, but also with a data-intensive calculation.

Conclusions

In this paper we have presented a novel Code Execution Framework (CEF) that is able to execute problem solving environment (PSE) source code in parallel, using a cloud infrastructure. With this framework the scientists are enabled to use different client applications to communicate with our system, (a) out of his/her problem solving environment, (b) Taverna workflow engine, and (c) from our Liferay Web portal. In the future we will implement different other clients (e.g. Galaxy Project), depending on the requests of the CEF users. Additionally, the scientist is able to execute different PSE source code without having the required PSE installed locally. This can be very important for closed source PSEs (e.g., MATLAB) to reduce the license costs. Depending on the cloud infrastructure used, the Code Execution Framework influences the total cost of ownership [46] (e.g., maintenance and ownership costs), as well. When using a self-owned cloud infrastructure, the hardware, maintenance and the energy costs are increasing, whereas when using Amazon Elastic Compute Cloud (EC2), the machines used must be paid per hour. The whole discussed design concept has been implemented in our first prototype. We implemented the framework for the breath analysis domain, however the system is independent of the underlying scientific field and thus can be used for different domains without any adoptions.

The performance test shows the time improvements while executing a CPU-intensive mathematical calculation. The transfer overhead mainly depends on the infrastructure used (e.g., local Eucalyptus or Amazon EC2), the processing speed depends on the VM-type used (e.g., CPU and available memory). If a given calculation can be parallelized by invoking the same method with different parameter sets, the provided easy to use Code Execution Framework will reduce the total execution time rapidly.

As the next step we will define and implement algorithms to predict the required execution time and to generate the best possible execution plan that fulfills the required conditions (e.g. costs, time). In addition to that we will continue our efforts to integrate our system in a workflow environment that can be extended to support our Kerberos based security concept.

Competing interests

The authors declare that they have no competing interests.

Authors' contributions

TL, TF and PB have all contributed to the Code Execution Framework concept. They designed the paper structure and gave their feedbacks to all its versions. TL has designed the architecture of the described system and was responsible for implementation and testing. PB and TF are the co-leaders of the Breath analysis project, in the context of which the solution presented in the paper was developed. All authors read and approved the final manuscript.

Authors' information

Thomas Ludescher

Thomas Ludescher is working at the university of applied sciences in Vorarlberg, Austria. He holds a M.Sc. in computer science from the university of applied sciences in Vorarlberg, Austria. Currently he is writing his Ph.D. at the university of Vienna in the field of high productivity e-Science frameworks. He worked several years as a computer scientist for the international breath research community in the context of the European BAMOD-project. His main duties there were to set up a novel database for volatile organic compounds and to develop tools for their automatize access within PSEs. His research interests include in cloud technologies, distributing time consuming problem solving environment calculations, and all aspects related to security frameworks in e-Science infrastructures.

Thomas Feilhauer

Thomas Feilhauer is a professor for Computer Science at the Fachhochschule Vorarlberg University of applied sciences in Dornbirn, Austria. He has been involved in the set-up of the diplom-program iTec, the bachelor-program Informatik (ITB), and the master-program Informatik (ITM). To extend his research activities, he became a founding member of the Research Center "Process and Product Engineering". His research interests are in areas of Distributed Systems, Grid & Cloud computing. Selected Project Experience: (a) Partner in the Austrian Grid project, funded by the Austrian Federal Ministry of Education, Science and Cultural Affairs; (b) SWOP (Semantic Web-based Open engineering Platform) - co-funded by the European Commission under FP6; (c) OptimUns - Josef Ressel-Lab, funded by FFG (Österreichische Forschungsförderungsgesellschaft).

Peter Brezany

Dr. Peter Brezany is a professor of Computer Science in the University of Vienna Faculty of Informatics. He received his Doctor of Philosophy in

Computer Science from the Slovak Technical University in Bratislava in 1980. He is known for his work in the areas of high performance programming languages and their implementation for input/output intensive scientific applications. Now his primary research interests focus on large-scale, high-productive data analytics. He leads the GridMiner project that developed the first full-fledged data mining system operating on data streams and data repositories connected to grids and clouds; the system is being used und further developed in other research projects. He published one book monograph, five book chapters and over one hundred papers.

Acknowledgements
The funding of the ABA-Project (Project No. TRP 77-N13) by the Austrian Federal Ministry for Transport, Innovation and Technology and the Austrian Science Fund is key to bringing the partners together and to undertaking the research. The entire research team contributed to the discussions that led to this paper and provided the environment in which the ideas could be implemented and evaluated. We thank all reviewers, whose comments and suggestions greatly helped to improve this paper.

Author details
[1]Fachhochschule Vorarlberg, University of Applied Sciences, Hochschulstrasse 1, 6850 Dornbirn, Austria. [2]Research Group Scientific Computing, Faculty of Computer Science, University of Vienna, Waehringer StraSSe 29, A-1090 Vienna, Austria.

References

1. IABR (2012) International Association for Breath Research. http://iabr.voc-research.at. Accessed Dec 2012
2. IOPscience (2012) Journal of, Breath Research. http://iopscience.iop.org/1752-7163. Accessed Dec 2012
3. The MathWorks (2012) Matlab - The Language Of Technical Computing. http://www.mathworks.com/products/matlab. Accessed Dec 2012
4. Eato JW (2012) Octave. http://www.gnu.org/software/octave. Accessed Dec 2012
5. The R Project for StatisticalComputing (2012). http://www.r-project.org. Accessed Dec 2012
6. The MathWorks (2012) Which MATLAB function benefit from multithreaded computations. http://www.mathworks.de/support/solutions/en/data/1-4PG4AN. Accessed Mar 2013
7. Armbrust M, Fox A, Griffith R, Joseph AD, Katz RH, Konwinski A, Lee G, Patterson DA, Rabkin A, Stoica I, Zaharia M (2009) Above the clouds: a Berkeley view of cloud computing In: Tech. Rep. UCB/EECS-2009-28. EECS Department, University of California, Berkeley. http://www.eecs.berkeley.edu/Pubs/TechRpts/2009/EECS-2009-28.html
8. IBM Research (2012) Global Technology Outlook 2012. http://www.research.ibm.com/files/pdfs/gto_booklet_executive_review_march_12.pdf. Accessed Dec 2012
9. Atkinson M (2013) The data bonanza: improving knowledge discovery in science, engineering, and business. Wiley Series on Parallel and Distributed Computing
10. Mell P, Grance T (2011) The NIST definition of cloud computing. National Institute of Standards and Technology. http://csrc.nist.gov/publications/nistpubs/800-145/SP800-145.pdf
11. Amazon (2012) Amazon Web Services. http://aws.amazon.com. Accessed Dec 2012
12. Eucalyptus Systems (2012) Open Source Private and Hybrid Clouds from Eucalyptus. http://www.eucalyptus.com. Accessed Dec 2012
13. Amazon (2012) Amazon simple storage service (Amazon S3). http://aws.amazon.com/s3. Accessed Dec 2012
14. Gallopoulos E, Houstis E, Rice J (1994) Computer as thinker/doer: problem-solving environments for computational science. Comput Sci, Eng, IEEE 1(2): 11–23
15. Michalowski T (2011) Applications of MATLAB in science and engineering. InTech. http://www.intechopen.com/books/applications-of-matlab-in-science-and-engineering
16. Scientific Computing (2009) ParallelR version 1.2. http://www.scientificcomputing.com/product-hpc-ParallelR-Version-1.2-031009.aspx. Accessed Apr 2012
17. Scientific Computing Associates Inc (2007) NetWorkSpacs for R user guide. http://nws-r.sourceforge.net/doc/nwsR-1.5.0.pdf. Accessed Dec 2012
18. Rickert JB (2010) R for Web-Services with RevoDeployR. http://info.revolutionanalytics.com/RevoDeployR-Whitepaper.html. Accessed Dec 2012
19. Chine K (2011) Elastic-R: A virtual collaborative environment for scientific computing and data analysis in the cloud. http://www.elasticr.net/doc/ElasticR-SC10-Tutorial.pdf. Accessed Dec 2012
20. Parallel Octave (2003). http://www.aoki.ecei.tohoku.ac.jp/octave. Accessed Feb 2013
21. Buehren M (2009) The 'multicore' package. http://octave.sourceforge.net/multicore. Accessed Feb 2013
22. Kepner DJ (2013) MIT Lincoln Laboratory: MatlabMPI. http://www.ll.mit.edu/mission/isr/matlabmpi/matlabmpi.html. Accessed Feb 2013
23. The MathWorks (2009) Parallel computing with MATLAB on amazon elastic compute cloud. Parallel Comput: 1–24. http://www.mathworks.com/programs/techkits/ec2_paper.html. Accessed Feb 2012
24. Cornell University Center for Advanced Computing (CAC) (2012) Red cloud. http://www.cac.cornell.edu/redcloud. Accessed Apr 2012
25. Jejkal T (2010) GridMate — The Grid Matlab Extension. In: Lin SC, Yen E (eds) Managed Grids and Cloud Systems in the Asia-Pacific Research Communit. Springer, US, pp 325–339. http://dx.doi.org/10.1007/978-1-4419-6469-4_24.
26. Geeknet Inc (2013) Octave as a cloud service. http://octaveoncloud.sourceforge.net. Accessed Mar 2013
27. EMBL-EBI (2013) R Cloud Workbench. http://www.ebi.ac.uk/Tools/rcloud. Accessed Mar 2013
28. Revolutions (2009) Running R in the cloud with Amazon EC2. http://blog.revolutionanalytics.com/2009/05/running-r-in-the-cloud-with-amazon-ec2.html. Accessed Mar 2013
29. University of Vienna (2013) Advanced Breath Analysis - ABA. http://aba.cloudminer.org. Accessed Feb 2013
30. Taverna (2012) Taverna - open source and domain independent Workflow Management System. http://www.taverna.org.uk. Accessed Dec 2012
31. National Science Foundation (2012) The kepler project. https://kepler-project.org. Accessed Dec 2012
32. Kranjc J (2012) ClowdFlows - A data mining workflow platform. http://clowdflows.org. Accessed Mar 2013
33. University of Waikato (2013) ADAMS - The Advanced Data Mining And Machine learning System. https://adams.cms.waikato.ac.nz. Accessed Mar 2013
34. Ludescher T, Feilhauer T, Brezany P (2012) Security concept and implementation for a cloud based e-Science infrastructure: pp.280-285. 2012 Seventh International Conference on Availability, Reliability and Security
35. Doucet A, De Freitas N, Gordon N (eds) (2010) Sequential Monte Carlo methods in practice (information science and statistics). Springer, US. [http://www.springer.com/statistics/physical-%26-information-science/book/978-0-387-95146-1]
36. Fachhochschule Vorarlberg - University of AppliedSciences (2012) ABA Community. http://aba.hostingcenter.uclv.net. Accessed Mar 2013
37. Liferay Inc (2013) Liferay. http://www.liferay.com. Accessed Feb 2013
38. The HDF Group (2012) ADF Group -HDF5. http://www.hdfgroup.org/HDF5. Accessed Dec 2012
39. The MathWorks (2012) How can I distribute an application that is developed using MATLAB. http://www.mathworks.de/support/solutions/en/data/1-GQC9MB. Accessed Feb 2013
40. Apache (2012) Apache CXF. http://cxf.apache.org. Accessed Dec 2012
41. CROSS CHECK networks (2012) Introduction to MTOM. http://www.crosschecknet.com/intro_to_mtom.php. Accessed Dec 2012
42. Yeung JHC, Tsang CC, Tsoi KH, Kwan BSH, Cheung CCC, Chan APC, Leong PHW (2008) Map-reduce as a programming model for custom computing machines. In: Proceedings of the2008 16th International Symposium on Field-Programmable Custom Computing Machines,

FCCM '08. IEEE Computer Society, Washington, pp 149–159. http://dx.doi.org/10.1109/FCCM.2008.19

43. Yahoo! Inc (2013) Hadoop tutorial. http://developer.yahoo.com/hadoop/tutorial/module3.html. Accessed Feb 2013

44. Liss J (2011) EC2 CPU benchmark: Fastest instance type (serial performance). http://www.opinionatedprogrammer.com/2011/07/ec2-cpu-benchmark-fastest-instance-type-for-build-servers. Accessed Feb 2013

45. Amazon (2013) Amazon EC2 instance types. http://aws.amazon.com/ec2/instance-types. Accessed Feb 2013

46. Agarwal S, McCabe L (2010) The TCO advantages of SaaS-Based budgeting, forecasting & reporting. www.hurwitz.com . [http://www.adaptiveplanning.co.uk/uploads/docs/Hurwitz_TCO_of_SaaS_CPM_Solutions.pdf]

5

Clustering-based fragmentation and data replication for flexible query answering in distributed databases

Lena Wiese

Abstract

One feature of cloud storage systems is data fragmentation (or sharding) so that data can be distributed over multiple servers and subqueries can be run in parallel on the fragments. On the other hand, flexible query answering can enable a database system to find related information for a user whose original query cannot be answered exactly. Query generalization is a way to implement flexible query answering on the syntax level. In this paper we study a clustering-based fragmentation for the generalization operator Anti-Instantiation with which related information can be found in distributed data. We use a standard clustering algorithm to derive a semantic fragmentation of data in the database. The database system uses the derived fragments to support an intelligent flexible query answering mechanism that avoids overgeneralization but supports data replication in a distributed database system. We show that the data replication problem can be expressed as a special Bin Packing Problem and can hence be solved by an off-the shelf solver for integer linear programs. We present a prototype system that makes use of a medical taxonomy to determine similarities between medical expressions.

Keywords: Fragmentation; Distributed database; Flexible query answering; Clustering; Load balancing; Data replication; Bin packing with conflicts

Introduction

In the era of "big data" huge data sets usually cannot be stored on a single server any longer. Cloud storage (where data are stored in a cloud infrastructure) offers the advantage of flexibly adapting the amount of used storage based on the growing or shrinking storage demands of the data owners. In a cloud storage system, a distributed database management system (DDBMS) can be used to manage the data in a network of servers. This allows for load balancing (data can be distributed according to the capacities of servers) and higher availability (servers can process user requests in parallel). In particular, when data are distributed over a wider area in different data centers, it is important that only few servers have to be contacted to answer user queries in order to reduce network delays; in the ideal case, these servers are also geographically close to the user.

Correspondence: wiese@cs.uni-goettingen.de
Institute of Computer Science, Georg-August-Universität Göttingen, Goldschmidtstraße 7, Göttingen, Germany

Depending on the data structure used in the DDBMS a variety of distribution models are possible. For relational data, the theory of fragmentation has a long history (see for example [1]) and several procedures have been analyzed for splitting tabular data into fragments and subsequently assigning fragments to servers. Other database systems with key-based access (like key-value stores, document databases, or column family stores) use range-based partitioning or consistent hashing to distribute data.

On the other hand, *flexible query answering* offers mechanisms to intelligently answer user queries going beyond conventional exact query answering. If a database system is not able to find an exactly matching answer, the query is said to be a *failing* query. Conventional database systems usually return an empty answer to a failing query. In most cases, this is an undesirable situation for the user, because he has to revise his query and send the revised query to the database system in order to get some information from the database. In contrast, flexible query answering systems internally revise failing user queries themselves and – by evaluating the revised query – return answers to the user that are more informative for the user than just an empty answer. *Query generalization* is one way to implement flexible query answering.

This paper revises and extends the previous results presented in [2]. In this paper we make the following additional contributions:

- We study how a standard clustering heuristic on a single relaxation attribute (that is, table column) can induce a horizontal fragmentation of a database table; in [2] a taxonomy-based fragmentation was used instead of a clustering-based fragmentation.
- We formally study the *data replication problem* for these fragments by representing it as a variant of the bin packing problem and solve it using an integer linear programming solver. This was not discussed in [2].
- We present a detailed query rewriting and query redirecting method that allows access to the distributed fragments. This was discussed in [2] only briefly.

The paper is organized as follows. Section Background provides background on data fragmentation, query generalization (in particular anti-instantiation) and data replication. Section Clustering-based fragmentation presents the main contribution on clustering-based fragmentation and its management with a lookup table; whereas Section Query rewriting talks about how to decompose a query to be distributed among the servers. Section Improving data locality with derived fragmentations extends the basic approach by allowing derived fragmentation in order to facilitate joins over multiple tables. Section Implementation and example presents the components of our prototype implementation. Section Related work surveys related work and Section Discussion and conclusion concludes the paper.

Background

In the following subsections we present prior work on **data fragmentation**, flexible query answering (with a focus on **anti-instantiation**) and **data replication**. These three techniques will be combined to obtain an intelligent distributed database system that can autonomously configure its replication mechanism while at the same time support users in finding relevant information by flexible query answering.

Data fragmentation

As the basic data model, we consider the case of data stored in relational tables. The relational data model is still widely applied today although alternatives exist (like tree- or graph-structured data or data stored in a simple key-value format).

Example 1. *As a running example, we consider a hospital information system that stores illnesses and treatments of patients as well as their personal information (like address and age) in the following three database tables:*

Ill	PatientID	Diagnosis
	8457	Cough
	2784	Flu
	2784	Asthma
	2784	brokenLeg
	8765	Asthma
	1055	brokenArm

Treat	PatientID	Prescription
	8457	Inhalation
	2784	Inhalation
	8765	Inhalation
	2784	Plaster bandage
	1055	Plaster bandage

Info	PatientID	Name	Address
	8457	Pete	Main Str 5, Newtown
	2784	Mary	New Str 3, Newtown
	8765	Lisa	Main Str 20, Oldtown
	1055	Anne	High Str 2, Oldtown

In relational database theory, several alternatives of splitting tables into fragments have been discussed (see for example [1]), for example:

- Vertical fragmentation: Subsets of attributes (that is, columns) form the fragments. Rows of the fragments that correspond to each other have to be linked by a tuple identifier. A vertical fragmentation corresponds to projection operations on the table.
- Horizontal fragmentation: Subsets of tuples (that is, rows) form the fragments. A horizontal fragmentation can be expressed by a selection condition on the table.
- Derived fragmentation: A given horizontal fragmentation on a primary table (the *primary fragmentation*) induces a horizontal fragmentation of another table based on the semijoin with the primary table. In this case, the primary and derived fragments with matching values for the join attributes can be stored on the same server; this improves efficiency of a join on the primary and the derived fragments.

The following three properties are considered the important *correctness properties* of a fragmentation:

- Completeness: No data should be lost during fragmentation. For vertical fragmentation, each column can be found in some fragment; in horizontal fragmentation each row can be found in a fragment.
- Reconstructability: Data from the fragments can be recombined to result in the original data set. For vertical fragmentation, the join operator is used on the tuple identifier to link the columns from the fragments; in horizontal fragmentation, the union

operator is used on the rows coming from the fragments.

- Non-redundancy: To avoid duplicate storage of data, data should be uniquely assigned to one fragment. In vertical fragmentation, each column is contained in only one fragment (except for the tuple identifier that links the fragments); in horizontal fragmentation, each row is contained in only one fragment.

In this paper we will compute semantically-guided horizontal fragmentations of a primary table. Each of these fragmentations will be based on clustering an attribute for which values should be relaxed to allow for flexible query answering. In contrast to the conventional applications of fragmentation, the clustering-based fragmentations will support flexible query answering in an efficient manner.

For other tables (those that can be joined with the primary table) a derived fragmentation will be computed that allows for data locality in a distributed database system.

Anti-instantiation

In this paper we focus on flexible query answering for conjunctive queries expressed as logical formulas. That is, we assume a logical language $\mathcal{L}$ consisting of a finite set of predicate symbols (denoting the table names; for example, *Ill*, *Treat* or *P*), a possibly infinite set *dom* of constant symbols (denoting the values in table cells; for example, *Mary* or *a*), and an infinite set of variables (*x* or *y*). A term is either a constant or a variable. The capital letter X denotes a vector of variables; if the order of variables in X does not matter, we identify X with the set of its variables and apply set operators – for example we write $y \in X$. We use the standard logical connectors conjunction $\wedge$, disjunction $\vee$, negation $\neg$ and material implication $\rightarrow$ and universal $\forall$ as well as existential $\exists$ quantifiers. An atom is a formula consisting of a single predicate symbol only; a literal is an atom (a "positive literal") or a negation of an atom (a "negative literal"); a clause is a disjunction of atoms; a ground formula is one that contains no variables; the existential (universal) closure of a formula ϕ is written as $\exists \phi$ ($\forall \phi$) and denotes the closed formula obtained by binding all free variables of ϕ with the respective quantifier.

A query formula Q is a conjunction of literals with some variables X occurring freely (that is, not bound by variables); that is, $Q(X) = L_{i_1} \wedge \ldots \wedge L_{i_n}$. By abuse of notation, we will also write $L_{ij} \in Q$ when L_{ij} is a conjunct in formula Q. A query $Q(X)$ is sent to a knowledge base Σ (a set of logical formulas) and then evaluated in Σ by a function *ans* that returns a set of answers containing instantiations of the free variables (in other words, a set of formulas that are logically implied by Σ); as we focus on the generalization of queries, we assume the *ans* function and an appropriate notion of logical truth given. A special

case of a knowledge base can be a relational database with database tables as in Example 1.

Example 2. *Query* $Q(x_1, x_2, x_3) = Ill(x_1, Flu) \wedge Ill(x_1, Cough) \wedge Info(x_1, x_2, x_3)$ *asks for all the patient IDs x_1 as well as names x_2 and addresses x_3 of patients that suffer from both flu and cough. This query fails with the given database tables as there is no patient with both flu and cough. However, the querying user might instead be interested in the patient called Mary who is ill with both flu and asthma. Query generalization will enable an intelligent database system to find this informative answer.*

As in [3] we apply a notion of generalization based on a model operator $\models$.

Definition 1 (Deductive generalization [3]). *Let Σ be a knowledge base, $\phi(X)$ be a formula with a tuple X of free variables, and $\psi(X, Y)$ be a formula with an additional tuple Y of free variables disjoint from X. The formula $\psi(X, Y)$ is a deductive generalization of $\phi(X)$, if it holds in Σ that the less general ϕ implies the more general ψ where for the free variables X (the ones that occur in ϕ and possibly in ψ) the universal closure and for free variables Y (the ones that occur in ψ only) the existential closure is taken:*

$$\Sigma \models \forall X \exists Y (\phi(X) \rightarrow \psi(X, Y))$$

The CoopQA system [4] applies three generalization operators to a conjunctive query (which – among others – can already be found in the seminal paper of Michalski [5]): **Dropping Condition** (*DC*) removes one conjunct from a query; **Anti-Instantiation** (*AI*) replaces a constant (or a variable occurring at least twice) in Q with a new variable y; **Goal Replacement** (*GR*) takes a rule from Σ, finds a substitution θ that maps the rule's body to some conjuncts in the query and replaces these conjuncts by the head (with θ applied). In this paper we focus only on the AI operator.

Example 3. *For query $Q(x_1, x_2, x_3) = Ill(x_1, Flu) \wedge Ill(x_1, Cough) \wedge Info(x_1, x_2, x_3)$ an example generalization with AI is $Q^{AI}(x_1, x_2, x_3, y) = Ill(x_1, Flu) \wedge Ill(x_1, y) \wedge Info(x_1, x_2, x_3)$. A non-empty answer (and hence informative answer) $Ill(2748, Flu) \wedge Ill(2748, Asthma) \wedge Info(2748, Mary, 'New Str 3, Newtown')$ is returned as an answer saying that Mary suffers from flu and asthma at the same time. However, another obtained answer is $Ill(2748, Flu) \wedge Ill(2748, brokenLeg) \wedge Info(2748, Mary, 'New Str 3, Newtown')$ saying that Mary suffers from flu and a broken leg.*

AI applies to constants and to variables and covers these special cases:

- turning constants into variables: $P(a)$ is converted to $P(x)$ (see [5])
- breaking joins: $P(x) \wedge S(x)$ is converted to $P(x) \wedge S(y)$ (introduced in [3])

- naming apart variables inside atoms: $P(x, x)$ is converted to $P(x, y)$

For each constant a all occurrences can be anti-instantiated one after the other; the same applies to variables x – however, with the exception that if x only occurs twice, one occurrence of x need not be anti-instantiated due to equivalence. For logical queries, anti-instantiation can be implemented as shown in the listing in Listing 1.

Listing 1 Anti-instantiation (AI)

Input: Query $Q(X) = L_1 \wedge \ldots \wedge L_n$ of length n
Output: Generalized query $Q^{AI}(X, Y)$ with Y containing one new variable
1: From $Q(X)$ choose a term t such that t is

- either a variable occurring in $Q(X)$ at least twice
- or a constant

2: Choose one literal L_j where t occurs
3: Let L'_j be the literal with one occurrence of t replaced with a new variable
4: **return** $L_1 \wedge \ldots \wedge L_{j-1} \wedge L'_j \wedge L_{j+1} \wedge \ldots \wedge L_n$

In this paper, we focus on the first application of anti-instantiation: turning constants into variables. In the following section, we present an approach that identifies those tuples in a relational table that are good candidates for answers to such an anti-instantiated query; these candidates are put into one fragment for storage in a distributed database system.

Data replication

To achieve fault tolerance, reliability and high availability, data in a distributed database system should be copied (that is, *replicated*) to different servers. Whenever one of the database servers fails, if it is too overloaded or geographically too far away from the requesting user, a data copy (that is, a *replica*) can be retrieved from one of the other servers.

The data replication problem (DRP; see [6]) is a formal description of the task of distributing copies of data records (that is, database fragments) among a set of servers in a distributed database system. The data replication problem is basically a Bin Packing Problem (BPP) in the following sense:

- K servers correspond to K bins
- bins have a maximum capacity W
- n fragments correspond to n objects
- each object has a weight (a capacity consumption) $w_i \leq W$
- objects have to be placed into a minimum number of bins without exceeding the maximum capacity

This BPP can be written as an integer linear program (ILP) as follows – where x_{ik} is a binary variable that denotes whether fragment/object i is placed in server/bin k; and y_k denotes that server/bin k is used (that is, is non-empty):

$$\text{minimize} \sum_{k=1}^{K} y_k \tag{1}$$

$$\text{s.t.} \quad \sum_{k=1}^{K} x_{ik} = 1, \qquad i = 1, \ldots, n \tag{2}$$

$$\sum_{i=1}^{n} w_i x_{ik} \leq W y_k, \qquad k = 1, \ldots, K \tag{3}$$

$$y_k \in \{0, 1\} \qquad k = 1, \ldots, K \tag{4}$$

$$x_{ik} \in \{0, 1\} \quad k = 1, \ldots, K, \ i = 1, \ldots, n \tag{5}$$

To explain, Equation 1 means that we want to minimize the number of servers/bins used; Equation 2 means that each object is assigned to exactly one bin; Equation 3 means that the capacity of each server is not exceeded; and the last two equations denote that the variables are binary – that is, the ILP is a so-called 0-1 linear program.

An extension of the basic BPP will be used to ensure that replicas will be placed on distinct servers: the Bin Packing with Conflicts (BPPC; [7-9]) problem allows constraints to be expressed on pairs of objects that should not be placed in the same bin. That is, one adds a conflict graph $G = (V, E)$ where the node set $V = \{1, \ldots, n\}$ corresponds to the set of objects. A binary edge $e = (i, j)$ exists whenever the two incident nodes i and j must not be placed in the same bin; note that (i, j) is meant to be undirected and hence identical to (j, i). In the ILP representation, a further constraint is added to avoid conflicts in the placements.

$$\text{minimize} \sum_{k=1}^{K} y_k \tag{6}$$

$$\text{s.t.} \quad \sum_{k=1}^{K} x_{ik} = 1, \qquad i = 1, \ldots, n \tag{7}$$

$$\sum_{i=1}^{n} w_i x_{ik} \leq W y_k, \qquad k = 1, \ldots, K \tag{8}$$

$$x_{ik} + x_{jk} \leq y_k \quad (i, j) \in E, \ k = 1, \ldots, K \tag{9}$$

$$y_k \in \{0, 1\} \qquad k = 1, \ldots, K \tag{10}$$

$$x_{ik} \in \{0, 1\} \quad k = 1, \ldots, K, \ i = 1, \ldots, n \tag{11}$$

Equation 9 ensures that no conflicting objects i and j are placed in the same bin k because otherwise the sum of the two x-variables x_{ik} and x_{jk} would be 2 and hence exceed y_k which is 1.

In this paper, we will extend the BPPC to ensure that a certain replication factor m for each fragment of the relational table is obeyed; that is, for each fragment stored at one server there are at least $m - 1$ other servers storing a copy of this fragment, too.

Clustering-based fragmentation

We now present our intelligent fragmentation and replication procedure that will support flexible query answering with anti-instantiation.

The anti-instantiation operator as stated above is a purely syntactic operator. For the application of turning constants into variables, any constant can be inserted in the answer. This syntactic operator is oblivious of whether the obtained answer is *semantically* close to the replaced constant in the original query or not. For example in Example 3, the two diseases cough and asthma are semantically closer to each other than the two diseases cough and broken leg. That is, the generalization operators can sometimes lead to overgeneralization where the generalized queries (and hence the obtained answers) are too far away from the user's original query intention. To avoid this overgeneralization and the overabundance of answers, a semantic guidance has to be added to the process. This semantic guidance can for example be given by a taxonomy on constants.

As an extension to [2], we will present a clustering heuristics attributes on which anti-instantiation should be applied. We call such attribute a *relaxation attribute*. The *domain* of an attribute is the set of values that the attribute may range over; whereas the *active domain* is the set of values actually occuring in a given table. For a given table instance F (a set of tuples ranging over the same attributes) and a relaxation attribute A, the active domain can be obtained by a projection π to A on F: $\pi_A(F)$. In our example the relaxation attribute is the attribute *Diagnosis* in table *Ill*. From a semantical point of view, the domain of *Diagnosis* is the set of strings that denote a disease; the active domain is the set of terms {*Cough, Flu, Asthma, brokenArm, brokenLeg*}.

Wiese 2013 [2] assumes a tree-shaped taxonomy on the active domain of a relaxation attribute where the active domain values can be found in the leave nodes connected by some intermediary nodes serving as a classification of the values. As an alternative, in this paper we only rely on the specification of a similarity value $sim(a, b)$ between any two values a and b in the active domain of a relaxation attribute. These similarity values, however, can indeed be calculated by using a taxonomy; we will briefly survey some of such similarity measures below when describing the prototype. Based on this similarity specification, we derive a clustering of the active domain of each relaxation attribute A in a relation instance F. We rely on a very general definition of a clustering as being a set of

subsets (the *clusters*) of a larger set of values. For a clustering to be reasonable, similarities of any two values inside one cluster should somehow be larger than between any two values from different clusters. This will be ensured below by relying on so-called *head* elements in the clusters and on a threshold value α that restricts the minimal similarity allowed inside a cluster: if c_i is a cluster, then $head_i \in c_i$ and for any other value $a \in c_i$ (with $a \neq head_i$) it holds that $sim(a, head_i) \geq \alpha$ The clustering of the active domain of A induces a horizontal fragmentation of F into fragments $F_i \subseteq F$ such that the active domain of each fragment F_i coincides with one cluster; more formally, $c_i = \pi_A(F_i)$. For the fragmentation to be complete, we also require the clustering C to be complete; that is, if $\pi_A(F)$ is the active domain to be clustered, then the complete clustering $C = c_1, \ldots, c_n$ covers the whole active domain and no value is lost: $c_1 \cup \ldots \cup c_n = \pi_A(F)$. These requirements are summarized in the definition of a *clustering-based fragmentation* as follows.

Definition 2 (Clustering-based fragmentation). *Let A be a relaxation attribute; let F be a table instance (a set of tuples); let $C = \{c_1, \ldots c_n\}$ be a complete clustering of the active domain $\pi_A(F)$ of A in F; let $head_i \in c_i$; then, a set of fragments $\{F_1, \ldots, F_n\}$ (defined over the same attributes as F) is a clustering-based fragmentation if*

- *Horizontal fragmentation: for every fragment F_i, $F_i \subseteq F$*
- *Clustering: for every F_i there is a cluster $c_i \in C$ such that $c_i = \pi_A(F_i)$ (that is, the active domain of F_i on A is equal to a cluster in C)*
- *Threshold: for every $a \in c_i$ (with $a \neq head_i$) it holds that $sim(a, head_i) \geq \alpha$*
- *Completeness: For every tuple t in F there is an F_i in which t is contained*
- *Reconstructability: $F = F_1 \cup \ldots \cup F_n$*
- *Non-redundancy: for any $i \neq j$, $F_i \cap F_j = \emptyset$ (or in other words $c_i \cap c_j = \emptyset$)*

Approximation algorithm for clustering

We use and adapt an established approximation algorithm for clustering originally presented by Gonzalez [10]. Its original presentation relies on a notion of distance between any two values. It has a running time of $O(kf)$ for clustering a set of k objects into f clusters. Each cluster is represented by one or more so-called head values; and each value is assigned to the cluster represented by a head with minimal distance to the value. In case the distance measure is metric (in particular, satisfies the triangular inequation), Gonzalez showed that the number of heads obtained by his algorithm is at most twice as much as the optimal number of heads (in other words, it is a 2-approximation of the optimal solution).

Rieck et al. [11] apply this algorithm to malware detection. Instead of fixing the number f of clusters, they use a threshold for the distances of values inside a cluster to the cluster head; hence the number of obtained clusters can differ. This functionality is also needed in our application. We however rely on the notion of similarity between two values (instead of distance) and provide a reformulation of the clustering algorithm here based on [10,11]. The algorithm starts by assigning all values of the active domain to an initial cluster c_1, choosing an arbitrary element of it as $head_1$ and then step by step choosing other head elements $head_2, \ldots, head_f$ that have lowest similarity to all other heads and moving other elements to the new clusters $c_2, \ldots, c_f$; an element is moved to a new cluster when it has higher similarity to the new head element than to the old head element. The algorithm continues finding new heads until a threshold α is reached; α limits the minimum similarity that elements inside a cluster may have to their cluster heads. Listing 2 shows a pseudocode for the clustering procedure.

Listing 2 Clustering procedure

Input: Set $\pi_A(F)$ of values for attribute A, similarity threshold α

Output: A set of clusters $c_1, \ldots, c_f$

1: Let $c_1 = \pi_A(F)$
2: Choose arbitrary $head_1 \in c_1$
3: $sim_{min} = min\{sim(a, head_1) \mid a \in c_1; a \neq head_1\}$
4: $i = 1$
5: **while** $sim_{min} < \alpha$ **do**
6:     Choose $head_{i+1} \in \{b \mid b \in c_j; b \neq head_j; sim(b, head_j) = sim_{min}; 1 \leq j \leq i\}$
7:     $c_{i+1} = \{head_{i+1}\} \cup \{c \mid c \in c_j; c \neq head_j; sim(c, head_j) \leq sim(c, head_{i+1}); 1 \leq j \leq i\}$
8:     $i = i + 1$
9:     $sim_{min} = min\{sim(d, head_j) \mid d \in c_j; d \neq head_j; 1 \leq j \leq i\}$
10: **end while**

Note that the clustering obtained by this heuristic is always complete: any value of $\pi_A(F)$ is assigned to some cluster c_i. And we also have the property that clusters do not overlap: $c_i \cap c_j \neq \emptyset$ for each $i \neq j$.

Example 4. *In our example, we assume that the pairwise similarities for the values in the active domain of the relaxation attribute Diagnosis are given. We assume further that the pairwise similarities in the subset {Cough, Flu, Asthma} and in the subset {brokenArm, brokenLeg} are higher than any similarity in between these two subsets. In the first clustering step, we choose head$_1$ arbitrarily – let us assume Flu – and the entire active domain forms cluster c$_1$. Now as head$_2$ the value with the lowest similarity is chosen – let us assume brokenArm. Now, all values with higher similarity to brokenArm (than to Flu) are moved to cluster c$_2$ – which*

will then consist of {brokenArm, brokenLeg}. If we choose threshold α to lie in between the minimum intra-cluster (of both c$_1$ and c$_2$) similarity and the maximum inter-cluster similarity (between pairs of values from c$_1$ and c$_2$), we will stop after this second iteration.

Fragmentation and lookup table

When considering only a single relaxation attribute A, we obtain a fragmentation of the corresponding table: a set of fragments F_i – each corresponding to a cluster c_i. A relational algebra expression for each fragment can be stated as follows (using the selection operator σ and a disjunction of equality conditions on A for each value a contained in the cluster):

$$F_i = \sigma_{condition(c_i)}(F)$$
$$\text{where } condition(c_i) = \bigvee_{a \in c_i}(A = a)$$

The selection operator results in a set of rows – hence a horizontal fragmentation is obtained. Because the clustering is complete, the fragmentation itself will also be complete; hence, in addition a reconstruction of the original instance F is possible by the union operator. Moreover, because clusters do not overlap, we also achieve nonredundancy in this fragmentation. Hence, all properties of Definition 2 will be ensured.

Example 5. *Based on the above clustering, we obtain two fragments of the Ill table.*

Respiratory	PatientID	Diagnosis
	8457	Cough
	2784	Flu
	2784	Asthma
	8765	Asthma

Fracture	PatientID	Diagnosis
	2784	brokenLeg
	1055	brokenArm

Fragmentation and replica management are usually supported by lookup tables [12] (also called root tables [13]) that store metadata – for example, information about in which fragment to look for matching tuples when a query arrives. In our case, as we enable flexible query answering in distributed database systems, we create a lookup table that contains:

- the fragment ID F_i that is used to solve the data replication problem
- the fragment name that will be used in queries to the fragment
- the head $head_i$ of the cluster c_i that was used to obtain the fragment F_i as a semantic representative of the values for relaxation attribute A inside fragment F_i
- the size w_i of fragment F_i that is used in the data replication problem; for simplicity, in this paper we

only count the number of rows – but more advanced size measures can be used, too

- an array of the IP addresses or names of the database servers that fragment F_i is assigned to

Example 6. *We insert the following data into the ROOT lookup table where ID is the fragment identifier, Name is the fragment name, S is the fragment size in number of tuples, and Host is the name of the server where the fragment is assigned to.*

ROOT	ID	Name	Head	S	Host
	F1	Respiratory	Flu	4	NULL
	F2	Fracture	brokenArm	2	NULL

The last missing information – identifying the database server hosting the fragment – is computed by solving a bin packing problem with conflicts (BPPC). The basic idea is that for f fragments we want to replicate m times, each fragment F_i is copied $m - 1$ times: for F_i (and $1 \leq i \leq f$) we obtain the copies $F_{f+i}, F_{2f+i}, \ldots, F_{(m-1)f+i}$ so that the total number of fragments will be $n = f \cdot m$. Furthermore any two copies of fragment F_i (and including F_i itself) must not be placed on the same server; this will be ensured by a conflict graph where there exist edges between all pairs of copies of F_i.

Example 7. *In our example, when we assume a replication factor of $m = 2$, we have to copy each fragment once. Hence we have that $F_1 = F_3 = Respiratory$ each with a size of 4; and $F_2 = F_4 = Fracture$ each with a size of 2. The conflict graph then consists of nodes $V = \{F_1, F_2, F_3, F_4\}$ and edges $E = \{(F_1, F_3), (F_2, F_4)\}$.*

As input information for the BPPC we hence need:

- the capacity W of each of the database servers based on some configuration information of the distributed database system
- the replication factor m based on some configuration information of the distributed database system
- F_i as well as $m - 1$ copies $F_{f+i}, F_{2f+i}, \ldots, F_{(m-1)f+i}$ of each F_i (where $1 \leq i \leq f$)
- the sizes w_i for each F_i (where $1 \leq i \leq n$) where the copies of a fragment have the same size as the fragment itself
- the conflict graph G where the set of $n = f \cdot m$ nodes is the set of fragments and their copies – that is, $V = \{F_1, F_2, \ldots, F_f, F_{f+1}, \ldots, F_n\}$ – and the set of undirected binary edges E consists of the sets E_i (where $1 \leq i \leq f$) of pairs (X, Y) of a fragment F_i and all its copies – that is, $E = \bigcup_{i=1}^{f} E_i$ where $E_i = \{(X, Y) \mid X, Y \in \{F_i, F_{f+i}, F_{2f+i}, \ldots, F_{(m-1)f+i}\}; 1 \leq i \leq f\}$.

When solving the usual ILP formulation of BPPC (as shown in Equations 6 to 11) with these inputs, we obtain a solution that occupies the minimal number of servers (bins) while respecting the different sizes w_i that the fragments (for a single relaxation attribute A) may have as well as ensuring the replication factor. An example with the ILP solver *lpsolve* is provided in an upcoming section.

As opposed to lookup tables for individual tuples [12], we only store a row per fragment (and only the appropriate cluster head). Due to this, the lookup tables are small and lookups can be faster. That is why we assume that there is only a master server for the lookup table; one hot backup server can be used that can take over the task of the master server in case of a failure. Alternatively, distribution of the lookup table to all replica servers can be used; however, this incurs extra overhead and consistency problems [12].

Query rewriting

Flexible query answering can now be executed on the obtained clustering-based fragmentation. Queries are rewritten and redirected to the appropriate fragment with the help of the lookup table as follows:

1. The user sends a query to the database system with a selection condition containing a constant a for the relaxation attribute A.
2. The database system checks if there is a head value $head_i$ in the lookup table such that $head_i = a$. Then the appropriate fragment F_i is already identified and the next three steps can be skipped.
3. Otherwise the database system reads all f head values from the lookup table.
4. The database system computes all similarities $sim(a, head_i)$ (for $1 \leq i \leq f$).
5. The database system chooses a head $head_i$ with maximum similarity to a and thereby identifies appropriate fragment F_i. A threshold β can be provided by the user to limit this similarity divergence.
6. The database system rewrites the query by replacing the original table name with the identified fragment name and removes the selection condition containing a for the relaxation attribute.
7. The rewritten query is redirected to the server that hosts the identified fragment.
8. The server can return the entire fragment for the rewritten query with the assertion that the distance threshold β is not exceed and hence the answers are relevant for the user.
9. If the query contains multiple selection conditions for the relaxation attribute, several query rewritings will be executed and theses queries can be redirected to different servers.

Example 8. *In the example query $Q(x_1, x_2, x_3) = Ill(x_1, Flu) \land Ill(x_1, Cough) \land Info(x_1, x_2, x_3)$ the constant Cough is anti-instantiated. The fragment matching the*

Cough constant is the one containing respiratory diseases because we assume that it holds that sim(Flu, Cough) > sim(brokenArm, Cough). The second constant for the relaxation attribute in this query is Flu; however, Flu is a head element of the corresponding fragment and hence no similarities have to be computed. The anti-instantiated query is

$$Q^{AI}(x_1, x_2, x_3, y, y') - Respiratory(x_1, y)$$
$$\wedge Respiratory(x_1, y') \wedge Info(x_1, x_2, x_3) \wedge y \neq y'$$

The inequality condition on the new variables is necessary to only obtain answers where the two disease values found in the Respiratory fragment differ. A distributed join on x_1 has to be executed to combine the data from the Info table with the data from the Respiratory fragment; we will later on discuss how this overhead can be avoided by using derived fragmentation. Because the query is redirected to the fragment with highest similarity, in this case only the first informative answer (see Example 3) with the disease asthma $Ill(2748, Flu) \wedge Ill(2748, Asthma) \wedge Info(2748, Mary, 'New Str 3, Newtown')$ is returned. In contrast, the answer for the disease brokenLeg is suppressed because it resides in the Fracture fragment.

The computation of distributed joins cannot be avoided if subqueries must be redirected to different server. We argue however, that with any other conventional data replication scheme (like [12,14]), distributed joins have to be processed, too; while with our scheme we have added support for flexible query answering.

Example 9. *Consider the example query*

$$Q(x_1, x_2, x_3) = Ill(x_1, brokenLeg)$$
$$\wedge Ill(x_1, Cough) \wedge Info(x_1, x_2, x_3)$$

The query has to be rewritten into the query

$$Q^{AI}(x_1, x_2, x_3, y, y') = Fracture(x_1, y)$$
$$\wedge Respiratory(x_1, y') \wedge Info(x_1, x_2, x_3)$$

which has to be answered by both Fracture the and the Respiratory fragment. It may happen that the Respiratory, Fracture and Info tables all reside on different servers and so we would have to compute a three-way distributed join on x_1.

Improving data locality with derived fragmentations

Apart from failure tolerance and load balancing, another important issue for cloud storage is *data locality*: Data that are often accessed together should be stored on the same server in order to avoid excessive network traffic and delays. That is why we propose to compute a *derived fragmentation* for each table that shares join attributes with the primary table (for which the clustering-based fragmentation was computed). Each derived fragment should

then be assigned to the same database server on which the primary fragment with the matching join attribute values resides.

Hence for a given fragmentation $\{F_1, \ldots, F_f\}$ of a primary table F we compute the corresponding fragmentation $\{G_1, \ldots, G_f\}$ of any table G sharing join attributes with F as a semijoin of G with each fragment F_i: $G_i = G \ltimes F_i$ – which is equivalent to the projection on the attributes of G of the natural join of G and F_i: $\pi_{Attr(G)}(G \bowtie F_i)$.

Example 10. *In our example we can join both the Treat as well as the Info table with the Ill table. Because we have two fragments of Ill, we obtain two derived fragments of Treat and Info as well: the first set of derived fragments is called Treat_resp and Info_resp based on a join on patient IDs occurring in the primary Respiratory fragment.*

Respiratory	PatientID	Diagnosis
	8457	Cough
	2784	Flu
	2784	Asthma
	8765	Asthma

Treat_resp	PatientID	Prescription
	8457	Inhalation
	2784	Inhalation
	8765	Inhalation
	2784	Plaster bandage

Info_resp	PatientID	Name	Address
	8457	Pete	Main Str 5, Newt.
	2784	Mary	New Str 3, Newt.
	8765	Lisa	Main Str 20, Oldt.

The second set of derived fragments is Treat_frac and Info_frac based on a join on patient IDs occurring in the primary Fracture fragment.

Fracture	PatientID	Diagnosis
	2784	brokenLeg
	1055	brokenArm

Treat_frac	PatientID	Prescription
	2784	Inhalation
	2784	Plaster bandage
	1055	Plaster bandage

Info_frac	PatientID	Name	Address
	2784	Mary	New Str 3, Newt.
	1055	Anne	High Str 2, Oldt.

Note that non-redundancy of derived fragments is difficult to achieve (this is also discussed in [1]). We opt for having some redundancy in the derived fragments for sake of better data locality and hence better performance of query answering. That is why the information for patient

Mary occurs in both derived fragments; the same applies to the treatment fragments.

Data replication for derived fragments

We maintain separate lookup tables for each (primary and derived) fragmentation of each table. Hence, the sizes of the derived fragments are also computed and stored in the corresponding lookup table. These sizes of the derived fragments must be taken into account for the data replication procedure and are encoded in the BPPC as follows. The capacity W, the replication factor m, the primary fragments and their $m - 1$ copies as well as the conflict graph stay the same as before; the only input that changes is sizes w_i assigned to the fragments:

- the sizes w_i are now computed as the sum of the size of the primary fragment F_i plus the size of any derived fragment G_i.
- solving the BPPC results in a placement where the primary fragment fits on the server together with all its derived fragments.
- the primary fragment and its derived fragments are hence assigned to the same server and the server information in the lookup tables is inserted accordingly.

Implementation and example

Our prototype implementation is based on PostgreSQL and the UMLS::Similarity implementation. In the following subsections we describe the steps that the prototype executes.

UMLS and its similarity measures

The Unified Medical Language System incorporates several taxonomies from the medical domain like the Systematized Nomenclature of Medicine–Clinical Terms (SNOMED CT), or Medical Subject Headings (MeSH). It unifies these taxonomies assigning Concept Unique Identifiers (CUI) to terms so that shared terms in the different taxonomies have the same identifier.

The Perl program UMLS::Similarity [15] offers an implementation of several standard similarity measures. They can be differentiated into measures based solely on path lengths in a taxonomy and measures taking the so-called information content [16] into account. The information content (IC) is computed from a pre-assigned estimated probability $p(c)$ of each leave term in the taxonomy (assuming a parent-child or is-a relationship in the taxonomy); for inner nodes that subsume other terms, this probability must be larger than for any child node (for example, by summing over all child nodes) because this concept covers all its child concepts. The information content is then defined as the negative log likelihood: $-\log p(c)$. In this way, the higher a term is

located in taxonomy, the more abstract the term it is, and the lower is its information content; where the unique root node of the taxonomy has IC 0 (or in other words, its probability is 1) – that is, no information content.

UMLS::Similarity offers implementations of the following measures based on path lengths:

- Path length (path) counts the nodes occurring on a path between two terms a and b and takes the inverse: $sim(a, b) = \frac{1}{length(path(a,b))}$.
- Leacock and Chodorow (lch) [17] use the length of the shortest path between two terms but also consider the overall maximum depth d_{max} of the taxonomy: $sim(a, b) = -\log \frac{length(path(a,b))}{2 \cdot d_{max}}$
- Wu and Palmer (wup) [18] consider the depth of terms – that is, the length of the path from the root node to the term. It first calculates the depths of the two terms and the depth of their least common subsumer (LCS) and then calculates similarity as twice the lcs depth divided by the sum of the depths of the two terms: $sim(a, b) = \frac{2 \cdot depth(lcs(a,b))}{depth(c)+depth(b)}$
- Conceptual distance (cdist) refers to the path length between two terms; while in the original case paths between terms were defined with respect to whether a meaning was narrower or broader ([19]), later on the paths in a parent-child (is-a) relationship were considered [20] – that is why in the latter case cdist coincides with path.
- Al-Mubaid and Nguyen (nam) [21] combine path length and depth into one measure; they consider the overall maximum depth d_{max} of the taxonomy, the depth of the least common subsumer of the two comparison terms, the shortest path length between the two terms. UMLS::Similarity returns the inverse of this distance measure, that is:
$$\frac{\log 2}{(length(path(a,b))-1) \cdot (d_{max}-depth(lcs(a,b)))+1}$$

UMLS::Similarity offers implementations of the following measures incorporating information content (IC):

- Resnik (res) [16] proposed to use the information content of the least common subsumer (LCS): $IC(lcs(a, b))$
- Jiang and Conrath (jcn) [22] use the inverse of a distance that is based on the IC of the two terms and the IC of the least common subsumer: $sim(a, b) = \frac{1}{IC(a)+IC(b)-2 \cdot IC(lcs(a,b))}$
- Lin (lin) [23] takes twice the IC of the LCS and divides it by the sum of the ICs of the two terms: $sim(a, b) = \frac{2 \cdot IC(lcs(a,b))}{IC(a)+IC(b)}$

We used the UMLS::Similarity web interface with the MeSH taxonomy to obtain the pair-wise similarity of the set of terms *asthma, cough, influenza, tibial fracture* and *ulna fracture*. Figure 1 shows how the terms are related by a is-a relationship in the MeSH taxonomy. Table 1 shows the similarity values obtained. Due to symmetry of the terms in the taxonomy (the path lengths and LCSs are mostly identical), the similarity values do not differ much in the two subsets *asthma, cough* and *influenza*, as opposed to *tibial fracture* and *ulna fracture*; the only difference is obtained with the two measures where the IC of the respective terms *a, b* are taken into account – namely jcn and lin.

Clustering and fragmentation

The clustering heuristics has been implemented as a Java module that calls the UMLS::Similarity web interface. When using the clustering heuristics with the given similarities, regardless of which heads we choose, after two steps we obtain the two clusters {*asthma, cough, influenza*}, and {*tibial fracture, ulna fracture*}: let us assume, we choose *asthma* as $head_1$, then we compute all similarities to *asthma*. The one with the lowest similarity is *ulna fracture* – which is taken to be $head_2$. Because *tibial fracture* has lower similarity to *ulna fracture* than to *asthma*, it is assigned to c_2. For an appropriate threshold α (depending on the similarity measure chosen) the process could stop here. If instead we now continue the clustering, we would eventually obtain a total clustering consisting of only singleton sets: *tibial fracture* would become $head_3$ (because it has minimal distance to $head_2$); later on, *cough* would become $head_4$ and *influenza* would be $head_5$.

Choosing the path similarity and a threshold $\alpha = 0.15$ results in the two mentioned clusters. A fragmentation of the base table *Ill* can hence be obtained by computing the following materialized views in the Postgres database.

```
CREATE MATERIALIZED VIEW Respiratory AS
  SELECT * FROM Ill WHERE Diagnosis
  IN ('Cough', 'Influenza', 'Asthma')

CREATE MATERIALIZED VIEW Fracture AS
  SELECT * FROM Ill WHERE Diagnosis
  IN ('Tibial fracture', 'Ulna Fracture')
```

Sophisticated size estimations for these fragments might be possible as stated previously. We obtain the sizes of the fragment by counting the number of rows:

```
SELECT count(*) FROM Respiratory
```

and

```
SELECT count(*) FROM Fracture
```

Next, we fill a lookup table containing information as.

```
INSERT INTO root_ill VALUES
('F1', 'Respiratory', 'asthma', 4, NULL);
  INSERT INTO root_ill VALUES
('F2', 'Fracture', 'ulna fracture', 2,
  NULL);
```

To obtain the placement of the fragments to servers we model the corresponding BPPC and use the solver lp_solve [24]. lp_solve has a simple human-readable syntax and can be accessed by a Java program via the Java Native Interface (JNI). An example input for $K = 5$ (maximum number of servers), $W = 5$ (capacity per server), $m = 2$ (replication factor) looks as shown in Listing 3.

Listing 3 Input to ILP solver

```
 1: min: y1 + y2 + y3 + y4 + y5;

 2:

 3: x11 + x12 + x13 + x14 + x15 = 1;
 4: x21 + x22 + x23 + x24 + x25 = 1;
 5: x31 + x32 + x33 + x34 + x35 = 1;
 6: x41 + x42 + x43 + x44 + x45 = 1;

 7:

 8: 4 x11 + 2 x21 + 4 x31 + 2 x41 <= 5 y1;
 9: 4 x12 + 2 x22 + 4 x32 + 2 x42 <= 5 y2;
10: 4 x13 + 2 x23 + 4 x33 + 2 x43 <= 5 y3;
11: 4 x14 + 2 x24 + 4 x34 + 2 x44 <= 5 y4;
12: 4 x15 + 2 x25 + 4 x35 + 2 x45 <= 5 y5;

13:

14: x11 + x31 <= y1; x21 + x41 <= y1;
15: x12 + x32 <= y2; x22 + x42 <= y2;
16: x13 + x33 <= y3; x23 + x43 <= y3;
17: x14 + x34 <= y4; x24 + x44 <= y4;
18: x15 + x35 <= y5; x25 + x45 <= y5;

19:

20: bin x11,x12,x13,x14,x15;
21: bin x21,x22,x23,x24,x25;
22: bin x31,x32,x33,x34,x35;
23: bin x41,x42,x43,x44,x45;

24:

25: bin y1,y2,y3,y4,y5;
```

The solution uses four servers (out of the five available ones): one for each of the two fragments and their copy. If the capacity is increased to $W = 6$, only two servers are used: the two fragments now fit on one server and the two copies on another server.

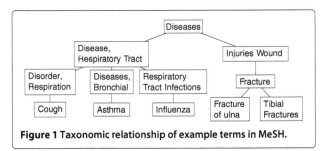

Figure 1 Taxonomic relationship of example terms in MeSH.

Table 1 Sample similarity obtained with UMLS::Similarity

	Asthma	Cough	Influenza	Tibial fracture	Ulna fracture
Asthma		(jcn) 0.3109	(jcn) 0.3844	(jcn) 0.1405	(jcn) 0.1282
	max	(cdist) 0.2	(cdist) 0.2	(cdist) 0.1429	(cdist) 0.1429
		(lin) 0.6175	(lin) 0.6662	(lin) 0.2116	(lin) 0.1968
		(wup) 0.6667	(wup) 0.6667	(wup) 0.5556	(wup) 0.5556
		(path) 0.2	(path) 0.2	(path) 0.1429	(path) 0.1429
		(res) 2.5963	(res) 2.5963	(res) 0.9555	(res) 0.9555
		(lch) 2.0794	(lch) 2.0794	(lch) 1.743	(lch) 1.743
		(nam) is 0.1621	(nam) 0.1621	(nam) 0.1483	(nam) 0.1483
Cough			(jcn) 0.2958	(jcn) 0.1266	(jcn) 0.1166
		max	(cdist) 0.2	(cdist) 0.1429	(cdist) 0.1429
			(lin) 0.6057	(lin) 0.1948	(lin) 0.1822
			(wup) 0.6667	(wup) 0.5556	(wup) 0.5556
			(path) 0.2	(path) 0.1429	(path) 0.1429
			(res) 2.5963	(res) 0.9555	(res) 0.9555
			(lch) 2.0794	(lch) 1.743	(lch) 1.743
			(nam) 0.1621	(nam) 0.1483	(nam) 0.1483
Influenza				(jcn) 0.1373	(jcn) 0.1256
			max	(cdist) 0.1429	(cdist) 0.1429
				(lin) 0.2079	(lin) 0.1936
				(wup) 0.5556	(wup) 0.5556
				(path) 0.1429	(path) 0.1429
				(res) 0.9555	(res) 0.9555
				(lch) 1.743	(lch) 1.743
				(nam) 0.1483	(nam) 0.1483
Tibial fracture					(jcn) 0.243
				max	(cdist) 0.3333
					(lin) 0.6295
					(wup) 0.7778
					(path) 0.3333
					(res) 3.4961
					(lch) 2.5903
					(nam) 0.1867
Ulna fracture					
					max

For improved efficiency, the root table is currently stored as a hash map in the Java frontend (instead of stored in a separate database table). The hash map is keyed by the head element, because the heads are necessary for the query rewriting module.

Query rewriting

The query rewriting procedure has to parse the SQL string inserted by the user. If a selection condition is given for the relaxation attribute, the root table is consulted to check for a matching head element. If none is found, again the UMLS::Similarity interface is consulted to obtain the similarities between head elements and the selection condition.

As a simple example considers the SQL query

```
SELECT * FROM Ill
WHERE Diagnosis = 'Bronchitis'
```

When comparing bronchitis to the first head (that is, asthma), UMLS::Similarity gives the following similarity results: 'The similarity of bronchitis (C0006277) and asthma (C0004096) using (jcn) is 1.0305, (cdist) is 0.3333, (lin) is 0.881, (wup) is 0.8, (path) is 0.3333, (res) is 3.5921, (lch) is 2.5903, (nam) is 0.1867'

Whereas comparing bronchitis to the second head (that is, tibial fracture), UMLS::Similarity gives the following similarity results: 'The similarity of bronchitis (C0006277) and tibial fracture (C0040185) using (jcn) is 0.1308, (cdist) is 0.1429, (lin) is 0.2, (wup) is 0.5556, (path) is 0.1429, (res) is 0.9555, (lch) is 1.743, (nam) is 0.1483'

Hence, asthma is more similar to bronchitis in every measure. The SQL query is rewritten by retrieving the appropriate fragment name and redirected to the appropriate server identified from the root table:

```
SELECT * FROM Respiratory
```

That is, the entire fragment is returned as it is the one with the most relevant answers for the user.

Experimental analysis

In general, any flexible query answering approach incurs a certain performance overhead compared to exact query answering. In our case, the clustering and fragmentation have to be compute but also the query answering incurs some extra overhead due to the fact that the appropriate fragment has to be identified and multiple answers are returned whereas exact query answering would simply have returned an empty answer set. With our approach however we aim to reduce this overhead by locating all related answers in the same fragment; any other fragmentation approach would need to recombine related answers from different fragments. For a performance evaluation of our prototype we used a test dataset consisting of values taken from the list of Medical Subject Headings (MeSH) [25]. The similarity computation during the clustering constituted an extreme overhead. That is why we computed pairwise similarities for 300 sample headings and stored these similarity values in a separate table. With these 300 values we randomly filled the disease column of a test table. We varied the row count between 10 and 1000 rows. Another parameter to vary is the threshold α for the intra-cluster similarity: the maximum similarity that values in a cluster may have to their respective

head. For a higher threshold, more clusters are computed (and hence more similarity computations are executed) than for a lower threshold. We tested similarity thresholds 0.1, 0.125, 0.3 and 0.5. We ran the clustering and fragmentation algorithm on a PC with 1.73 GHz and 4GB RAM. The observed runtimes and number of obtained fragments are reported in Table 2. For the lower threshold values 0.1 and 0.125 runtimes are in the range of some seconds up to around 17 minutes. For a row count of 1000 rows the higher similarity values lead to a high number of fragments and runtimes are hence prohibitively high. Due to the high amount of pairwise comparisons, obtaining the similarity values is still the bottleneck of the clustering procedure. In future work we will follow two ways of improving scalability of the clustering: optimizing the access to the similarity values and investigating implications of a parallel implementation of the clustering procedure.

Related work

We divide the related work survey into approaches for flexible query answering and approaches for data fragmentation and replication.

Flexible query answering

The area of flexible query answering (sometimes also called cooperative query answering) has been studied extensively for single server systems. Some approaches have used taxonomies or ontologies for flexible query answering but did not consider their application for distributed storage of data: CoBase [26] used a type abstraction hierarchy to generalize values; Shin et al. [27] use some specific notion of metric distance in a knowledge abstraction hierarchy to identify semantically related answers; Halder and Cortesi [28] define a partial order between cooperative answers based on their abstract interpretation framework; Muslea [29] discusses the relaxation of queries in disjunctive normal form. Ontology-based query relaxation has also been studied for non-relational data (like XML data in [30]).

All these approaches address query relaxation at runtime while answering the query. This is usually prohibitively expensive. In contrast, our approach

Table 2 Runtime and fragment count obtained for MeSH dataset

α	10 rows		100 rows		1000 rows	
	Runtime (ms)	Fragment count	Runtime (ms)	Fragment count	Runtime (ms)	Fragment count
0.1	971	2	18200	4	709627	12
0.125	1211	3	32900	7	1038085	17
0.3	2658	8	201959	45	4132254	94
0.5	2415	10	244161	69	7428473	233

precomputes the clustering and fragmentation so that query answering does not incur a performance penalty.

Data fragmentation and replication

There are some approaches for fine-grained fragmentation and replication on object/tuple level; however none of these approaches support the flexible query answering application aimed at in this paper. In contrast they are mostly workload-driven and try to optimize the locality of data that are covered in the same query. However, they only support exact query answering. In contrast to this, we do not consider workloads but a generic clustering approach that can work with arbitrary workloads providing the feature of flexible query answering by finding semantically related answers. While some approaches are adaptive to updates, no quality guarantee after an update is reported. We intend to extend our approach in the future by bringing robust optimization to the data replication area. Loukopoulos and Ahmad [6] describe data replication as an optimization problem; they focus on fine-grained geo-replication for individual objects. They include an assumed number of reads and writes for each site as well as communication costs between sites. They reduce their problem to the Knapsack problem. In particular, they devise an adaptive genetic algorithm that can reallocate data to different sites. We aim to follow a different path to support this adaptive behavior: the notion of robust optimization is briefly discussed in Section Discussion and conclusion.

Curino et al. [14] represent database tuples as nodes in a graph. They assume a given transaction workload and add hyperedges to the graph between those nodes that are accessed by the same transactions. By using a standard graph partitioning algorithm, they find a database fragmentation that minimizes the number of cut hyperedges. In a second phase, they use a machine learning classifier to derive a range-based fragmentation. Then they make an experimental comparison between the graph-based, the range-based, a hash-based fragmentation on tuple keys and full replication. Lastly, they also compare three different kinds of lookup tables to map tuple identifier to the corresponding fragment: indexes, bit arrays and Bloom filters. Similar to them, we apply lookup tables to locate the replicated data; however we apply this to larger fragments and not to individual tuples.

Quamar et al. [31] also model the fragmentation problem as minimizing cuts of hyperedges in a graph; for efficiency reasons, their algorithm works on a compressed representation of the hypergraph which results in groups of tuples. In particular, the authors criticize the fine-grained (tuple-wise) approach in [14] to be impractical for large number of tuples which is similar to our approach. The authors propose mechanisms to handle changes in the workload and compare their approach to random and tuple-level partitioning.

Tatarowicz et al. [12] assume three existing fragmentations: hash-based, range-based and lookup tables for individual keys and compare those in terms of communication cost and throughput. For an efficient management of lookup tables, they experimented with different compression techniques. In particular they argue that for hash-based partitioning, the query decomposition step is a bottleneck. While we apply the notion of lookup tables, too, the authors do not discuss how the fragments are obtained, whereas we propose a semantically guided fragmentation approach here.

Discussion and conclusion

In this paper we proposed an intelligent fragmentation and replication approach for a distributed database system; with this approach, cloud storage can be enhanced with a semantically-guided flexible query answering mechanism that will provide related but still very relevant answers for the user. The approach combines fragmentation based on a clustering with data replication. For the user, this approach is totally invisible: he can send queries to the database system unchanged. The distributed database system autonomously computes the fragmentation (where the only additional information needed is the clustering backed by a taxonomy specific to the domain of the anti-instantiation column) and can use an automatic data replication mechanism that relies on the size information of each fragment and generates a bin packing input for an Integer Linear Programming (ILP) solver. As most of the related approaches, we assume a static dataset with mostly read-only accesses. When receiving a user query, the database system can autonomously rewrite the query and redirect subqueries to the appropriate servers based on the maintenance of a root table. The proposed method hence offers novel self-management and self-configuration techniques for a user-friendly query handling. While the user provides the original table and the desired similarity threshold as input, the database system can autonomously distribute the data while minimizing the amount of database servers. Hence we see our approach as a first step towards an intelligent cloud database system. For full applicability in a cloud database, automatic reconfiguration after updates, failure-tolerance as well as parallelization of our clustering approach (for example with map-reduce) will be necessary; these topics will be handled in future work.

The work presented in this paper can be extended in various research directions. We give a brief discussion of possible extensions.

- So far, the fragmentation process is only centered around a single relaxation attribute. The current approach can of course be executed in parallel for several relaxation attributes in parallel (with separate fragmentations and root tables for each relaxation attribute); however, this will lead to a massive (possibly unnecessary) replication of the data. We are currently investigating a more fine-grained support for multiple relaxation attributes with a more sophisticated data replication approach that can also be stated as a bin packing problem.

- In order to have a full-blown distributed flexible query answering system, the interaction of the proposed fragmentation with other generalization operators (like dropping condition and goal replacement) must be elaborated.

- When multiple fragments are assigned to one server, data locality can be improved by assigning fragments that are semantically close to each other to the same server.

- Our main focus for future work is to study the effect of updates on data (deletions and insertions) in the fragments: it must be studied in detail how fragments can be reconfigured and probably migrated to other server without incurring too much transfer cost.

Regarding the update problem, we plan to apply a special optimization approach to database replication: the notion of recovery robust optimization [32] describes optimization methods that compute a solution that can later on adapt to changing conditions which so far have been used mostly for timetabling applications [33] or job sequencing [8] or telecommunication networks [34]; in this respect it is important to ensure a worst case guarantee as in [8]. This is a different approach than presented here and its implications will hence be the topic of future work.

Competing interests
The author declares that she has no competing interests.

Acknowledgements
I would like to thank Anita Schöbel and Marie Schmidt for helpful discussions and Florian Henke for implementation and evaluation of the prototype. I acknowledge support by the German Research Foundation and the Open Access Publication Funds of Göttingen University.

References
1. Özsu MT, Valduriez P (2011) Principles of distributed database systems, Third Edition. Springer, Berlin/Heidelberg
2. Wiese L (2013) Taxonomy-based fragmentation for anti-instantiation in distributed databases. In: 3rd International Workshop on Intelligent Techniques and Architectures for Autonomic Clouds (ITAAC'13) collocated with IEEE/ACM 6th international conference on utility and cloud computing. IEEE, Washington, DC. pp 363–368
3. Gaasterland T, Godfrey P, Minker J (1992) Relaxation as a platform for cooperative answering. JIIS 1(3/4):293–321
4. Inoue K, Wiese L (2011) Generalizing conjunctive queries for informative answers. In: Flexible query answering systems. Springer, Berlin/Heidelberg. pp 1–12
5. Michalski RS (1983) A theory and methodology of inductive learning. Artif Intell 20(2):111–161
6. Loukopoulos T, Ahmad I (2004) Static and adaptive distributed data replication using genetic algorithms. J Parallel Distributed Comput 64(11):1270–1285
7. Gendreau M, Laporte G, Semet F (2004) Heuristics and lower bounds for the bin packing problem with conflicts. Comput OR 31(3):347–358
8. Epstein L, Levin A, Marchetti-Spaccamela A, Megow N, Mestre J, Skutella M, Stougie L (2010) Universal sequencing on a single machine. In: Integer programming and combinatorial optimization. Springer, Berlin/Heidelberg. pp 230–243
9. Sadykov R, Vanderbeck F (2013) Bin packing with conflicts: a generic branch-and-price algorithm. INFORMS J Comput 25(2):244–255
10. Gonzalez TF (1985) Clustering to minimize the maximum intercluster distance. Theor Comput Sci 38:293–306
11. Rieck K, Trinius P, Willems C, Holz T (2011) Automatic analysis of malware behavior using machine learning. J Comput Secur 19(4):639–668
12. Tatarowicz A, Curino C, Jones EPC, Madden S (2012) Lookup tables: Fine-grained partitioning for distributed databases. In: Kementsietsidis A, Salles MAV (eds). IEEE 28th International Conference on Data Engineering (ICDE 2012). IEEE Computer Society, Washington, DC. pp 102–113
13. Chang F, Dean J, Ghemawat S, Hsieh WC, Wallach DA, Burrows M, Chandra T, Fikes A, Gruber RE (2008) Bigtable: a distributed storage system for structured data. ACM Trans Comput Syst 26(2):4:1–4:26
14. Curino C, Zhang Y, Jones EPC, Madden S (2010) Schism: a workload-driven approach to database replication and partitioning. Proc VLDB Endowment 3(1):48–57
15. McInnes BT, Pedersen T, Pakhomov SVS, Liu Y, Melton-Meaux G (2013) Umls::similarity: Measuring the relatedness and similarity of biomedical concepts. In: Vanderwende L, Daumé H III, Kirchhoff K (eds). Human language technologies: conference of the North American chapter of the association of computational linguistics. The Association for Computational Linguistics, Stroudsburg. pp 28–31
16. Resnik P (1999) Semantic similarity in a taxonomy: an information-based measure and its application to problems of ambiguity in natural language. J Artif Intell Res (JAIR) 11:95–130
17. Leacock C, Chodorow M (1998) Combining local context and wordnet similarity for word sense identification. WordNet: Electron Lexical Database 49(2):265–283
18. Wu Z, Palmer MS (1994) Verb semantics and lexical selection. In: Pustejovsky J (ed). 32nd annual meeting of the association for computational linguistics. Morgan Kaufmann Publishers/ACL, Stroudsburg. pp 133–138
19. Rada R, Mili H, Bicknell E, Blettner M (1989) Development and application of a metric on semantic nets. IEEE Trans Syst Man Cybernet 19(1):17–30
20. Caviedes JE, Cimino JJ (2004) Towards the development of a conceptual distance metric for the umls. J Biomed Inform 37(2):77–85
21. Al-Mubaid H, Nguyen HA (2006) New ontology-based semantic similarity measure for the biomedical domain. IEEE, Washington, DC. pp 623–628
22. Jiang JJ, Conrath DW (1997) Semantic similarity based on corpus statistics and lexical taxonomy. CoRR cmp-lg/9709008
23. Lin D (1998) An information-theoretic definition of similarity. In: Shavlik JW (ed). Proceedings of the fifteenth international conference on machine learning. Morgan Kaufmann, San Francisco. pp 296–304
24. lp_solve. http://lpsolve.sourceforge.net/
25. U.S. National Library of Medicine: Medical Subject Headings. http://www.nlm.nih.gov/mesh/
26. Chu WW, Yang H, Chiang K, Minock M, Chow G, Larson C (1996) CoBase: a scalable and extensible cooperative information system. JIIS 6(2/3):223–259
27. Shin MK, Huh S-Y, Lee W (2007) Providing ranked cooperative query answers using the metricized knowledge abstraction hierarchy. Expert Syst Appl 32(2):469–484
28. Halder R, Cortesi A (2011) Cooperative query answering by abstract interpretation. In: SOFSEM2011. LNCS, vol. 6543. Springer, Berlin/Heidelberg. pp 284–296
29. Muslea I (2004) Machine learning for online query relaxation. In: Knowledge Discovery and Data Mining (KDD). ACM, New York. pp 246–255

30. Hill J, Torson J, Guo B, Chen Z (2010) Toward ontology-guided knowledge-driven XML query relaxation. In: Computational Intelligence, Modelling and Simulation (CIMSiM). IEEE, Washington, DC. pp 448–453

31. Quamar A, Kumar KA, Deshpande A (2013) Sword: scalable workload-aware data placement for transactional workloads. In: Guerrini G, Paton NW (eds). Joint 2013 EDBT/ICDT conferences. ACM, New York. pp 430–441

32. Barber F, Salido MA (2014) Robustness, stability, recoverability, and reliability in constraint satisfaction problems. Knowl Inf Syst 41(2):1–16

33. Liebchen C, Lübbecke M, Möhring R, Stiller S (2009) The concept of recoverable robustness, linear programming recovery, and railway applications. In: Robust and online large-scale optimization. Springer, Berlin/Heidelberg. pp 1–27

34. Büsing C, Koster AM, Kutschka M (2011) Recoverable robust knapsacks: the discrete scenario case. Optimization Lett 5(3):379–392

## 6

Self-service infrastructure container for data intensive application

Ibrahim K Musa[1*], Stuart D Walker[1], Anne M Owen[2] and Andrew P Harrison[2]

Abstract

Cloud based scientific data management - storage, transfer, analysis, and inference extraction - is attracting interest. In this paper, we propose a next generation cloud deployment model suitable for data intensive applications. Our model is a flexible and self-service container-based infrastructure that delivers - network, computing, and storage resources together with the logic to dynamically manage the components in a holistic manner. We demonstrate the strength of our model with a bioinformatics application. Dynamic algorithms for resource provisioning and job allocation suitable for the chosen dataset are packaged and delivered in a privileged virtual machine as part of the container. We tested the model on our private internal experimental cloud that is built on low-cost commodity hardware. We demonstrate the capability of our model to create the required network and computing resources and allocate submitted jobs. The results obtained shows the benefits of increased automation in terms of both a significant improvement in the time to complete a data analysis and a reduction in the cost of analysis. The algorithms proposed reduced the cost of performing analysis by 50% at 15 *GB* of data analysis. The total time between submitting a job and writing the results after analysis also reduced by more than 1 *hr* at 15 *GB* of data analysis.

Keywords: Cloud computing; Microarray data analysis; Bioinformatics; Cells-As-A-Service

Introduction

Large scale data are increasingly generated from a wide variety of sources such as scientific experiments and monitoring devices. Consequently, there is a compelling need to store, analyse, query, manage, understand, and respond to such data for knowledge extraction and decision making. The emergence of cloud computing presents a new and promising paradigm to handle these challenges [1]. The model allows the use of configurable resources on a pay-as-you-go basis, thereby eliminating upfront investments. Scientific clouds [2] deployed on large heterogeneous research projects have shown good performance in handling burgeoning data volumes in an economic and efficient manner [3].

As the interest in cloud adoption for scientific applications intensifies, it is necessary to cope with the challenges of adhering to service level agreements, achieving high service elasticity, and the complexity of managing large scale cloud datacentre resources [4-6]. Another critical research issue [1,7] in cloud computing is the notion of enabling users to automatically consume cloud services without necessarily understanding the complexities associated with the new paradigm. To address these challenges, numerous techniques including effective provisioning strategies [8,9] and flexible job allocation [9] have been proposed.

This article presents a container-based model of cloud computing where all resources (virtual machines, storage, and interconnecting networks) and the logic to manage these resources are packaged in a virtual container and delivered to users. We refer to this model as Virtual Cells-As-A-Service (vCAAS) and each container as a vCell. The paper proposes a strategy similar to the research in [10,11]. vCAAS is an IAAS/PAAS model enabled with application specific resource management functionalities such as provisioning, job allocation, and holistic optimization [12]. The functionalities are created from platform as a service (PAAS). The resources are then consumed as an IAAS service similar to the Biolinux virtual instance.

Our proposal is a self-service container model inspired by the concept of a biological cell [13] on the premise that nature has successfully managed complexity. This

*Correspondence: ikmusa@essex.ac.uk
[1] School of Computer Science and Electronic Engineering, University of Essex, Wivenhoe Park, Colchester CO4 3SQ, Essex, UK
Full list of author information is available at the end of the article

new approach aims to address the challenges of using cloud services for large scale data analysis. Our approach assumes VMs interact and complement each other to perform tasks. In vCAAS, each vCell is isolated from other tenants in the datacentre and the owner controls the entire components of the service cell from a simple template via a service console. The virtual container model provides a portable infrastructure platform for deploying self-contained and self-service IAAS.

This work demonstrates the strength of our model with an analysis from the area of bioinformatics. The GeneChips technology called GeneChips from the company Affymetrix is widely used by biologists and other life scientists to perform experiments on tissue samples. We use the microarray datasets from GeneChips in the analysis of RNA sequence to measure tissue samples. We use the microarray datasets to determine whether significant bias is encountered in this gene expression data. This bias could be introduced by the technology of the GeneChips rather than by the biology being tested. The work follows on from that pursued by Shanahan and colleagues [14].

The rest of the paper is organized as follows. The Section "Related works" presents related works in the area, the Section "Container-based cloud framework" describes our proposed framework, the Section "Container-based cloud model for bioinformatics" describes the specific implementation of the framework for bioinformatics experiment, the Section "Implementation and results" presents the experiment set-up and the result of experiment conducted, and finally the Section 'Conclusion' ends the paper and suggests ways in which the research can be expanded.

Motivation

Despite numerous developments in the adoption of cloud computing for scientific research, scientists employing the capabilities of cloud computing to perform experiments face the challenges of achieving efficient and cost effective use of cloud resources. This is attributed to the need to understand often complex cloud specific technologies (e.g. virtualization, job scheduling), to build and submit the required work flow, to choose the right virtual machine for the problem, to configure the purchased resources for the chosen experiment, and to choose the right number of resources for the given task [3,15]. Numerous projects, such as Biolinux [16,17], attempt to solve some of these problems by allowing cloud users to clone and use fully-packaged virtual machines containing scientific data analysis tools. This approach unifies scientific activities, reduces time to perform experiments, and offers cost-effective infrastructure. However, the challenges of efficiently and effectively running a large number of such packaged workstations still need to be addressed. As a result, this work is motivated by the following issues:

- Most current cloud computing models applied to solve problems in application areas (e.g. Biological sciences, Physics) are yet to clearly address the complete automation of domain specific resource management tasks such as initial capacity and the internal organization of resources as a holistic entity. Such intelligent resource management is needed to properly unlock the full advantage of cloud computing.
- Cloud users from specific domain areas are forced to understand and perform complex resource management tasks, thereby making the application of cloud computing in these areas more difficult.
- The need for cloud applications to explore the economic benefit of a holistic and complimentary interrelationship between set of purchased resources deployed for the execution of a task.
- The need to achieve more transparent interaction between a container management service and the underlying physical infrastructure.
- The need to implement proactive job monitoring services that apply historical pattern inference to determine status of jobs. Most current cloud platforms are yet to provide a full monitoring service at the job level. This often leads to high cost as a running VM with a failed job incurs unnecessary expense until the problem is detected and the failed job reassigned. This task is often left to the scientist running the experiment.

The main aim of this article is to present a next generation cloud computing model based on a holistic organization of resources in a virtual infrastructure container. The proposed framework optimises the provisioning of resources, automates the coordination of activities in a virtual service container, and efficiently allocates task to the resources provisioned as part of the container.

Related works

Enormous interest surrounds the application of cloud computing to support large scale biological data analysis [2,18-22]. A distributed system enabled by an intelligent agent in [19], data and software sharing using a central repository [18], and a publicly available packaged VM such as Biolinux [16] are already proposed. At extremely large scale, research projects such as CloudBurst [23], CloudBlast [24], and Galaxy [25] provide standard environments and algorithms for analyzing large data generated from scientific experiments. These development paves the way for cloud-based data analysis for bioinformatics. For instance, in [26] more than 1 billion short sequence reads were proposed using a cloud base algorithm available in [23].

Various models of holistic infrastructure services for cloud computing have been proposed [10,27-29]. Perhaps the proposals in [27,29] and [28] are the closest to the approach in this article. The proposals describe PAAS/IAAS container-based next generation cloud architecture created as a subset of a typical datacentre. The FP7 project 4Caast [29] described an enabling platform for an advanced PAAS cloud capable of offering an optimized programming interface for next generation internet application. The strategy outlined in [27] envisions the provision of compute, storage, and network services to a large number of multi-tenants each with specific performance criteria such as delay, security, and flexibility all defined in an Extensible Mark-up Language (XML) template. Each service user is assign a view isolated from other services. Another study in [28] describes the integration of both PAAS and IAAS in a VM set model. The proposal in [28] uses a data repository to store the configuration about available hardware and virtual resources which can be accessed using service oriented infrastructure (SOI). The attempt in [10] is to improve on the scalability of cloud services with a holistic resource view across a multi cloud environment.

Strategies for data transfer, cloud resource provisioning and job allocation have been proposed in the literature. A Stream-based data transfer strategy presented in [21] proposed a data compression technique to reduce the data transfer overhead associated with large data. In [30], various strategies for provisioning of virtual machines and workflow scheduling are described. Another similar survey in [9] tested various on-demand execution and waiting time provisioning policies.

vCAAS and other cloud computing models share many functional and structural features of existing technologies such as service grid, utility, and cluster computing (CCom). Cluster computing is a type of parallel and distributed system, which consists of a collection of interconnected stand-alone computers working together as a single integrated computing resource [31]. Computer clusters are often built around proprietary technologies and applications needs to be re-architected to meet policies [32]. In cluster computing, a service model is virtually absent and limited user requirement integration is offered during the resource composition. vCAAS, on the other hand, emphasizes user-driven service delivery of virtual components with the aim of creating business value. Service grids are, on the other hand, aimed as collaborative ventures with no apparent business objectives.

The VPC adopts a logical view where a cloud infrastructure appears as though it is operated solely for an organization. It may be managed by the organization or a third party and may exist on-premises or off-premises or some combination of these options [33]. Current deployment models of VPC concentrate mainly on extending an existing public cloud with secured virtual private network(VPN) services. On the other hand, the original concept of vCAAS, like similar previous proposals, envisions a flexible [27], user-driven [28], and self-managed [29] cloud service beyond the extension offered by laying VPN atop a public cloud as proposed in the VPC [7]. vCAAS aim to provide automated provisioning of resources, allocation of task, and failure management.

The next section describes our proposed framework for a virtual infrastructure container as well as the functionalities and actors coordinated to realise the vCAAS model.

Container-based cloud framework

The main component of our proposed framework (Figure 1) are the Delivery layer, Service layer, Control and Virtualization layer, and Physical fabric layer.

Delivery layer

This layer facilitates the submission of a vCell request and provides the enabling environment for the vCell. Technical requirements such as bandwidth, load balancing, priority, service discovery mechanisms, communication protocols, delay, and response time are properly identified and submitted using appropriate description language. Business objectives such as deadline, cost, accounting, and auditing are also submitted using this interface. Figure 1 shows a typical virtual infrastructure container framework.

Additionally, as shown in Figure 1 each vCell is enabled with the delivery layer which consist of four main subcomponents that interact to realize vCell functionalities.

The service console

enables the functionalities to interact with users and accept/update requests for vCell creation. The module allows simple and complex workflow specifications. VXDL [34] allows the complex request presentation required in a holistic cloud delivery model [28]. Complex parameters such as virtual timeline description, dynamic resource configuration, and components' behaviour during the service life cycle can be modelled. Fundamental features such as aggregate capacity and lease time of the submitted request is, however, subject to approval by the underlying service layer. This way the mediation function of the service layer controls and secures the subsequent activities of the vCell. For instance, a vCell manager cannot create resources beyond the maximum capacity or lease period.

Report interface

This provides monitoring capabilities to report (to the vCell Manager) jobs and virtual resource status and activities in the vCell. The module maintains and updates the

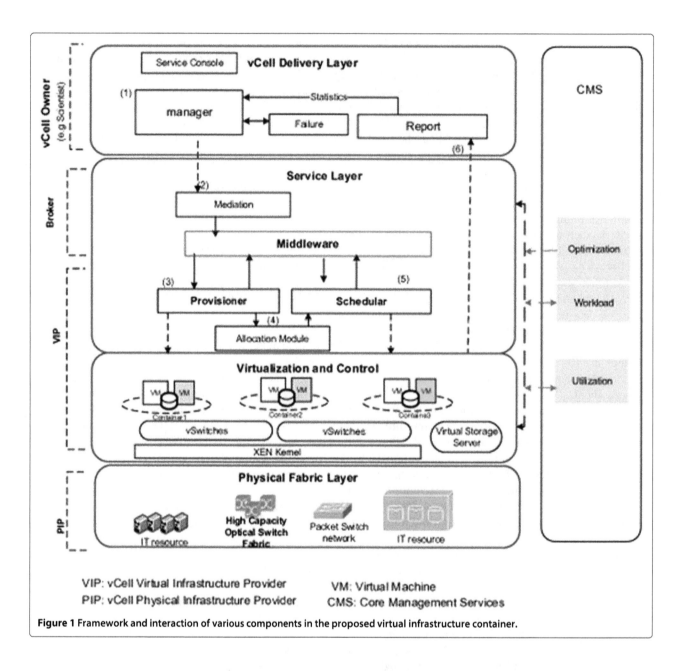

Figure 1 Framework and interaction of various components in the proposed virtual infrastructure container.

activities database of all components in the vCell. It maintains the record of finish times and provides time series data to the cell manager for use in predicting future task finish times. The functionalities provided by this interface enable additional failure detection and management capabilities. Each report is a tuple (S, T, F) of source, S, traffic type T, and feature F. The traffic type can be update, completion time, processed data e.t.c. F is a 2 tuple (Z, U) with size Z (e.g.in bytes or milliseconds) and unit U (e.g. s, MB, GB, Gbps).

vCell manager
All dynamic behaviour of the vCell is organized and coordinated by this module. This module is projected with

privileged functionalities to perform management functions at cell level. This effectively reduces the management spaces making them small and correct. All ingress and egress traffic is controlled by this module. All the vCell managers are configured to send and receive messages in the cloud datacentre. However in receiving messages only those targeted to the vCell are treated while all others are discarded. This forms the initial basis for vCell isolation where all other components in the vCell are not exposed to receiving such messages - thereby isolating the components from broadcast messages. Although the manager receives these high communication signals, all other components are shielded from unnecessary communication overhead. The obvious problem is the performance of the CM. This research envisions cell-based management that eliminates high communication overload at the CM's interface.

Central to the functions provided by the module is the template-base mechanism for organizing and controlling the activities of components in a vCell. Each vCell is identified by a template which is used by the manager to create components, allocate resources, reconfigure existing components, and achieve all interactions with the underlying infrastructure and with other vCells. The request description received at the delivery layer is stored as a template for organizing the activities of vCell.

The request for vCell creation is submitted to the middleware residing in the global service layer. The service layer then creates the CM with basic service management functions projected into it as a privileged virtual machine. Subsequently, any additional component to be created in the vCell is initiated by the CM which queries available capacity and creates the required resources. The virtual switch connecting the newly created component (if computing or storage node) is added to the list v of virtual switches controlled by the CM. Two basic communications allowed in vCAAS are Intra and Inter vCell communication. In the former, two or more components interact to fulfil the submitted task. The vCell manager (CM) is equipped with the necessary control functionalities to configure network slice on the vSwitch. To isolate each of the vCells, a FlowVisor [35] is installed between the flows controller and cell manager. This way the CM control flows in the slice allocated for the vCell. This also provides to the vCell owner an illusion of unique isolated network infrastructure.

Inter-vCell communication exists between multiple vCells owned by one entity. This form of communication is regulated by the two vCell Managers in the communicating vCells. In the middle is the mediation layer which provide additional regulation by identifying the communication request and applying drop or allow policy. An example of the mediation layer is the SDN controller and a vSwitch. The controller maintains a set of rules each identified by the source and the destination of the traffic. The rules are matched and the appropriate decision such as forward to specific port, drop traffic, or add to certain queue is inserted into the forwarding table of the distributed virtual switch. Next time the same traffic appears, the vSwitch is equipped with the right set of rules in its forwarding table for the inter-vCell traffic.

Service layer

This enables the functionalities for container-based cloud service creation. It performs the provisioning of resources (e.g. CPU time, memory, storage, and network bandwidth) to a vCell, interacts with the underlying layer, and

performs additional global scheduling. Interpretation of a submitted vCell request, and virtual resource requests are mediated by the layer. Privileged functionalities such as resource provisioning and job allocation are projected into each vCell during creation. The Template Engine provides functionalities for parsing job requests submitted by the owner (or function). The layer is capable of parsing both XML and Virtual Infrastructure Description Language (VXDL) file formats into canonical parameters.

Information about provider resources available for vCells to purchase are published as set of service units which can be acquired via the mediation layer. In Figure 2, WS-Net and WS-IT provide information about available network (e.g. bandwidth, links) and IT(computational and storage resources) respectively. The privileged VM in a vCell is capable of accessing the service units for scaling or task execution.

Virtualization and control layer

In the vCAAS model, an adaptive virtual interface (VIF) is created for each virtual node (VM). The VIF connects a VM to a distributed virtual switch (vSwitch) forming a virtual link. Combinations of these virtual links and connected virtual nodes (Figure 2) constitute the definition of a virtual network topology (VNT). This article employs an adaptive vSwitch-based traffic shaping strategy for vCAAS. Each VM in a vCell is assigned a virtual switch (vSwitch) port with initial bandwidth, based on request, and allowed to expand capacity relative to the unused bandwidth in the vCell. This way, the VMs adapt dynamically to various traffic conditions under the control of a distributed vSwitch (DVS) enabled with openflow protocol. To protect the service level agreement (SLA) of each container, traffic isolation mechanisms are applied at DVS level to control VM activity and one vCell does not have an adverse effect on the performance of other VMs in different vCells. The DVS maintains a database of entries for the policies in the network. Functionalities enabled by this module are under the control of a virtual infrastructure provider.

In the isolation strategy for vCAAS, each VM interacts with the vCell manager and other VMs, in hub and spoke arrangement, to complete work flow tasks. A VM experiencing high traffic (such as a storage VM) consumes high vCell's bandwidth. Other VMs require less bandwidth. At the time of creating a vCell, a variable super port with the equivalent capacity of bandwidth requested by a vCell is assigned. This super port can be viewed as an aggregation of fixed capacity ports. The bandwidth available for any VM is computed as:

$$A_{i,k} = B_{i,k} + \sum U_{j,k} \tag{1}$$
$$i, j, k = 1, 2, \ldots N, \ i \neq j$$

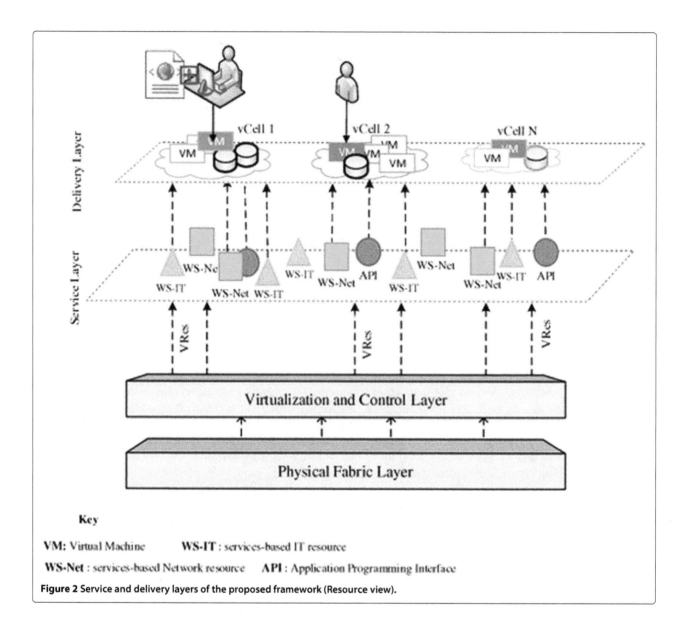

Figure 2 Service and delivery layers of the proposed framework (Resource view).

where Bi;k is the allocated bandwidth for VM i in virtual container k, Uj;k is the available bandwidth of VM j in virtual container k. The summation on the right of equation 1 is the unused bandwidth in vCell which can be utilized by a transmitting VM. Thus all bandwidth request β_i from VM i are accepted as long as $A_{i,k} \geq \beta_i$. This is demonstrated in Figure 3.

Physical fabric layer

This layer comprises heterogeneous physical IT interconnected with electrical and optical network in a hierarchical topology to enable cloud service. Network management services (NMS) are installed by the and access allowed to create a virtual resource.

Container-based cloud model for bioinformatics

This section presents the real world application of our virtual service cell. The concept of packaging application logic and resource management logic as a holistic resource container is implemented to perform large biological microarray data analysis. Virtual machines and the interconnecting network are created from a subset of the cloud datacentre and are configured to coexist and operate in concert during the execution of the data analysis tasks. Furthermore, the fundamental logic for job specific resource provisioning, jobs allocations, and optimization strategies [12] are packaged in a privileged virtual machine and delivered as part of the container. The framework for the cloud based container is shown in Figure 4. The section also presents the models adopted for the vCell automation.

Listing 1 Request for a vCell

```
<vxdl:vCell>
<vxdl:storageLocation>.6.1/NFSServer/GSE</vxdl:storageLocation>
<vxdl:vm>
      <vxdl:PE>2</vxdl:PE>
      <vxdl:MinMemory>2048</vxdl:MinMemory>
      <vxdl:NIC>1</vxdl:NIC>
      <vxdl:vNet>
          <vxdl:Duration>Read</vxdl:Duration>
            <vxdl:networkName>R</vxdl:networkName>
      </vxdl:vNet>
      <vxdl:vNet>
            <vxdl:Duration>Write</vxdl:Duration>
              <vxdl:networkName>W</vxdl:networkName>
          </vxdl:vNet>
      <vxdl:vNet>
            <vxdl:Duration>Computation</vxdl:Duration>
              <vxdl:networkName>C</vxdl:networkName>
      </vxdl:vNet>
      <vxdl:hdSize>
          <vxdl:min>20</vxdl:min>
          <vxdl:unit>GB</vxdl:unit>
      </vxdl:hdSize>
</vxdl:vm>
<vxdl:network>
      <vxdl:name>R</vxdl:name>
      <vxdl:Number>1</vxdl:Number>
      <vxdl:BW>
          <vxdl:min>2</vxdl:min>
          <vxdl:unit>GB</vxdl:unit>
      </vxdl:BW>
      <vxdl:dedicated>true</vxdl:dedicated>
        <vxdl:timeline>T1</vxdl:timeline>
</vxdl:network>
</vxdl:vCell>
```

Various roles

In the proposed model, clear separation of actors ensures flexibility of vCell creation and isolation. Various actors (Figure 5) interact to achieve the proposed vCAAS. Physical resources owned by vCAAS physical Infrastructure Providers (vCAAS-PIP) are accessed and virtualized by vCAAS Virtual Infrastructure Provider (vCAAS-VIP). vCell service starts with the submission of requests from the scientist performing the experiment - who also acts as the vCell owner (IAAS or PAAS user). The vCell owner submits a request for specific composition of network and computation to the Broker/vCAAS-VIP. Where a Broker exists, the actor then queries all vCAAS-VIPs and selects one. To meet the requirements of the vCell owner, the Broker evaluates the existing resource pool and consults vCAAS-VIP to appraise available resources suitable for the submitted request. vCAAS-VIP then virtualizes and offers the vCell to satisfy the initial request (Figure 5). The proposed framework combined the functionalities of the actors and is realised as an IAAS/PAAS model. The sequence of operation for the interaction between the various actors during the creation of a vCell are shown in Figure 6.

vCAAS automation

To properly operate as a self-service infrastructure for data intensive applications, each vCell is capable of the following key features:

1. Automatically compute the initial and dynamic capacity requirements of the container. There should be mechanisms for estimating the initial VMs and the configuration requirements of the data analysis to be performed by the vCell.
2. Optimally allocating the submitted jobs to VMs using the estimated current and future states of virtual machines in the vCell.
3. Adapt to the changing capacity availability in the virtual container in a holistic manner.

Enabling these features in vCell requires a dynamic model with the mechanism for continuous learning and update. This way, properties of the vCell and the resources contained can be properly characterized and managed without user intervention.

A Markov Chain offers a type of automation model that uses a stochastic process to determine or estimate the states of a system in a tractable manner. The Markov process uses observable and hidden features of the components to estimate future states. The latter feature is enabled by a kind of a hidden Markov Model (HMM) [36].

Within a vCell, component's status, such as the total workload, consists of both observable (e.g. average throughput) and hidden features (e.g. operating system's background processes). Using HMM in vCAAS enables automation features by estimating the future status of resources in vCell and reconfiguring components to adapt without user intervention. HMMs have been successfully applied in many problem domains including speech recognition, bioinformatics, and artificial intelligence. A basic HMM consists of set of states Θ, a set of initial states $\pi = P[q_1 = \Theta_m]$ such that $1 \leq m \leq N$, a transition probabilities distribution $A = \{a_{i,j}\}$ for transition from states Θ_i to Θ_j, and a set of observations distribution $O = b_j(k)$ where

$$b_n(k) = P[v_k \, at \, t \mid q_t = \Theta_n] \qquad (2)$$

for $1 \leq n \leq N$, $1 \leq k \leq M$. The set of states is defined by

$$\Theta = \Theta_1, \Theta_2, \dots, \Theta_N \qquad (3)$$

In the proposed vCell, the HMM states can be characterized as high, medium, and small workloads. These states may vary at various task execution phases such as reading data, performing computation, and writing results.

The next section demonstrates the application of HMM to achieve dynamic resource provisioning and allocation. We define provisioning as the task of creating and configuring the cloud resources for job execution. The task of allocation involves scheduling and submitting jobs to the created resources for execution.

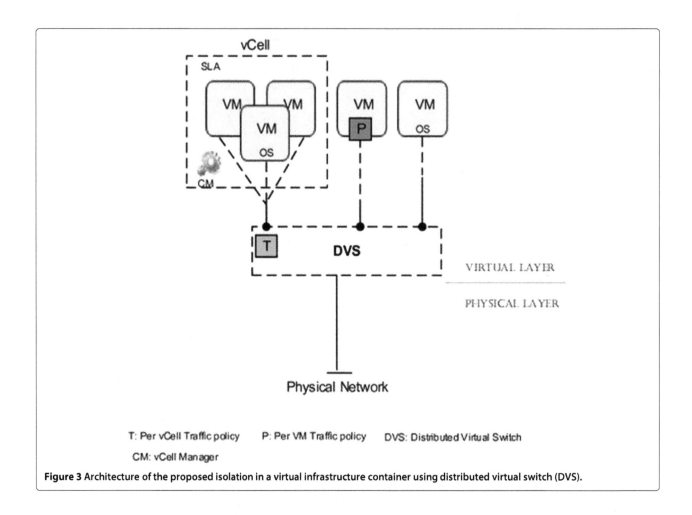

T: Per vCell Traffic policy   P: Per VM Traffic policy   DVS: Distributed Virtual Switch

CM: vCell Manager

Figure 3 Architecture of the proposed isolation in a virtual infrastructure container using distributed virtual switch (DVS).

Finish time

Our model relies on the finish times (predicted by the vCell manager) of jobs on a virtual machine to optimize the provisioning of virtual resources and allocation of jobs. The finish time F_j^t of job j at any t is computed as:

$$F_j^t = \frac{S_j + \beta}{C_v} + \frac{S_j}{L_c} \tag{4}$$

S_j is the size of job j, C_v is the processing capacity of virtual machine v that the job j is submitted to, L_c is the available link capacity, and β is VM processing policy such that $\beta = 0$ if the policy is single processor allocation policy and β is a value that denotes other workloads at time t and is defined as:

$$\beta = \begin{cases} 0 & \text{if single worker processor} \\ \ell & \text{otherwise} \end{cases} \tag{5}$$

ℓ is the predicted size of jobs concurrent on machine i at time t. For central storage servers (e.g. network file servers

or NFS), ℓ is the workload exerted by virtual machines accessing the data stored on the server. Estimating ℓ is particularly challenging due to a number of factors. Firstly, the notion of virtualization means that a large number of VMs sprawl on physical servers. This makes the observable workload values incomplete due to background processes and resource contention. Secondly, task execution exerts a time varying workload on the virtual machine. A task in execution has different workload patterns at various stages of the execution. For instance, the data loading process takes a considerable amount of time in dataintensive allocation after which the execution is a memory intensive process and exerts less demand for IO. Consider a simple model where the task execution overhead is given as:

$$\Psi_i(t) = \Sigma_{j \in J} \left(R_{i,j} + N_{i,j} - E_{i,j} \right) * X_{i,j}(t) \tag{6}$$

where $X_{i,j} = \{0, 1\}$ is a binary variable indicating whether virtual machine i is executing job j at time t, $R_{i,j}$ is the computation overhead of job j on machine i, $N_{i,j}$ is the network overhead incurred during data access, and finally $E_{i,j}$ is the total time spent on the execution of job j at time t.

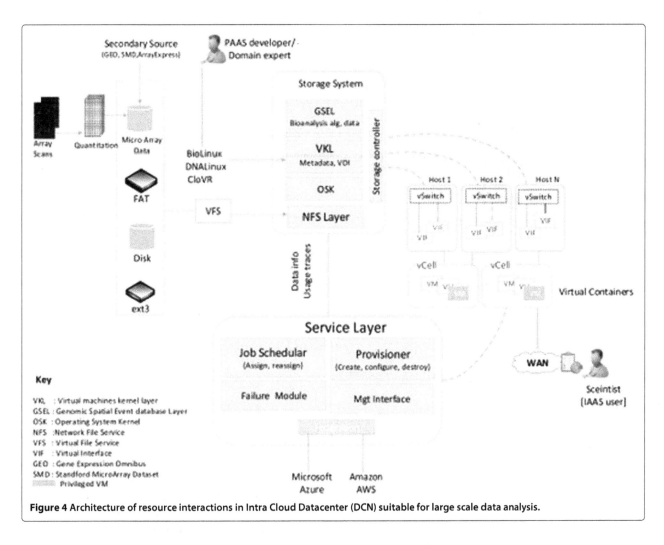

Figure 4 Architecture of resource interactions in Intra Cloud Datacenter (DCN) suitable for large scale data analysis.

To predict ℓ we adopt an inference mechanism based on the posterior distribution of a parameter for any given observation traces, X. Specifically, we adopt the Naive Bayes Classifier (NBC) and Markov Chain states model to predict the jobs concurrent on i at a given time t. NBC is a supervised learning classifier used in data mining [37]. Using the notation $X_{1:t-1}$ to mean all the observations $X_1, X_2, \ldots, X_{t-1}$, we seek to estimate the state Ψ_t at any time t using all the previous observations $X_{1:t-1}$. From Bayesian rule we have the posterior probability for any A, B, and C as:

$$P(A/BC) = \frac{P(B/C)P(B/A)C}{P(B/C)} \qquad (7)$$

Applying bayesian recursive property to equation 6 we obtain:

$$P(\Psi_t \mid X_{1:t-1}) = \Sigma_{\Psi_{t-1}} P(\Psi_t \mid \Psi_{t-1})P(\Psi_{t-1} \mid X_{1:t-1}) \qquad (8)$$

Equation 8 depends only on the previous state and the observations at time t-1. For $i \in V$ machines and given

transitional states as the workload Ψ, the probability of a VM i having workload $\ell_i(t) = P(\Psi_t \mid X_{1:t-1})$ is thus given by equation 8 irrespective of the observation at t.

Initial VM

We formulate a technique to determine the capacity of VMs for a job submitted. This work uses joint VM provisioning in a container based model. We propose the cost model $f(M_h, P_t, B)$ to estimate the initial capacity C. Given a budget of B units, the cost model estimates the initial capacity C of VMs using time series [8] of similar tasks. We compute the capacity C for each container as a function of the user defined budget B, standard machine hour M_h cost, and the processing time F_j^t obtained from equation 4. The capacity of VMs required is computed as:

$$C = \frac{B(S, \varphi)}{M_h * \sum_{j \in S} F_t^j} \qquad (9)$$

φ is the concession, per unit cost invested, that the cell owner is willing to allow and is inversely related to the budget. S is the job size submitted for analysis.

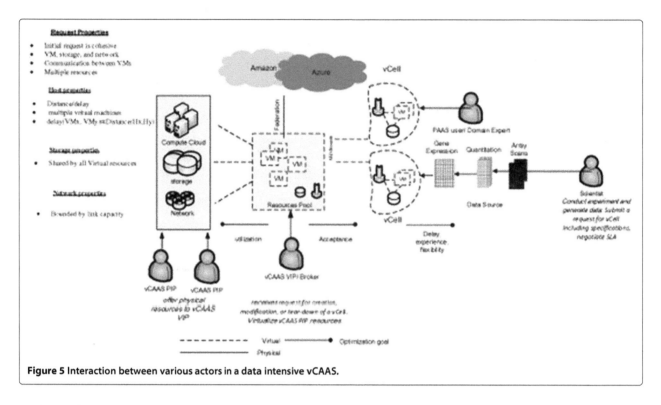

Figure 5 Interaction between various actors in a data intensive vCAAS.

Understanding the microarray data

For several years, biologists and life scientists have been using GeneChip technology to analyze gene expression in cells. Affymetrix supplies small glass slide arrays on which many probes of 25 bases of DNA or RNA sequence data are established. The probes are designed so that sets of probes on the GeneChip will test for the expression of particular genes. The data read from one array is stored in one CEL file, which has a standard format but can be either binary or character text which results in a variation in the size of the CEL files. Researchers tend to use several arrays to test different conditions so that one set of experiments which have a connection with each other are stored in related CEL files in a folder called a GSE (GEO Series Experiment).

The microarray data from many experiments are uploaded to public databases such as GEO (Gene Expression Omnibus) [38], for other scientists to use in their research. In this work, some of the experiments which use the Human GeneChip called HG-U133A were downloaded and analyzed. The analysis, carried out using the R statistical language, was to determine whether runs of guanine in the probe sequences (runs of 4 or more 'G's) were producing a significant bias in the gene expression data [14,39].

The microarray data from many experiments are often uploaded to public databases [40] such as GEO and Array-Express, for other scientists to use in their research. The microarray data studied in this work has the following characteristics:

- All jobs are submitted at the initial phase of the experiment.
- All CEL files in a GSE folder must be processed to complete a successful analysis.
- Each GSE folder contains between 10 and 700 CEL files each between $4MB$ and $32MB$ in size.
- To process each folder, depending on the size, requires memory capacity in the range $1\ GB$ to $16\ GB$.
- All data to be processed must be loaded in the main memory.
- Time to process data depends on the number of CEL files and total GSE folder size.
- Data access time varies considerably depending on the size of CEL files in the GSE folder.

Implementing the data analysis container

Our work considers self-service and dynamic algorithms for initial VM size, VM provisioning, and job allocation. The proposed algorithms are implemented in 4 steps. To perform analysis of this type of data, the following steps are required:

Step 1: Read job configuration settings.

Step 2: Estimate the number of VMs for the given data to analyse and provision the required VMs. For the chosen microarray data analysis, this step requires the classification of the data into sub group and the types of virtual machines with

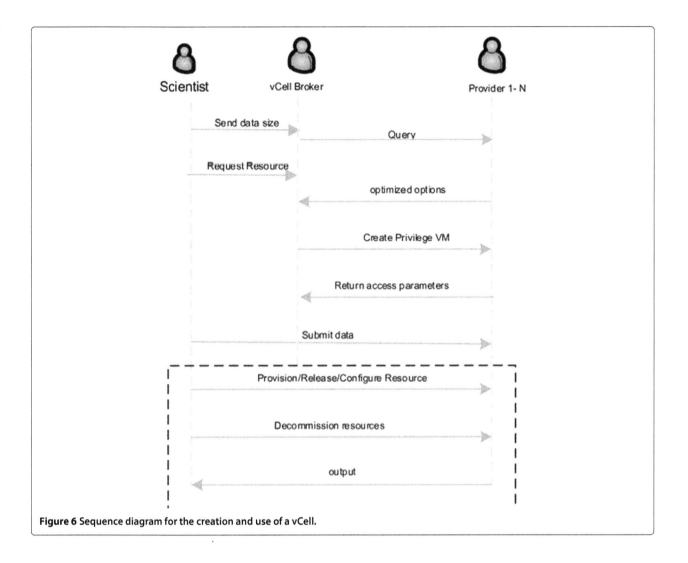

Figure 6 Sequence diagram for the creation and use of a vCell.

required memory for each group created. The dynamic classification provides automation and eliminates the need to manually assign the jobs thereby reducing the delay and, subsequently, the cost associated with manual resource creation and release. This works well for data intensive tasks. However, for other application types with different requirements other than memory, a different scheme is required. In both cases, knowledge of the domain and the historical output trace of previously executed related jobs are valuable inputs to the inference mechanism to determine the relationship between the task requirements and capacity (e.g. bandwidth, memory, CPU) of the VMs.

Step 3: Creation of virtual network (VIF) for the created VM. This stage takes into consideration both the task stage requirement.

Step 4: Configuring the created VMs with required software packages and network address to enable interaction using the VIF.

Step 5: Allocate submitted jobs to the VMs.

Step 6: Release the VMs and scale-down the vCell resources if there are no more jobs to process.

The major challenges for scientists using cloud computing to effectively and efficiently analyse this type of data are steps 2–5. For instance, the time between creating a resource and then submitting the job adds to the total idle time of the VM. This incurs additional cost as a result. Similarly, VMs not released after job execution further incur additional cost as most public clouds charge per hour [41]. The next subsection proposes dynamic mechanisms to achieve these steps without user intervention. Novel provisioning, job allocation, and adaptive clustering algorithms [42] are presented to enable the self-service data analysis.

Virtual machines provisioning

The provisioning problem for any given set of folders J each of size S_i and set of virtual machines M each $VM_j \in M$ of capacity C_j. The problem is to find the 1-to-1 mapping $J_i \longrightarrow M_j$ such that $Si \in Mj$ at any time t.

In a similar way to a biological cell, the strict requirement for all initial functional VMs (control, report, failure, and service console) to be created is enforced; otherwise the vCell request is rejected. All the algorithms considered in this work make use of the holistic view and complement each other to execute the submitted task cohesively.

To estimate the initial VMs' capacity we use equation 9 with $N = 3$ number of states (Θ) to predict the finish time (equation 4). For the data described, we identify the states in terms of workload size as high (Θ_3), medium (Θ_2), and low (Θ_1). Each VM processes a submitted job through all or part of the states. Each state varies depending on the current process. We identify three such distinct observed current processes as read (xR), write (xW), and computation (xC). It is evident as shown in Figure 7, that the average time spent on data access constitutes less than 30% of the total job finish times. This signifies that job processing is read intensive (xR) at the beginning of microarray data analysis and then compute intensive (xP) afterwards. Notice that the data access time depend on the number of VMs concurrently accessing the data stored at the NFS server. The higher the number of VMs accessing the NFS server concurrently, the more workload at the NFS server and hence slower data access time may be experienced by the VMs. In the Figure 7, jobs 9 and 10 seems to be accessing the NFS server at the same time and hence the large data access time. The job allocation strategy proposed in this research is to vary the data access period of the VMs to reduce concurrent access and consequently reduce the data access times.

We choose the initial state in Θ based on the hidden state probabilities distribution $\phi = \phi_i$ for $1 \leq i \leq N$. Tables 1, 2, and 3 shows the initial state probabilities distribution, observation distribution, and transition probabilities respectively for each VM in the vCell. Although the ϕ is chosen based on observable job processing cycle, it has been shown in [36] that the selection and update process in Markov Chain modelling eliminates the initial error over long iteration of equation 8.

LJF-KQ algorithm

To provision the required VMs, we proposed a variation of [30] as Largest Job First on the K Queues (LJF-KQ) strategy. In this scheme (Algorithm 1), we implement a K-queue on-demand provisioning policy that leases VM instances based on K job categories (classified based on size). If we denote $Q_1, Q_2, \ldots, Q_K$ as the queues of large, medium, and small jobs; then the algorithm proceeds as follows. Initially, one VM for each queue type is created on the first fit host starting with Q_1 and then Q_2. Subsequently, one VM per each Q_K job is created until the maximum allowable number of VMs are reached. Idle VMs are assigned new jobs from the job category they are created for. Once all jobs from a particular category Q_n are completed successfully, the resource allocated to the VMs for Q_n is reclaimed and re-allocated to create virtual machine(s) for other job categories in the global queue.

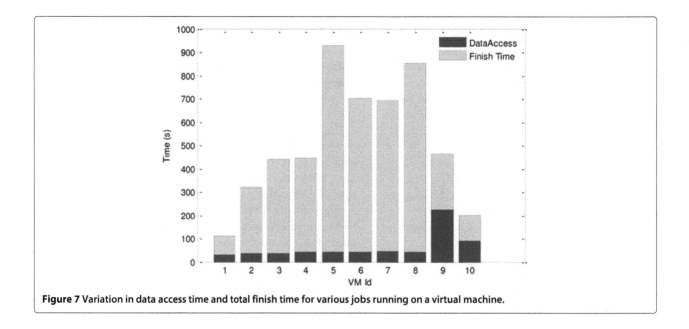

Figure 7 Variation in data access time and total finish time for various jobs running on a virtual machine.

Algorithm 1 LJF-KQ (K Queue Largest Job first)

Input: J – job list, trace- previous job completion time, M_H – standard cost of machine hour, C – container capacity requested in terms of bandwidth RAM and MIPS, minC – minimum capacity, K - job queue types, Type – distinct job categories , C_i – capacity of virtual machine i, B - Budget

Output: V – list of VMs created

1: Set B
2: T ← $trace(Size(J))$ {estimate time required to complete job}
3: C ← $B/(M_H * T)$
4: Type = KMeans(J,K)
5: **SORT** Type in descending {sort the job categories}
6: count=0
7: **for** t = size(Type) to 1 **do**
8:     count=0
9:     Create virtual machine V_{count} for Type(t) {one VM from each category except last category }
10:     C ← $C - C_{count}$ {update available capacity}
11:     V ← $V \bigcup V_{count}$
12:     count= count+1
13: **end for**
14: **while** $C > 0$ **do**
15:     Create virtual machine V_{count} for Type(t) {one VM from each category except last category }
16:     C ← $C - C_{count}$ {update available capacity}
17:     V ← $V \bigcup V_{count}$
18:     count= count+1
19: **end while**
20: Return V

Algorithm 2 below shows the pseudo code for the classification using K-Means. The initial cluster K is determined by the available classes of VMs. Amazon AWS, for instance, offers many instance types (small, medium, large) based on capacity (memory, storage, bandwidth) and target optimization.

Algorithm 2 K-Means

Input: Training Data - J, job clusters - K,

Output: Classified jobs - Type

1: n=**length**(J)
2: Initialize K clusters centroids $\mu = \mu_1, \mu_2, \ldots,$ $\mu_k \in R^n$
3: **repeat**
4:   **for** i=1 to n **do**
5:     $c^{(i)} = index(1 : K) \in \mu$ Closest to $J^{(i)}$
6:     $Type(J^{(i)}) \leftarrow c^{(i)}$
7:   **end for**
8:   $\Delta = 0$
9:   **for** k=1 to K **do**
10:     $mu'_k = \mu_k$
11:     μ_k = average mean of points assigned to cluster k
12:     $\Delta = \Delta + \triangledown(\mu', \mu)$
13:   **end for**
14: **until** $\Delta = 0$
15: Return Type

Table 1 Sample initial state probabilities distribution

Θ_1	Θ_2	Θ_3
0.5	0.3	0.2

LJF-KQ-L algorithm

The Largest Job First on K Queues with Lookup (LJF-KQ-L) algorithm is a variation of LJF-KQ with lookup for finish times. The finish times F is obtained from pilot data. Just like LJF-KQ, a large VM is created for Q_n jobs initially. However, in creating VMs for the next job categories one VM per job is created from Q_{n-1} while the estimated finish time of the jobs is less than the finish time of Q_n. This continues until n = 1. Then the process begins with Q_n again. This continues until the maximum VMs size is reached or vCell capacity is reached. The algorithm can be summarized as follows:

- Classify the submitted jobs based on size and files count using K-Means clustering
- Select a job from the job classes and create the VM for the chosen job size.
- SORT in descending order
- N = 0
- SELECT job category L_N
- Set current large job as L_N
- CREATE one VM for L_N with capacity $C(L_N)$

1. Create VMs from next large job L_{N-1} with capacity $C(L_{N-1})$ until capacity allocated for L_N is reached
2. Set $N = N + 1$
3. Repeat 1–3 until maximum capacity is reached

Algorithm 3 gives the detail steps in the proposed algorithm

Table 2 Sample discrete observations probabilities

State| Operations	xR	xW	xC
Θ_1	0.1	0.6	0.3
Θ_2	0.2	0.4	0.4
Θ_3	0.3	0.3	0.4

Algorithm 3 LJF-3Q-L (K Queue Largest Job first)

Input: J – job list, trace- previous job completion time, M_H – standard cost of machine hour, C – container capacity requested in terms of bandwidth RAM and MIPS, minC – minimum capacity, K - job queue types, Type – distinct job categories , C_i – capacity of virtual machine i, B - Budget

Output: V – all VMs created

Ensure: C > 0

1: Set B
2: T $\leftarrow$ trace(Size(J)) {*estimate time required to complete job*}
3: C $\leftarrow$ B/(M_H * T)
4: Type = KMeans(J,K)
5: **SORT** Type in descending {*the job categories*}
6: N=**length**(Type)
7: count=0 , n=N
8: **while** n > 0 **do**
9:     count=0
10:     Create virtual machine V_{count} for Type(n) {*one VM from each category except last category* }
11:     C $\leftarrow$ C − C_{count} {update available capacity}
12:     V $\leftarrow$ V $\bigcup V_{count}$
13:     cummB $\leftarrow V_{count}$
14:     count= count+1, sum=0, η=n-1
15:     **while** η > 0 **do**
16:         **while** C > 0 **AND** sum < C_{cumB} **do**
17:             Create virtual machine V_{count} for Type(η) {*one VM from this category* }
18:             sum = sum + C_{count}
19:             C $\leftarrow$ C − C_{count} {update available capacity}
20:             V $\leftarrow$ V $\bigcup V_{count}$
21:             count= count+1
22:         **end while**
23:         η=η-1
24:     **end while**
25: **end while**
26: Return V

Job allocation algorithm

Next we present the algorithms for job allocation considered in this work. The use of container based resource provisioning enables the sharing of statistics between the vCell manager and other resources in the vCell. This interaction is computationally and network transfer wise

expensive if implemented for the whole datacentre. At the boot, all VMs register with the resource database in the cell manager module. The virtual machines are allocated bandwidth to satisfy the current job requirement (computed from time series). At the end of the data access time, the bandwidth allocated is reconfigured to allow other VMs to utilize the container's overall capacity.

SJF-KQ

The shortest job first algorithm on K queues (SJF-KQ) is a variation of Shortest Job First (SJF). In this approach, jobs are ordered in decreasing order of size and submitted to the suitable category, K, of VMs created during the provisioning stage. This algorithm executes the submitted jobs based on the resource queues implemented in the provisioning phase.

SJF-KQ-L

The shortest job first algorithm on K queues with Lookup (SJF-KQ-L) is a variation of SJF-KQ. However, the expected finish time of each job is utilized to vary the data access period of the jobs. If the data access time of the job i is T_i, then the input/output overhead at storage server contributed by i at each point in F_i- T_i is zero. This variation on data access is exploited to reduce the overheads associated with data access by the virtual machines during jobs execution. The algorithm carefully schedules the job execution of VMs to ensure that the number of concurrent VMs accessing the NFS server is reduced. This way, the makespan is consequently reduced.

FCFS-KQ-L

The First Come First Serve algorithm on K queues with Lookup(FCFS-KQ-L) is a variation of SJF-KQ-L that is based on the widely used First Come First Serve (FCFS) discipline instead of the SJF.

Implementation and results

This section demonstrates the implementation stages of adopting a holistic view to resource management and job allocation in performing large data analysis. The approach taken is to implement well-known ordering disciplines - FCFC and SJF - in provisioning of cloud resources and then apply the container-based model to measure the benefits of our approach. Java code and R script are implemented to provide the features of the perceived vCAAS for the analysis of a large data intensive application.

Infrastructure setup

A room is dedicated to the cloud facility that served as a testbed cloud within the School of Computer Science and Electronic Engineering at the University of Essex. The following are the hardware infrastructure (Figure 8) deployed for the experiment consisted of:

Table 3 Sample state transition probabilities

States	Θ_1	Θ_2	Θ_3
Θ_1	0.1	0.4	0.5
Θ_2	0.4	0.4	0.2
Θ_3	0.2	0.4	0.4

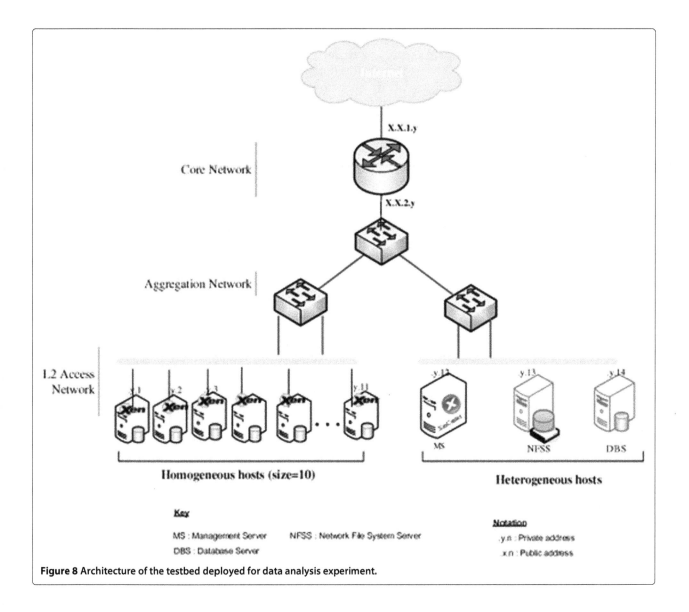

Figure 8 Architecture of the testbed deployed for data analysis experiment.

1. Ten homogeneous 64 bit Dell OptiPlex systems with 4 *GB* RAM, core 2 Duo processor running at 3.33*GHz*, and 300 *GB* hard disk storage capacity. Each computer has 4 virtual cores per processor. The internal prototype experiment cloud is therefore created on the 40 virtual cores of total processing capacity and 80 *GB* of total RAM. We deploy XEN Cloud Platform (XCP) [43] on all the 10 servers for hosting virtual machines. Deploying XCP enable us to combine all the capacities into one large pool of memory and processing capacity.

2. One 64 bit Dell OptiPlex system with 8 *GB* Ram and core 2 Duo processor running at 3.33*GHz* is set aside for the NFS server (NFSS). The computer has a total usable storage capacity of 20*TB* comprising the internal hard disk and the external storage array directly attached to the server.

3. One 64 bit Dell OptiPlex system with 8 *GB* RAM, core 2 Duo processor running at 3.33*GHz* and 4 virtual cores, and a hard disk storage capacity of 300 *GB* is set aside for the management server (MS) which also serves as the Middleware server.

4. One 64 bit Dell OptiPlex system with 8 *GB* Ram, core 2 Duo processor running at 3.33*GHz* is set aside for storing results of gene expression in a MySQL database server (*DBS*). The *DBS* has a capacity of 300 *GB* hard disk and 4 virtual cores per processor.

The experiment set-up to demonstrate the data analysis is depicted in Figure 8. In the experiment set-up the following features are employed:

- Cheap commodity network and IT hardware are deployed for the experiment.

- Physical hosts are connected in 3-layered hierarchical network topology (Figure 8) comprising aggregation, edge, and access layers.
- Basic modules presented in Section 'Container-based cloud framework' are created and packaged in a privileged virtual machine.
- The privileged VM is created and configured with functionalities for resource provisioning and dynamic job allocation. This packaged virtual machine is created in the requested container.
- Each virtual service cell is equipped with basic service functionalities suitable for the microarray data analysis.
- Experiment data stored in various storage media are made available via a standard network file system.
- The functionalities available in the vCell estimate finish time based on previous time series statistics of finished job and dynamically adjust the operations of various components.
- Provisioning and job allocation algorithms are tested using the value K = 3 for the job queues.

The classes to enable the main datacentre functionalities (Figure 9) are written in java and installed in the MS. The classes to implement the storage service are also written in Java and installed in the NFSS as set of Java objects. And finally a stand-alone MySQL Server 5.1. is installed at the DBS to save the results of the microarray data analysis.

vCell implementation
The code to realize the proposed virtual infrastructure container is divided into five sets of modules. Each module is created to perform interdependent task. The modules are for vCell creation, vCell request creation, storage access, gene expression identification, and the result writer. vCell creation is performed by the datacentre main classes. The datacentre main module provides all the functionalities for parsing submitted vCell request in VXDL format, create and initializes the privilege VM (pVM) to enable the function of vCell Manager. The functions of provisioning, allocation, and report writing are projected into the pVM. The provisioning is invoked by the pVM which starts the operation of the provisioner.

The vCell resources (VM, VIF) creation modules reside in pVM enabled with a subset of the service layer. Resource provisioning, task classification and allocation, resource release and update, and inference learning are all performed by this module. The class diagram for this module is shown in Figure 9. The provisioning process starts with an estimation of the required initial VMs. Initial VMs capacity for the vCell is computed from the implementation of equation 9. The capacity is then used as input to XEN API libraries to create the required VMs. The Provisioner classifies the submitted GSE data into

groups using an implementation of dynamic K-Means strategy shown in algorithm 2. After the classification, the function *getSuitableHost*() is called to invoke the host service wrapper class (HostServiceWrapper). The HostServiceWrapper replies with the set of available physical hosts and their available capacities. pVM then chooses the most suitable as guided by the SLA parameters in vCell's submitted request.

After the selection of suitable host, the required Xen Api (XEN) VM class is invoked to create all the required initial VMs. The VIF class instance is then invoked to create a network of links and virtual interfaces. One virtual interface is created for each network definition in the VXDL request file. Using the initial task inference from the dynamic Markov chain model, an initial virtual interface is selected as the default for communication. The allocated bandwidth to a VM is constantly updated by the pVM to reflect the various phases of job execution at the VM. This process ensures that available bandwidth in the vCell are properly budgeted.

Each created VM is started via the implementation of a call to the VM.start method. The VMs are configured with a standard socket to listen, on a specific port, for any incoming job submitted by pVM. The class RScript starts the R script, if it is not running, and set the current working directory of the R workspace to the directory where the data to be analysed is saved. At the end of computation the results are written back to the VM class which subsequently write the final result to the MySQL database server.

We implement virtual file service (VFS) functionalities in combination with allocation and control to provide an effective and flexible storage server. Figures 8 and 9 show the realization of the storage access module. Our approach attempts to minimize the IO overhead overtime caused by VM sprawl. Each VM is enabled with a microarray data analysis algorithm and accesses the required files in a "just in time" policy. This approach allows ease in relocation of jobs since only the required data is copied and the relocation to any idle resource is easily achieved.

The pVM periodically checks all running instances and decides, based on the status information (failed, running, idle, halt) obtained, whether to reassign the job. The functionalities provided include: initiate termination of a VM, report reclaim resources to resident vCell manager, and initiate creation of new virtual resource. This way, the job status can be determined and, where necessary, relocation of the job to a new instance initiated. The set-up determines job status by computing completion time as a function of GSE folder size, available memory in allocated VM, and data transfer delay. After the expected finished time, VM is marked inaccessible and the job running in the VM marked as failed. If status is failed, the module notifies the provisioning module which then destroys the

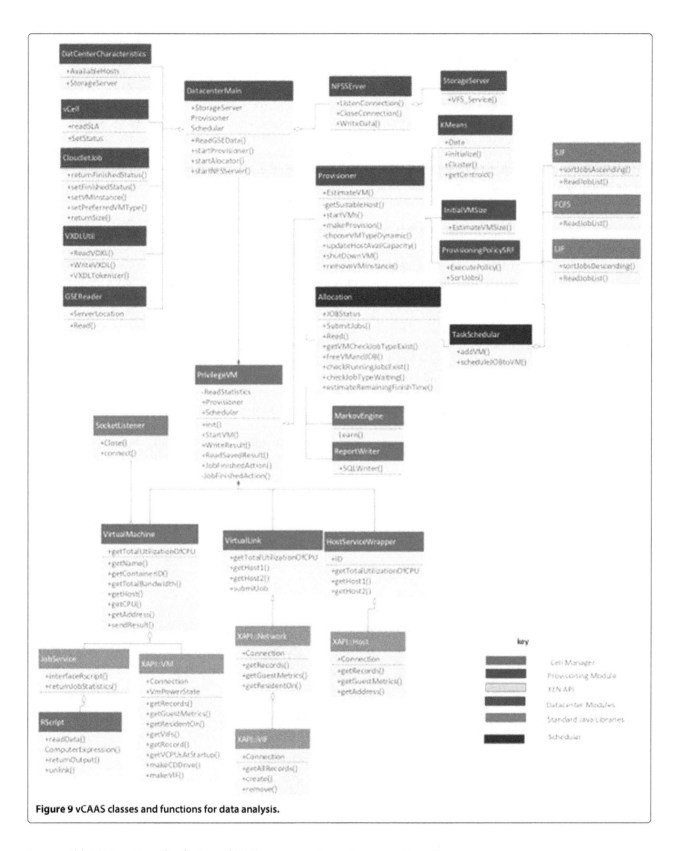

Figure 9 vCAAS classes and functions for data analysis.

inaccessible VM, assigns the destroyed VM's resources to create new VM, and finally reassigns the failed job to the newly created VM.

Experiment results

In this section we present the results of our data intensive experiment on a private cloud. Our work investigates the impact of adopting cohesive operational behaviours among the VMs to exploit the differences in data access times and implement effective resource provisioning and job scheduling. Each virtual machine requests bandwidth of a certain size to satisfy the job submitted. After the duration of data access, the virtual machines bandwidth is reduced to the basic bandwidth. This is achieved by inserting new action table entry in the software-defined enabled virtual switch introduced in Section 'Container-based cloud framework'. The residual bandwidth from the reconfiguration is made available for other VMs.

Our first experiment investigates the performance of our proposed provisioning algorithms. The algorithm that utilizes the predicted finished time lookup during provisioning is compared using three well-known [30] on-demand algorithms for virtual machines provisioning. Figure 10 show that our proposed algorithms reduced the thrashing rate - frequency of creation and destruction of virtual machines. High thrashing rate increases the workload on a provisioner and the instability of the data analysis process as resources are created and released. Since cloud services are normally charged per hour, the creation and release of virtual machines incur additional overhead cost. Hence, a small value for the thrashing rate is required to maintain a stable and, consequently, cost effective job execution. We use First Come First Serve (FCFS), Largest Job First (LJF), and Shortest Job First (SJF) to demonstrate (Figure 10) that predicting the finish time and taking the prediction into consideration during the classification of jobs into groups during resource provisioning phase reduces the thrashing rate.

In all the experiment, we set the value of K = 3 for the algorithms presented in Section 'Container-based cloud model for bioinformatics'. For example example, LJF-KQL becomes LJF-3QL. The result in Figure 10 shows that the algorithms ('Thrash overhead 3QL') implemented with a lookup outperformed those without lookup ('Thrash overhead 3Q'). In the experiment, a maximum of ten virtual machines and one privilege VM instances are instantiated per vCell. The budget size for the chosen experiment is set to $100. The experiment involved the analysis of 30 *GB* of microarray data. The values on the y-axis in Figure 10 shows the number of times a VM is released and new one created to accommodate new analysis job.

In the Figure 10, all our three algorithms that enhanced common provisioning disciplines (FCFS, SJF, and LJF) with a group classification and finished time lookup outperformed those without such enhancement. This is possible as each VM in the vCell operate alongside members of the vCell as a complementary component. Note that achieving such enhanced provisioning is made possible due to the small size of vCell. Implementing the same

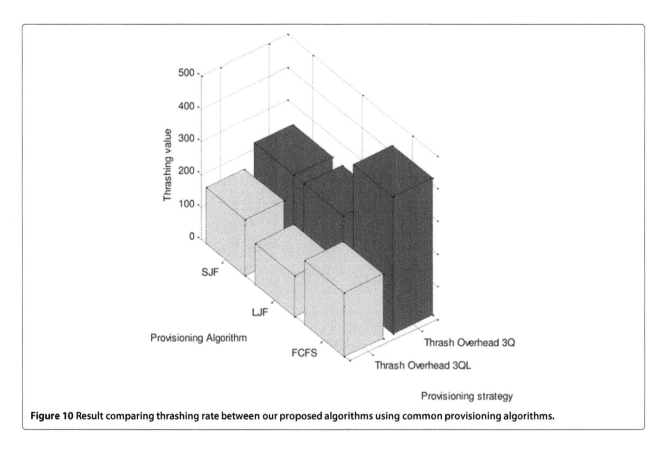

Figure 10 Result comparing thrashing rate between our proposed algorithms using common provisioning algorithms.

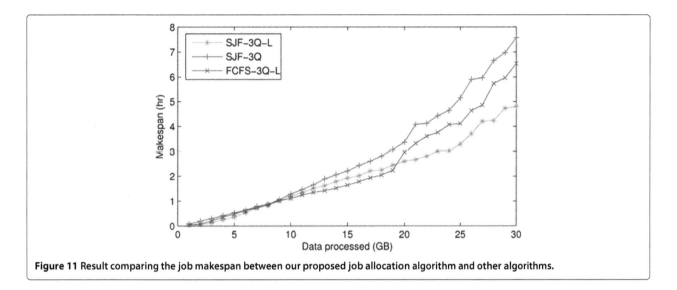

Figure 11 Result comparing the job makespan between our proposed job allocation algorithm and other algorithms.

finished time lookup and grouping of jobs to complement each other at the whole datacentre level will amount to large computation in the domain of NP-hard problem.

We continue with a comparison between our modified versions of SJF task allocation algorithms as SJF-3Q and SJF-3Q-L respectively. Figure 11 shows the result obtained from analyzing up to 30 *GB* of microarray data. We first defined the makespan as the time difference between the start and finish of the data analysis and include time to read the required data, performs compuation to identify gene expression, and write the output result to the DBS. In the figure, SJF-3Q-L outperformed the other two algorithms with shorter makespan at various job sizes. We attribute this higher performance to the ability of our vCell manager to assign jobs based on expected finished times.

We then investigate the impact of using our proposed holistic view of cloud resources on the cost of data analysis. As demonstrated in Figure 12, the cost of analysing

the data is lower for algorithm utilizing the finish times of jobs on virtual machines. We attribute the performance strength of SJF-3Q-L on two features:

- the small size of VM thrashing reduces the cost of resource usage since VMs are only created gradually as resources are released by the large number of small VMs.
- by carefully utilizing the jobs statistics from the report interface module, we can allocate jobs in a way that reduces concurrent data access and improves the performance.

In summary, the combined results in Figures 10, 11, and 12 highlights that holistic view of resources improved the performance of well-known algorithms for resource provisioning and job allocation. Quantitatively, the cost of performing analysis is reduced by 50% at 15 GB of data

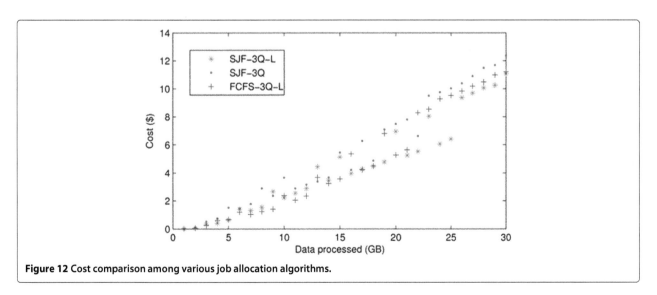

Figure 12 Cost comparison among various job allocation algorithms.

analysis. The makespan also reduces by more than 1 hr at 15 GB of data analysis.

Conclusion

There is a general perception [44,45] that the next wave of cloud services to be dominated by PAAS value added services. The virtual container described in this work is a step toward this advancement. In our case, the value added service is created by the bioinformatician and packaged as a virtual machine. The scientist performing the experiment request this virtual machine and other required resources as a self-service and dynamic container. Our work demonstrates the strength of this next generation cloud framework in performing cost effective analysis of microarray data on commodity hardware. Flexibility, dynamic configuration, and elasticity were enabled by creating a self-service infrastructure container which allows the scientist performing the experiment to submit an abstract description of requirements. Furthermore, the cloud framework proposed in this work allows VMs to operate in concert with each other and with the enabling logic. The dynamic feature of the model reduces the need to understand technical cloud computing concepts.

The virtual container presented in this work is enabled with Markov Chain learning and prediction that allows the container to manage itself using previous observations from job execution traces. We use the automation capability to estimate initial VMs' capacity without the intervention of a user.

This article demonstrates the concept in a prototype experiment cloud built on commodity hardware. The cloud environment is created using XEN Cloud Platform (XCP). The proposed privileged virtual machine is equipped with necessary XAPI compliant java modules.

A significant difference between the strategy described in this work and existing clouds is the holistic view of the resource. Also in the proposed framework, use of an observed pattern of data analysis is applied to automate the whole data analysis process. Using the variation in instant virtual machine bandwidth requirements, our proposed algorithms improved the performance and led to considerable reduction in cost at a performance that guarantees the same experience as commercial cloud services. Although this work focused on a data intensive cloud application, the same logic can easily be extended to other cloud applications. In the future, our work aims to implement the same container model for parallel and distributed cloud applications.

Competing interests
The authors declare that they have no competing interests.

Authors' contributions
IKM developed the algorithms to dynamically provision virtual resources and allocate submitted jobs in vCAAS. IKM built the cloud environment to test the proposed cloud model. AMO and APH provided the domain specific expertise

of the chosen biological data and helped develop the algorithm for the data analysis. SW verifies the applicability of the model in the chosen application area and supervised the development and testing of the models proposed. All authors read and approved the final manuscript.

Acknowledgement
IKM wish to thank Abubakar Tafawa Balewa University Bauchi Nigeria for awarding him the scholarship to study in the UK. The authors would like to express their thanks to Hugh P. Shanahan and Farhat N. Memon for the original data analysis algorithm [14], and to Graham J.G. Upton who contributed to it.

Author details
[1] School of Computer Science and Electronic Engineering, University of Essex, Wivenhoe Park, Colchester CO4 3SQ, Essex, UK. [2] Department of Mathematical Sciences and Biological Sciences, University of Essex, Wivenhoe Park, Colchester CO4 3SQ, Essex, UK.

References
1. Michael A, Armando F, Rean G, Joseph AD, Katz RH, Andrew K, Gunho L, David AP, Ariel R, Matei Z (2009) A view of cloud computing. Commun ACM 53(4):50–58
2. Srirama S, Batrashev O, Vainikko E (2010) Scicloud: scientific computing on the cloud. In: Proceedings of the 2010 10th IEEE/ACM international conference on cluster, cloud and grid computing. IEEE Computer Society, pp 579–580
3. Hines MR, Deshpande U, Gopalan K (2009) Post-copy live migration of virtual machines. ACM SIGOPS Oper Syst Rev 43(3):14–26
4. Al-fares M, Radhakrishnan S, Raghavan B, Huang N, Vahdat A (2010) Hedera: dynamic flow scheduling for data center networks. In: NSDI, pp 19–19
5. Benson T, Akella A, Maltz DA (2010) Network traffic characteristics of data centers in the wild. In: Proceedings of the 10th Annual Conference on Internet Measurement. IMC '10. ACM, New York, pp 267–280
6. Wang G, Andersen DG, Kaminsky M, Kozuch M, Ng TSE, Papagiannaki K, Glick M, Mummert L (2009) Your data center is a router: the case for reconfigurable optical circuit switched paths. Comput Sci Dep:62
7. Zhang Q, Cheng L, Boutaba R (2010) Cloud computing: state-of-the-art and research challenges. J Internet Serv Appl 1(1):7–18
8. Meng X, Isci C, Kephart J, Zhang L, Bouillet E, Pendarakis D (2010) Efficient resource provisioning in compute clouds via vm multiplexing. In: Proceedings of the 7th international conference on autonomic computing. ACM, pp 11–20
9. Vinothina V, Shridaran DR, Ganpathi DP (2012) A survey on resource allocation strategies in cloud computing. Int J Adv Comput Sci Appl 3(6):97–104
10. Ferrer AJ, Hernández F, Tordsson J, Elmroth E, Ali-Eldin A, Zsigri C, Sirvent R, Guitart J, Badia RM, Djemame K (2012) Optimis: a holistic approach to cloud service provisioning. Future Generat Comput Syst 28(1):66–77
11. Banerjee P, Friedrich R, Bash C, Goldsack P, Huberman BA, Manley J, Patel C, Ranganathan P, Veitch A (2011) Everything as a service: Powering the new information economy. Computer 44(3):36–43
12. Musa IK, Stuart W (2014) Multi objective optimization strategy suitable for virtual cells as a service. In: Innovations in bio-inspired computing and applications. Springer, pp 49–59
13. Zorov DB, Kobrinsky E, Juhaszova M, Sollott SJ (2004) Examining intracellular organelle function using fluorescent probes from animalcules to quantum dots. Circ Res 95(3):239–252
14. Shanahan HP, Memon FN, Upton GJG, Harrison AP (2012) Normalized affymetrix expression data are biased by G-quadruplex formation. Nucleic Acids Res 40(8):3307–3315
15. Schatz MC, Langmead B, Salzberg SL (2010) Cloud computing and the dna data race. Nat Biotechnol 28(7):691
16. Field D, Tiwari B, Booth T, Houten S, Swan D, Bertrand N, Thurston M (2006) Open software for biologists: from famine to feast. Nat Biotechnol 24(7):801–804
17. Krampis K, Booth T, Chapman B, Tiwari B, Bicak M, Field D, Nelson KE (2012) Cloud biolinux: pre-configured and on-demand bioinformatics computing for the genomics community. BMC Bioinformatics 13(1):42

18. Dudley JT, Butte AJ (2010) In silico research in the era of cloud computing. Nat Biotechnol 28(11):1181–1185
19. Bajo J, Zato C, de la Prieta F, de Luis A, Tapia D (2010) Cloud computing in bioinformatics. In: Distributed Computing and Artificial Intelligence. Springer, pp 147–155
20. Autosomes Chromosome X (2012) An integrated map of genetic variation from 1,092 human genomes. Nature 491:1
21. Kienzler R, Bruggmann R, Ranganathan A, Tatbul N (2012) Incremental dna sequence analysis in the cloud. In: Scientific and statistical database management. Springer, pp 640–645
22. Stein LD (2010) The case for cloud computing in genome informatics. Genome Biol 11(5):207
23. Schatz MC (2009) Cloudburst: highly sensitive read mapping with mapreduce. Bioinformatics 25(11):1363–1369
24. Matsunaga A, Tsugawa M, Fortes J (2008) Cloudblast: Combining mapreduce and virtualization on distributed resources for bioinformatics applications. In: eScience 2008, eScience'08. IEEE fourth international conference on. IEEE, pp 222–229
25. Goecks J, Nekrutenko A, Taylor J (2010) Galaxy: a comprehensive approach for supporting accessible, reproducible, and transparent computational research in the life sciences. Genome Biol 11(8):R86
26. Langmead B, Hansen KD, Leek JT (2010) Cloud-scale rna-sequencing differential expression analysis with myrna. Genome Biol 11(8):R83
27. Banerjee P, Friedrich R, Bash C, Goldsack P, Huberman BA, Manley J, Patel C, Ranganathan P, Veitch A (2011) Everything as a service: powering the new information economy. Computer 44(3):36–43
28. Jarzab M, Kosiński J, Zieliński K, Zieliński S (2012) User-oriented provisioning of secure virtualized infrastructure. In: Building a national distributed e-infrastructure–PL-Grid. Springer, pp 73–88
29. Díaz FEO, Gómez SG (2012) 4caast technical value proposition. 4CaaSt consortium. http://4caast.morfeo-project.org/wp-content/uploads/2011/02/ValueProposition_Whitepaper.pdf, Accessed: 2013-09-30
30. Genaud S, Gossa J (2011) Cost-wait trade-offs in client-side resource provisioning with elastic clouds. In: Cloud computing (CLOUD), 2011 IEEE international conference on. IEEE, pp 1–8
31. Adam C, Stadler R (2005) Adaptable server clusters with qos objectives. In: Integrated network management, 2005. IM 2005. 2005 9th IFIP/IEEE international symposium on. IEEE, pp 149–162
32. Buyya R (1999) High performance cluster computing. Prentice Hall PTR, Upper Saddle River. 99017906 edited by Rajkumar Buyya. ill. ; 25 cm. Includes bibliographical references and indexes. v. l. Architectures and systems – v. 2. Programming and applications.
33. Wood T, Gerber A, Ramakrishnan KK, Shenoy P, Van der Merwe J (2009) The case for enterprise-ready virtual private clouds. Usenix HotCloud https://www.usenix.org/legacy/events/hotcloud09/tech/full_papers/wood.pdf, Accessed: 2011-01-3
34. Koslovski GP, Primet PV-B, Charão AS (2009) VXDL: virtual resources and interconnection networks description language. In: Networks for grid applications. Springer, pp 138–154
35. Sherwood R, Gibb G, Yap K-K, Appenzeller G, Casado M, McKeown N, Parulkar G (2009) Flowvisor: a network virtualization layer. OpenFlow Switch Consortium, Tech. Rep
36. Rabiner LR (1989) A tutorial on hidden markov models and selected applications in speech recognition. Proc. IEEE 77(2):257–286
37. Webb GI, Boughton JR, Wang Z (2005) Not so naive bayes: aggregating one-dependence estimators. Mach Learn 58(1):5–24
38. Barrett T, Troup DB, Wilhite SE, Ledoux P, Rudnev D, Evangelista C, Kim IF, Soboleva A, Tomashevsky M, Edgar R (2006) NCBI GEO: mining tens of millions of expression profiles–database and tools update. Nucleic Acids Res 35(Database issue):760–765
39. Memon FN, Owen AM, Sanchez-Graillet O, Upton GJG, Harrison AP (2010) Identifying the impact of G-quadruplexes on Affymetrix 3' arrays using cloud computing. J Integr Bioinform 7(2):111
40. Ball CA, Brazma A, Causton H, Chervitz S, Edgar R, Hingamp P, Matese JC, Parkinson H, Quackenbush J, Ringwald M (2004) Submission of microarray data to public repositories. PLoS Biol 2(9):317
41. Armbrust M, Fox A, Griffith R, Joseph AD, Katz RH, Konwinski A, Lee G, Patterson DA, Rabkin A, Stoica I, Zaharia M (2009) Above the clouds: a berkeley view of cloud computing. Technical Report No. UCB EECS-2009-28, 2009–200928
42. Chinrungrueng C, Sequin CH (1995) Optimal adaptive k-means algorithm with dynamic adjustment of learning rate. IEEE Trans Neural Network 6(1):157–169
43. Williams DE (2007) Virtualization with Xen (tm): including XenEnterprise, XenServer, and XenExpress. Syngress
44. Garcia-Gomez S, Jimenez-Ganan M, Taher Y, Momm C, Junker F, Biro J, Menychtas A, Andrikopoulos V, Strauch S (2012) Challenges for the comprehensive management of cloud services in a paas framework. Scalable Comput: Pract Exp 13(3)
45. Natis YV, Lheureux BJ, Pezzini M, Cearly DW, Knipp E, Plummer DC (2011) Paas road map: a continent emerging. Gartner Res. Gartner (Inc)

## 7

THUNDER: helping underfunded NPO's distribute electronic resources

Gabriel Loewen[*], Jeffrey Galloway, Jeffrey Robinson, Xiaoyan Hong and Susan Vrbsky

Abstract

As federal funding in many public non-profit organizations (NPO's) seems to be dwindling, it is of the utmost importance that efforts are focused on reducing operating costs of needy organizations, such as public schools. Our approach for reducing organizational costs is through the combined benefits of a high performance cloud architecture and low-power, thin-client devices. However, general-purpose private cloud architectures are not easily deployable by average users, or even those with some computing knowledge. For this reason, we propose a new vertical cloud architecture, which is focused on ease of deployment and management, as well as providing organizations with cost-efficient virtualization and storage, and other organization-specific utilities. We postulate that if organizations are provided with on-demand access to electronic resources in a way that is cost-efficient, then the operating costs may be reduced, such that the user experience and organizational efficiency may be increased. In this paper we discuss our private vertical cloud architecture called THUNDER. Additionally, we introduce a number of methodologies that could enable needy non-profit organizations to decrease costs and also provide many additional benefits for the users. Specifically, this paper introduces our current implementation of THUNDER, details about the architecture, and the software system that we have designed to specifically target the needs of underfunded organizations.

Introduction

Within the past several years there has been a lot of work in the area of cloud computing. Some may see this as a trend, whereas the term "cloud" is used simply as a buzzword. However, if viewed as a serious contender for managing services offered within an organization, or a specific market, cloud computing is a conglomerate of several very desirable qualities. Cloud computing is known for being scalable, which means that resource availability scales up or down based on need. Additionally, cloud computing represents highly available and on-demand services, which allow users to easily satisfy their computational needs, as well as access any other required services, such as storage and even complete software systems. Although there is no formal definition for cloud computing, we define cloud computing as a set of service-oriented architectures, which allow users to access a number of resources in a way that is elastic, cost-efficient, and on-demand. General cloud computing can be separated into three categories: Infrastructure-as-a-Service (IaaS), Platform-as-a-Service (PaaS), and Software-as-a-Service (SaaS). Infrastructure-as-a-Service provides access to virtual hardware and is considered the lowest service layer in the typical cloud stack. An example of Infrastructure-as-a-Service is the highly regarded Amazon EC2, which is subsystem of Amazon Web Services [1]. At the highest layer is Software-as-a-Service, which provides complete software solutions. An example software solution, which exists as a cloud service is Google Docs. Google Docs is a SaaS which gives users access to document editing tools, which may be used from a web browser. In between SaaS and IaaS is Platform-as-a-Service, which allows users to access programming tools and complete API's for development. An example of a PaaS is Google AppEngine, which gives developers access to robust API's and tools for software development in a number of different languages. We are beginning to see many software services being offered by a number of public cloud providers, including image editing software, email clients, development tools, and even language translation tools. However, these tools are all offered by different providers and are not necessarily free for general use.

*Correspondence: gloewen@crimson.ua.edu
Department of Computer Science, The University of Alabama, Tuscaloosa, AL, USA

Considering that non-profit organizations cannot always afford to purchase access to software, we propose that these organizations should simply maintain their own private cloud, which could decrease the costs associated with software licensing. There are several freely available cloud architectures that may be considered. However, general-purpose cloud architectures are not suitable for organization that do not have highly trained professionals to manage such a system. This downfall of most general-purpose architectures is due to the lack of an easy to use user interface and somewhat complicated deployment process. Many architectures, such as Eucalyptus [2] and OpenStack [3], rely heavily on the command line for interfacing with the system, which isn't desirable for markets that do not have experts readily available for troubleshooting. A cloud architecture designed for these specific markets must have the following attributes: ease of deployment, user friendly interface, energy efficiency, and cost effectiveness. In consideration of these qualities we have designed a new IaaS cloud architecture, which we call THUNDER (THUNDER Helps Underfunded NPO's Distribute Electronic Resources). THUNDER utilizes the notion of simplicity at all levels in order to ensure that all users, regardless of their technical experience, will be able to use the system or redeploy the architecture if necessary.

Most IaaS cloud architectures rely upon the general case model. In the general case, an IaaS cloud architecture supports low-level aspects of the cloud stack, such as hardware virtualization, load balancing of virtual machine instances, elastic storage, and modularity of physical hardware. Vertical clouds, on the other hand, are defined by a specific market, and therefore, are able to abstract the general case IaaS cloud model to provide features that are tailored for a specific set of uses. We see vertical clouds predominantly in the healthcare sector with the e-health cloud architecture. The THUNDER architecture is an abstraction of the general case model by taking care of the low-level details of hardware virtualization, load balancing, and storage in a way that is considerate of the technical maturity of the users, as well as the level of expertise expected from the administrators. This abstraction is possible in a vertical cloud designed for the non-profit sector because we can make an assumption about the maximum number of virtual machines, the type of software required, and the expected level of experience of the users. We assume the number of virtual machine instances is congruent to the number of client devices in an office or computer lab. Additionally, the software available on the cloud is defined by a set of use cases specific to the organization. For example, THUNDER deployed to a school may be used in conjunction with a mathematics course, which would be associated with a virtual machine image containing mathematics software, such as Matlab or Maple. Additionally, we assume that the technical experience of

administrators and instructors in a school setting is low. Therefore, by deviating from the general case model of an IaaS cloud architecture, and by considering the special needs of the market, we can minimize the complexity of deployment by removing the necessity of a fine-tuned configuration.

In the following sections we discuss related background work in private vertical cloud architectures, our proposed architecture, future work, and we end with a summary and conclusion.

Background and motivation

There has been much discussion on the topic of cloud computing for various administrative purposes at educational institutions. However, cloud computing is a topic that until recently has not been widely considered for the high school grade bracket. Due to the nature of cloud computing, being a service oriented architecture, there is a lot of potential in adopting a cloud architecture that can be used in a classroom [4]. Cloud computing in the classroom could be used to provide valuable educational tools and resources in a way that is scalable, and supportive of the ever-changing environment of the classroom. Production of knowledgeable students is not a trivial task. Researchers in education are focused on providing young students with the tools necessary to be productive members of society [4]. The past decade has seen, in some cases, a dramatic decrease in state and local funding for public secondary education. This reduction in funding indicates that a paradigm shift in how technology is utilized in the classroom is necessary in order to continue to provide high quality education. The authors of [4-7] believe that cloud computing may be a viable solution to recapture students' interests and improve student success.

Education

Researchers at North Carolina State University (NCSU) have developed a cloud architecture, which is designed to provide young students with tools that help to engage students in the field of mathematics [4]. This cloud architecture, known as "Virtual Computing Lab" or "VCL", has been provided as a public service to rural North Carolina 9th and 10th grade algebra and geometry classes. The goal of this study is to broaden the education of STEM related topics using the VCL in these schools, and two applications were selected to be used in the course curriculums: Geometer's Sketchpad 5, and Fathom 2. The authors describe a set of key challenges that were encountered during the study, including: diversity of software, software licensing, security, network availability, life expectancy of hardware, affordability, as well as technical barriers. Software availability is a prime concern when it comes to provisioning educational tools for academic use.

The specific needs of the classroom, in many cases, require specific software packages. When deploying software to a cloud architecture, it is not always possible to provide certain software packages as cloud services. For this reason, it is common to bundle software with virtual machine images, which are spawned on an IaaS cloud. A virtual machine image is a single file that contains a filesystem along with a guest operating system and software packages. Additionally, software packages may have some conflicts with one another that can create an issue with the logistics of the system [4]. Another software concern is related to software-specific licensing, and how it affects the cloud. Many software packages require licensing fees to be paid per user of the system, or as a volume license, which may or may not impose a maximum number of users allowed access to the software. Therefore, depending on the specific requirements of the school and course, software licensing fees must be paid for accordingly. For example, when geometers sketchpad was deployed to the VCL, the authors made sure that the software licensing fees were paid for in accordance with the software publishers' license agreement. The necessity for licensing does affect the cost effectiveness of using a cloud in this setting, however it is no different than licensing software for traditional workstations [4].

The authors of [8] have created a private cloud architecture, called CloudIA, which supports e-Learning services at every layer of the cloud stack. At the IaaS layer, the CloudIA architecture supports an automated virtual machine image generator, which utilizes a web interface for creating custom virtual machine images with predefined software packages installed. At the PaaS layer, the CloudIA architecture supports computer science students with a robust API for writing software that utilizes cloud services. At the SaaS layer, the CloudIA architecture supports collaborative software for students to utilize for projects and discussion.

The authors of [9] describe the benefits of cloud computing for education. The main point that the authors make is that cloud computing provides a flexible and cost effective way to utilize hardware for improving the way information is presented to students. Additionally, the authors describe details about the ability of cloud computing to shift the traditional expenses from a distributed IT infrastructure model to a more pay-as-you-go model, where services are paid for based on specific needs.

Authors of [5] discuss "Seattle", which is a cloud application framework and architecture, enabling users to interact with the cloud using a robust API. By using this platform students can execute experiments for learning about cloud computing, networking, and other STEM topics. The authors also describe a complimentary programming language built upon Python, which gives students easy access to the Seattle platform.

The authors of [10] discuss a new model for SaaS, which they have named ESaaS. ESaaS is defined as a Software-as-a-Service cloud architecture with a focus on providing educational resources. The authors discuss the need for a managed digital library and a global repository for educational content, which is easily accessible through a web interface. The proposed architecture is meant to integrate into existing secondary and post-secondary institutions as a supplementary resource to their existing programs.

LTSP
One approach is the use of thin client devices, which have been used in other educational endeavors, such as the Linux Terminal Server Project (LTSP) [11]. Thin client solutions, when paired with an IaaS cloud, offer low power alternatives to traditional computing infrastructures. The authors of [12] analyze energy savings opportunities in the thin-client computing paradigm.

Authors of [13] discuss design considerations for a low power and modular cloud solution. In this study the LTSP [11] architecture is reviewed and compared to the authors cloud architecture design. LTSP is a popular low power thin client solution for accessing free and open source Linux environments using a cluster of server machines and thin client devices. The LTSP architecture provides services, which are very similar to an IaaS cloud architecture with a few notable limitations. Firstly, LTSP only offers Linux environments, which differs from an IaaS cloud in that the cloud can host Linux, Windows, and in some instances Apple OSX virtual machine instances. Additionally, LTSP does not utilize virtualization technology, rather it provides several minimal Linux and X windows environments on the same host computer. Interfacing with an LTSP instance also differs from an IaaS cloud in that an LTSP terminal will boot directly from the host machine using PXE or NetBoot, which is a remote booting protocol. A client connected to an IaaS cloud will typically rely upon the Remote Desktop Protocol (RDP) for accessing Windows instances, or the Virtual Network Computing (VNC) protocol for Linux instances.

Other work
All of the previous work relate to educational resources and services in the cloud. However, most of the related work is integrated using public cloud vendors and is specific towards one particular subject, as is presented in [4] and [5]. The authors of [14] present their solution, SQRT-C, which is a light-weight and scalable resource monitoring and dissemination solution using the publisher/subscribe model, similar to what is described in this manuscript. The approach considers three major design implementations as top priority: Accessing physical

resource usage in a virtualized environment, managing data distribution service (DDS) entities, and shielding cloud users from complex DDS QoS configurations. SQRT-C can be deployed seamlessly in other cloud platforms, such as Eucalyptus and OpenStack, since it relies on the libvirt library for information on resource management in the IaaS cloud.

In [15], the authors propose a middleware for enterprise cloud computing architectures that can automatically manage the resource allocation of services, platforms, and infrastructures. The middleware API set used in their cloud is built around servicing specific entities using the cloud resources. For end users, the API toolkit provides interaction for requesting services. These requests are submitted through a web interface. Internal interface APIs communicate between physical and virtual cloud resources to construct interfaces for users and determine resource allocation. A service directory API is provided for users based on user privileges. A monitoring API is used to monitor and calculate the use of cloud system resources. This relates to the middleware introduced in this manuscript; however, it addresses architectures more suitable for large enterprises.

The authors of [16] propose a resource manager that handles user requests for virtual machines in a cloud environment. Their architecture deploys a resource manager and a policy enforcer module. First, the resource manager decides if the user has the rights to request a certain virtual machine. If the decision is made to deploy the virtual machine, the policy enforcer module communicates with the cloud front-end and executes an RPC procedure for creating the virtual machine.

Authors of [17] describe how cloud platforms should provide services on-demand that helps the user complete their job quickly. Also mentioned is the cloud's responsibility of hiding low-level technical issues, such as hardware configuration, network management, and maintenance of guest and host operating systems. The cloud should also reduce costs by using dynamic provisioning of resources, consuming less power to complete jobs (within the job constraints), and by keeping human interaction to cloud maintenance to a minimum.

Development of cloud APIs is discussed in [18]. The author mentions three goals of a good cloud API: Consistency, Performance, and Dependencies. Consistency implies the guarantees that the cloud API can provide. Performance is relatively considered in forms of decreasing latency while performing actions. Cloud dependencies are other processes that must be handled, other than spawning virtual machines and querying cloud resource and user states. These three issues are considered in the development process of our own IaaS cloud architecture.

Proposed architecture

Our focus is to provide underfunded non-profit organizations with the means to facilitate the computing needs of their users in a cost-effective manner. The THUNDER architecture is composed of a special purpose private cloud stack, and an array of low power embedded systems, such as Raspberry Pi's [19] or other low-power devices. The THUNDER stack differs from the general-purpose private cloud model in a number of ways. General purpose cloud stacks, such as Eucalyptus [2] and OpenStack [3], are focused on providing users with many different options as to how the cloud can be configured. These general-purpose solutions are great for large organizations because the architecture is flexible enough to be useful for diverse markets. However, non-profit organizations do not typically have the resources to construct a general-purpose cloud architecture. Therefore, a special-purpose or vertical cloud architecture is desirable because it circumvents the typical cloud deployment process by making assumptions about the use of the architecture. THUNDER may be utilized by various NPO's and for various purposes, but a secondary focus of THUNDER is focused on the education market. Research in cloud computing for education has shown that educational services in high school settings are successful in motivating students to learn and achieve greater success in the classroom [4].

The THUNDER cloud stack utilizes a number of commodity compute nodes, in addition to persistent storage nodes with a redundant backup, as well as a custom DHCP, MySQL, and system administration server. Each compute node is capable of accommodating four Windows virtual machines or twelve Linux virtual machines. The lab consists of low-power client devices with a keyboard, mouse, and monitor connected to a gigabit network. A custom web-based interface allows users to login, select their desired virtual machine from a list of predefined images, and then launch the virtual machine image. For example, students taking a course in Python programming might be required to use a GNU/Linux based computer for development. However, a receptionist in an office setting might be required to use a Microsoft Windows system. Therefore, regardless of the user requirements, THUNDER will be able to provide all necessary software components to each user independently. Figure 1 illustrates the THUNDER network topology. The THUNDER network topology resembles a typical cloud topology, where the compute cluster is connected to a single shared LAN switch, and support nodes share a separate LAN switch. Additionally, the topology shows the client devices and how they interface with the rest of the system. Table 1 shows a power cost comparison between THUNDER and a typical 20 PC lab, and shows a possible savings of 50% when compared to a traditional computer lab.

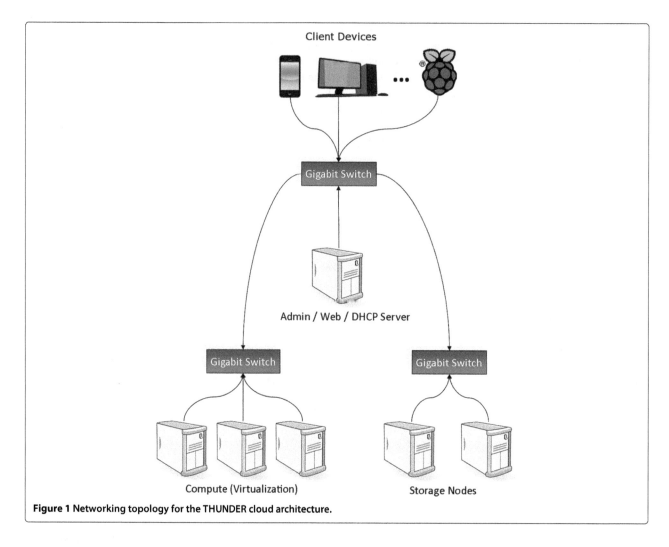

Figure 1 Networking topology for the THUNDER cloud architecture.

Network topology

The THUNDER network topology in Figure 1 is most cost efficient when combined with low-power or thi–client devices, but can also be paired with regular desktop and laptop computers. One of the common advancements in wired Ethernet technology is the use of switches.

Table 1 Power cost comparison between THUNDER and a typical lab

Typical lab			THUNDER		
#	Hardware	Watts	#	Hardware	Watts
20	PC Desktops	6,000	20	Thin client	60
20	Display	2,000	20	Display	2,000
			3	Compute node	1,200
			2	Storage node	500
			1	Admin/Web	250
Total		8,000	Total		4,010
Monthly bill: $152			Monthly bill: $77		

Ethernet switches allow for adjacent nodes connected to the switch to communicate simultaneously without causing collisions. The network interface cards used in all of the devices of THUNDER support full duplex operation, which further allows nodes to send and receive data over the network at the same time. Ethernet is a Link-Layer protocol, which determines how physical devices on the network communicate. The clients communicate with THUNDER through simple socket commands and a virtual desktop viewing client, such as VNC or RDP viewers.

Compute and store resources

THUNDER compute and storage resources will consume a considerable amount of network bandwidth. The compute nodes are responsible for hosting virtual machines that are accessed by the clients. These compute nodes will mount the user's persistent data as the virtual machine is booting. Each compute node will communicate with the THUNDER cloud resources and the client devices using a 1 Gbps network interface. The client devices should be equipped with a 10/100/1000 Mbps network adapter, and considering the limited number of cloud servers, it is unlikely that the 1 Gbps network switch will become completely saturated with traffic. Userspace storage nodes are connected to the same switch as the compute nodes, which allows for tighter coupling of storage nodes and compute nodes, decreasing the potential delay for persistent file access. Backup storage nodes are connected to a separate network switch, and are used to backup the cloud system in case of a system failure.

Administrative resources

The THUNDER administrative resources include a MySQL database, Web interface, and Networking services. These services are hosted on a single physical machine, with a backup machine isolated to the same network switch. There will be no need for a high amount of resources in the administrative node since the numbers of compute and storage nodes determine the amount of clients that can be connected to THUNDER. The THUNDER cloud, when accessed from devices external to the organization's private network, can be routed to a secondary administrative node, such that the on-site users will not experience any quality of service issues.

Network provisioning for low latency

Using a top down approach, the amount of bandwidth (maximum) needed for a twenty node THUNDER lab can be described. If we assume that each client device requires a sustained 1 Mbps network throughput, we would need to accommodate for sustaining 20 Mbps within the network switch used by the clients. Since the network switch is isolated to communicating with the resources of THUNDER, this throughput needs to be sustainable on the uplink port. This is relatively easy, given the costs of gigabit switches on the market today. The specification that needs close attention is the total bandwidth of the switch backplane. Making the assumption that this bandwidth is the number of ports multiplied by the switch speed is not always true. In our case, the bandwidth needed, 20 Mbps, is much lower than the maximum throughput of a twenty-four port gigabit switch.

There is little to no communication between THUNDER compute node resources. These devices are used to host virtual machines that are interfaced to the clients directly. Given a THUNDER lab size of twenty clients, the network bandwidth needed on the isolated network containing the compute nodes should be above 20 Mbps, assuming each client consumes 1 Mbps of bandwidth.

The THUNDER storage node resources are also isolated to the same gigabit network switch as the compute node resources. When the user logs into THUNDER and requests a virtual machine, their persistent storage is mounted inside the virtual machine for them to use. The data created by the users has to be accessed while they are using a virtual machine.

Middleware design and implementation

One of the core components in building a cloud architecture is the development of a middleware solution, allowing for ease in resource management. Additionally, in order to improve the quality of service (QOS) an emphasis on minimizing resource utilization and increasing system reliability is desirable. Our reasoning for developing a new cloud middleware API is to address issues that we have encountered in current cloud middleware solutions, which are centered upon ease of deployment and ease of interfacing with the system. Additionally, we have utilized our API to build a novel cloud middleware solution for use in THUNDER. Specifically, this middleware solution is designed for management of compute resources, including instantiation of virtual machine images, construction and mounting of storage volumes, metadata aggregation, and other management tasks. We present the design and implementation for our cloud middleware solution and we introduce preliminary results from our study into the construction of THUNDER, which is our lightweight private vertical IaaS cloud architecture.

Management of resources is a key challenge in the development of a cloud architecture. Moreover, there is a necessity for minimizing the complexity and overhead in management solutions in addition to facilitating attributes of cloud computing, such as scalability and elasticity. Another desirable quality of a cloud management solution is modularity. We define modularity as the ability to painlessly add or remove components on-the-fly without the necessity to reconfigure any services or systems. The field of cloud management exists within several overlapping domains, which include service management, system deployment, access control management, and others. We address the requirements of a cloud management middleware API, which is intended to support the implementation of the private cloud architecture currently in development. Additionally, we compare our cloud management solution to solutions provided by freely available private IaaS cloud architectures.

When examining the current state of the art in cloud management, there are few options. We are confined to free and open source (FOSS) cloud implementations, such as Eucalyptus [2] and Openstack [3]. Cloud management solutions used in closed-source, and often more popular cloud architectures, such as Amazon EC2, are out of reach from an academic and research perspective due to their closed nature. However, there has been an effort to make Eucalyptus and Openstack compatible with Amazon EC2 by implementing a compatible API and command line tools, such as eucatools [20] and Nova [21], respectively. The compatibility of API's makes it easy to form a basis of comparison between different architectures. Although, this compatibility may also serve as a downfall because if one API suffers from a bug, it may also be present in other API's.

Eucalyptus discussion

The methodology for management of resources in Eucalyptus is predominantly reliant upon establishing a control structure between nodes, such that one cluster is managed by one second-tier controller, which is managed by a centralized cloud controller. In the case of Eucalyptus, there are five controller types: cloud controller, cluster controller, block-based storage controller (EBS), bucket-based storage controller (S3), and node controller. The cloud controller is responsible for managing attributes of the cloud, such as the registration of controllers, access control management, as well as facilitating user interaction through command-line and, in some cases, web-based interfacing. The cluster controller is responsible for managing a cluster of node controllers, which entails transmission of control messages for instantiation of virtual machine images and other necessities required for compute nodes. Block-based storage controllers provide an abstract interface for creation of storage blocks, which are dynamically allocated virtual storage devices that can be utilized as persistent storage. Bucket-based storage controllers are not allocated as block-level devices, but instead are treated as containers by which files, namely virtual machine images, may be stored. Node controllers are responsible for hosting virtual machine instances and for facilitating remote access via RDP [22], SSH [23], VNC [24], and other remote access protocols.

OpenStack discussion

Similar to the methodology used by Eucalyptus, OpenStack also maintains a control structure based on the elements present in the Amazon EC2 cloud. OpenStack maintains five controllers: compute controller (Nova), object-level storage (Swift), block-level storage (Cinder), networking controller (Quantum), and dashboard (Horizon). There are many parallels between the controller of OpenStack and the controllers of Eucalyptus. The Nova controller of OpenStack is similar to the node controller of Eucalyptus. Similarly we see parallels between Swift in OpenStack with the bucket-based controller in Eucalyptus, and Cinder in Openstack with the block-based storage of Eucalyptus. There seems to be a discretion in implementation between the highest-level controller in each architecture. OpenStack maintains different controllers for interfacing and network management, while Eucalyptus maintains a single cloud controller combining these functionalities. Additionally, OpenStack does not maintain a higher-level control structure for managing compute components, which is a deviation from the cluster controller mechanism present in Eucalyptus.

Middleware interfacing, communication, and authentication

In developing our middleware solution we encountered challenges regarding the method by which it would interface with the various resources in the cloud. Many different methodologies were considered. However, we decided to use an event-driven mechanism, which is similar to remote procedure calls (RPC).

One of the prime differences in the way Eucalyptus and OpenStack perform management tasks is in the means of communication. Eucalyptus utilizes non-persistent SSH connections between controllers and nodes in order to remotely execute tasks. OpenStack, on the other hand utilizes remote procedure call, or RPC's. In keeping with the methodology introduced by OpenStack and its current momentum in the open source cloud computing community, we utilize an event driven model, which presents a very similar mechanism to that of RPC. However, these two architectures share a common component. They both utilize the libvirt [25] library, which is the same library that we utilize in our architecture.

Additionally, authentication was a challenge because in reducing the complexity of authentication we introduce new possible security threats. Although, we believe the security threats posed by our authentication model are minimal, additional threats could be uncovered during system testing. We believe that this solution is important because we address concerns regarding the overall usage of the cloud architecture, and our initial performance results in Figure 2 show that our middleware performs well when compared to Eucalyptus [2].

Node-to-node communication scheme

In contrast to the methodologies used by Eucalyptus, OpenStack, and presumably Amazon, our cloud middleware API addresses resource management in a simplified and more direct manner. The hierarchy of controllers used in Eucalyptus introduces extra complexity that we have deemed unnecessary. For this reason, our solution utilizes a simple publisher/subscriber model by which compute, storage, and image repository nodes may construct a closed network. The publisher/subscriber system operates in conjunction with event driven programming, which allows events to be triggered over the private network to groups of nodes subscribed to the controller node. Figure 3 shows the logical topology and lines of communication constructed using this model.

In constructing the communication in this manner we are able to broadcast messages to logical groups in order to gather metadata about the nodes subscribed to that group. Message passing is useful for retrieving the status

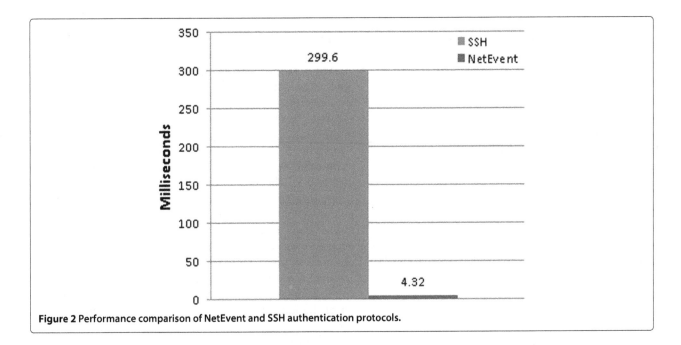

Figure 2 Performance comparison of NetEvent and SSH authentication protocols.

of nodes, including virtual machine utilization, CPU and memory utilization, and other details pertaining to each logical group. Additionally, we are able to transmit messages to individual nodes in order to facilitate virtual machine instantiation, storage allocation, image transfer, and other functions that pertain to individual nodes.

Registration of nodes

Communication between nodes utilizes non-persistent socket connections, such that the controller node maintains a static pre-determined port for receiving messages, while other nodes may use any available port on the system. Thus, each node in the cloud, excluding the controller node, automatically selects an available port at boot time. Initial communication between nodes is done during boot time to establish a connection to the controller node. We utilize a methodology for automatically finding

and connecting to the controller node via linear search over the fourth octet of the private IP range (xxx.xxx.xxx.0 to xxx.xxx.xxx.255). Our assumption in this case is that the controller node will exist on a predefined subnet that allows us to easily establish lines of communication without having to manually register nodes. Additionally, we can guarantee sequential ordering of IP addresses with our privately managed DHCP server. Once a communication link is established between a node and the controller node, the node will request membership within a specific logical group, after which communication between the controller node and that logical group will contain the node in question.

The registration methodology used in our middleware solution differs from the methodology used by Eucalyptus and OpenStack. For example, Eucalyptus relies upon command line tools to perform RSA keysharing and for

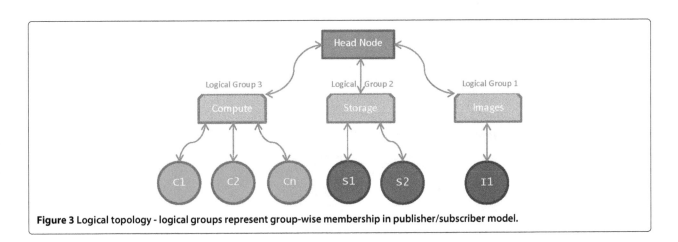

Figure 3 Logical topology - logical groups represent group-wise membership in publisher/subscriber model.

establishing membership with a particular controller. We do not perform key sharing, and instead rely upon a pre-shared secret key and generated nonce values. This approach is commonly known as challenge-response [26], and it ensures that nodes requesting admission into the cluster are authentic before communication is allowed. When a node wishes to be registered as a valid and authentic node within a cluster, a nonce value is sent to the originating node. The node will then encrypt the nonce with the pre-shared key and transmit the value back to the controller. We validate the message by comparing the decrypted nonce produced by the receiver and the nonce produced by the sender. Thus, we do not rely upon manual sharing of RSA keys beforehand, and instead we eliminate the need for RSA keys altogether and utilize a more dynamic approach for validation of communication during the registration process. Figure 4 presents the registration protocol.

Middleware API

As stated in the introduction, our methodology for constructing a middleware API for cloud resource management centers around the decreasing overhead when compared to general-purpose solutions. In order to facilitate a simple middleware solution, our API was designed to provide a powerful interface for cloud management while not introducing excessive code overhead. We have titled our API "NetEvent", which is indicative of its intended purpose as an API for triggering events over a

network. This API is utilized within our private IaaS cloud architecture as a means for communication, management of resources, and interaction with our cloud interface. Figures 5 and 6 illustrate the manner in which the API is accessed. Although, the code examples presented here are incomplete, they illustrate the simplicity of creating events to be triggered by the system for management of resources.

In Figure 5 we present sample code for the creation of a controller node, which is responsible for relaying commands from the web interface to the cloud servers. In Figure 6 we present a skeleton for the creation of a compute node with events written for instantiation of virtual machine images and for retrieving the status of the node. Although, we do not present code for the implementation of storage or image repository nodes, the implementations are similar to that of the compute node. In addition, the code examples presented in this paper show only a subset of the functionality contained within the production code.

The API presented here provides a powerful interface for implementing private cloud architectures. By means of event triggering over a private network we are able to instantiate virtual machine images, mount storage volumes, retrieve node status data, transfer virtual machine images, monitor activity, and more. The implementation of the system is completely dependent upon the developer's needs and may even be used in distributed systems, which may or may not be implemented as a

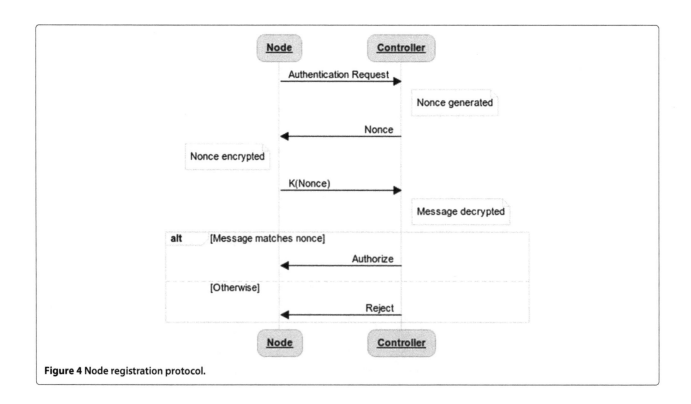

Figure 4 Node registration protocol.

```
1 function main
2    // Instantiate NetEvent object
3    // Listen on port 6667 with a
4    // role of ADMIN
5    netEvent = NetEvent(6667, 'ADMIN')
6
7    // Register an event for invoking commands
8    netEvent.registerEvent('INVOKE', invoke)
9 end
10
11 // Invoke a command within the system.
12 // Allows for the retrieval of information
13 // and triggering of events in other nodes.
14 function invoke(params)
15    if (params[0] == 'GET_CLIENT_LIST')
16       return netEvent.getClientList()
17    elseif (params[0] == 'GROUP')
18       groupName = params[1]
19       event = params[2]
20       res = netEvent.publishToGroup(groupName, event)
21       return res
22    else
23       ...
24    endif
25 end
26
27 main()
```

Figure 5 Example controller node service written in pseudocode.

cloud architecture. This approach is different than the more traditional approach of remote execution of tasks by means of SSH tunneling.

User interfacing

In the previous section we introduced our middleware API for managing cloud resources. However, another important component is a reasonable way to interface with the middleware solution. Although, the middleware API solution is completely independent from the interface, we have chosen to use a message passing approach that is different from that of general-purpose architectures. In this approach our web interface, which is written in PHP, connects to the controller node in order to trigger the "INVOKE" event. By interfacing with the controller node we are able to pass messages to groups or individual nodes in order to manage the resources of that node and receive responses. The ability to interface in this manner allows our interface to remain decoupled from the logical implementation, while allowing for flexibility in the interface and user experience. Figure 7 shows an example PHP script for interfacing with the resources in the manner described in this section.

```
1 function main
2    // Create NetEvent object
3    netEvent = NetEvent()
4
5    // Register events
6    netEvent.registerEvent('INSTANTIATE', instantiate)
7    netEvent.registerEvent('STATUS', status)
8
9    // Set the logical group name
10   netEvent.associateGroup('COMPUTE')
11
12   // Find and connect to controller node
13   netEvent.findController()
14 end
15
16 // Instantiate virtual machine, return
17 // private IP address of instance
18 function instantiate(params)
19   // params[0] -> name of image
20   ...
21   return ip_addr
22 end
23
24 main()
```

Figure 6 Skeleton for compute node service written in pseudocode.

```
 1 class Communication {
 2   var $sock;
 3
 4   /* Insert socket connect/send/receive code here */
 5
 6   function getStatus($group) {
 7     $this->connect();
 8     $this->send('INVOKE GROUP ' .
 9               $group .
10               ' STATUS');
11     $response = $this->receive();
12     $this->close();
13     if ($response == '') {return array();}
14     return explode('\;',$response);
15   }
16
17   function getClusterList() {
18     $this->connect();
19     $this->send('INVOKE CONTROL GET_CLUSTER_LIST');
20     $response = $this->receive();
21     $this->close();
22     if ($response == '') {return array();}
23     return explode('\;',$response);
24   }
25 }
```

Figure 7 Example communication interface in PHP.

The PHP interface presented in Figure 7 illustrates the methodology behind how we may capture and display data about the nodes, as well as provide a means for user interaction in resource allocation and management. Although, we do not present the full source code in this paper, additional functions could be written. For example, a function could be written that instructs compute nodes to instantiate a particular virtual machine image. One important aspect of this system is that the mode of communication remains consistent at every level of the cloud stack. Every message sent is implemented via non-persistent socket connections. This allows for greater data consistency without modifying the semantics of messages between the different systems. Figure 8 shows an example interface for metadata aggregation of a logical compute group. Figure 9 presents a sequence diagram for the VM selection interface.

Supporting storage services

Pinnacle to the development of a complete cloud architecture, and a pre-requisite to supporting compute services is the ability for a cloud middleware to support the mounting and construction of persistent storage volumes. Storage service support is a pre-requisite of compute services because it is common for virtual machine images to reside on a separate image repository or network attached storage device. Therefore, before compute services can be fully realized it is necessary to be able to mount the image repository, such that the local hypervisor may have access to the virtual machine images. We can support storage services using the storage driver provided by libvirt. Figure 10 shows the XML specification provided to libvirt, which is required by the storage driver.

Once the storage pool has been mounted, then the user of the cloud may be provided access to storage space, if it is persistent userspace. Alternatively, if the share is a image repository, then the compute node will be given access to the virtual machine images provided by the storage pool.

Supporting compute services

The NetEvent API allows for services to be written and distributed to nodes within a private cluster. These services utilize the NetEvent API as a means for triggering events remotely. Within cloud architectures there are a few important events that must be supported. Firstly, the instantiation of virtual machine images must be supported by all cloud architectures. Compute services may be supported by combining the flexibility of the NetEvent API and a hypervisor, such as KVM. A proper compute service should maintain an image instantiation event which invokes the hypervisor and instructs it to instantiate a specific virtual machine image.

The steps involved in supporting compute services start with mounting the storage share containing the virtual machine images. This is made possible with the function, *mountVMPool*, which constructs a storage pool located in the directory "*/var/lib/iibvirt/images*", and is the default location by which libvirt may locate the available domains or virtual machine images available to the system. Once the virtual machine pool is mounted then a specific virtual machine may be instantiated, which is made possible with the function, *instantiateVM*. This function looks up the virtual machine, and if it exists in the storage pool, it will be instantiated. Once the VM is instantiated, a domain object will be returned to the node, which provides the methods for managing the virtual machine instantiation.

Node 1

IP Address: 192.168.1.106
Operating system: Linux (Ubuntu 12.04 precise)
Kernel: 3.2.0-29-generic

Total RAM: **1992.87 Mbytes**
Free RAM: **696.27 Mbytes**
CPU Load: **0.02** (1 min.), **0.02** (5 min.), **0.05** (15 min.)

(0 = no load, 1.0 = max load, >1.0 = max load with waiting jobs)

Node 2

IP Address: 192.168.1.145
Operating system: Linux (Ubuntu 12.04 precise)
Kernel: 3.2.0-36-generic

Total RAM: **984.86 Mbytes**
Free RAM: **83.2 Mbytes**
CPU Load: **0.92** (1 min.), **0.28** (5 min.), **0.13** (15 min.)

(0 = no load, 1.0 = max load, >1.0 = max load with waiting jobs)

Figure 8 Example interface for metadata aggregation with two nodes being polled for data.

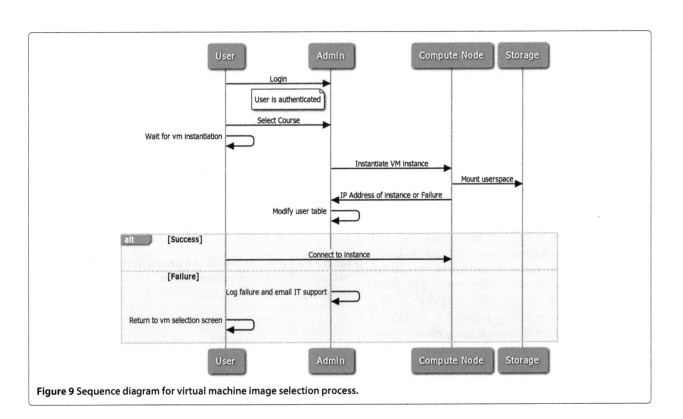

Figure 9 Sequence diagram for virtual machine image selection process.

```
1  <pool type="netfs">
2    <name>Name_libvirt</name>
3    <source>
4      <host name="Hostname"/>
5      <dir path="Name_share"/>
6      <format type='Format'/>
7    </source>
8    <target>
9      <path>Mountpoint</path>
10   </target>
11 </pool>
```

Figure 10 Storage pool XML specification required by libvirt.

Supporting metadata aggregation

Metadata aggregation refers to the ability to retrieve data about each node within a specific group. This data may be used for informative purposes, or for more complex management tasks. Example metadata includes the nodes IP address, operating system, and kernel. Additionally, dynamic data may be aggregated as well, including RAM availability and CPU load. We can support metadata aggregation in each service by introducing events that retrieve the data and transmit it to the controller node.

Performance results

One of the many reasons for not using SSH, which seems to be the industry standard approach for inter-node communication in general-purpose cloud architectures, is that SSH produces excessive overhead. The communication approach used by NetEvent is very simplified and does not introduce data encryption or a lengthy handshake protocol. The downfall of simplifying the communication structure is that the system becomes at risk for loss of sensitive data being transmitted between nodes. However, in the case of this system no sensitive data is ever transmitted, and instead only simple commands are ever sent between nodes. For this reason encryption is unnecessary. However, authentication is still required in order to determine if nodes are legitimate. In testing the performance of NetEvent we compared the elapsed time for authenticating a node with the controller and establishing a connection with the elapsed time for SSH to authenticate and establish a connection. We gathered data over five trials, which is presented in Table 2. Additionally, Figure 2 presents the average latencies between SSH and NetEvent.

From the performance comparison we draw the conclusion that general-purpose cloud architectures that utilize SSH connections, such as Eucalyptus, sacrifice up to a 99% loss in performance when compared to traditional sockets. However, this comparison is being made at optimal conditions, because the servers are under minimal load. More data needs to be gathered to determine how much the performance is affected when the servers are overloaded.

Supporting software services

The preceding sections discussed our implementation of the software system necessary for supporting IaaS cloud services, namely hardware virtualization and persistent storage. Building upon virtualization of hardware, we are able to provide software services as custom virtual machine instances. The approach that THUNDER takes is instantiation of server virtual machine images, which deploy web services for user collaboration, research, and other tools and utilities. By implementing services in this fashion, no modifications are required to the infrastructure of the cloud, and administrators may easily start services by allocating hardware resources and stop services by deallocating resources. This approach differs from typical SaaS architectures in that no additional configuration is necessary outside of what is required for regular instantiation of virtual machines. The only difference is that regular users do not have access to connecting to service instances directly using VNC.

Future work and conclusion

We would like to introduce this architecture in a select number of organizations in order to determine the effectiveness and usability of the architecture from both the user's and administrator's perspectives. Based on the results of the study, we will alleviate any possible concerns from users or administrators. We plan to form an incremental process, such that various aspects of the system are studied in different organizational environments, then small changes will be made to the system

Table 2 Performance results comparing NetEvent to traditional SSH-based authentication

Trial #	SSH (ms)	NetEvent (ms)
1	298	3.1
2	301	3.2
3	302	9.2
4	298	3.1
5	299	3.0

before running another study. In this fashion, we will have more control over which features are beneficial to organizations, and which features are least significant. Currently, the THUNDER cloud is comprised of a set of standalone servers which are not organized in a shared structure, such as a rack-style chassis. We would like to build a complete prototype that is presentable and able to be easily taken to organizations for demonstration purposes. One of the key challenges in building a cloud infrastructure is the development of a middleware solution, which allows for ease in resource management. The work presented in this paper demonstrates that a middleware solution does not have to be as complex as those found in the popular cloud architectures, Eucalyptus and Openstack. We also introduced the model by which our middleware API offers communication between nodes, namely utilizing event driven programming and socket communication. We have developed our API to be efficient, light weight, and easily adaptable for the development of vertical cloud architectures. Additionally, we showed the manner in which a web interface may interact with the middleware API in order to send messages and receive responses from nodes within the cloud. For future work we would like to investigate approaches for fault tolerance in this architecture. Additionally, we would like to perform an overall system performance benchmark and make comparisons between other cloud architectures. We would also like to implement a method for obfuscation of management traffic such that the system may not be as susceptible to malicious users.

We have presented our work in designing and implementing a new private cloud architecture, called THUNDER. This architecture is implemented as a vertical cloud, which is designed for use in non-profit organizations, such as publicly funded schools. We leverage a number of technologies, such as Apache2 web server, and MySQL for implementation of the architecture. Additionally, we introduce socket programming and RPC as a viable alternative to the more common SSH based solution for inter-node communication. We have established that the primary goal of THUNDER is not to replace traditional private cloud architectures, but to serve as an alternative, which is custom tailored for reducing complexity, costs, and overhead in underprivileged and underfunded markets. We also demonstrate that if an organization were to adopt the THUNDER architecture they could benefit by reducing up to 50% of their power bill due to the low power usage when compared to a traditional computer lab. We believe that the power and cost savings, when combined with the features and qualities of THUNDER as presented in this paper, make THUNDER a desirable architecture for school computer labs and other organizations. Further studies and analysis will validate the effectiveness of the architecture.

Competing interests
The authors declare that they have no competing interests.

Authors' contributions
GL performed the research, design, and development of the THUNDER architecture. JG and JR revised the manuscript and contributed to the background work. XH provided insight and guidance in developing the networking model for THUNDER. SV edited and revised the final manuscript. All authors read and approved the final manuscript.

References
1. Amazon Web Services. [http://aws.amazon.com/]. Accessed: 12/18/2012
2. Eucalyptus Enterprise Cloud. [http://eucalyptus.com/]
3. OpenStack. [http://openstack.org/]
4. Stein S, Ware J, Laboy J, Schaffer HE (2012) Improving K-12 pedagogy via a Cloud designed for education. Int J Informat Manage. [http://linkinghub.elsevier.com/retrieve/pii/S0268401212000977]
5. Cappos J, Beschastnikh I (2009) Seattle: a platform for educational cloud computing. ACM SIGCSE 111–115. [http://dl.acm.org/citation.cfm?id=1508905]
6. Donathan K, Ericson B (2011) Successful K-12 outreach strategies. In: Proceedings of the 42nd ACM technical symposium on Computer science education, pp 159–160. [http://dl.acm.org/citation.cfm?id=1953211]
7. Ercan T (2010) Effective use of cloud computing in educational institutions. Procedia - Social and Behavioral Sci 2(2):938–942. [http://linkinghub.elsevier.com/retrieve/pii/S1877042810001709]
8. Doelitzscher F, Sulistio A, Reich C, Kuijs H, Wolf D (2010) Private cloud for collaboration and e-Learning services: from IaaS to SaaS. Comput 91: 23–42. [http://www.springerlink.com/index/10.1007/s00607-010-0106-z]
9. Sultan N (2010) Cloud computing for education: A new dawn? Int J Inform Manage 30(2):109–116. [http://linkinghub.elsevier.com/retrieve/pii/S0268401209001170]
10. Masud M, Huang X (2011) ESaaS: A new education software model in E-learning systems. Inform Manage Eng 468–475. [http://www.springerlink.com/index/H5547506220H73K1.pdf]
11. Linux Terminal Server Project. http://ltsp.org/. [Accessed: 12/23/2012]
12. Willem Vereecken LD (2010) Energy efficiency in thin client solutions. GridNets 25:109–116
13. Cardellini V, Iannucci S (2012) Designing a flexible and modular architecture for a private cloud: a case study. In: Proceedings of the 6th international workshop on Virtualization Technologies in Distributed Computing Date, VTDC '12. ACM, New York, NY, USA, pp 37–44. [http://doi.acm.org/10.1145/2287056.2287067]
14. An K, Pradhan S, Caglar F (2012) Gokhale AA publish/subscribe middleware for dependable and real-time resource monitoring in the cloud. In: Proceedings of the Workshop on Secure and Dependable Middleware for Cloud Monitoring and Management, SDMCMM '12. ACM, New York, NY, USA, pp 1–3:6. [http://doi.acm.org/10.1145/2405186.2405189]
15. Lee SY, Tang D, Chen T, Chu WC (2012) A QoS Assurance middleware model for enterprise cloud computing. In: IEEE 36th Annual Computer Software and Applications Conference Workshops (COMPSACW), 2012, pp 322–327
16. Apostol E, Baluta I, Gorgoi A, Cristea V (2011) Efficient manager for virtualized resource provisioning in cloud systems. In: IEEE International Conference on Intelligent Computer Communication and Processing (ICCP), 2011, pp 511–517
17. Khalidi Y (2011) Building a cloud computing platform for new possibilities. Computer 44(3):29–34
18. Pallis G (2010) Cloud computing: the new frontier of internet computing. IEEE Int Comput 14(5):70–74
19. Raspberry Pi Foundation (2013). http://www.raspberrypi.org/ [Accessed: 11/15/2012]
20. EC2 Tools (2013). [http://www.eucalyptus.com/eucalyptus-cloud/tools/ec2]
21. OpenStack Nova (2013). [http://nova.openstack.org/]

22. Surhone L, Timpledon M, Marseken S (2010) Remote desktop protocol.
    VDM Verlag Dr. Mueller AG & Company Kg, Saarbruecken, Germany
23. Barrett DJ, Silverman RE, Byrnes RG (2005) SSH, The secure shell: the
    definitive guide. O'Reilly Media, Sebastopol, CA, USA
24. VNC - Virtual network computing (2013). [http://www.hep.phy.cam.ac.uk/
    vnc_docs/index.html]. [Accessed: 12/18/2012]
25. libvirt - The virtualization API (2013). http://libvirt.org/.
    [Accessed: 7/21/2013]
26. M'Raihi D, Rydell J, Bajaj S, Machani S, Naccache D "OCRA: OATH
    Challenge-Response Algorithm", RFC 6287. June 2011

Efficient parallel spectral clustering algorithm design for large data sets under cloud computing environment

Ran Jin[1,2*], Chunhai Kou[1], Ruijuan Liu[1] and Yefeng Li[1]

Abstract

Spectral clustering algorithm has proved be more effective than most traditional algorithms in finding clusters. However, its high computational complexity limits its effect in actual application. This paper combines the spectral clustering with MapReduce, through evaluation of sparse matrix eigenvalue and computation of distributed cluster, puts forward the improvement ideas and concrete realization, and thus improves the clustering speed of the distinctive clustering algorithm. According to the experiment, with the processing data scale being enlarged, the clustering rate is in nearly linear growth, and the proposed parallel spectral clustering algorithm is suitable for large data mining. The research results provide research basis to better design a clustering partition algorithm in large data and high efficiency.

Keywords: Large data; Spectral clustering algorithm; Clustering analysis; Parallel Lanczos; K-means

Introduction

The clustering analysis is an important and active research field in data mining, and the research is about the classification of data objects. In order to conveniently expound and understand the data objects and extract inherent information or knowledge hidden in the data, it is necessary to use cluster analysis technology. Its main idea is to divide the data into several classes or clusters, so as to make the objects in same cluster become the most similar while objects in different clusters vary greatly. On the whole, the algorithm can be divided into partition method, hierarchical method, density method, and model method and so on [1]. Generally, the traditional clustering algorithm has following drawbacks: low efficiency in clustering, long processing time in large data and difficulty in meeting the expected effect. For these problems, a popular research idea is correspondingly formed: combining clustering analysis, parallel computing and cloud computing, and designing an efficient parallel clustering algorithm [2,3]. This paper adopts the classical spectral clustering

algorithm as the research foundation of clustering partition algorithm as for large-scale data, analyzes how to dig valuable, understandable data information out of large data in a rapid and efficient way and at low costs. Parallel computing is a process that simultaneously uses various computing resources to solve calculation problem, which has the advantages of speeding up program execution and saving investments. Owing to the clustering, many cheap computers can be used to replace the expensive servers, and the data mining services under the parallel computing environment greatly reduces data processing costs. Besides, the cloud computing can provide scalability, reliability and stability when operating large-scale application in virtual computing environment. Based on the characteristics of cloud computing in large application, namely - distributivity, isomerism and mass data, it is suitable for data intensive application and processing [3,4].

Clustering analysis has following common problems: difficulty in handling mass data and distribution data, difficulty in determining parameters, low efficiency and poor clustering quality. In recent years, some researchers have been focusing on how to accelerate spectral clustering algorithm [5-12]. Fowlkes et al. propose to use the Nyström approximation to avoid calculating the whole similarity matrix. That is to say, they trade accurate similarity values

* Correspondence: ran.jin@163.com
[1]College of Information Science and Technology, Donghua University, Shanghai, P.R.C
[2]School of Computer Science and Information Technology, Zhejiang Wanli University, Ningbo, P.R.C

for shortened computational time. Dhillon et al. presupposed the availability of the similarity matrix and proposes a method which does not use eigenvectors. Although these methods can reduce computational time, they trade clustering accuracy for computational speed gain, and they do not address the bottleneck of memory use. To get rid of the memory capacity limit and computational bottleneck, many people like Yang utilized MPI (Message passing Interface) to build a distributed environment. Nevertheless, MPI mechanism increased the consumption of communication between machines and the network. More importantly, it is more complex if realization program uses MPI to deserialize. After all, it requires the whole cluster communication to be controlled, which is not so convenient and easy comparing with Hadoop. The Hadoop is better in fault tolerance. To make the algorithm work normally in mass data, researchers like *Meng* raised the method of using matrix sparsification - closest method, and finally used the matrix spared through the nearest neighbor method to the parallel implementation of spectral clustering. Finally, by proving the algorithm through learning experience of documents data, they proved that the algorithm can effectively cope with the problem of mass data. In this paper, we first calculate the similar matrix and sparsification according to the data point identification segmentation, then use Lanczos distributed computing and parallel computing to get the feature vector when we store the Laplace matrix in the distributed file system HDFS for calculating the characteristic vector by way of using, finally get clustering results by efficient parallel K-means clustering in terms of the transposed matrix of the feature vector. At each step, different parallel strategies are used in algorithm, and the whole algorithm grows fast.

Paper structure is organized as follows: in Section Relevant concepts and description, the MapReduce paradigm is briefly introduced and traditional spectral clustering algorithm is inspected. In Section Parallel spectral clustering algorithm design based on Hadoop, our design and implementation of PSCA(Parallel Spectral Clustering Algorithm) are presented. Performance evaluation is presented in Section The analysis of experiment and result. In Section Conclusion, conclusion is drawn and future works are discussed.

Relevant concepts and description

From above analysis, we can know that the parallel algorithm design is based on Hadoop, so the users' main job is to design and realize the Map and Reduce functions, including input and output the type of < key, value > key value and specific logic of Map and Reduce functions, etc.

Hadoop platform

With the appearance of Google's MapReduce distributed platform, some calculation of high computational complexity can be completed in acceptable time. Based on MapReduce's thought, Apache foundation developed Hadoop Open Source Project. As an open source project, Hadoop's distributed computing framework can be used to construct cloud computing environment (distributed computing). With the help of the computing power, it can be even distributed to many computing nodes in the cluster, thus realizing the huge computation ability about large data. Hadoop has high data throughput, and realizes the high fault tolerance, high reliability and scalability. It is composed of two main parts: HDFS (distributed file system) and MapReduce programming model. At the same time, by combining spectral clustering, serial traditional algorithm and MapReduce programming model, it is transplanted into Hadoop platform to conduct distributed data mining calculation by adopting corresponding parallel strategy. However, if the Hadoop platform technology is applied to the data mining algorithms, key problem is how to achieve the parallelization implementation of traditional data mining algorithm [13]. Among these modes, MapReduce (mapping and specification) programming model can make the user conveniently develop distributed computing program without caring about details. In the whole operation process, MapReduce model is always using key value of < key, value > to input and output about the form. It simplifies the programming model of parallel computing, and only provides available interface to upper users. Working processes at each stage of MapReduce calculation model is as follows:

(1) Input: An application based on the Hadoop platform and MapReduce framework that often need a pair of Map and Reduce functions by realizing appropriate interface or providing abstract class. It should also specify the locations of both input and output, and other operating parameters. This stage will divide big data under the input directory into several independent data blocks.

(2) Map: MapReduce framework treats the application input as a group of < key, value > key value pairs. At this stage, the framework will call the Map function that user defines to process each < key, value > key value pairs. At the same time, it will create some new intermediate < key, value > key value pairs. The types of the two groups of key value pairs may be different.

(3) Shuffle: In Shuffle stage, in order to ensure that Reduce input is output in sequence that Map has already sequenced, the frame gets all related < key, value > key value pairs in Map output for each Reduce through HTTP; according to the key value, MapReduce framework groups are the input in Reduce stage (There are maybe same key for different Map's outputs).

(4) Reduce: This stage will be full of intermediate data, and for each unique key, implement the user-defined Reduce function. The input parameter is "<key, {list of values} >", and the output is a new < key, value > key value pairs.

(5) Output: This stage will write the result output from Reduce in the designated location of output directory. In this way, a typical MapReduce process is completed.

Traditional spectral clustering algorithm

Spectral clustering algorithm is a dot pair cluster algorithm, and it is first used in computer vision, VLSI design and other fields, and then it is used in machine learning, and rapidly becomes research focus in the field of international machine learning. It has very promising application prospects for data clustering. The idea of this algorithm is derived from the spectrogram partition theory. If each data sample is considered as the vertex V in the chart, give weight value W to edge E between vertex in accordance with similarity degree between samples, then the undirected weighted graph $G=(V, E)$ based on similarity degree can be obtained. So in the graph G, the clustering problem can be transformed into partition problem on graph G. The optimal classification criterion based on graph theory is to make the internal similarity degree of the two subgraphs the largest, and similarity degree between subgraphs the smallest.

The standard serial spectral clustering algorithm steps are as follows:

(1) By computation, obtain the similar matrix $S \in R^{n \times n}$ and then sparse it;
(2) Construct diagonal matrix D;
(3) Compute the standard Laplace matrix L;
(4) Compute k minimum eigenvectors of matrix L, and compose matrix $Z \in R^{n \times k}$ which contains k minimum eigenvectors and are regarded as the columns of the matrix Z;
(5) Standardize it as $Y \in R^{n \times k}$
(6) Use K-Means algorithm to cluster the data point $y_i \in R^k (i = 1, ..., n)$ into k clusters.

Parallel spectral clustering algorithm design based on Hadoop

In the standard serial spectral clustering algorithms, we know that algorithm computational complexity is mainly presented in the construction of similar matrix, calculation of k minimum feature vector(s) in Laplace matrix and k-means the clustering. The parallel design of spectral clustering algorithm is processed from the above three aspects.

Calculate similar matrixes in parallelized ways

Because the Hadoop MapReduce can provide outstanding distributed computing framework, we realize our parallel spectral clustering algorithm in the Hadoop MapReduce. Firstly, we put the data point $x_1, ..., x_n$ in HBase chart, which can be accessed by each machine, and the line key (row key) of each data point x_i is set as the subscript $i \in \{1, ..., n\}$ of the data point. Then we use a Reduce function to automatically distribute the similar values between the calculated data points. For each data point x_i with identification i, Reduce function will only clear those whose subscripts are equal to or bigger than i with the data point of $x_j (j = i, ..., n)$ and the similar value of x_i. We can call it "the similar value calculation of subscript i". In this way, the similar value between each pair of data points can be calculated only once. The apparent "similar value calculation of subscript i" and "similar value calculation of other subscripts" are independent from each other. Therefore, if we distribute different subscripts to different machines, then "similar value calculation of subscript i" can be operated in distributed environment.

Especially, "similar value calculation of subscript i" needs to calculate the similar value $\{< x_i, x_i >, < x_i, x_{i+1} >, ..., < x_i, x_n >\}$ of $n - i + 1$ data point pairs. That is to say, the first subscript 1 needs to compute similar value of n data point pairs, and the last subscript n only needs to compute the similar value of a data point, that itself is $< x_n, x_n >$. In order to balance the calculation of similar value, we put the "similar value calculation of subscript 1" and "similar value calculation of subscript n" together, and "similar value calculation of subscript 2" and "similar value calculation of subscript $n - 1$" together, and so on (see Figure 1). When the calculation of similar values is completed, put them back on HBase table and they will be used to calculate the Laplace matrix in later steps. The process of parallel construction of similar matrix can be shown in Algorithm 1.

Algorithm 1 parallelized constructing the reduce function in similarity matrix

Input: <key, value>, key is the subscript index of data point, and value is supposed as null.
Output:<key', value' > = < key,value>
1. index = key, another Index = n-key + 1
2. For i in{index,another Index}
    i_content = get Content From HBase(i):
    For j = i to n do
        j_content = get Content From HBase(j);
        sim = compute Similarity(i_content,j_content);
        store Similarity(i, j, sim) into HBase table;
    End For
    End For
3. Output < key,null>
4. End.

Parallel computing k minimum eigenvectors

Lanczos algorithm is an iterative algorithm invented by Cornelius Lanczos. The algorithm was invented and used

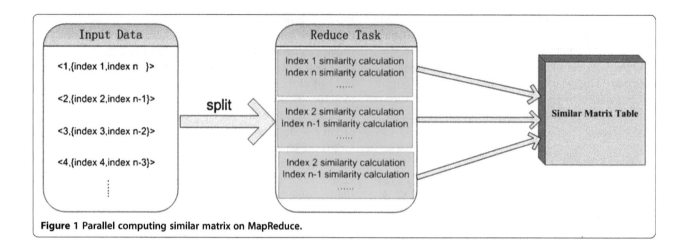

Figure 1 Parallel computing similar matrix on MapReduce.

to compute the eigenvalue and feature vector of square matrix, or the singular value decomposition of rectangular matrix [14]. Especially for the very large and sparse matrix, Lanczos' algorithm is very effective [15-17]. When calculating the maximum (or minimum) k feature vector of the matrix, the Lanczos is more suitable, for it can find out the k feature vectors by only iterating k times [15,16].

Lanczos transforms the original Laplace matrix L into a real and symmetric tri-diagonal matrix: $T_{mm} = V_m^* L V_m$ with the diagonal elements marked as $\alpha_j = t_{jj}$ and the off-diagonal elements as $\beta_j = t_{j-1j}$. Notice that T_{mm} is a symmetric matrix, so $t_{j-1j} = t_{jj-1}$. Lanczos algorithm is shown in Algorithm 2:

Notice that (x, y) is the dot product of two vectors, and after the iteration, we get a tridiagonal matrix composed of α_j and β_j:

$$T_{mm} = \begin{pmatrix} \alpha_1 & \beta_2 & & & & 0 \\ \beta_2 & \alpha_2 & \beta_3 & & & \\ & \beta_3 & \alpha_3 & \ddots & & \\ & & \ddots & \ddots & \beta_{m-1} & \\ & & & \beta_{m-1} & \alpha_{m-1} & \beta_m \\ 0 & & & & \beta_m & \alpha_m \end{pmatrix}$$

After we get the matrix T_{mm}, because T_{mm} is a tridiagonal matrix, it is easy to obtain its eigenvalues and feature vector through other ways (such as QR algorithm). It can be proved that the eigenvalue (feature vector) is the similar value to original Laplacian matrix L's eigenvalue (feature vector).

Algorithm 2 Lanczos algorithm

1. $v_1 \leftarrow norm$ is the random vector of 1

   $v_0 \leftarrow 0$

   $\beta_1 \leftarrow 0$

2. Iteration: for $J = 1, 2, ..., m$

   $w_j \leftarrow Lv_j - \beta_j v_{j-1}$

   $\alpha_j \leftarrow (w_j, v_j)$

   $w_j \leftarrow w_j - \alpha_j v_j$

   $\beta_{j+1} \leftarrow \|w_j\|$

   $v_{j+1} \leftarrow w_j / \beta_{j+1}$

3. Return

From Lanczos' algorithm, we can see that the multiplication Lv_j of matrix and vector is a time-consuming process. If the matrix is put into memory, then L must be removed every time when it is multiplied by a vector, thus consuming a lot of time consumes. The distributed function provided by Hadoop MapReduce and HDF adopts an excellent idea: mobile computing to near the data that is to be operated saves time than to calculation program. We adopt a similar Distributed Matrix to store the matrix L that is to be decomposed on HDFS, and the storage of matrix L on HDFS is according to segmentation. Then Lanczos' each iteration doesn't remove the distributed matrix L on HDFS. On the contrary, what should be moved is a vector (i.e. mobile computing). Every time, the vector vj, which is going to multiply matrix, should be sent to the location that matrix L stores in HDFS, and then the product of vector vj and matrix L on each line (see Figure 2) should be calculated in a parallelized way. The product Lv_j between matrix L

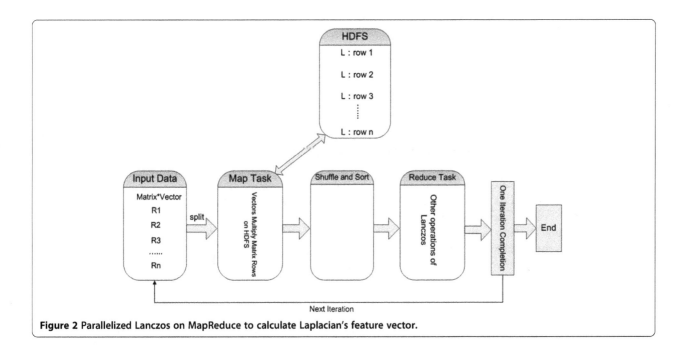

Figure 2 Parallelized Lanczos on MapReduce to calculate Laplacian's feature vector.

and vector v_j is the primary time-consuming operation in Lanczos algorithm. But now with matrix L's distributed storage in HDFS, this operation can be completed by Map/Reduce. If the former k feature vector (s) is needed, just send the vector for k times to the data storage of matrix for calculation.

Parallelization of K-means clustering

In parallelization of K-means clustering algorithm, a file including initialization k cluster (s) center is created, and can be accessed by each machine in the cluster when it is placed on the HDFS. Obviously, the distance calculation between a data point and the k center and other data points and k center is independent of each other. Therefore, the distance calculation between different data points and k center can be performed in parallel in the MapReduce framework. In terms of research on parallel K-means clustering algorithm, there are many achievements, taking literatures [18,19] for instance. In the paper, our designed parallelized K-means clustering algorithm mainly consists of Map function and Reduce function, with Combine operation being added after Map function.

Map function design

The Map function task is to calculate the distance between each record and the center point and remark the focus clustering category. The input is all recorded data for clustering and iterated clustering center from the previous round, with the record data form of < key, value > pairs as < line number, recording line>; each

Map function will read the described file of clustering center, and the Map function will calculate the nearest class center to the input recording point and make a new category marking; the form of output intermediate result < key, value > is < cluster category ID, record attribute vector >. The pseudo code of Map function is as follows:

```
void Map(Writable key, Text point){
    The initialization of variable mindis is the possible
    maximum value;
    for(i = 0;i < k;i++){
        if (dis(point, cluster [i]) < mind is){
            mindis = dis(point, cluster[i]);
            current cluster ID = i;}}
    output (current clusterID, point);}
```

When data is large and those objects of each data subset after partition are rather approximate, the middle k value produced in the process of map will be more likely to be repeated. For example, thousands of such records < key j, value j > produced in Map process will be sent through the network to the designated reduce function. It certainly wastes valuable network resources, makes the delay increase, and reduces the I/O performance. Therefore, after the map process is executed, an optional Combiner function is added. Combiner function will firstly merge the output of map function at locality and output < key j, list (value j) > list, and then make use of the partition function hash (key) mod R, halve the intermediate key/value produced by Combiner function into R different partitions, and distribute each partition to the designated reduce function. Figure 3 is the K-means parallel process.

Reduce function design

The task of Reduce function is to calculate the new clustering center in accordance with the intermediate results of Map function, and is for next round of MapReduce Job. The form of input data < key, value > pair is < cluster category ID, {record attribute vector set} >; all the records with same key (i.e., records of same category ID) will receive a Reduce task– accumulate the number of points with same key and the sum of the records and get the average value and then a new clustering center description file; form of the output result < key, value > pair is < cluster category ID, average vector >. The pseudo code of Reduce function is as follows:

```
void Reduce(Writable key, Iterator < Point Writable >
points){
   Initialize the variable num, record the total number
   of samples distributed to the same cluster, the initial
   value is of 0;
   While (points. Has Next()){
      Point Writable current point = points. next();
      Num + =current point. get num();
```

```
for(i = 0;i < dimension;i++){
   sum[i] + =current point. point [i];}
for(i = 0;i < dimension;i++)
   mean[i] = sum[i]/num;
out(key, mean);}
```

This iteration continues until each class cluster center is not changed any more, or the iterated number reaches a preset value.

Analysis of complexity of algorithm
Parallel computing of similar matrix

Before giving detailed analysis, assume that the time complexity of computing data points on similar value S (x_i, x_j) is $O(1)$, and assume that m is the number of machines in cluster. It is mentioned that "similar value calculation of subscript i" needs to compute the similar value of $n - i + 1$ data points. We can obtain that the time complexity of "similar value calculation of subscript 1" is $O(n)$, the time complexity of "similar value calculation of subscript 2" is $O(n-1)$, and the like, the time complexity of "similar value calculation of subscript n" is $O(1)$. So the time complexity of computing similar matrix is $O(n + (n - 1) ... + 1) = O((n^2 + n)/2)$. Because the calculation of similar matrix is evenly executed on m machines, the time complexity of parallel similar matrix calculation is $O((n + (n - 1) ... + 1)/m) = O((n^2 + n)/(2m))$.

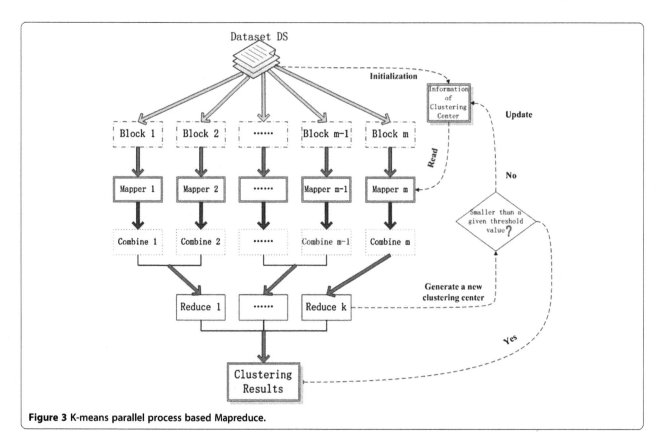

Figure 3 K-means parallel process based Mapreduce.

Parallel computing of k minimum feature vector(s)

Under the non-parallel condition, the time complexity of using Lanczos to compute Laplacian L's k vector(s) of different characteristics is $O(kL^{op} + k^2 n)$ [20], in which L^{op} is the time that matrix L multiplies vector vj. Because the matrix L has already been segmented into lines and stored on HDFS, multiplication of matrix L and vector vj is distributed and executed on the machines. And under ideal conditions, the time complexity of each multiplication is L^{op}/m, so the time complexity of parallel computation front $k$feature vector(s) is $O(kL^{op} + k^2 n)$.

Parallelization of K-means clustering

New expression form y_i of each data point is k-dimensional, hence in each iteration, the distance calculation will be executed between itself and k centers. In this way, the distance computing time complexity of each data point is $O(k^2)$. Therefore, the time complexity of iterating the distance calculation of all points each time is $O(nk^2)$. If the condition is ideal, then all the distance calculation of data points is evenly distributed to each machine and in parallel execution, so the time complexity is reduced to $O(nk^2/m)$ * (*numofiterations*).

The analysis of experiment and result

Experimental environment

In this experiment, we use 10 computers to set up the Hadoop cluster. Among them, 8 computers are in dual-core 2.6 GHZCPU, 4 GB memory and operating system of Ubuntu10.04; two in quad core 2.8 GHZCPU, 8 GB memory together with the operating system of Ubuntu10.04. The Hadoop version is 0.20.2, and each machine uses gigabit Ethernet card and is connected through switch machine.

The experiments adopts the classic data set DataSet1 provided by KDD Cup' 99 to test the correctness of the proposed parallel spectral clustering algorithm; we use respectively 10000(Data Set DS1), 50000(Data Set DS2), 100000(Data Set DS3), 1000000(Data Set DS4), 5000000 (Data Set DS5) to verify the superiority of the proposed

parallel algorithm, and data samples is the multidimensional data listed in literature [20,21].

In the experiment, both the speedup ration and scaleup ration are deemed as evaluation indicators.

Experimental results

Correctness validation

Table 1 shows the clustering results of data set DataSet1 in stand-alone and the proposed parallel spectral clustering algorithm mode. It can be seen from Table 1, both the proposed parallel spectral clustering algorithm and the serial algorithm have clustering results of higher consistency. The error rate of them is less than 2%, they both achieve a better clustering results and effectiveness, the spectral clustering algorithm proposed in the paper is correct.

Test of speedup ratio

Speedup ratio is defined by parallel computing to reduce the running time and improve the performance. It is an important indicator to verify the performance of parallel computing. The greater speedup ratio is, the less time parallel computing consume relatively, and the higher parallel efficiency and performance improve. Under changing the number of Hadoop cluster nodes, respectively use the results of speedup ratio performance tests according to 10000, 50000, 100000, 1000000, 5000000 pieces of data. Table 2 is the running time of datasets under different nodes. Figure 4 shows the results.

It can be seen from Table 2 and Figure 4, with the increase scale of data set, the algorithm speed-up ratio performance is getting better and better. The reasons are mainly as following: 1) in this paper, the set of < key, value > pair in the stage of Map and Reduce of the proposed parallel spectral clustering algorithm is rather reasonable; 2) we add Combine operation after the stage Map, which greatly reduces the communication costs between the master node and slave nodes. Therefore, as the data quantity becomes large, the speed-up ratio performance will be substantially enhanced.

Table 1 Comparison of clustering accuracy of stand-alone mode and parallel algorithm mode proposed in the paper

Type	Data volume	Stand-alone mode		The proposed parallel algorithm by the paper	
		Correct number	Wrong number	Correct number	Wrong number
Normal	18183	17818	365	17892	291
u2r	267	263	4	265	2
Dos	17408	17132	276	17221	187
R2l	3897	3795	102	3808	89
Probe	4672	4571	101	4600	72
Average error rate		1.98%		1.45%	

Table 2 Comparison of running time

Data volume	Machines	Similar matrix (sec)	Eigenvector (sec)	K-means (sec)	Total time (sec)
DS1 (10000)	1	0.386	0.481	0.156	1.023
	2	0.532	1.099	3.436	5.067
	4	0.186	0.364	1.137	1.687
	6	0.096	0.175	0.582	0.853
	8	0.038	0.065	0.231	0.334
	10	0.025	0.050	0.204	0.279
DS2 (50000)	1	7.251	9.315	2.947	19.513
	2	9.814	12.879	4.139	26.832
	4	3.162	3.963	1.376	8.501
	6	2.299	2.829	1.239	6.367
	8	1.477	1.881	0.910	4.268
	10	1.218	1.555	0.887	3.660
DS3 (100000)	1	19.228	23.982	8.572	51.782
	2	11.234	14.409	4.414	30.057
	4	5.736	6.538	2.246	14.520
	6	4.007	5.587	1.432	11.026
	8	2.965	4.056	0.901	7.922
	10	2.359	3.453	0.654	6.466
DS4 (1000000)	1	7671.580	9603.573	3422.564	20697.717
	2	37.590	46.058	16.678	100.326
	4	19.629	23.755	8.719	53.103
	6	10.126	18.473	6.475	35.074
	8	8.797	13.532	4.865	27.194
	10	6.894	11.415	3.852	22.161
DS5 (5000000)	1	31602.604	39909.984	16630.820	88143.408
	2	150.853	191.559	80.850	423.262
	4	75.164	98.906	39.213	213.283
	6	50.273	70.427	22.087	142.787
	8	40.032	53.142	18.521	111.695
	10	30.841	42.112	13.940	86.893

When the data volume is less than 50000, because in the parallel process, the data volume of each node is not big enough, the speed is smaller than the serial spectral clustering algorithm. However, with the increase of data volume, the speed of parallel algorithm is gradually increased, especially when the data volume is over 1000000, the speedup ratio grows significantly. The running time of stand-alone mode is 3.667 times as long as that of ten computers when dataset volume is 10000. However, it is 1014.39 times when dataset is 5000000. But, it can be seen from Figure 4, when the number of nodes increases to 8 or more, the increasing range of speed-up will narrow. It can be illustrated that the execution efficiency of the parallel spectral clustering algorithm based on Hadoop platform is higher than that of conventional spectral clustering algorithm.

Analysis of scalability

This paper introduces the concept of the efficiency of parallel algorithms. Efficiency of parallel algorithms represents the utilization of a cluster during the execution of parallel algorithms. The formula is $n = {S_p}/{N}$, wherein, S_p represents the speedup ratio, N means the number of cluster nodes. Figure 5 shows the efficiency of parallel algorithms proposed in the paper. For a more general, this paper test the scalability of dataset 100000, 1000000 and 5000000.

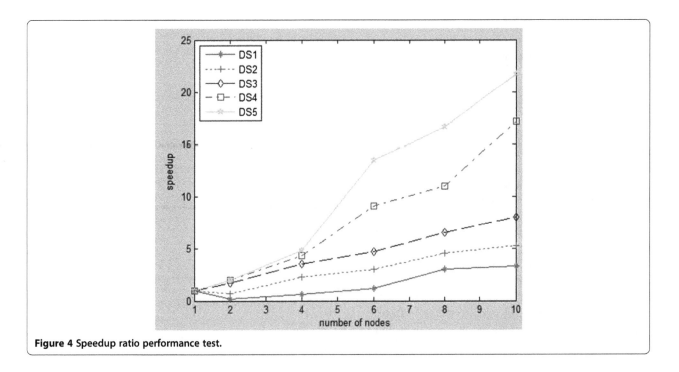

Figure 4 Speedup ratio performance test.

It can be seen from Figure 5, their efficiency curve goes down overall. This is mainly because as the growth of computing nodes in the cluster, the communication overhead increased gradually between nodes. As the data size increases, the efficiency value of parallel algorithm proposed in this paper is larger, namely the better scalability is, the more stable efficiency curve is. Experimental results show that the parallel algorithm proposed in this paper has better scalability in large data sets.

Conclusion

Those data on the Internet exist in vast scale and grow rapidly, so it is urgently required in technology to mine high-value information from the mass data. As a kind of unsupervised learning method, clustering algorithm is a technique commonly used in data statistics and analysis which contains data mining, machine learning, pattern recognition, image analysis, and many other areas. The traditional serial clustering algorithm has two problems

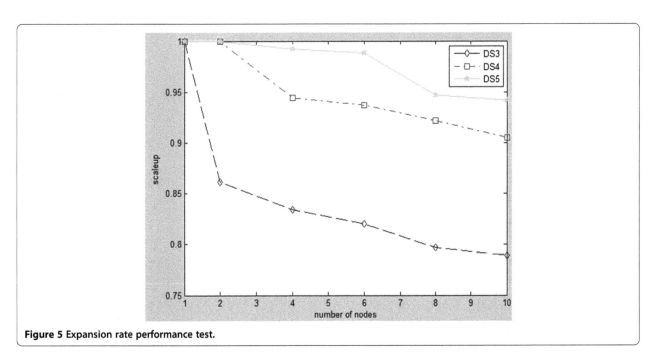

Figure 5 Expansion rate performance test.

and it is difficult to meet the needs of practical applications: the first one is that the speed of clustering is not fast enough and the efficiency is not high; the other one is that in the face of mass data, subject to the limits of memory capacity, it often cannot run effectively. This paper studied the traditional spectral clustering algorithm and designed efficient parallel spectral clustering algorithm. The strategy of parallel spectral clustering algorithm is to compute similar matrix and sparse according to data points segmentation; when computing eigenvectors, store the Laplacian matrix on the distributed file system HDFS, use distributed Lanczos to compute and get the eigenvectors by parallel computation; at last, in terms of the transposed matrix of eigenvectors, adopt the improved parallel K-Means cluster to obtain the clustering results. Through adopting different parallel strategies about each step of the algorithm, the whole algorithm gets linear growth in speed. The experimental results show that the proposed parallel spectral clustering algorithm is suitable for applying in mass data mining. We hope that the research achievements of this paper can provide inspiration and application value for subsequent research developers.

Competing interest
The authors of this paper have no competing interest.

Authors' contributions
The contributions of the paper are twofold: The use of Hadoop to design an improved parallel spectral clustering algorithm for large data sets. The use of speedup ratio and scalability to verify the superiority of the parallel algorithm. All authors read and approved the final manuscript.

Acknowledgement
This work was supported by the Science and Technology Research Program of Zhejiang Province, under grant No.2011C21036, and by the Shanghai Natural Science Foundation under grant No.10ZR1400100, and by Projects in Science and Technique of Ningbo Municipal under grant No. 2012B82003.

References
1. Hartigan, JA (1975) Clustering Algorithms. Wiley, USA.
2. Cui J, Li Q, Yang LP (2011) Fast algorithm for mining association rules based on vertically distributed data in large dense databases. Comput Sci 38:216–220
3. Zheng P, Cui LZ, Wang HY, Xu M (2010) A data placement strategy for data-intensive applications in cloud. Comput Sci 33:1472–1480
4. Wang P, Meng D, Zhan JF, Tu BB (2010) Review of programming models for data-intensive computing. J Comput Res Dev 47:1993–2002
5. Fowlkes C, Belongie S, Chung F, Malik (2004) Spectral grouping using the nyström method. IEEE Trans Pattern Anal Mach Intell 26:214–225
6. Dhillon IS, Guan Y, Kulis B (2007) Weighted graph cuts without eigenvectors: a multilevel approach. IEEE Trans Pattern Anal Mach Intell 29:1944–1957
7. Kumar S, Mohri M, and Talwalkar A (2009) Sampling techniques for the nyström method [C]. Paper presented at the 12th conference on artificial intelligence and statistics, University of California, 16–18 April 2009
8. Zhang K, Tsang I, Kwok J (2008) Improve nyström low-rank approximation and error analysis. Paper presented at the 25th International Conference on Machine Learning, Helsinki, 5–9 July 2008
9. Yan D, Huang L, Jordan MI (2009) Fast approximate spectral clustering. Paper presented at the 15th ACM SIGKDD International Conference on Knowledge Discovery and Data Mining, Paris, 28 June-1 July 2009
10. Gropp E, Skjellum A (1999) Using MPI-2: advanced features of the message-passing interface. MIT Press, USA
11. Song Y, Chen W, Bai H, Lin C, Chang E (2008) Parallel spectral clustering. In: European Conference, ECML PKDD. The joint conference on Machine Learning and Knowledge Discovery in Databases, Belgium, September 2008. Lecture notes in computer science (Lecture notes in artificial intelligence), vol 5212. Springer, Heidelberg, p 374
12. Maschhoff K, Sorensen D (1996) A portable implementation of ARPACK for distributed memory parallel architectures. Paper presented at the 4th Copper Mountain Conference on Iterative Methods, Colorado, 9–13 April 1996
13. Yang C (2010) The research of data mining based on HADOOP. Dissertation, Chongqing University
14. Cullum J, Willboughby RA (1985) Lanczos Algorithms for Large Symmetric Eigenvalue Computations volume I. Birkhauser Boston Inc, USA
15. Golub GH, Loan CFV (1996) Matrix Computations. The Johns Hopkins University Press, Maryland
16. Cullum J, Willboughby RA (1981) Computing eigenvalues of very large symmetric matrices: an implementation of a lanczos algorithm with no reorthogonalization. J Comput Phys 44:329–358
17. Mahadevan S (2008) Fast Spectral Learning Using Lanczos Eigenspace Projections. The 23th national conference on artificial intelligence, Chicago, 13–17 July
18. Zhao WZ, Ma HF, Fu YX, Shi ZZ (2011) Research on parallel K-means algorithm design based on hadoop platform. Comput Sci 38:166–176
19. Niu XZ, She K (2012) Study of fast parallel clustering partition algorithm for large data set. Comput Sci 39:134–151
20. Feng LN (2010) Research on parallel K-Means clustering method in resume data. Dissertation, Dissertation. Yunnan University
21. Jin R, Kou CH, Liu RJ, Li YF (2013) A Co-optimization routing algorithm in wireless sensor network. Wireless Pers Comm 70:1977–1991

## 9

Automatic verification technology of software patches for user virtual environments on IaaS cloud

Yoji Yamato

Abstract

We propose here a technique for automatic verification of software patches for user virtual environments on Infrastructure as a Service (IaaS) Cloud to reduce the cost of verifying patches. IaaS services have been spreading rapidly, and many users can customize virtual machines on IaaS Cloud like their own private servers. However, users must install and verify software patches of the OS or middleware installed on virtual machines by themselves. This task increases the user's operation costs. Our proposed method replicates user virtual environments, extracts verification test cases for user virtual environments from a test case database (DB), distributes patches to virtual machines in the replicated environments, and executes the test cases automatically on the replicated environments. To reduce test cases creation efforts, we propose an idea of two-tier abstraction which groups software to software groups and function groups and selects test cases belonging to each group. We applied the proposed method on OpenStack using Jenkins and confirmed its feasibility. We evaluated the effectiveness of test case creation efforts and the automatic verification performance of environment replications, test cases extractions, and test case executions.

Keywords: OpenStack; Cloud Computing; IaaS; Managed service; Automatic verification; Automatic patch distribution; Jenkins

Introduction

Infrastructure as a Service (IaaS) cloud computing has advanced recently, and users can use virtual resources such as virtual machines, virtual networks, virtual routers, virtual storage, and virtual load balancers on demand from IaaS service providers (for example, Rackspace public cloud [1]). Users can install OS and middleware such as DBMS, Web servers, application servers, and mail servers to virtual machines by themselves and can customize virtual machines as if they were their own private servers.

Software vendors periodically issue software patches for OS and middleware deployed on virtual machines in order to protect them from security vulnerabilities or provide additional functions. In most cases of IaaS virtual machines, users manually select and install these patches to their virtual machines. Because there is a risk of system failure when these patches are distributed, most service

providers state in a contract that the application of patches is the user's responsibility. Therefore, users need to distribute patches to their virtual machines and verify the health of their systems by themselves. This task increases users' virtual machine operation costs.

If service providers distributed patches and verified the health of user systems after distributing the patches, the users' operation costs would decrease. With existing shared hosting services, only service providers configure OS or middleware. Meanwhile, in the case of IaaS cloud computing, users can customize virtual machine OS or middleware. Therefore, it would take a lot of effort for service providers to verify distributed patches because the environment and configuration of each user's virtual machine are different. Thus, no service provider currently verifies patch normality after a patch distribution to user virtual machines.

In this paper, we propose automatic verification technology of software patches for various user virtual environments on the IaaS Cloud to reduce users' costs of verifying patches. The service model is such that users pay

Correspondence: yamato.yoji@lab.ntt.co.jp
NTT Software Innovation Center, NTT Corporation, 3-9-11 Midori-cho, Musashino-shi 180-8585, Japan

optional service fees for patch verifications to providers. Because it typically takes more than a day's effort for a user to verify a patch (for example, the paper [2] evaluates regression test efforts for each release, and most regression tests take more than a day), we believe that some fees would most likely be acceptable to a user who would like to reduce his/her operational cost especially in software patch verification.

Our proposed method replicates user virtual environments, extracts verification test cases for user virtual environments from a test case database (DB), distributes patches to virtual machines on the replicated environments, and executes those test cases automatically on the replicated environments. To reduce test cases creation efforts, we propose an idea of two-tier abstraction which groups software to software groups and function groups and selects test cases belonging to each group. We implemented the proposed method on OpenStack [3] using Jenkins and confirmed the feasibility of automatic selection and execution of test cases based on user virtual environments. Using the implementation, we evaluated the effectiveness of test case creation efforts by the idea of two-tier abstraction. We also evaluated the automatic verification performance.

The rest of this paper is organized as follows. In Section Problems with existing technologies, we introduce IaaS platforms such as OpenStack, review existing automatic test tools, and clarify problems of virtual machine patch verification for service providers. In Section Proposal of automatic verification technology of virtual machines patches, we propose automatic software patch verification technology for user virtual machines and describe a design to solve the problems of existing methods. In Section Evaluation of automatic verification technology of virtual machines patches, we explain how we implemented the proposed method, confirmed its feasibility, and evaluated test case creation costs and automatic verification performance. We compare our work to other related work in Section Related work and summarize the paper in Section Conclusion.

Problems with existing technologies
Outline of IaaS platforms
According to the definition of the National Institute of Standards and Technology (NIST) [4], cloud service models can be divided into SaaS (Software as a Service), PaaS (Platform as a Service), and IaaS (Infrastructure as a Service). Virtual machines' OS and middleware of SaaS and PaaS are managed by service providers. When the providers verify software patches for OS or middleware, they only repeat the same regression tests because there are only pre-known configuration settings, and verification efforts are minimal. However, IaaS provides hardware computer resources for the CPU or Disk via networks. Therefore, OS and middleware of virtual machines can be customized by

users, and users need to apply patches by themselves. This paper targets patches for virtual machines on IaaS cloud.

OpenStack [3], CloudStack [5], and Amazon Web Services [6] are major IaaS platforms. The basic idea of our proposed method is independent from the IaaS platform. For the first step, however, we implement a prototype of the proposed method on OpenStack (see Section Evaluation of automatic verification technology of virtual machines patches). Therefore, we use OpenStack as an example of an IaaS platform in this section. Note that functions of OpenStack are similar to other IaaS platforms such as CloudStack and Amazon Web Services. For example, our method uses Heat [7], which is a template deployment technology of OpenStack; Amazon Web Services have a similar deployment function called Amazon CloudFormation [8].

OpenStack is composed of plural function blocks. Some function blocks provide coordinate functions such as authentication, orchestration and monitoring of other function blocks. And other function blocks provide management functions of logical/virtual resources. Figure 1 shows a diagram of OpenStack function blocks. Neutron manages virtual networks. OVS (Open Virtual Switch) [9] and other software switches can be used as virtual switches, and Neutron controls to create these virtual switches or virtual routers. Nova manages virtual machines. KVM (Kernel based Virtual Machine) [10], Xen [11], and others can be used as hypervisors, and Nova controls to create virtual machines on these hypervisors. OpenStack provides two storage management function blocks: Cinder for block storage and Swift for object storage. Both types of storage are used for retaining data. Glance manages image files for virtual machines. Heat orchestrates these function blocks and provisions multiple virtual resources according to a template text file. Keystone is a function block that enables single sign-on authentication among other OpenStack function blocks. The functions of OpenStack are used through REST (Representational State Transfer) APIs. There is also a Web GUI called Horizon that uses the functions of OpenStack. Ceilometer is a monitoring function of virtual resource usage.

Major versions of OpenStack are released once every six months; the latest version is called Juno.

Problems with existing verification technologies
Regarding Linux patches, distributors such as RedHat confirm function degradation when they release a patch or upgraded version, and users can adopt a stable software version provided by distributors. However, distributors only confirm functions of OS and do not check middleware behavior on Linux. Therefore, users need to verify middleware behavior on Linux to check whether a Linux patch affects it. It is also said that distributors do not check the performance of each patch, so system performance

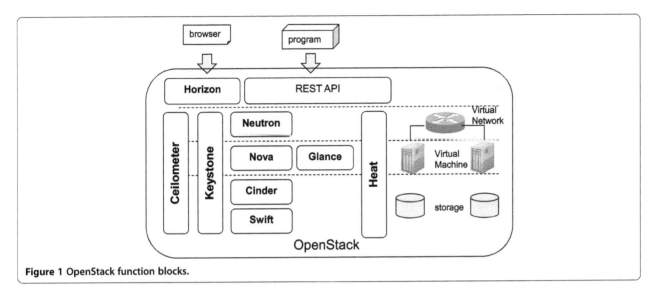

Figure 1 OpenStack function blocks.

degradation checks are necessary after patch distributions. For example, to check the transaction performance of a Web three-tier model, it is better to run a TPC-C (Transaction Processing Performance Council benchmark) test on a user virtual environment.

Some tools enable automatic tests, for example, Jenkins [12] and Selenium [13]. Jenkins is a tool to support Continuous Integration and is useful not only for building software but also for executing regression test cases for software that is changed during the software life cycle. Selenium is a tool to enable automatic Web tests; it captures actions of Web browsers and repeats captured Web actions or conducts Web actions described by Selenium IDE scripts.

However, the objectives of these tools are recurrent executions of the same regression test cases. There are two problems with IaaS virtual machine patch verifications.

i) Service providers cannot execute different test cases for multiple user virtual environments with different configurations. For example, we consider the case in which user A installed a Windows 2012 server and MySQL 5.1 to a virtual machine, and user B installed a Windows 2012 server and Apache 2.1 to a virtual machine. In this case, the same patch for the Windows 2012 server is distributed to both virtual machines, but the verification test cases should be different in order to confirm the health of each user's system.

ii) Preparing automatic test cases for each user environment beforehand is not realistic because service providers would have to make extensive preparations. A method to enable effective regression tests for Cloud platform development using Jenkins and Selenium was reported [2]. However, the paper [2] targeted IaaS platform development, and regression tests of user virtual machines deployed on an IaaS platform are out of scope. The paper [2] also describes that three to five times of the amount of work are needed for automatic test case creations using Jenkins and Selenium compared with manual regression test executions.

Proposal of automatic verification technology of virtual machines patches

We propose technology for automatically verifying software patches for user virtual environments on IaaS cloud to reduce users' patch verification costs. In Automatic verification steps, we explain the automatic verification steps. The figure shows OpenStack, but OpenStack is not a precondition of the proposed method. In Test case extraction method, we explain the process of selecting automatic test cases, which is a core process of the verification steps.

Automatic verification steps

Our proposed system is composed of automatic verification functions (hereinafter, AVFs), Jenkins, a test case DB, and an IaaS controller such as OpenStack. Figure 2 shows the processing steps of automatic verification when a software patch is released.

Service providers manage a customer DB in which each user's policy of patch verification such as whether a user would like to verify a released patch or not. For example, we consider a case in which a patch was issued for a Windows 2012 server. Service providers extract users who would like to verify the Windows 2012 patch for their virtual machines from the customer DB. The automatic verification steps when a patch is released from a software vendor are as follows.

1. Operators specify a patch and a user tenant (logical space for each user where virtual resources are deployed) to which a patch is distributed to AVFs. A user is extracted from the customer DB. A tenant is a logical space for each user where virtual resources such as virtual machines, virtual routers, and volumes are deployed. We assume both use cases of a manual verification start or automatic verification start. AVFs provide

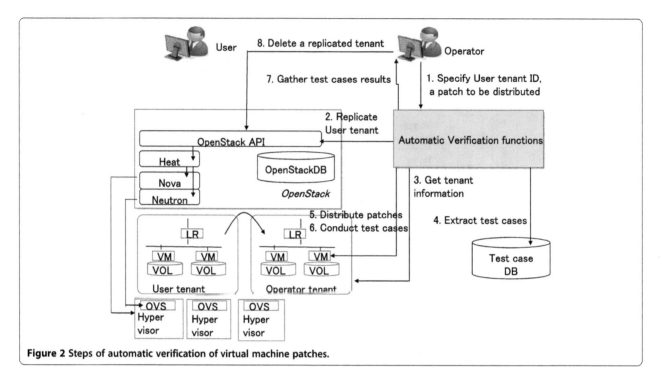

Figure 2 Steps of automatic verification of virtual machine patches.

not only the GUI but also the API to start verifications. When verifications are handled for many users, a provider prepares a script program that extracts verification target users from a customer DB, manages released patches to be verified, schedules orders of each user tenant verification, and calls the AVF API to start verifications.

2. AVFs replicate a user virtual environment. First, AVFs request the IaaS controller to extract a template of a user tenant of virtual resources. A template is a JSON text file with virtual resource structure information and is used by OpenStack Heat or Amazon CloudFormation to provision virtual resources in one batch process. Note that the current OpenStack Heat cannot extract a template from a user tenant directly; we use complementary technology to Heat [14] for OpenStack tenant replication cases.

Second, AVFs request the IaaS controller to deploy an extracted template with the target tenant ID; then the IaaS controller provisions virtual resources of the user tenant on the specified tenant. When volumes are replicated, volumes data such as installed software are extracted as a RAW image file; then the image file data are copied to a volume on the specified replicated tenant. Replicated virtual resources are deployed on tenants managed by service providers so as not to charge users. Our technology main targets are users who do not have sufficient skills in using OpenStack, or sufficient resources for verifications. Therefore,

we extract a template from an actual user environment in this step. However, there are some users who can utilize OpenStack Heat templates sufficiently. If these users would like to verify patches by themselves, our technology does not support them, but if they would like to use our automatic verifications, AVFs skip a process of template extraction and receive their own templates to build test tenants, then we can help them to verify patches based on their templates.

3. AVFs acquire environmental data of installed software. Specifically, the data of the software that is installed on each virtual machine is acquired from replicated virtual environments.

4. AVFs select test cases for patch verifications from the test case DB. Test cases are executed after patch distributions to virtual machines, but some test cases may need to set verification data before distributing patches. To select test cases, virtual resources structure template information (step 2), and software environmental data (step 3) are used. This is a core step of automatic verification; thus, we explain it in detail in Test case extraction method.

5. AVFs distribute a specified patch to replicated virtual machines. Existing patch distribution methods corresponding to virtual machine software can be used. Here, we explain an example of windows update case. As a prerequisite, cygwin module is installed on a windows virtual machine and patches are stored in a server which can be accessed from a

windows virtual machine. Firstly, AVFs login to the windows virtual machine by SSH. AVFs copy patches to the windows virtual machine by scp command. AVFs apply these patches to the windows virtual machine by wusa (Windows Update StandAlone) command. AVFs confirm validity of patches application by event logs through powershell Get-WinEvent command. Finally, AVFs reboot the Windows vitual machine by shutdown command. Note that all virtual machines on a replicated environment are supplied with a patch in this step. This is because gaps in software versions between virtual machines may cause unexpected behavior. For example, software versions of DBMS need to be the same in high-availability clusters of DB servers.

6. AVFs execute test cases selected in Step 4 for replicated virtual environments with distributed patches.

There are three kinds of test case confirmation targets after applying a patch; one is a confirmation of normal functioning, one is a data normality confirmation, and the other is a confirmation of performance. In the data normality confirmation test cases, data to be confirmed need to be prepared before patch distribution; therefore, AVFs set sample data to virtual resources between Steps 4 and 5. For example, to confirm a Japanese web page expression, a test case needs to set a Japanese sample html before the patch and check whether html characters are garbled after the patch.

Both remote tests and local tests are executed based on extracted test cases. For example, in local tests to check performance, performance test tools are deployed on virtual machines and are started using SSH login from AVFs. Note that SSH login ID and password are acquired from customer DB data. Although a patch is distributed only to virtual machines, verification test cases are executed for all virtual resources in a replicated user tenant. In a case where virtual machines with web servers are under one virtual load balancer, web server verifications after patch distributions need to be tested via the virtual load balancer.

We use an existing tool, Jenkins, to execute test cases selected from the test case DB. Jenkins is installed on a server in which AVFs also work. The AVFs request Jenkins to execute extracted test cases, and then Jenkins executes test cases and gathers results.

7. AVFs collect the results of test cases for each user environment using Jenkins functions. Collected data are sent to operators or reported to users. Users can judge patch adoptions to actual user tenants based on reports. If users agree to automatic patch distributions beforehand, AVFs distribute patches to virtual machines on actual user tenants when all test case results on replicated user environments are positive.

8. Operators may retain replicated environments to skip step 2 in the next verification when there are sufficient physical resources for virtual resource deployment. Otherwise, operators may delete replicated virtual resources after patch verification if they do not have a lot of physical resources. By deleting virtual resources on which patch verification is already completed, operators can verify patches implemented on other user virtual environments using the same physical resources. Because OpenStack Heat provides a stack-delete API, operators can delete virtual resources directly by one OpenStack API call. Note that AVFs do not have to provide deleting functions of virtual resources.

Test case extraction method

In this subsection, we explain in detail step 4 of test case selection, which is a core step of our proposal.

The test case DB retains two types of information. One is software relation information. The relations between software and the software group, which is a concept grouping different versions of software, and the function group, which is a concept grouping same functions software, are stored. The other is test case information of test cases themselves that can be executed by Jenkins as well as attribute information of the test cases.

Table 1 shows an example of software relation information. We consider a case where a function group is the DB, and the software groups include Oracle, MySQL, and Postgre SQL. Each software group contains specific kinds of software; for example, the Oracle software group includes Oracle 10 g and 11 g. Function groups can be defined by operators, for example, the OS, DB, mail server, web server, and application server.

Table 1 Example of software relation

Function group	Software group	Software
OS	Windows	Windows Server 2012
OS	Windows	Windows 8.1
OS	RHEL	RHEL 7.0
OS	RHEL	RHEL 6.1
DB	Oracle	Oracle 11g
DB	Oracle	Oracle 10g
DB	MySQL	MySQL 5.0
DB	MySQL	MySQL 4.0
Web	Apache	Apache 2.1
Web	Apache	Apache 2.2
Web	IIS	IIS 8.0
Web	IIS	IIS 8.5

Table 2 shows an example of test case information. The test case DB stores a test case itself and its attribute data. A test case class is information that indicates the test case is intended for which software, which software group, or which function group. A target subject is information on whether the verification target is a function, data, or performance. A test site is information on whether the test is executed remotely or locally.

For example, DB table CRUD (Create, Read, Update, Delete) is a test case of CRUD operations using SQL and can be commonly used for the DB function group because all relational DBs have SQL CRUD functions. Also, the DB table CRUD target is to confirm a function; thus, the target subject is "function." In another example, a test case of a registered Japanese character garbling check is a test case of the DB function group, and data to be checked are data registered before patch distribution; thus the target subject is "data." If the target subject is "data," AVFs need to prepare and insert confirmation data before patch distribution. In another example, a TPC-C test measures the performance of a transaction, so the target subject is "performance". In another example, table data CRUD by phpMyAdmin is a test case for the MySQL software group, and the target subject is "function" because phpMyAdmin is a Web GUI access tool only for MySQL.

Figure 3 shows an entity-relationship diagram of the test case DB. The function group is a bundle of software groups that relates function group test cases. The software group is a bundle of software that relates software group test cases. Software relates software test cases.

Service providers prepare these data and test cases in the test case DB before patch verifications. Next, we explain the procedure for selecting test cases for each user environment using software relation data and test case attribute data when a new patch is released.

AVFs extract software information of the OS and middleware that user virtual machines use from the step 3 environmental information of the replicated user tenant. From the information in the list of installed software, AVFs search what software group the software belongs to and what function group the software group belongs to.

AVFs select test cases using this software relation information. Specifically, AVFs select corresponding function group test cases, corresponding software group test cases, and corresponding software test cases respectively for each installed software.

Although the test case DB can retain software test case data, the test case creation and preparation costs for service providers are too high for each software. Therefore, it is better for service providers to prepare as many upper-tier (function group or software group) test cases as possible. This means that service providers do not have to prepare software test cases in practical use. By abstracting software to software groups and function groups in our proposed idea, service providers can verify virtual machine patches by preparing only a small number of test cases. We call this idea "two-tier abstraction of software and test cases".

Here, we clarify the division of roles in test case creation. Service providers prepare OS and middleware functions and performance regression test cases for patch verifications. Because service providers cannot create application-specific test cases, users need to create them if application-specific tests are needed. AVFs also provide a user interface to register users' application-specific tests to the test case DB. Thus, not only OS or middleware tests but also application-specific tests can be executed on replicated user environments if users create and register their test cases.

We have implemented AVFs GUI/API interfaces of verification start and test case registration. By releasing GUI to users, users can register their application-specific test cases. A user registers a test case and its attribute data to a test case DB via GUI. Registered test cases need to be invoked by Jenkins. And registered attribute data need to have information of for which tenant and for which virtual machines. For user registrations, we add two additional columns of exclusive tenant ID and virtual machine ID to a test case table. By setting exclusive tenant ID, registered test is only used on the specified tenant. By setting virtual machine ID, AVFs can distinguish which virtual machine in the tenant is tested by the test case.

After user test case registration, the verification is preceded as follows. In Step 1, a user or an operator starts to verify by specifying a tenant ID. In Step 4, AVFs extract not only test cases corresponding to software information but also registered user test cases corresponding to the specified tenant ID and AVFs executed them in Step 5.

Table 2 Example of test case information

Function group	Software group	Software	Test case	Test case class	Target subject	Test site
DB			Table CRUD	DB function group	function	remote
DB			Japanese character garbling check	DB function group	data	remote
DB			TPC-C benchmark test	DB function group	performance	local
DB	MySQL		Access by phpMyAdmin	MySQL software group	function	remote

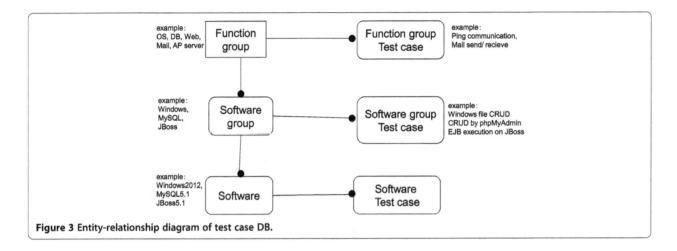

Figure 3 Entity-relationship diagram of test case DB.

We also explain supplemental information of test case preparations and upgrades. Regarding to test case preparations, some free test cases of open source software can be re-used for our system such as PostgreSQL regression tests. And regarding to test cases upgrades, we think frequent upgrades are not needed because our tests are regression tests. We need to upgrade test cases when software major version upgrade is released. But major middleware such as MySQL or Apache major version upgrade is less than once a year, then upgrade efforts are not so much.

Evaluation of automatic verification technology of virtual machines patches

In this section, we describe how we implemented the proposed method and confirmed the feasibility of automatic verification for virtual machine patches. We also discuss test case creation costs and performance using implemented functions.

Implementation of automatic verification functions

We implemented AVFs of Figure 2 on OpenStack Folsom. Folsom is the name of the previous (not the latest) OpenStack version. AVFs were implemented on OS Ubuntu 12.04, Tomcat 6.0, and Jenkins 1.532.2 by Python 2.7.3. The implemented Python code was less than 10 K lines.

We confirmed the expected behavior of the AVFs using the environments described in subsection Performance evaluation of automatic verification. Specifically, we confirmed that verification test cases were selected differently based on each installed middleware when the same OS patch was distributed to one virtual machine with MySQL and another virtual machine with Postgre SQL.

Evaluation of test case preparation costs for automatic verification

Our method is expected to reduce the number of prepared test cases by two-tier abstraction of installed software and

test cases. Currently, providers need to prepare and execute regression test cases on each patch for their services. For example, about 300 regression test cases are executed for a production hosting service that is mainly used for mail and web functions [15].

In this subsection, we explain how our method is able to execute appropriate regression test cases when each virtual machine has different software. We also confirm that abstracting software to a software group or function group was able to reduce the number of prepared test cases.

Test case evaluation conditions

Patch type: CentOS 6 periodic patches.

User numbers with virtual machines of CentOS 6: 12 users.

User environment configuration:

- Each user tenant has two virtual machines, two volumes, two virtual Layer-2 networks, and one virtual router. Two virtual machines have the same DBMS software.
- The virtual machines of each tenant respectively used MySQL 4.1, MySQL 5.1, MySQL 5.5, MySQL 5.6, PostgreSQL 8.4, PostgreSQL 9.1, PostgreSQL 9.2, PostgreSQL 9.3, Oracle 11.1, Oracle 11.2, Oracle 12.1.0.1, and Oracle 12.1.0.2. To represent different software, the 12 users used different versions or different vendor DBMS in this experiment.

Number of verification test cases after patch distributions:

- DB function group test cases: 10. For example, a test case of CRUD by SQL, which can be commonly used for all relational DBs.
- Each software group test case: 5. The MySQL, Postgre SQL, and Oracle software groups each have 5 test cases. For example, phpMyAdmin CRUD

check is a test case of the MySQL software group. (In this test, a sample data is inserted, referred, updated and deleted through phpMyAdmin)
- Each software test case: 0. We do not prepare test cases for specific types of software.

An outline of test case evaluation conditions is given in Table 3.

Evaluation of test cases preparation results

Using the implemented function, we executed automatic verification test cases after applying CentOS 6 patches for 12 user virtual machines.

In the results, 15 test cases were executed for each user virtual machine, and total of 180 test cases were executed automatically. Only 25 test cases were prepared by service providers, but our proposed idea of software group and function group abstraction was able to effectively select test cases based on user environments. Although, automatic test cases preparations of Jenkins took about three times the amount of work of normal manual test cases executions [2], but it was more effective than executing each user and each software test case manually.

Performance evaluation of automatic verification

The implemented AVFs of virtual machine patches replicate virtual resources by using OpenStack Heat, distribute patches to virtual machines, and execute selected test cases. We evaluated the performance of the total processing time and each section processing time with changing the concurrent processing number when CentOS 6 patches were distributed.

Note that when we verify a large number of virtual machines, we need to schedule order of verifications to keep concurrent processing number of verifications within a certain number. Keeping the concurrent processing number is for reducing negative impact on the actual user environments. Our previous work in cloud platform development [16] showed that more than three concurrent volume replications of OpenStack greatly affected storage.

Measurement conditions

Processing steps of automatic verification to be measured:

Case 1: template and image extraction, template deployment, tester resource preparation such as

Internet connection settings, environment information acquisition, patch distribution, test case execution, virtual resource deletion.
Case 2: environment information acquisition, patch distribution, test case execution. (We consider the case where service providers replicate virtual resources beforehand and do not delete them after verifications)
Case 3: template extraction, template deployment except for volumes, tester resource preparation such as Internet connection settings, environment information acquisition, patch distribution, test case execution, virtual resource deletion except for volumes. (We consider the case where service providers replicate only volumes beforehand and do not delete them after verifications)

User tenant configuration:

Tenant pattern A
- Each user tenant has two virtual machines, two volumes, two virtual Layer-2 networks, and one virtual router. The structure of virtual resources is shown in Figure 4(a).
- Each virtual machine's specifications are: one CPU with one Core, 1-GB RAM, and one attached volume with a size of 10 GB, and the installed OS is CentOS 6.
- Either MySQL 5.6 or Postgre SQL 9.3 is installed on each volume for virtual machine DBMS software.
Tenant pattern B
- Each user tenant has two virtual machines, two volumes, one virtual Layer-2 network, one virtual router, and one virtual load balancer. The structure of virtual resources is shown in Figure 4(b).
- Each virtual machine's specifications are: one CPU with one Core, 1-GB RAM, and one attached volume with a size of 10 GB; the installed OS is CentOS 6.
- Either Apache 2.4 or nginx 1.6 is installed on each volume, and http requests are load-balanced to two virtual machines by a virtual load balancer.

Selected number of test cases: 15.

- 10 for the DB function group and 5 for the MySQL software group or Postgre SQL software group.
- 10 for the Web server function group and 5 for the Apache software group or nginx software group.

Table 3 Outline of test case evaluation conditions

User numbers	12
User tenant configuration	2 virtual machines, 2 volumes, 2 virtual Layer 2 networks, 1 virtual router.
Each virtual machine installed software	MySQL 4.1, MySQL 5.1, MySQL 5.5, MySQL 5.6, PostgreSQL 8.4, PostgreSQL 9.1, PostgreSQL 9.2, PostgreSQL 9.3, Oracle 11.1, Oracle 11.2, Oracle 12.1.0.1, Oracle 12.1.0.2.
Test cases	10 for DB function, 5 for MySQL group, 5 for PostgreSQL group, 5 for Oracle group.

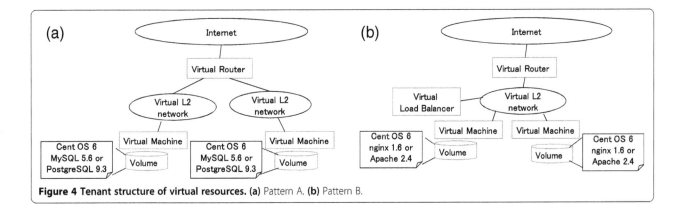

Figure 4 Tenant structure of virtual resources. (a) Pattern A. **(b)** Pattern B.

Concurrent processing numbers:

− 1, 3, 5, 10, 20

1, 3, 5 for tenant pattern A measurement and 1, 3 for tenant pattern B measurement. We only measured performances with 10 and 20 concurrent processing for Case 3 & pattern A to confirm the effectiveness of Case 3. Automatic verifications are started by a command line interface, and concurrent processing is managed by a simple script program in this performance measurement.

An outline of the performance measurement conditions is presented in Table 4.

Performance measurement environment

Figure 5 shows the performance measurement environment. Maintenance servers such as syslog, or backup servers and redundant modules such as heartbeat have been omitted. Meanwhile there are many servers for OpenStack virtual resources, the main server of this measurement is an automatic verification server. These servers are connected with Gigabit Ethernet.

In detail, Figure 5 shows the physical and virtual servers and the modules in each server. For example, in the OpenStack API server case, this server is a virtual server, it is in both the Internet segment and the Control segment, and its modules are a Cinder scheduler, Cinder API, nova-api, keystone, glance-registry, and nova-scheduler. Two servers are used for redundancy. Other servers are the proposed automatic verification server, a user terminal and an operator terminal, Glance application servers for image upload, NFS storage for images, template servers for tenant replication, a DB for OpenStack and test cases, OpenStack servers for virtual resources, iSCSI storage for the data of these servers, and load balancers for load balancing.

Table 5 lists the specifications and usage for each server. For example, in the DB case (6th row), the hardware is HP ProLiant BL460c G1, the server is a physical server, the name is DB, the main usage is OpenStack and Test case DB, the CPU is a Quad-Core Intel Xeon 1600 MHz*2 and the number of cores is 8, RAM is 24 GB, the assigned HDD is 72 GB, and there are four NICs (Network Interface Cards).

Performance measurement results

Figure 6 (a) shows each processing time of automatic verification of Case 1 & tenant pattern A, and Figure 6 (b) shows each processing time of Case 1 & tenant pattern B. In Figure 6 graphs, average execution times

Table 4 Outline of performance measurement conditions

Processing step cases	**Case 1** template and image extraction, template deployment, tester resources preparation, environment info acquisition, patch distribution, test cases execution, virtual resources deletion.	**Case 2** environment information acquisition, patch distribution, test cases execution.	**Case 3** template extraction, template deployment except for volumes, tester resources preparation, environment info acquisition, patch distribution, test cases execution, virtual resources deletion except for volumes.	
User tenant patterns	**Pattern A** 2 virtual machines, 2 volumes, 2 virtual Layer 2 networks, 1 virtual router.	**Pattern B** 2 virtual machines, 2 volumes, 1 virtual Layer 2 network, 1 virtual router, 1 virtual load balancer.		
Selected tests	10 for DB function, 5 for MySQL group, 5 for PostgreSQL group.	10 for Web server function, 5 for Apache group, 5 for nginx group.		
Concurrent processing number	1	3	5	10 20

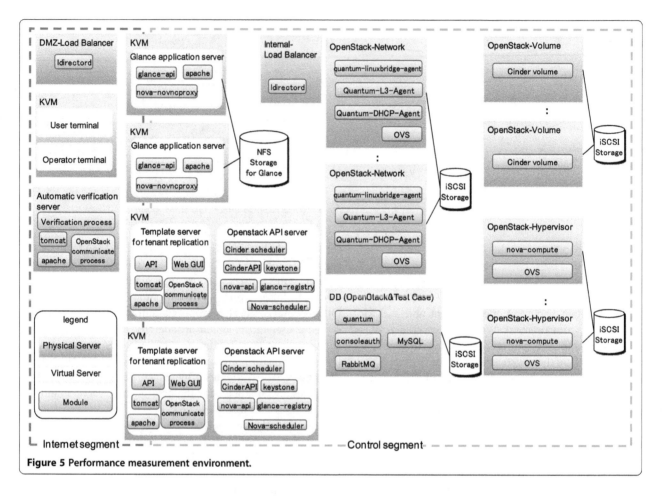

Figure 5 Performance measurement environment.

of concurrent processing are showed. In all cases of concurrent processing (1, 3, and 5), the template and image extraction and template deployment take a lot of time while a patch distribution and test case executions take only 4–5 minutes. It is clear that OpenStack tenant replication processing becomes a bottleneck. Comparing results of tenant pattern A and B, the processing time of pattern B became rather longer because a virtual load balancer resource creation needs much computer resource compared to other virtual resources in OpenStack but processing time characteristics were similar to pattern A.

If it takes a lot of time to extract and deploy templates, the total processing time becomes very long, and service providers cannot distribute the released patches quickly. Therefore, our idea to complete the replications of user environments before patch verifications timing (all virtual resource replications in Case 2 and only volume replications in Case 3) is thought to be an effective countermeasure to this.

Figure 6 (c) shows each processing times for Case 2 & tenant pattern A, and Figure 6 (d) shows each processing times for Case 2 & tenant pattern B. In Case 2, we skip step 2 (tenant replication) and step 8 (replicated virtual resource deletion). In this case, because the OpenStack

load is light, the AVFs can verify multiple user environments in parallel, and it takes only 4–5 minutes for total processing even with 5 concurrent processing.

Figure 6 (e) shows each processing times for Case 3 & tenant pattern A, and Figure 6 (f) shows each processing times for Case 3 & tenant pattern B. In Case 3, we skip volume replications and volume deletions. In this case, AVFs can verify multiple user environments in parallel, and it takes about 85 minutes for total processing even with 20 concurrent processing. Because each tenant has two virtual machines in this test, the results mean about 670 virtual machines (2*20*24*60/85 = 677) can be verified in one day.

These experiments indicate that the Case 3 method is appropriate for many virtual machine verifications because the Case 1 method takes a lot of time to verify, and the Case 2 method needs twice as many servers and twice as much storage for replicated virtual resources.

The Case 3 method is advantageous in that it reduces the cost of keeping virtual resources except for volumes compared to the Case 2 method. User volumes are generally separated into a system volume that stores OS or middleware and a data volume that stores user data. We can reduce replication costs by only replicating system

Table 5 Specifications and usage of each server

Hardware	Physical or VM	Name	Main usage	CPU		RAM (GB)	HDD	NIC
				model name	core		logical (GB)	
HP ProLiantBL460c G6	physical	KVM host		Quad-Core Intel Xeon 2533 MHz×2	8	48	300	4
	VM	OpenStack API server	OpenStack stateless process such as API		assign: 4	assign: 8	assign: 60	
	VM	Template server	template management for tenant replication		assign: 4	assign: 8	assign: 60	
HP ProLiantBL460c G6	physical	KVM host		Quad-Core Intel Xeon 2533 MHz×2	8	48	300	4
	VM	Glance application server	receive requests related to glance		assign: 8	assign: 32	assign: 150	
HP ProLiantBL460c G1	physical	DB	OpenStack & Test case DB	Quad-Core Intel Xeon 1600 MHz×2	8	24	72	4
HP ProLiantBL460c G1	physical	OpenStack-Network	used for OpenStack logicalnetwork resources	Quad-Core Intel Xeon 1600 MHz×2	8	18	72	6
HP ProLiantBL460c G1	physical	OpenStack-Volume	used for OpenStacklogical volume resources	Quad-Core Intel Xeon 1600 MHz×2	8	18	72	6
HP ProLiantBL460c G1	physical	OpenStack-Hypervisor	used for OpenStack VM resources	Quad-Core Intel Xeon 1600 MHz×2	8	24	72	4
IBM HS21	physical	Automatic verification server	proposed automatic verification server	Xeon E5160 3.0GHz×1	2	2	72	1
IBM HS21	physical	DMZ-Load Balancer	Load Balancer for Internet access	Xeon E5160 3.0GHz×1	2	2	72	1
IBM HS21	physical	Internal-Load Balancer	Load Balancer for Internal access	Xeon E5160 3.0GHz×1	2	2	72	1
IBM HS21	physical	KVM host		Xeon E5160 3.0GHz×1	2	2	72	1
	VM	User VM	VM for user terminal		assign: 1	assign: 1	assign: 20	
	VM	Operator VM	VM for operator terminal		assign: 1	assign: 1	assign: 20	
EMC VNX5300	physical	iSCSI storage	iSCSI storage for user volume				500	
EMC VNX5300	physical	NFS storage	NFS storage for Image				500	

volumes because a patch mainly affects the OS or middleware of system volumes. Of course, a verification of user data volume is needed in few cases such as a patch converts data format. For these cases, providers receive requests from users to replicate not only system volumes but also data volumes.

The Case 3 method has a risk of gaps between the actual user volumes and the replicated user volumes. Therefore, when we launch this option verification service, we will replicate user system volumes about once a month and will send patch verification results with the replicated date information to users. (We also plan to set SLA of verification period that IaaS providers verify patches within a certain period).

The storage cost in Case 3 for keeping replica user system volumes is not high compared to the cost of keeping all IaaS resources such as the CPU, RAM, and a global IP address for virtual machines or virtual routers,

because virtual resources except for volumes are only created during about 85 minutes verifications even with 20 concurrent processing. For example, based on service fees of cloudn [17] which is an NTT IaaS cloud service, the additional equipment cost for verifications is about several USD/(virtual machine*month). We believe this cost can be recovered by an option service fee of automatic patch verification.

If we need to verify more than 670 virtual machines within a day, we need to build a new AZ (Availability Zone) to verify virtual machines in parallel with existing AZs. Note that hypervisors or storage are not shared in different AZs, parallel verifications can be executed in different AZs.

Related work

Other types of open source IaaS software in addition to OpenStack [3] are OpenNebula [18], Ecalyptus [19], and CloudStack [5]. OpenNebula is a virtual infrastructure

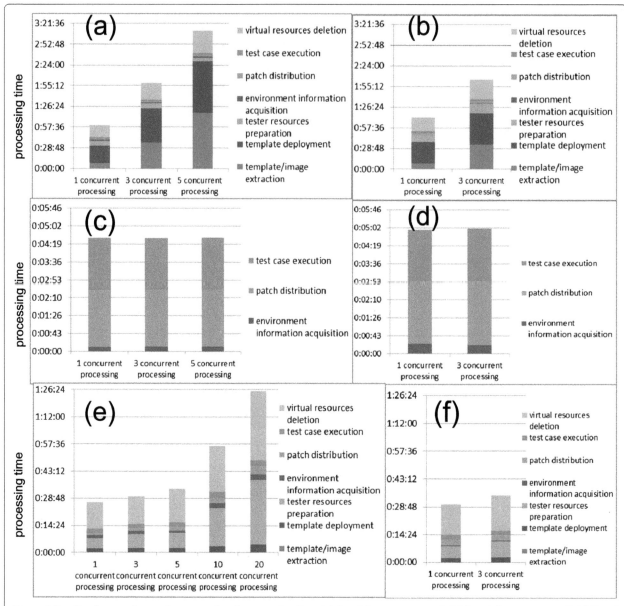

Figure 6 Results of measuring performance of each processing time. (a) Case 1 & tenant pattern A. **(b)** Case 1 & tenant pattern B. **(c)** Case 2 & tenant pattern A. **(d)** Case 2 & tenant pattern B. **(e)** Case 3 & tenant pattern A. **(f)** Case 3 & tenant pattern B.

manager of IaaS function blocks. OpenNebula manages virtual machines, storage, and networks of companies and virtualizes system resources to provide Cloud services. Eucalyptus is characterized by its interoperability with Amazon EC2; moreover, Xen, KVM, or many hypervisors can be used on Eucalyptus. CloudStack functions are similar to OpenStack and Amazon Web Services. CloudStack is developed mainly by Citrix, and many organizations have adopted it because of its usability and degree of completeness. We also contribute to the development of OpenStack itself. Some bug fixes of OpenStack are our contributions.

Amazon CloudFormation [8] and OpenStack Heat [7] are major template deployment technologies on the IaaS Cloud. However, there are no works using these template deployment technologies for automatic patch verifications of virtual machines. We use Heat to replicate user virtual environments to verify patches in the background of users' actual usage. Heat cannot extract a template from an existing tenant, so we use the technique of [14] for template extraction.

Some tools enable automatic tests, for example, Jenkins [12] and Selenium [13]. However, these tools are aimed at executing automatic regression tests during the software development life cycle, and there is no tool to extract test cases dynamically based on each user environment. Our proposed method can conduct different verification test cases for different user environments. The work of [2] enables effective regression tests for Cloud platform development using Jenkins, and it explains that three times the effort is needed for automatic test case preparations with Jenkins compared with executing normal test cases. Our proposed two-tier abstraction of software installed on each virtual machine can reduce test case preparation costs.

CASTE [20] is a cloud-based automatic software test environment. It provides automatic test execution using a concentrated DB with testing environments and test scripts. CASTE requires a lot of test scripts beforehand. Our proposed method can reduce the number of prepared test cases by the two-tier abstraction idea. The method proposed by Willmor and Embury is intended to generate automatic test cases of DB [21]. It needs the specifications of pre-conditions and post-conditions for each DB test case. However, collecting user system specifications is impossible for IaaS virtual machine users. Our approach is to restrict the verification targets to OS or middleware patch normality to reduce users' operation costs.

Conclusion

In this paper, we proposed a technique for automatic verification of software patches for user virtual environments on IaaS Cloud to reduce users' costs of verifying patches. Our proposed method replicates user virtual environments, extracts verification test cases for user virtual environments from a test case DB, distributes patches to virtual machines on the replicated environments, and conducts those test cases automatically on the replicated environments. We implemented our method on OpenStack using Jenkins and evaluated the feasibility of its functions, the effectiveness of reducing test case preparation costs, and the performance of automatic verification.

We confirmed the automatic selection and conduction of verification test cases on user virtual environments by the implemented AVFs. We confirmed the effectiveness of test case preparations by a service provider because our method abstracts software of user virtual machines to software groups and function groups and selects the corresponding verification test cases of each tier. In our evaluation, only 25 test cases were prepared for DB middleware, but 15 test cases were executed respectively for 12 user virtual machines with different kinds of DB middleware (total of 180 test cases were executed). Performance measurements showed that automatic verification of virtual environment replications, patch distributions, and execution of test cases took more than 60 minutes with 1 concurrent processing. However,

those processes took about 85 minutes when we replicated user volumes beforehand even with 20 concurrent processing. The automatic verifications are executed on replicated environments, because it is preferable to run them in the background of a user's actual usage.

In the future, we will implement AVFs of software patches not only for OpenStack but also for other IaaS platforms such as CloudStack and Amazon Web Services. We will also increase the number of test cases for actual use cases of IaaS virtual machines. Then, we will cooperate with IaaS Cloud service providers or VPS (Virtual Private Server) [22] hosting providers to provide managed services in which service providers distribute software patches to user virtual machines using our AVFs.

Competing interests
The author declares that he has no competing interests.

Authors' contributions
YY carried out the automatic verification technology studies, implementations, evaluations and drafted the paper. YY has read and approved the final manuscript.

Authors' information
Yoji Yamato received his B. S., M. S. degrees in physics and Ph.D. degrees in general systems studies from University of Tokyo, Japan in 2000, 2002 and 2009, respectively. He joined NTT Corporation, Japan in 2002. Currently he is a senior research engineer of NTT Software Innovation Center. There, he has been engaged in developmental research of Cloud computing platform, Peer-to-Peer computing and Service Delivery Platform. Dr. Yamato is a member of IEEE and IEICE.

Acknowledgements
We thank Kenichi Sato and Hiroshi Sakai who are managers of this development.

References
1. Rackspace public cloud powered by OpenStack web site, http://www.rackspace.com/cloud/.
2. Yamato Y, Shigematsu N, Miura N (2014) Evaluation of agile software development method for carrier cloud service platform development. IEICE Trans Inf Syst E97-D(No.11):2959–2962
3. OpenStack web site. http://www.openstack.org/.
4. Mell P and Grance T. "The NIST Definition of Cloud Computing," National Institute of Standards and Technology, SP 800-145, Sep. 2011. http://csrc.nist.gov/publications/nistpubs/800-145/SP800-145.pdf.
5. CloudStack web site. http://cloudstack.apache.org/.
6. Amazon Elastic Compute Cloud web site. http://aws.amazon.com/ec2.
7. OpenStack Heat web site. https://wiki.openstack.org/wiki/Heat.
8. Amazon CloudFormation web site. http://aws.amazon.com/cloudformation/.
9. Pfaff B, Pettit J, Koponen T, Amidon K, Casado M, Shenker S (2009) Extending Networking into the Virtualization Layer. In: Proceedings of 8th ACM Workshop on Hot Topics inNetworks (HotNets-VIII)
10. Kivity A, Kamay Y, Laor D, Lublin U, Liguori A (2007) kvm: the Linux virtual machine monitor. In: OLS'07: The 2007 Ottawa Linux Symposium., pp 225–230
11. Barham P, Dragovic B, Fraser K, Hand S, Harris T, Ho A, Neugebauer R, Pratt I, Warfield A (2003) Xen and the art of virtualization. In: Proceedings of the 19th ACM symposium on Operating Systems Principles (SOSP'03)., pp 164–177
12. Jenkins web site. http://jenkins-ci.org/.
13. Selenium web site. http://www.seleniumhq.org/.
14. Yamato Y, Muroi M, Tanaka K and Uchimura M, "Development of Template Management Technology for Easy Deployment of Virtual Resources on

OpenStack," Springer J Cloud Comput, DOI: 10.1186/s13677-014-0007-3, July 2014.

15. Yamato Y, Naganuma S, Uenoyama M, Kato M, Parmer M, Olsen B (2012) Development of low user impact and low cost server migration technology for shared hosting services. IEICE Trans Commun J95-B(No.4):547–555, in Japanese

16. Yamato Y, Nishizawa Y, Muroi M, Tanaka K (2015) Development of resource management server for carrier IaaS services based on OpenStack. J Inf Process 23(1):58–66

17. cloudn web site. http://www.ntt.com/cloudn_e/.

18. Milojicic D, Llorente IM, Montero RS (2011) OpenNebula: A Cloud Management Tool. IEEE Internet Comput 15(2):11–14

19. Nurmi D, Wolski R, Grzegorczyk C, Obertelli G, Soman S, Youseff L, Zagorodnov D (2008) The Eucalyptus Open-source Cloud-computing System. In: Proceedings of Cloud Computing and Its Applications

20. Peng F, Deng B, Qi C (2011) CASTE: a Cloud-Based Automatic Soft'ware Test Environment", World Academy of Science, Engineering & Technology. Issue 71:1502–1505

21. Willmor D, Embury SM (2006) An intensional approach to the specification of test cases for database applications. In: Proceedings of the 28the interanational conference on Software engineering., pp 102–111, ACM

22. Kamp P-H, Watson RNM (2000) Jails: Confining the Omnipotent root. In: Proceedings of the 2nd International SANE Conference

## 10

Utilising stream reasoning techniques to underpin an autonomous framework for cloud application platforms

Rustem Dautov[1]*, Iraklis Paraskakis[1] and Mike Stannett[2]

Abstract

As cloud application platforms (CAPs) are reaching the stage where the human effort required to maintain them at an operational level is unsupportable, one of the major challenges faced by the cloud providers is to develop appropriate mechanisms for run-time monitoring and adaptation, to prevent cloud application platforms from quickly dissolving into a non-reliable environment. In this context, the application of intelligent approaches to Autonomic Clouds may offer promising opportunities. In this paper we present an approach to providing cloud platforms with autonomic capabilities, utilising techniques from the Semantic Web and Stream Reasoning research fields. The main idea of this approach is to encode values, monitored within cloud application platforms, using Semantic Web languages, which then allows us to integrate semantically-enriched observation streams with static ontological knowledge and apply intelligent reasoning. Using such run-time reasoning capabilities, we have developed a conceptual architecture for an autonomous framework and describe a prototype solution we have constructed which implements this architecture. Our prototype is able to perform analysis and failure diagnosis, and suggest further adaptation actions. We report our experience in utilising the Stream Reasoning technique in this context as well as further challenges that arise out of our work.

Keywords: Cloud computing; Autonomic computing; Monitoring; Analysis; Stream reasoning

Introduction

Cloud computing impacts upon almost every aspect of daily life and the economy – pervasive cloud services are revolutionising the way we do business, maintain our health, and educate and entertain ourselves. Along with recent advances in computing, networking, software, hardware and mobile technologies, however, come emerging challenges to our ability to ensure that cyberspace resources and services are properly regulated, maintained and secured. The ubiquitous insertion of increasingly automated processes and procedures into traditional personal, scientific and business activities dictates a need to design such systems carefully, so as to guarantee that these associated challenges are properly met. Managing such large scale systems effectively inevitably means that

resources will need to become increasingly "autonomous", capable of managing themselves – and cooperating with one another - without manual intervention.

In particular, the Platform-as-a-Service (PaaS) segment of cloud computing has been steadily growing over the past several years, with more and more software developers choosing cloud application platforms as convenient ecosystems for developing, deploying, testing and maintaining their software. Following the principles of Service-Oriented Computing (SOC), such platforms offer their subscribers a wide selection of pre-existing and reusable services, ready to be seamlessly integrated into users' applications. However, by offering such a flexible model for application development, in which software assets are assembled from existing components just like a Lego® construction set, cloud platform providers increasingly find themselves in a situation where the ever-growing complexity of entangled cloud environments poses new challenges as to how such systems should be monitored and managed.

*Correspondence: rdautov@seerc.org
[1] South-East European Research Centre, International Faculty of the University of Sheffield, City College, 24 Proxenou Koromila Street, 54646 Thessaloniki, Greece
Full list of author information is available at the end of the article

In this context, we present a novel approach to developing autonomic cloud application platforms, based on our vision of treating cloud platforms as sensor networks [1]. Our approach makes intelligent re-use of existing solution strategies and products (specifically, Stream Reasoning and the Semantic Web technology stack), to create a general-purpose autonomous framework. In this paper we consider how cloud application platform providers can benefit from our approach. As will be explained in more detail below, our approach relies on annotating monitored values with semantic descriptions, thereby enabling the framework to combine observation streams with static ontological knowledge and perform run-time formal reasoning. This in turn opens promising opportunities for performing run-time analysis, problem diagnosis, and suggesting further adaptation actions. We also discuss potential shortcomings of our approach and consider ways of overcoming them.

The rest of the paper is organised as follows. Section "Background and motivation" is dedicated to background information and motivation of the research presented in this paper. It briefs the reader on the current state of the art and known limitations in service-based cloud environments and also summarises existing research efforts in the area of managing the ever-expanding complexity of cloud application platforms. Section "Related technology: stream reasoning" introduces the reader to Stream Reasoning – a promising combination of traditional stream processing systems with Semantic Web technologies. This section also explains why these techniques are suitable for developing monitoring and analysis mechanisms. In Section "Description of the framework" we present the autonomous framework: we present a high-level conceptual architecture based on the MAPE-K reference model, then describe the prototype implementation of the framework, and finally summarise our initial experimental results.

Background and motivation

A fundamental goal of cloud computing is to achieve economies of scale by providing seemingly unlimited access to computing resources, while at the same time avoiding the sunk costs associated with acquiring dedicated systems and personnel. The core underlying architecture of the cloud is, accordingly, one of service-oriented computing (SOC): services are provided as basic building blocks from which applications can be constructed both rapidly and cheaply, without compromising on reliability or security [2]. Today's providers consequently need to host an ever-increasing number of online services, and make these available both reliably and securely to large numbers of users spread across a wide range of geographical locations. Meeting these demands has naturally shaped the way services are provided: it has long been recognised

that the 'service cloud' will ultimately comprise a federated collection of resources distributed across multiple infrastructure providers [3], and cloud application platforms can be expected to play an important role in this context. Creating and maintaining the required infrastructure is, inevitably, an increasingly complex issue, and one that needs careful consideration.

As in all industries, cloud service providers face the problem of monitoring their customers' changing needs, and responding in an appropriate and timely manner. This is particularly problematic in the context of cloud services, because these are, by definition, targeted at users whose needs can be expected to change both rapidly and, at times, dramatically. Providers therefore need to monitor service usage in real time, so as to identify bottlenecks and failures that might undermine their ability to honour their customers' service-level agreements (SLAs) – and having identified 'broken' services, these need to be replaced seamlessly with new services whose behaviour is, in some contractually meaningful sense, equivalent to those being replaced. Given that services also need to be ubiquitous and available to customers using them in new and potentially unexpected ways, it is clear that cloud services will need to become increasingly autonomous and self-describing, reusable, and highly interoperable. This is particularly important at the PaaS level, given the large and increasing number of generic platform services and apps that are available, offering everything from basic calculator functionality to multi-environment distributed business processing [4].

Such cloud platforms, which not only provision customers with an operating system and run-time environment, but additionally offer a complete supporting environment to develop and deploy service-based applications, including a range of generic, reliable, composable and reusable services, are known as cloud application platforms (CAPs) [5,6] (see Figure 1). By offering integrated services in this way, CAPs further reduce the human effort and capital expenses associated with developing complex software systems. This means that software developers – CAP end users – can concentrate on their immediate, domain-specific tasks, rather than expend effort on, for example, developing their own authentication or e-billing mechanisms – instead, existing components are offered, managed and maintained by the CAP. The integration of users' applications with platform services usually takes place by means of APIs, through which software developers can easily couple necessary services with their applications and also perform further service management. Some of the most prominent and commercially successful CAPs already provision their subscribers with tens of built-ins and third-party services. For example, Google App Engine [7] offers 38 services, and Microsoft Azure [8] provides 20 built-in services and 35 add-ons (i.e., third-party services

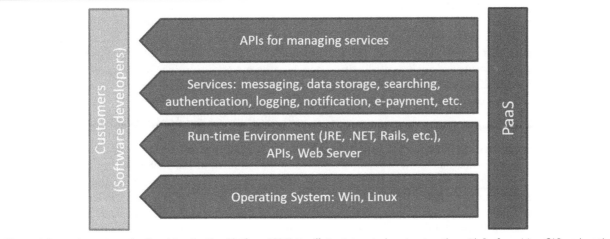

Figure 1 General structure of a Cloud Application Platform (CAP). By offering integrated services together with PaaS provision, CAPs reduce the costs associated with complex development.

registered with the platform). Appealing opportunities to significantly decrease time to market, introduced by the combination of cloud computing and SOC, has been attracting more and more attention over the past several years. Gartner forecasts that the PaaS market will grow from $900 M (in 2011) to $2.9B (in 2016) with the aPaaS (application Platform-as-a-Service) as the largest segment [9]. IDC, another leading IT market research and analysis agency, predicts that in 2014 "value will start to migrate "up the stack", from IaaS to PaaS and from generic PaaS to data-optimized PaaS" [10].

From SOC to clouds and its consequences

Given the continuing shift towards cloud computing, the complexity of next-generation service-based cloud environments is soon expected to outgrow our ability to manage them manually [11,12]. For instance, Heroku [13] already offers more than 120 different 'add-ons', including such services as data storage, searching, e-mail and SMS notification, logging and caching, and more. These can be re-used and integrated by users, generating complex interrelationships between services and user applications – indeed, add-ons are already being replicated across multiple computational instances, coupled to more than a million deployed applications [14,15].

Maintaining the ever-expanding software environment of a CAP is, consequently, a major challenge. Platform providers must be able to monitor the resulting "tangled" environment for failures and sub-optimal behaviours, while simultaneously addressing the needs of customer SLAs. They must be able to exercise control over all critical activities taking place on the platform, including the introduction of new services and applications and the modification of existing ones to maintain the platform's and deployed applications' stability and performance [16].

As we have argued above, this requires the introduction of autonomic features to the system, thereby allowing services, and the platform as a whole, to adapt their behaviours as required, following the principles of self-management, self-tuning, self-configuration, self-diagnosis, and self-healing [17].

While cloud providers arguably offer suitable adaptation mechanisms at the Infrastructure-as-a-Service (IaaS) level [18] - mainly dealing with load-balancing and elasticity - the same does not appear to be true at the PaaS level, where providers do not currently provide prompt, timely, and customisable self-management mechanisms [4] – mechanisms which would support intelligent, flexible, prompt and timely analysis of monitored values and detection of potential failures. At the PaaS level, a vast stream of data is constantly being generated and processed by a far wider range of agents than are present at the IaaS level, including a wide variety of platform components, generic and third-party services, deployed applications, and more.

For instance, WhatsApp – the world's leading instant messaging application for mobile devices [19] – is hosted on Google App Engine, utilises its XMPP-compatible chat messaging service and reports activity of 400 million monthly active users [20]. Heroku also reports several notable examples [21]: *PageLever*, an analytics platform for measuring a brand's presence on Facebook, processes 500 million Facebook API requests/month, which are then stored in a database. *Quiz Creator* saw activity peaks of over 10,000 user requests/minute. *Playtomic*, an application for run-time game analytics, claims to have around 15-20 million gamers generating over a billion events per day at the rate of 12,000 requests/second. Heroku itself hosts over one million deployed applications at a smaller scale and offers more than one hundred add-ons (20 of which are purely concerned with data storage). As these examples demonstrate, systems as dynamic as CAPs must handle numerous rapidly-generated streams of raw data at an unpredictable rate – that is, they must be capable of performing continuous monitoring and analysis of all critical activities taking place within the platform in order to maintain the overall stability of the platform and hosted applications.

State of the art in cloud self-management

Maintaining cloud environments has been a task of paramount importance ever since the emergence of cloud computing. Such complex environments clearly dictate the need for automated monitoring and analysis of vast amounts of dynamically flowing data so as to perform, for example, resource planning and management, billing, troubleshooting, SLA and performance management, security management, etc. [18].

According to [22,23], a cloud can be logically represented in terms of seven interconnected layers: facility, network, hardware, operating system (OS), middleware, application and user. Accordingly, monitoring and analysis activities can be performed at each of these layers or in a cross-layer manner. Based on this taxonomy, Aceto et al. [18] recently surveyed 28 existing cloud monitoring tools and solutions with respect to such criteria as scalability, timeliness, autonomicity, adaptability, reliability, accuracy, resilience, extensibility, intrusiveness and others. Most of the analysed works are specifically designed to perform low-level monitoring [24] (at facility, network, hardware and OS levels) – that is, to monitor the Infrastructure-as-a-Service (IaaS) level of cloud computing. Performing monitoring activities at this level primarily enables cloud providers to adapt to varying volumes and types of user requests by allocating the incoming workload across computational instances (i.e., load balancing), or by reserving and releasing computational resources upon demand (i.e., elasticity) [25,26].

However, more sophisticated adaptation scenarios at higher levels (middleware and application), such as modifying the actual structure and/or behaviour of a deployed application at run-time, are much more difficult to automate, and are currently beyond the capabilities of common CAPs. Unfortunately, at the moment there seem to be no self-management mechanisms of such a kind at the Platform-as-a-Service (PaaS) level. Even though there are several approaches which perform monitoring at the middleware level, the values they collect are primarily used to perform adaptations at theIaaS, rather than PaaS, level – for example, instead of replacing a "slow" service with an equivalent (but faster) alternative (PaaS-level adaptation), additional computational resources are provisioned to the given service (IaaS-level adaptation).

An alternative approach to PaaS-level adaptations performed by CAP providers is to require deployed applications to implement their own built-in adaptation functionality. As with IaaS solutions, this means that platform providers do not offer solutions which would allow hosted applications to modify their internal structure and/or behaviour at run-time by adapting to changing context (e.g., by substituting one service for another). Instead, this task has been shifted to the Software-as-a-Service (SaaS) level – that is, it has been left to software developers, the target customers of the PaaS offerings, to implement self-adaptation logic within their applications.

Given these considerations, we believe that self-adaptation capabilities at the PaaS level itself, and in CAPs in particular, are as yet immature and not well theorised. It is our belief that self-management at the PaaS level is equally important, and that development of self-adaptation mechanisms at this level is essential in order to prevent cloud platforms from dissolving into "tangled" and unreliable environments. Our goal in this paper is to present and justify one possible strategy for addressing this gap.

Related technology: stream reasoning

Since the early 2000s, when data volumes started exploding, the challenge of data analytics has grown considerably. Nowadays, the problem is not just about giant data volumes ("Big Data") – it is also about an extreme diversity of data types, delivered at various speeds and frequencies [27]. In the modern world, heterogeneous data streams are to be found everywhere – sensors networks, social media sites, digital pictures and videos, purchase transaction records, and mobile phone GPS signals, to name a few [28] – and on-the-fly processing of newly generated data has become an increasingly difficult challenge. Two important aspects of traditional database management systems make them unsuitable for processing continuously streamed data from geographically distributed sources at unpredictable rates, so as to obtain timely responses to complex queries [29], namely: (i) data is (persistently) stored and indexed before it can be processed, and (ii) data is processed only when explicitly queried by users, i.e. asynchronously with respect to its arrival. In contrast, streamed data cannot sensibly be stored for any length of time if it is to be used for real-time adaptation; and we cannot rely on users issuing one-off queries. Rather, we need some way for adaptation to be triggered automatically, as and when problems arise.

To cope with the unbounded nature of streams and temporal constraints, so-called continuous query languages [30] have been developed to extend conventional SQL semantics with the notion of windows. This approach restricts querying to a specific window of concern which consists of a subset of statements recently observed on the stream, while older information is (usually) ignored, thereby allowing traditional relational operators to be applied [31].

The concepts of unbounded data streams and windows are visualised in Figure 2. The small circles represent tuples continuously arriving over time and constituting a data stream, whereas the thick rectangular frame illustrates the window operator applied to this unbounded sequence of tuples. As time passes and new values are appended to the data stream, old values are pushed out of the specified window, i.e. they are deemed irrelevant and may be discarded (unless there is a need for storing historical data for later analysis).

Stream Reasoning goes one step further by enhancing continuous queries with run-time reasoning support – that is, with capabilities to infer additional, implicit knowledge based on already given, explicit facts. The concept was introduced by Barbieri et al. [32], who defined it as "reasoning in real time on huge and possibly noisy data streams, to support a large number of concurrent decision processes". In the Big Data paradigm, for example, where data streams are becoming increasingly pervasive, the combination of stream processing techniques with dynamically generated data, distributed across the Web, requires new ways of coping with the typical openness and heterogeneity of the Web environment – in this context, Semantic Web technologies facilitate data integration in open environments, and thus help to overcome these problems by using uniform machine-readable descriptions to resolve heterogeneities across multiple data streams [33]. The primary segment of Big Data processing, where Stream Reasoning is being adopted is the Semantic Sensor Web [34] – "an attempt to enable more expressive representation and formal analysis of avalanches of sensor values in such domains as traffic surveillance, environmental monitoring, house automation and tracking systems, by encoding sensor observation data with Semantic Web languages" [35]. Other problem domains, where Stream Reasoning techniques are expected to be effective, include, e.g., analysis of social media streams, understanding users' behaviour based on their click streams, and analysis of trends in medical records to predict spread of a disease over the world. [36].

As Semantic Web technologies are mainly based on Description Logics, their application to data stream processing also offers new opportunities to perform reasoning tasks over continuously and rapidly changing flows of information. In particular, Stream Reasoning utilises and benefits from the following Semantic Web technologies:

- Resource Description Framework (RDF), as a uniform format for representing streamed heterogeneous data as a collection of (subject, predicate, object) triples using a vocabulary defined in an OWL ontology;
- OWL ontologies and SWRL rules, as a source of static background knowledge. OWL ontologies may also act as a vocabulary of terms for defining RDF triples;
- SPARQL-based continuous query languages, as a way of querying RDF streams and performing reasoning tasks by combining them with the static background knowledge.

As a result, several prominent Stream Reasoning approaches have emerged, including, e.g., C-SPARQL [37], CQELS [38], ETALIS [39], and SPARQLstream [30]. These systems aim at preserving the core value of data stream processing, i.e. processing streamed data in a timely fashion, while providing a number of additional features [33]:

- Support for advanced reasoning: depending on the extent to which Stream Reasoning systems support reasoning, it is possible not only to detect patterns of events (as Complex Event Processing already does [29]), but in addition to perform more sophisticated

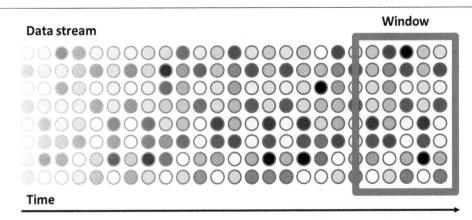

Figure 2 Querying of streamed data. Continuous query languages address the problem of querying an unbounded data stream by focussing on a well-defined window of interest.

and intelligent detection of failures by inferring implicit knowledge based on pre-defined facts and rules (i.e., static background knowledge).

- Integration of static background knowledge with streamed data: it is possible to match data stream values against a static background knowledge base (usually represented as an ontology), containing various facts and rules. This separation of concerns allows for seamless and transparent modification of the analysis rules constituting the static knowledge base.

- Support for expressive queries and complex schemas: ontologies also serve as a common vocabulary for defining complex queries. This means that the classes and properties constituting an ontology provide "building blocks" and may be used for defining queries of any required expressivity.

- Support for logical, data and temporal operators: to cope with the unlimited nature of data streams, Stream Reasoning systems extend conventional SQL-based logical and data operators with temporal operators. This allows us to limit an unbounded stream to a specific window, and also to detect events following one after another chronologically.

- Support for time and tuple windows: windows may be specified either by time-frame, or else by the number of entries to be retained, regardless of arrival time. Taken together, these features facilitate evaluation of expressive queries over streamed data and, as a result, have the potential to allow us to benefit from increased analysis capabilities when processing data streams, such as monitored values within CAPs. However, no solution is ever perfect, and Stream Reasoning at its current state is not an exception. Accordingly, in order to realise its potential in the context of analysing large data streams of CAPs, we need to address following shortcomings [35]:

- Need for unified data representation format: before formal reasoning can be applied, heterogeneous values have to be represented in a common format – RDF. Although this process can be seen as a way of tackling, e.g., the "variety" aspect of Big Data [40], it requires establishing mappings between source data formats and their RDF representations, which has to be performed manually.

- No standards yet: the lack of common standards resulted in several independent and hardly interoperable approaches.

- Immature reasoning support: as opposed to static SPARQL reasoning capabilities, querying over dynamic data streams with the reasoning support is not fully implemented yet, and the conventional SPARQL 2.0 specification is not supported by any of the existing Stream Reasoning approaches.

- Low performance: the Stream Reasoning research area is still in its infancy, and suffers from low performance. Since expressivity of a query language is known to be inversely related to its performance [33], evaluation of rich and complex queries always bears the penalty of performance, which is particularly critical when performing data analytics on very large data streams.

- Low scalability: one of the main shortcomings of formal reasoning, both static and stream, is that it is not linearly scalable [41]. This means that the larger the knowledge base over which reasoning is performed, the slower this process is. In the context of analysing large data sets within CAPs, this shortcoming becomes a major concern and cannot be neglected.

In summary, Stream Reasoning is not a "silver bullet" – its shortcomings, unless properly addressed, may outweigh its positive aspects and seriously hinder the implementation of the autonomous framework.

Description of the framework

In this section we explain the underlying organisation of the autonomous framework, starting from a high-level description of the architecture and then going into implementation details. Through our experiments with Heroku, we discovered that simply deploying the autonomous framework to a cloud is not enough. Shortcomings associated with Stream Reasoning required us to address unexpected performance and scalability issues relating to our approach, as will be further discussed in Subsection "Evaluation and future work" below.

Conceptual architecture

We will describe our approach by sketching out a high-level architecture of the framework, taking the established MAPE-K framework [17] as our underlying model for self-adaptation (see Figure 3). In order to support both self-awareness and context-awareness of the managed elements, we need to employ some kind of architectural model describing the adaptation-relevant aspects of the cloud environment (e.g., platform components, available resources, connections between them, etc.) and the managed elements (e.g., entry-points for monitoring and execution). We therefore used OWL ontologies to represent the self-reflective knowledge of the system. Such an architectural model also serves as a common vocabulary of terms shared across the whole managed system, and corresponds to the Knowledge component of the MAPE-K model. Moreover, our ontological classes and properties, as explained below, also serve as "building blocks" for creating RDF streams, SPARQL queries and SWRL rules.

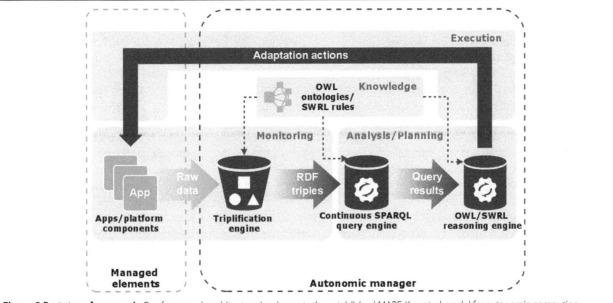

Figure 3 Prototype framework. Our framework architecture implements the established MAPE-K control model for autonomic computing.

Within the framework, raw data generated by sensors passes through three main processing steps:

- The triplification engine is a software component responsible for consuming and "homogenising" the representation of incoming raw observation values. The use of time-stamped RDF triples, incorporating OWL-based subjects, predicates and objects, promotes human-readability while at the same time allowing us to exploit the extensive capabilities of SPARQL query languages.
- The continuous SPARQL query engine is a software component which supports situation assessment by taking as input the continuous RDF data streams generated by the triplification engine and evaluating them against pre-registered continuous SPARQL queries. By registering appropriate SPARQL query against a data stream, we are able to detect critical situations – for example, service failures, high response time from services, overloaded message queues and network request time outs – with minimal delay: the continuous SPARQL engine will trigger as soon as RDF triples in the stream match the WHERE clause of any registered query. Using SPARQL and RDF triples in this way also makes it possible to benefit from inference capabilities – in addition to querying data and detecting complex event patterns, we are able to perform run-time analysis by reasoning over RDF triples [35]. Employing existing RDF streaming engines with "on-the-fly" analysis of constantly flowing observations from hundreds of sensors is expected to help us achieve near real-time

behaviour [36] of the adaptation framework (as opposed to "static" approaches where monitored data is first stored on the hard drive before being analysed) – a key requirement when developing an adaptation mechanism.

- The OWL/SWRL reasoning engine is the software component responsible for generating a final diagnosis and an appropriate adaptation plan whenever a critical condition is detected, a process which typically requires rather complex reasoning over the possible roots of a problem, and the identification of multiple potential adaptation strategies. We address this challenge (at least partially) using OWL ontologies and SWRL rules, since these provide sufficient expressivity to define adaptation policies [42], while at the same time avoiding the potentially error-prone and intensive task of implementing our own analysis engines from scratch. Instead, we apply the built-in reasoning capabilities of OWL and SWRL, so that the routine of reasoning over (i.e., analysing) a set of situations and adaptation alternatives is achieved using an existing, tested, and highly optimised mechanism. This also enhances opportunities for reuse, automation and reliability [12].

Prototype implementation

As a first step towards a proof of concept, a prototype solution implementing the conceptual architecture has been developed. As a test bed for our experiments we have chosen Heroku – a well-established and trustable cloud PaaS offering with sufficient levels of support and documentation for our purposes. As outlined in Section "Background and motivation", Heroku qualifies as a cloud application platform, and it offers a range of add-on services to experiment with. The main criteria used when choosing services for our experiments were: (i) pervasive use by deployed applications to make sure that the service is widely used and thus emits enough data to be monitored and analysed, (ii) easy and straightforward provisioning of the service, and (iii) presence of clear and simple metrics for monitoring. Accordingly, from the more than 100 Heroku add-ons available, we chose for our experiments an implementation of the RabbitMQ messaging queue service called CloudAMQP [43] – a widely adopted solution for decoupled communication between various components of cloud-based distributed applications. We then developed the following simple use-case scenario, both to test the viability of our general approach, and to identify directions for further work and experimentation.

Let us consider a typical cloud-based scenario, in which worker applications responsible for background processing of various tasks are decoupled from the main application by means of a messaging queue service. At some point, the job queue gets overloaded and workers spend too much time processing their tasks. This may happen, for example, on a cheaper subscription plan when the rate of incoming messages is faster than the queue

service can write to disk, or the volume of incoming messages exceeds the available memory [44]. In order to satisfy SLAs we wish to detect such situations in a timely manner and, where possible, launch additional worker instances to offload the job queue. In investigating this scenario our main focus has been on the monitoring and analysis steps of the MAPE-K model, whereas the planning and execution steps have been left aside (this example is intended only to demonstrate the viability of our approach, and is correspondingly simplified).

Figure 4 shows the architecture of the prototype and illustrates the steps constituting the use-case scenario. The client application sends tasks to the RabbitMQ job queue, which are then picked up and processed by an available worker instance on a first-come first-served basis. Once a job task is processed, the worker acknowledges the queue of accomplishing the task.

Accordingly, in order to support proper functioning of this simple application system, we are interested in monitoring the following metrics associated with the messaging queue:

(i) Size of the message queue (i.e., current number of messages in the queue).
(ii) Message queuing time (i.e., difference between the time when a message is published to the queue and the time when it is consumed by a worker).

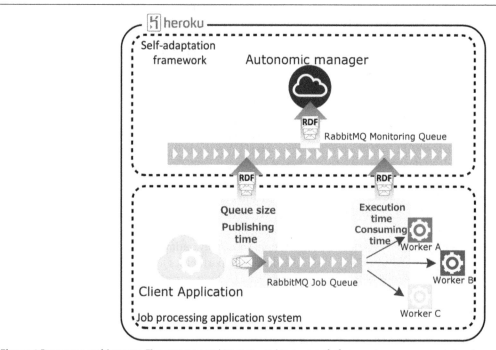

Figure 4 Prototype architecture. The prototype architecture used in our proof-of-concept use-case scenario involves real-time monitoring of service performance by an Autonomic Manager. The Autonomic Manager responds to critical situations at the PaaS level by identifying when 'slow' services should be replaced by faster alternatives.

(iii) Workers' execution time (i.e., time between the moment when a worker picks up a message from the queue and the moment when it acknowledges the queue of accomplishing the task).

We chose these particular metrics because they are easily monitored within Heroku (hence suitable for test purposes), and when violated they unambiguously indicate a critical situation. Simultaneous violation of threshold values of these three metrics represents a critical situation where the current number of worker instances is not able to cope with the workload, so that additional instances have to be launched to prevent the whole system from crashing.

To implement this simple use-case, we used Java as a programming language, Eclipse IDE (with the Heroku plug-in) for coding and testing, and Protégé IDE [45] for developing the OWL ontology and SWRL rules. We also used OWL API [46] to create, manipulate and reason over the OWL ontology and SWRL rules programmatically, and the C-SPARQL library [47] to create and query RDF streams.

The main components we implemented were:

- The RabbitMQ job queue – used to decouple the client application from workers, and for transferring tasks. The CloudAMQP implementation of RabbitMQ, offered by Heroku, is easy to use and configure within Java applications.
- Client – a GUI application responsible for sending jobs to the corresponding queue. From the GUI it is possible to specify the number of parallel threads sending tasks to the queue.
- Workers – computational instances responsible for picking tasks from the queue, executing them and notifying the queue when the task is accomplished.
- Sensors – pieces of programming code responsible for measuring: (i) size of the message queue – every time the client sends a new task to the queue, it receives back the current number of awaiting messages; (ii) time when a new task is published and time when it is consumed by a first available worker; (iii) workers' execution times – workers calculate their own execution time by subtracting the time when a job was picked up from the queue from the time when it was processed. The measured values are then transformed into RDF triples using terms from the OWL vocabulary, and sent to the RabbitMQ monitoring queue. The following three samples demonstrate how data, generated by sensors as described in the above-mentioned cases, is represented in the RDF format (where ex is shorthand notation for a purpose-built ontology containing corresponding classes and properties):

```
(i)   ex:queue13 ex:hasQueueSize ex:QS81
      ex:QS81    ex:hasValue "15500"^^xsd:int
(ii)  ex:task782 ex:isPublishedAt ex:time231
      ex:time231 ex:hasValue "11:12:13.555"^^xsd:time
      ex:task782 ex:isConsumedAt ex:time298
      ex:time298 ex:hasValue "11:12:19.213"^^xsd:time
(iii) ex:worker7 ex:hasExecutionTime ex:ET98
      ex:ET98    ex:hasValue "11.54"^^xsd:float
```

The main components constituting the monitoring framework are:

- The RabbitMQ monitoring queue – used to collect monitored values of the job queue workload and workers' response times.
- Autonomic Manager – this is the core component of the framework responsible for collecting and analysing monitored values, detecting/predicting critical conditions, and generating corresponding adaptation actions. By registering appropriate C-SPARQL queries against the monitoring queue, the Autonomic Manager is notified as soon as the RDF triples in the stream satisfy the WHERE clause of the query. Let us now consider the following queries for each of the monitored metrics:

```
(i)   REGISTER QUERY QueueSizeQuery
      AS PREFIX ex:<http://seerc.org/ontology.owl#>
      SELECT ?queue ?qs ?v
      FROM STREAM <http://seerc.org/stream>
          [RANGE 1m STEP 1s]
      WHERE {?queue ex:hasQueueSize ?qs .
          ?qs ex:hasValue ?v . FILTER (?v >= 10000)}
```

This query is triggered whenever the number of awaiting messages exceeds 10000.

```
(ii)  REGISTER QUERY QueuingTimeQuery
      AS PREFIX ex:<http://seerc.org/ontology.owl#>
      SELECT ?q ?qs ?v
      FROM STREAM <http://seerc.org/stream>
          [RANGE 1m STEP 1s]
      WHERE {?task ex:isPublishedAt ?t1 .
          ?t1 ex:hasValue ?v1 .
          ?task ex:isConsumedAt ?t2 .
          ?t2 ex:hasValue ?v2 .
          FILTER ((?v2 - ?v1) > 10000)}
```

This query is triggered whenever the difference between the time when a message is published and the time when it is consumed exceeds 10 seconds.

```
(iii) REGISTER QUERY ExecutionTimeQuery
      AS PREFIX ex: <http://seerc.org/ontology.owl#>
      SELECT ?worker ?t ?v
      FROM STREAM <http://seerc.org/stream>
          [RANGE 1m STEP 1s]
      WHERE {?worker ex:hasExecutiontime ?t .
          ?t ex:hasValue ?v . FILTER (?v >= 5000)}
```

This query is triggered whenever the execution time of a worker exceeds 5 seconds.

Querying over the RDF stream allows the autonomic manager to detect if there are too many messages in the queue, and to identify execution time violations. Once queries are triggered, fetched values are added to the OWL ontology in order for traditional static reasoning to be applied. The Autonomic Manager is able to deduce that the overloaded queue and workers represent a critical situation for which a possible adaptation strategy would be the launching of additional worker instances. These activities are performed by reasoning over the OWL ontology and SWRL rules, which are declaratively defined by platform administrators at design-time with respect to given SLAs, and can be modified at run-time if needed. The following is illustrates a typical SWRL rule, which allows the Autonomic Manager, based on the violated values received at the querying stage, to deduce that the observed critical situation requires some adaptation actions – that is, that additional worker instances have to be launched:

```
Worker(?w), Queue(?q), isSubscribedTo(?w, ?q),
  hasQueueSize(?q, ?qs), hasValue(?qs, ?v1),
  greaterThan(?v1, 10000), Task(?t),
  hasQueuingTime(?t, ?qt), hasValue(?qt, ?v2),
  greaterThan(?v2, 10000),
  hasExecutionTime(?t, ?et), hasValue(?et, ?v3),
  greaterThan(?v3, 5000)
    -> needsAdditionalInstances(?w, true)
```

We have run initial experiments on Heroku's Cedar stack using a free account – each computational instance (or dyno in Heroku terminology) has 512 MB of RAM and 1GB of swap space (1.5 GB RAM in total), and 4 CPU cores (Intel Xeon X5550 2.67 GHz). Single instances of the autonomic manager and the client application and three worker instances were deployed on separate dynos. To simulate the critical workload on the queue we: (i) completely turned workers off to let messages accumulate to reach critical level (the threshold level we specified in a corresponding C-SPARQL queue was set to 10000 messages); and (ii) made workers "sleep" for 1000 ms every time they picked a task from the queue (the threshold level of message queuing time was set to 10000 ms, and the threshold level of workers' execution times was set to 5000 ms). These initial experiments show that we are able to detect all critical conditions within 1 second – this is the minimum time frame between two consecutive evaluations of registered queries against the data stream which is allowed by the current implementation of the C-SPARQL engine.

Evaluation and future work

Unfortunately, as the number of incoming RDF triples increases, the performance of the framework decreases.

As explained in Section "Related technology: stream reasoning", Stream Reasoning on its own currently suffers from performance and scalability issues. Existing experiments suggest that with the increase of RDF data sets from 10K to 1M triples, the average execution time of C-SPARQL queries increases at least 50 times [38]. Such performance drops make our framework potentially incapable of monitoring and analysing large data sets within CAPs and need to be addressed, especially if at some later stage we wish to expand the technique to handle Big Data scenarios.

A possible solution to this problem, to be investigated in the next stage of our work, is to parallelise reasoning tasks across several instances of the Autonomic Manager [48] by fragmenting incoming data streams into sub-streams, so that each instance only deals with a subset of the incoming values. Unlike static data fragmentation, where the set of values is finite, partitioning of streamed data, due to its unbounded nature and unpredictable rate, is associated with a risk of splitting semantically connected RDF triples into separate streams, which in turn may result in incorrect deductions. Therefore, careful design of the fragmentation logic is crucial in order to confirm that no valuable data is misplaced or lost.

In order to address this challenge, there already exist several technologies, both commercial (e.g., Oracle Fast Data solutions [49] and IBM InfoSphere Streams [50]) and open-source (e.g. Apache S4 [51] or Storm [52]). These solutions provide infrastructure and tooling in order to handle massive data streams, and as the next step we will integrate our autonomous framework with one of these data stream solutions. We anticipate that this will allow us to address two of the five Stream Reasoning challenges identified in Section "Related technology: stream reasoning", namely, scalability and performance.

We also want to emphasise that we expect our main contribution to be in the area of prompt, dynamic and intelligent analysis of the monitored values (which is quite difficult to benchmark), rather than in terms of performance. We also anticipate that further on-going developments in Stream Reasoning will see the resolution of two further shortcomings – the immature reasoning support and the lack of standards. The requirement to homogenise data and represent it in RDF format is expected to be less problematic. There already exist tools for converting data stored in relational databases into RDF, using special mapping languages (e.g., R2RML [53]), and analogous tools can be envisaged for RDF stream generation.

Our prototype case study suggests that once we have implemented the whole MAPE-K chain for a small number of key parameters (e.g., the number of messages in the queue, message queuing time, and the execution times from workers), the introduction of additional monitoring parameters becomes a trivial task, and does not necessarily bring scientific contribution. Rather than create a comprehensive adaptation framework which would monitor and analyse all possible metrics of a cloud platform, our future research activities will therefore focus on further enriching the background knowledge base (i.e. OWL/SWRL policies) to see what kind of knowledge can be inferred from a limited number of observed parameters to support the analysis and diagnosis of potential failures.

We also plan to experiment with other continuous query engines, such as CQELS and SPARQLstream, and compare them in terms of the analytical support they can offer. At the moment, on-the-fly reasoning support of continuous SPARQL query languages is quite limited (at least compared to traditional static SPARQL) [35], and depends on the supported entailment regimes of particular query languages. Research in the direction of bridging the gap between static and dynamic reasoning support in SPARQL queries is continuing, and we can also reasonably hope for truly run-time reasoning to appear in the relatively near future.

Conclusion

In this paper we have presented a novel approach to enhancing cloud platforms with self-managing capabilities. It utilises the Semantic Web technology stack for annotating observation values with semantic descriptions, and techniques from Stream Reasoning for performing run-time analysis and problem diagnosis within cloud application platforms. We have also introduced a conceptual architecture which follows the MAPE-K reference model to implement closed adaptation loops, and a prototype framework developed in Java and deployed on Heroku. Initial experiments demonstrate the viability of the proposed approach, both in terms of performance and in terms of the analysis capabilities of the autonomous framework. More specifically, the framework is able not only to monitor values, but also to detect and diagnose critical situations, and to propose a simple adaptation strategy within 1 second. Our results are, however, based on a relatively small-scale case study, and we have identified further challenges associated with Stream reasoning that will need to be overcome for the approach to become adopted in practice. Even so, we believe that the application of Stream Reasoning and Semantic Web – two areas where intelligence lies at the very core – to Autonomic Clouds is a promising direction.

Competing interests
The authors declare that they have no competing interests.

Authors' contributions
The research presented in this paper is part of the Ph.D. dissertation of the first author under the supervision of the second and the third authors. All authors equally contributed to the paper. All authors read and approved the final manuscript.

Acknowledgements
The research leading to these results has received funding from the European Union's Seventh Framework Programme (FP7-PEOPLE-2010-ITN) under grant agreement n°264840.

Author details
[1] South-East European Research Centre, International Faculty of the University of Sheffield, City College, 24 Proxenou Koromila Street, 54646 Thessaloniki, Greece. [2] Department of Computer Science, University of Sheffield, Regent Court, 211 Portobello Street, S1 4DP Sheffield, UK.

References
1. Dautov R, Paraskakis I (2013) A vision for monitoring cloud application platforms as sensor networks. In: Proceedings of the 2013 ACM Cloud and Autonomic Computing Conference. CAC '13. ACM, New York, pp 25–1258
2. Papazoglou MP, Traverso P, Dustdar S, Leymann F (2008) Service-oriented computing: a research roadmap. Int J Coop Inf Syst 17(2):223–255
3. Clayman S, Galis A, Chapman C, Toffetti G, Rodero-Merino L, Vaquero LM, Nagin K, Rochwerger B (2010) Monitoring service clouds in the future internet. In: Tselentis G, et al. (eds) Towards the future internet – Emerging trends from European research. IOS Press, Amsterdam, pp 105–114
4. Wei Y, Blake MB (2010) Service-oriented computing and cloud computing: Challenges and opportunities. Internet Comput IEEE 14(6):72–75
5. Kourtesis D, Bratanis K, Bibikas D, Paraskakis I (2012) Software co-development in the era of cloud application platforms and Ecosystems: The case of CAST. In: Camarinha-Matos LM, Xu L, Afsarmanesh H (eds) Collaborative networks in the internet of services, vol. 380. Springer, Berlin Heidelberg, pp 196–204
6. Ried S, Rymer JR (2011) The Forrester Wave™: Platform-As-A-Service For Vendor Strategy Professionals. Q2 2011. Technical report, Forrester Research, Cambridge, MA, USA
7. Google App Engine. http://appengine.google.com/
8. Windows Azure. http://www.windowsazure.com/
9. Gartner Says Worldwide Platform as a Service Revenue Is on Pace to Reach $1.2 Billion. http://www.gartner.com/newsroom/id/2242415
10. IDC Predicts 2014 Will Be a Year of Escalation, Consolidation, and Innovation as the Transition to IT's "Third Platform" Accelerates. http://www.idc.com/getdoc.jsp?containerId=prUS24472713
11. Brazier FM, Kephart JO, Van Dyke Parunak H, Huhns MN (2009) Agents and service-oriented computing for autonomic computing: a research agenda. Internet Comput IEEE 13(3):82–87
12. Dautov R, Kourtesis D, Paraskakis I, Stannett M (2013) Addressing self-management in cloud platforms: a semantic sensor web approach. In: Proceedings of the 2013 international workshop on hot topics in cloud services. ACM, New York, pp 11–18
13. Heroku. http://www.heroku.com/
14. Harris D Heroku Boss: 1.5M Apps, Many Not in Ruby. http://gigaom.com/2012/05/04/heroku-boss-1-5m-apps-many-not-in-ruby/
15. Heroku – CrunchBase Profile. http://www.crunchbase.com/company/heroku
16. Kourtesis D (2011) Towards an ontology-driven governance framework for cloud application platforms. Technical report. South-East European Research Centre (SEERC), Thessaloniki, Greece
17. Kephart JO, Chess DM (2003) The vision of autonomic computing. Computer 36(1):41–50
18. Aceto G, Botta A, de Donato W, Pescapè A (2013) Cloud monitoring: a survey. Comput Netw 57(9):2093–2115
19. WhatsApp Leads The Global Smartphone Messenger Wars With 44 Percent Market Share. http://www.1mtb.com/whatsapp-leads-the-global-mobile-messenger-wars-with-44-pc-market-share/
20. 400 Million Stories. http://blog.whatsappcom/index.php/2013/12/400-million-stories/
21. Heroku – Success. http://success.heroku.com/
22. Spring J (2011) Monitoring cloud computing by layer, part 1. Secur. Priv. IEEE 9(2):66–68
23. Spring J (2011) Monitoring cloud computing by layer, part 2. Secur Priv IEEE 9(3):52–55

24. Caron E, Desprez F, Rodero-Merino L, Muresan A (2012) Auto-scaling, load balancing and monitoring in commercial and open-source clouds. In: Benatallah B (ed) Cloud computing: methodology, systems, and applications. CRC Press, Boca Raton, pp 301–323

25. Armbrust M, Fox A, Joseph A, Katz R, Konwinski A, Lee G, Patterson D, Rabkin A, Stoica I, Zaharia M (2009) Above the clouds: a berkeley view of cloud computing, EECS-2009-28. Technical report, University of California Berkeley, Berkeley, CA, USA

26. Natis YV, Knipp E, Valdes R, Cearley DW, Sholler D (2009) Who's who in application platforms for cloud computing: the cloud specialists. Technical report, Gartner Research, Stamford, CT, USA

27. Russom P (2011) Big data analytics. TDWI Best Practices Report, Renton, WA, USA

28. Botts M, Percivall G, Reed C, Davidson J (2008) OGC® sensor web enablement: overview and high level architecture. In: Nittel S, Labrinidis A, Stefanidis A (eds) GeoSensor Networks. Lecture Notes in Computer Science, vol. 4540. Springer, Berlin Heidelberg, pp 175–190

29. Cugola G, Margara A (2012) Processing flows of information: from data stream to complex event processing. ACM Comput Surv (CSUR) 44(3):15

30. Calbimonte J-P, Jeung H, Corcho O, Aberer K (2012) Enabling query technologies for the semantic sensor web. Int J Semantic Web Inform Syst (IJSWIS) 8(1):43–63

31. Barbieri D, Braga D, Ceri S, Della Valle E, Grossniklaus M (2010) Stream reasoning: where we got so far. In: Proceedings of the 4th workshop on new forms of reasoning for the semantic web: scalable & dynamic. Springer, Berlin Heidelberg, pp 1–7

32. Della Valle E, Ceri S, Barbieri DF, Braga D, Campi A (2009) A first step towards stream reasoning. In: Future Internet–FIS 2008. Springer, Berlin Heidelberg, pp 72–81

33. Lanzanasto N, Komazec S, Toma I (2012) Reasoning over real time data streams. http://www.envision-project.eu/wp-content/uploads/2012/11/D4.8-1.0.pdf

34. Sheth A, Henson C, Sahoo SS (2008) Semantic sensor web. Internet Comput IEEE 12(4):78–83

35. Dautov R, Stannett M, Paraskakis I (2013) On the role of stream reasoning in run-time monitoring and analysis in autonomic systems. In: Proceedings of the 8th south east European doctoral student conference. Thessaloniki, Greece

36. Valle ED, Ceri S, van Harmelen F, Fensel D (2009) It's a streaming world! Reasoning upon rapidly changing information. Intell Syst IEEE 24(6):83–89

37. Barbieri DF, Braga D, Ceri S, Della Valle E, Grossniklaus M (2009) C-SPARQL: SPARQL for continuous querying. In: Proceedings of the 18th international conference on World Wide Web. ACM, New York, pp 1061–1062

38. Le-Phuoc D, Dao-Tran M, Parreira JX, Hauswirth M (2011) A native and adaptive approach for unified processing of linked streams and linked data. In: The semantic Web–ISWC 2011. Springer, Berlin Heidelberg, pp 370–388

39. Anicic D (2011) Event Processing and Stream Reasoning with ETALIS. PhD thesis, Karlsruher Institut für Technologie (KIT), Karlsruhe, Germany

40. IBM: Four Vs of Big Data. http://www.ibmbigdatahub.com/infographic/four-vs-big-data

41. Baader F (2003) The description logic handbook: theory, implementation, and applications. Cambridge University Press, Cambridge

42. Hitzler P, Krotzsch M, Rudolph S (2011) Foundations of semantic web technologies. Chapman & Hall/CRC, Boca Raton

43. CloudAMQP – RabbitMQ as a Service. https://addons.heroku.com/cloudamqp

44. Message Throughput in RabbitMQ Bigwig. http://bigwig.io/docs/message_throughput/

45. The Protégé Ontology Editor and Knowledge Acquisition System. http://protege.stanford.edu/

46. OWL API. http://owlapi.sourceforge.net/

47. Continuous SPARQL (C-SPARQL) Ready To Go Pack. http://streamreasoning.org/download/csparqlreadytogopack

48. Urbani J (2010) Scalable and parallel reasoning in the Semantic Web. In: The semantic web: research and applications. Springer, Berlin Heidelberg, pp 488–492

49. Oracle Fast Data Solutions. http://www.oracle.com/us/solutions/fastdata/index.html

50. IBM - InfoSphere Streams. http://www-03.ibm.com/software/products/en/infosphere-streams

51. Apache: S4: Distributed Stream Processing System. http://incubator.apache.org/s4/

52. Storm – Distributed and Fault-tolerant Realtime Computation. http://storm-project.net/

53. R2RML: RDB to RDF Mapping Language (W3C Recommendation 27 September 2012). http://www.w3.org/TR/r2rml/

## 11

An on-demand scaling stereoscopic 3D video streaming service in the cloud

Maximilian Hoecker[*] and Marcel Kunze

Abstract

We describe a web service providing a complete stereoscopic 3D video multi-stream cloud application to serve a potentially very large number of clients over the Internet. The system architecture consists of a stream provider that leverages highly scalable and reliable cloud computing and storage services, with automatic load balancing capability for live and content streaming. By use of a suiting flash media plugin the content is displayed on a wide variety of 3D capable devices like for example 3D workstations or smart TV sets. Videos are made available by an on-line stream provider for live broadcasting or by cloud storage services. Compared to conventional 3D video streaming over satellite channels there are considerable savings in cost as well as a wider range of applicability and functional improvements. Possible areas of application are medical surgery, live concerts, and sports events.

Introduction

The conventional method of distributing high definition stereoscopic 3D live video streams is the transmission via satellite links. While the provisioning of the necessary bandwidth via satellite is technically feasible, live transmission is very costly: An hour of satellite channel costs approximately 700$ and the rental of a transmission vehicle adds up to 2,000$ per day. Furthermore, secure satellite transmission usually works point-to-point only especially when stream encryption is used. It would thus be interesting to develop methods to mass distribute 3D live content over cheaper Internet broadcasting channels. However, the Internet up to now has played a minor role in this context due to the high bandwidth demand of high definition 3D video streams. New compression methods like H.264 and encoders as well as improvements in the available bandwidth, however, have changed the situation: While professional streams in medical applications with quadruple HD may require up to 40 MBit/s uncompressed, the typical bandwidth consumption of a compressed stereoscopic 3D video stream in 720p quality is 2 MBit/s, ranging up to 5 MBit/s for 1024p.

The cloud application presented in this paper discusses the live broadcasting of stereoscopic 3D video over the Internet by use of automatically scaling media clusters and user interface portals based on commodity cloud services.

The paper is organized as follows: First we describe the application context with its specific requirements. In the next chapter we discuss the architectural aspects of an on-demand, scaling live video broadcasting environment. Then we present performance studies and the paper concludes with a summary and outlook.

Stereoscopic 3D video streaming

Stereoscopic 3D video presents each eye of the observer with a slightly different perspective to enable a realistic 3D experience. A corresponding video streaming setup thus has to transport two pictures synchronously, one for each eye. Various techniques have been employed to provide stereoscopic video such as anaglyph 3D, polarization 3D, active shutter, and side-by-side that are already embedded in actual 3D TV sets. A comprehensive streaming application should thus not be limited to a particular type of stereoscopic format in order to reach a large audience. There are tools and encoders on the market that allow to handle a wide spectrum of formats such as the Invistra multi converter [1] and Adobe Flash plugin [2] that have been chosen to support the research described in this paper.

Download vs. streaming

The transmission of video and audio data over the Internet has become very prominent. File sharing services are usually offering files to download in a web browser or they

---
*Correspondence: maximilian.hoecker@uni-heidelberg.de
Karlsruhe Institute of Technologie (KIT), Karlsruhe, Germany

leverage specific file sharing protocols like BitTorrent [3]. However, the download of files has its problems with fault tolerance and it is difficult to steer the bandwidth consumption. If a media file is downloaded, the client keeps on transferring data in the background while the content is being consumed. If a client navigates forward, the already transferred portions of the file have to be skipped and it might happen that there is a waiting time until the client may continue at the new location. Usually the "header" information of a media file is located at the end of the file.

An example for a standard download method is Apple's PodCast. A PodCast file has to be downloaded completely before it is able to be played because the header information is at the end of a file. The technique of progressive download transfers a header at the start of the file in addition to the content that contains information to navigate in the media. This makes it possible to play the file while it is still downloading. Various companies like Adobe, Apple, and Microsoft offer proprietary protocols to support HTTP based applications with progressive download. The corresponding implementations mainly differ in the supported CODECs.

Streaming on the other hand is a technology that transfers a data stream from a service to a client with quality control. Server and client exchange state information and quality metrics as well as meta data describing the stream by means of a streaming protocol.

Protocols

A streaming protocol contains two layers: A transport stream and a control stream. The transport stream carries the media data and it may be based on both transfer protocols, UDP and TCP. The control stream takes care of the Quality of Service (QoS) and its implementation depends on the specific transfer protocol in use.

A prominent implementation of a streaming protocol is the Real Time Protocol (RTP) that has been specified in RFC 3550 [4]. It is based on UDP and uses the Real Time Control Protocol (RTCP) for QoS. The Real Time Messaging Protocol (RTMP) has been published by Adobe in 2009 [5]. It uses TCP and guarantees the correct order of the datagrams in the stream. On the server side RTMP implements command messages, data messages, shared object messages to embed e.g. Flash events, media messages, and aggregate messages to combine various messages gaining efficiency. On the client and server side RTMP offers user control messages to notify about events like stream begin or end. There are several variants of RTMP that allow to tunnel through firewalls (RTMP-T), to encrypt the media streams (RTMP-E, RTMP-S), and a combination of both (RTMP-TE) [6]. Examples for RTMP streaming clients are the VLC player [7] and the browser based FlowPlayer [8].

Streaming services

Streaming servers are able to transport almost arbitrary video streams in almost any format. They offer capabilities such as live transmission, live transcoding into various formats, quality control, and digital rights management. Examples are the Adobe Flash Media Server [2] or the Wowza media server [9]. The Amazon Web Services (AWS) [10] offer paid instances of media servers that may be rented by the hour, thus implementing a dynamically scalable streaming service. We are utilizing these cloud based streaming services to construct our scalable media service based on RTMP.

Security

Broadcasting of video streams over the internet works on a global scale. Hence, a corresponding video streaming service should ensure the secure and reliable transmission of content. Depending on the application context, stream access control is needed e.g. in commercial portals selling video-on-demand. In addition the service may consume large amounts of bandwidth, especially when 3D videos in HD quality are distributed. A single stream may consume a bandwidth between 2 MBit/s and 40 MBit/s.

Several possibilities exist to transport live video data from a source to a streaming client: One could deploy a peripheral mesh network where each client is a stream distributor for many other clients, or a central streaming cluster multiplying streams locally.

The application presented in this paper is focussing on stereoscopic 3D live broadcasting in the public cloud combined with secure transmission of video as an aliased stream with optional encryption. A stream represented by an aliased name prevents replaying content on several clients. Stream aliasing is realized by masquerading real stream names with an alphanumeric hash derived from the stream name, current time, client IP-Address, and a customer specific secret key.

Architecture
Blueprint

Figure 1 shows an architectural blueprint of a system to transport stereoscopic 3D live content from a source to a potentially large number of viewers. The design philosophy is that all components may be instantiated as virtual machines in the public cloud. Video clients are requesting a live stream via a video streaming portal. The portal forwards the request to a streaming origin server accessing the content provided by a stream provider. The origin server delivers the stream to a dynamically scaling cluster of edge servers. The edge servers deliver the live stream to the requesting streaming clients. The whole system is managed and monitored by a management server (3Distribute). The management server is composed of

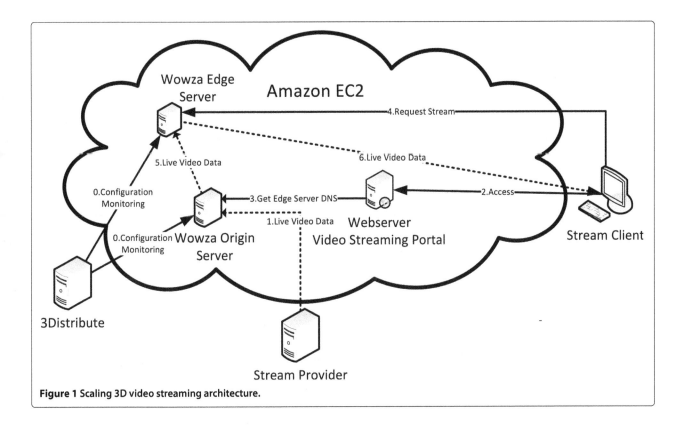

Figure 1 Scaling 3D video streaming architecture.

an application interface server (API-Server) and a user interface server (UI-Server).

Logical components

The core part of our system is the API-Server. Key functionalities are: Starting and configuring of virtual machines, as well as managing and monitoring of the media streaming cluster, including dynamic scaling of the cluster size. As shown in Figure 2 the API-Server consists of three layers of components, each of which abstracts the layer below: The very low layer consists of connectors to utilize IaaS services of various providers (Cloud connector) and grants access to virtual machine resources (Machine connector). A cluster and monitoring component abstracts this first layer and represents the basic functionality to manage a virtual cluster of machines. Finally, an application is able to access the system by use of the top level control component that constructs and steers instances of the cluster component. All components are defined by interfaces to provide the possibility to choose or change a specific implementation.

Cloud connector

The *cloud connector* component realizes transparent access to the proprietary API of an IaaS cloud service offering. Each individual implementation of this component has to provide the following functionalities:

- Launch and terminate virtual machines of a cloud service.
- Capture and collect performance metrics of virtual machines as a basis to perform service analysis.
- Associate reserved IP addresses with instances.

Machine connector

Controlling virtual machines with different protocols and connections is the task of the *machine connector* component. The machine connector takes care of the following tasks:

- Grant remote access to a machine in order to submit and execute remote procedures. Each task returns a result indicating if a command has been run successfully or not. Additionally the standard output and error messages of the remote command may be transferred.
- Provide a file transfer method to e.g. distribute configuration files.

The standard implementation of the machine connector is establishing connections via Secure Shell (SSH) and uses a Secure Copy (SCP) session for file transfers. It is possible to re-implement the connector with different protocols to transmit commands or local files to a remote machine. The portability of the component could be helpful to support different operating systems and media services.

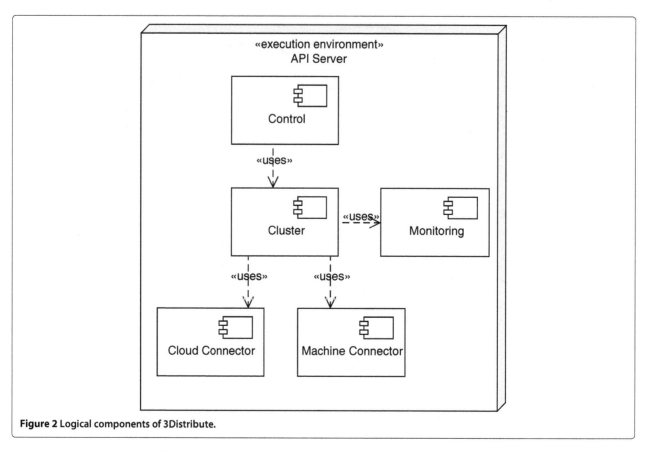

Figure 2 Logical components of 3Distribute.

Cluster component

The *cluster component* has been designed to construct a virtual cluster of virtual machines. It depends on all components located in the layer below and is organized as follows:

- A component called *scenario* is representing a data model providing information about virtual machine properties in a cloud environment. Instances of a cluster component scenario contain one ore more so-called *scenario parts*. Scenario parts represent a deployment information knowledge base for different independent parts of the cluster containing e.g. machine size and image information, key pair names, and files. Using scenario parts, different types of virtual machines in the cloud may be orchestrated in a cluster.

- In addition to the scenario part, a *machine configuration* represents another data model containing a set of ordered commands and local files to be uploaded and executed to configure a virtual machine dynamically during cluster startup or sizing operations.

- A central subcomponent is the *cluster machine* representing abstract access methods to interact with the virtual machines in a cloud. The main task of the

cluster machine is to update internal state relevant for cluster sizing and to control the connected virtual machines in the cloud using the connector components.

- Finally, the *clustering component* manages all subcomponents described above. It is creating and controlling all cluster machines and maps scenario parts and machine configurations accordingly.

Analysis component

The *analysis component* allows to monitor and control the cluster in a regular fashion. To provide this functionality, the component is organized as follows:

- The *cluster machine analyzer* analyzes the state of single cluster machines using data of metrics generated by a cloud connector. A report is generated including a qualitative measurement of the current streaming load of a cluster machine.

- Based on this report the *cluster analyzer* component prepares another report providing qualitative and quantitative information about the streaming load of a video streaming cluster as a whole.

- The *actions catalogue* component is able to determine the action needed to handle a specific load condition taking into account both, cluster and cluster machine reports.

A separate thread triggers the analysis of all clusters, including all necessary actions determined by the catalogue.

One possible action is resizing a cluster: If a cluster overload condition occurs, the number of virtual machines is dynamically increased by an upsizing process. On the other hand, if idle machines exist a downsizing process takes care to decrease the number of virtual machines by sending a termination or stop signal to underutilized machines. As a boundary condition the API server ensures the cost effectiveness of the operation as the resource usage accounting model may vary for different IaaS cloud providers. For example, the Amazon Web Services (AWS) compute service EC2 [11] charges any started hour of instance usage independent of the actual utilization profile (wallclock time). Thus it would be interesting to stop machines right before the end of the hour in order to take full advantage of an already billed resource. Another accounting model applied by Google [12] or Profitbricks [13] continuously charges the actually consumed resources (CPU time). The current implementation is utilizing AWS services and instances are therefore terminated on an hourly basis.

Control component

This component builds an abstract layer of all components below and provides functionalities to control, launch and terminate clusters. First of all the control component performs validity and integrity checks of parameters supplied to instantiate a cluster component instance. After the instantiation the cluster is passed to the analysis component taking over responsibility of cluster operations. The current implementation of the web interface uses an RMI Interface to connect to the API server.

User interface

The user interface consists of an administrative console and a web front end to play and watch stereoscopic content. The administrative console allows to configure and manage the complete environment and perform detailed monitoring of the system. The web front-end has to support a wide range of stereoscopic 3D formats, such as anaglyph 3D, polarization 3D, active shutter, and side-by-side. For this purpose a web browser plugin has been developed based on Adobe Flash technology [2]. A Microsoft Silverlight [14] implementation exists in addition to support NVIDIA 3D vision shutter glasses for desktop PCs [15]. The plugin supports to play a wide range of formats via a popup selection bar and is also used in the enduser interface of the commercial product. In principal, the control component may be embedded into arbitrary web pages in order to support customer specific portals with stereoscopic 3D content delivery.

Automated load balancing and scaling

Live streaming events like e.g. a medical congress or the transmission of a concerto may attract an unpredictable number of requesting streams. One of our targets during the design phase was to create a system scaling in every instance of time taking into account parameters like load and cost. A new streaming request is always redirected to the video streaming server having the highest load and the capacity to feed further clients. In case of a potential overload condition the next less loaded server is chosen. This procedure maximizes the usage efficiency of a video streaming server and minimizes the cost since servers are only kept online in case of a need.

We developed a load balancing Plugin for the Wowza Media Server to cover these requirements based on the heartbeat architecture pattern. An architecture including a heartbeat pattern consists of a master server and multiple slave nodes. Our setup implements the origin server as master node and edge servers as slave nodes sending heartbeats. The master node collects all load information (heartbeats) of each streaming server in the cluster by use of Remote Procedure Calls (RPC) via an encrypted protocol. The number of connections on a server as well as the outgoing network traffic is transmitted in a message. When a streaming request of a user is submitted as shown in Figure 1 (step 2) the IP-Address of an edge server is requested (step 3), selected and delivered by the load balancer plugin.

It is a challenge to scale the streaming capacity up and down in near-realtime. For EC2 the AWS CloudWatch service provides a time-aggregated view of the system performance at intervals of every one or five minutes. The delivered aggregation dataset holds a small collection of statistical metrics like average, minimum and maximum value of each system state. However, the CloudWatch service may take to long if QoS needs to be guaranteed.

In order to avoid this kind of delays and to minimize the time to scale, we implemented a faster scaling method in the API Server calling a specific entry of the load balancing plugin each 10 seconds. The encrypted call transmits collective cluster information consisting of all edge server heartbeats including a timestamp. A history of the last minute of heartbeats is kept in memory to determine the actual progression of load. Depending on the load history the necessary measures like cluster resizing are initiated by the API Server.

Measurement of server loads and capacity

An important role plays the load balancing in dependence of resource analysis and monitoring. We define a metric called `streaming capacity` which indicates the current workload. The metric is implemented as a percentage value, where 100% describes the best condition (no load) and 0% represents the least capacity left (cluster is fully loaded), respectively.

For the determination of the streaming capacity the application uses monitoring data that are provided and elevated by the cloud connector interface.

The main metric to calculate the streaming capacity is called `performance`. The performance is computed on the basis of the performance measurements of each scenario part. The *actions catalogue* component offers specific actions for the analysis report of each scenario part. The computation proceeds according to the following procedure:

One scenario part determines the streaming capacity at a certain point in time depending on the available streaming capacity of the individual streaming cluster machines of the scenario part. The application additionally discretizes the numerical metric into a nominal metric with the possible values *capable* and *overloaded*. This nominal value is determined by comparison to a threshold. If the actual streaming capacity of the cluster falls below the threshold, the nominal value is set to *overloaded*.

Figure 3 shows a sample graph of progressing streaming capacity with a threshold of 23%. At time step 24 the streaming capacity of the cluster falls below the threshold. The cluster is, per definition, overloaded at this point in time.

Each scenario part is separately analyzed and reported. Possible actions are extending or shrinking the cluster size in a specific scenario or leaving the cluster size untouched in case of optimal load conditions. In order to create a report for a scenario part, the *cluster analyzer* component computes the streaming capacity according to the following procedure:

First of all, a value named `derivation` is computed to indicate the difference of the status quo to the minimum required streaming capacity.

$$derivation = threshold - performance_{scenariopart}. \quad (1)$$

Another value called `streaming capacity reserve` is defined by $reserve = -1 * derivation$ and defines a metric for a reserve or lack of streaming capacity of a complete cluster.

In a second step the total media server streaming capacity of a scenario part cluster is compared to the threshold value with the possible conditions in equation

$$\sum_{i=1}^{n}(performance_i) <> threshold$$

If the sum of all available streaming capacity is smaller than the threshold, the derivation value is rounded to the next higher number. This rounded value defines the number of additional media servers to be started in addition to the actual number of cluster machines.

If the streaming capacity of a cluster complies to the threshold, the cluster size remains unchanged. If the threshold is defined low enough to accept a large number of streams on one streaming server in a stable streaming environment even if the stream bandwidth changes, this reflects the most cost effective point of operation.

The third situation indicates that the cluster is underutilized. In this case the `reserve` value of the cluster corresponds to the number of media servers to be removed from the corresponding streaming cluster.

Evaluation
Test setup
All studies have been performed with public cloud services offered by the AWS [10] and Wowza Media Server

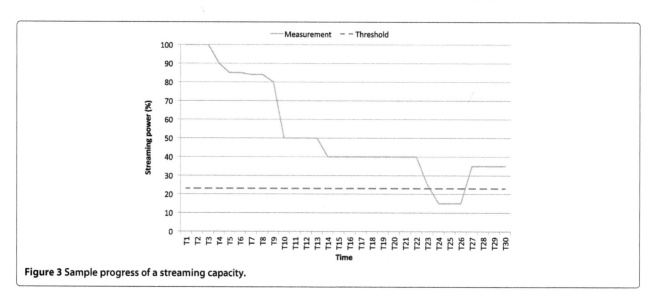

Figure 3 Sample progress of a streaming capacity.

[9]. For scalability and quality measurements we have used Flazr[16], a small command line tool to simulate a defined set of parallel video streaming consumers. In addition to this basic feature, advanced options like saving or consumption of encrypted video streams are also provided by this tool.

All testing procedures were subject to a well-defined topological setup:

- A set of 3Distribute API-Server and UI-Server located in a private context.
- One stream publisher that streams stereographic 3D content to a public iaaS based on AWS EC2.
- Virtual machines hosted in the AWS EC2 availability zone "eu-west-1", implementing a streaming service provided by a streaming cluster (Origin server and edge servers).
- Another cluster of virtual machines hosted in the AWS EC2 availability zone "us-west-1", simulating users consuming the content provided by the streaming service.

The deployment of the streaming cluster is the first step performed by the setup procedure. 3Distribute initializes and configures a video streaming cluster in the European availability zone, initially composed of a single origin server and one edge server. In order to put a load on the video streaming cluster a consumer virtual machine is instantiated in the availability zone "us-west-1".

After the streaming cluster has been deployed and configured, the stream publisher is manually enabled to launch the transmission of stereoscopic 3D live video content to the origin server of the streaming cluster. The consumption of streams is additionally started on the virtual machine in the other availability zone using Flazr. The number of streams to be consumed is initially calculated regarding the bandwidth of the stream and the network output capacity of the edge server.

Various quality attributes have been investigated and evaluated during the testing that are described in the following subsections.

Scalability
The current implementation of 3Distribute has limitations regarding the number of media servers. Due to the layered origin/edge server setup and the maximum networking bandwidth of a virtual machine in the cloud, a streaming cluster is able to provide a maximum of

$$n_{max} = \frac{origin_{max} * edge_{max}}{streambandwidth^2}$$

streams. The factors $origin_{max}$ and $edge_{max}$ denote the maximum possible outgoing networking bandwidth of the virtual machines available to the origin or edge servers.

Cluster Compute Instances (CCI) of the AWS EC2 service provide a 10 GBit ethernet connection. Thus, with CCI it would be possible to achieve a maximum of 25 million independent output streams in presence of a 2 MBit input stream. This limit could be expanded by introduction of a meshed cluster architecture. In a meshed cluster the edge servers would have the possibility to connect to a further layer of edge servers, implementing a tree-like streaming network to transmit a potentially unlimited number of streams.

The number of streams in a meshed setup is calculated by $n_{total} = n_{OriginServer} * n_{EdgeServer}^h$. The exponent h corresponds to the height of the spanned tree. As a boundary condition it is required that each height of a leaf in the tree is identical.

However, meshed video streaming clusters have another limitation: If a video streaming cluster is located in just a single availability zone of a cloud, it is possible to saturate the maximum available networking bandwidth of the provider. Whereas it is possible to support 25 Million streams with a tree height of one, a streaming cluster could theoretically already transmit $125*10^9$ streams with a height of two, resulting in a networking output bandwidth of 250 PBit per second. Such a load could only be handled, if the cluster would be operated in a multi cloud environment or across various availability zones.

In order to determine the streaming capacity of a cluster it is necessary to measure the streaming capacity of a single streaming server in the cloud with the test setup described in subsection "Test setup".

If the AWS EC2 service is used, it is relevant to understand which instance type should be deployed to provide the service for origin and edge servers. A 2.4 Mbit video encoded in full HD format has been selected as an input to study the streaming behavior of specific AWS EC2 instance types. The I/O classifications of AWS EC2 instance types can be reviewed in [17]. Table 1 shows the maximum number of stable streams and the corresponding maximum measured networking bandwidth per instance type. From a provisioning point of view, all instance types in the table have a GBit networking interface. It is an interesting observation that only the large instance types in reality reach GBit bandwidth; the small instance types seem to be throttled by the provider.

As described above, Flazr was used to generate a load on the streaming cluster. Each virtual machine running Flazr

Table 1 Average maximum number of streams and bandwidth provided by AWS instance types

AWS Instance Type	I/O	n_{max}	$\sum$ Bandwidth
m1.small	Moderate	110	ca. 308 Mbit/s
m1.large	High	300	ca. 830 Mbit/s
c1.xlarge	High	330	ca. 918 Mbit/s

was configured to pull up to a hundred streams from an edge server. With a binary search approach, the number of maximum streams was identified. As a start condition an initial maximum number of 500 streams was defined. To check if a streaming server is capable to provide the number of streams, a single stream has been watched visually as a control sample. If this control sample didn't show any deterioration of audio or video, the number of streams was set acceptable to be provided by the streaming server. During an initial measurement the test video consumed a bandwidth of 2.78 Mbit on average.

We designed and developed a special tool to measure the total bandwidth using the Wowza Media Systems API able to monitor bandwidth according to a one second precision. The tool takes measurements each five seconds yielding 12 measurements per minute. In addition, the median and average values are calculated and checked against the measurements of the AWS CloudWatch API to have a plausibility test. We observed a deviation of 5.4% between both measurements that may be explained by the measurement method of the CloudWatch API. CloudWatch measures in a one minute interval with an undefined number of values. The measurements contain values for all possible I/O performance and Wowza image combinations. Currently there is no possibility to deploy a Wowza image on a virtual machine having a "very high" or "low" I/O Performance.

Figure 4 shows the results and demonstrates, that the potential network traffic and the number of possible streams vary by almost a factor of three. The measurements illustrate that the utilized bandwidth is increasing linearly with the number of streams provided. If the server is not able to provide additional streams any more, the bandwidth for each stream (and for all streams summarized) would be decreasing. This behavior may be explained by the scheduling of multiple virtual machines on a single hypervisor of a host in a cloud, resulting in a specific profile for each I/O type to schedule the resources.

Figure 5 illustrates the limit of possible stable streams for a specific instance type. An origin server using a virtual machine of instance type "m1.small" is capable of providing 110 streams. If more streams are requested on the same server, the bandwidth per stream is decreasing until artifacts, audio or video glitches are observed. It became evident that artifacts occurred once the bandwidth of a video stream fell below 2.7 MBit. In Figure 5 the graph shows an analogue behavior for instance type "c1.xlarge" and "m1.large". Both figures indicate a variation by a factor three in streaming bandwidth per stream between small and large instance types. Since the allocation of virtual machines with different instance types on a physical host is not fixed, all measurements have been repeated multiple times using a freshly deployed cluster per measurement.

These measurements are specific for AWS EC2 and the conclusions may not be generally applicable to other cloud providers and environments. However, we can anticipate that different hypervisors or virtualization technologies of other cloud providers may deliver different results but of similar characteristics.

Availability

Cloud systems should be fault tolerant as a service should be available at all times. An evaluation regarding availability of the 3Distribute software and video streaming clusters is performed in this subsection. The consequences of a component failure will be discussed for customers, monitoring processes, or for the stream providers. The term *failure* in this context refers to the termination of virtual machines in the cloud or to the crash of a software component.

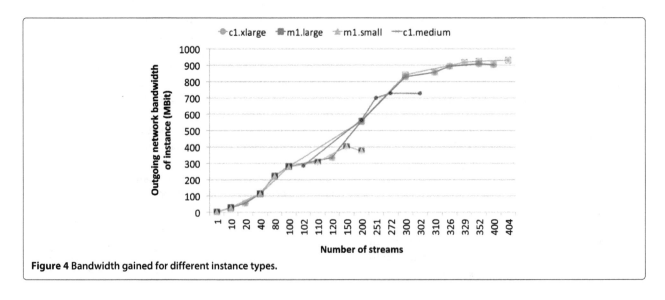

Figure 4 Bandwidth gained for different instance types.

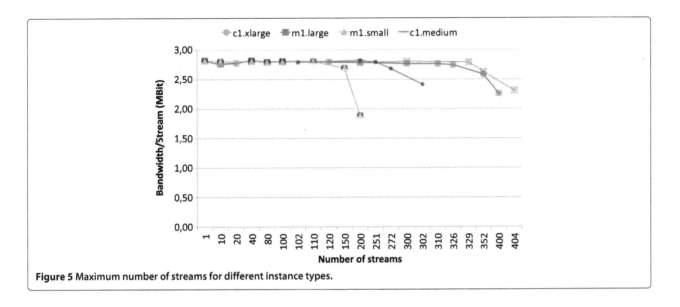

Figure 5 Maximum number of streams for different instance types.

A crash of the complete 3Distribute management system would result in a situation where the streaming cluster is not monitored and managed anymore. While operation continues in this case, scaling up or down in size would not be possible. This could cause two problems over time: Either the cost could be too high due to over provisioning, or the quality of the video stream could degrade due to a lack of video streaming server capacity. This scenario would result in a potential graceful degradation of the system.

However, failures of origin servers in a hierarchical origin/edge server setup is a yet unsolved open issue. If the origin part of a cluster is missing, no edge server would get any video data and no client could receive a video stream anymore. One possible preventive method to solve this issue is the setup of two or more spare origin servers. Each origin server would be receiving the same stream from the stream provider independently. Using a playlist, a multi-origin setup could be manually realized in all edge servers. A special configuration would deploy a second or third video streaming cluster just consisting of one origin server in hot standby mode. The switching between the origin servers may be done automatically by the Wowza streaming server itself. If one stream is ending (because of a failure), the next origin server is requested to jump in and deliver the stream. During the failover procedure a user would observe a small interrupt or artifact caused by the RTMP handshake between edge and origin server. This time period of switching is comparable to the initial handshake during a client connect initialization. In the clients view, the switchover is done transparently since the stream delivery from edge server to a final client is not interrupted.

Failures of edge servers would affect just the viewers consuming streams from the corresponding location. The streaming client would simply reconnect requesting a new edge server from the origin server. On the client side the player would react on an edge server fault automatically.

Related work

A substantial number of providers already offer video streaming services in the Internet, but almost any of these host 2D video applications only. The most prominent video service, YouTube [18], only works in the area of static content and has recently established the possibility to upload 3D videos in modest quality. KUK Filmproduktion is producing stereoscopic 3D live concert events, but only via satellite and into movie theaters [19]. There are some companies experimenting with 3D HD video live transmission of endoscopic medical surgery [20]. In the area of media oriented protocols there are developments in the direction of predictable reliability and predictable delivery (PRPD) to minimize the amount of required bandwidth [21]. In this context there are research efforts in the area of adaptive coding to optimize the coding parameters such that they are producing the minimal amount of redundancy. Another field of interest are Peer-to-Peer (P2P) solutions for live streaming video. AngelCast [22] is a system extending a P2P network with the resources of a cloud provider. AngelCast networks are capable to streami videos live and may be extended by cloud resources using a controller. The Elastic Stream Cloud (ESC) [23] represents a concept to connect multiple smaller private clouds for video streaming. ESC does not make use of specific cloud resources but provides the delivery model that has been implemented as a decentralized SaaS, forcing streaming providers to run a proprietary web OS with self defined protocols.

The authors in [24] describe an application called MediaWise Cloud Content Orchestrator (MCCO) for the delivery of static (recorded) content. MCCO deploys a multi-cloud content delivery network (CDN) using public cloud resources and consists of a specific three tier architecture controlled by widgets in the front-end tier.

The CDN architecture typically deploys a load balanced setup with distributed cache servers spread geographically around the world in order to optimize latency, bandwidth, and cost of networking [25,26], leading to data replication into various centers and a static tier hierarchy.

A live streaming application as described in this paper, however, demands dynamic adaptation of networking and streaming capacity. In order to achieve this, content is distributed with small partial buffers (0-3 seconds) in the media servers across the deployed tree topology, growing in height and width as clients connect.

Monitoring services are a major architectural component of any cloud application to support scaling and QoS [27]. As the cloud monitoring systems offered by providers very often bear technical limitations application architects tend to work out their own individual setup. Hence, we defined a specifically well suited QoS metric for our application called streaming capacity as described in section "Measurement of server loads and capacity".

Conclusions and future work

Cloud services have a huge potential to support the broadcasting of stereoscopic 3D live events over the Internet. The rapidly growing IP-TV market with its 3D enabled smart TV sets could benefit a lot by corresponding service offerings. The architecture presented in this paper has been implemented to support Trivido [28], a 3D live video portal run by the startup Invistra [1]. The client side of the application is currently based on proprietary Flash and Silverlight enabled endpoints. The transition to HTML5 is on the roadmap and would offer a broader support of devices by the corresponding 3D TV application stores. As there is a growing uptake of LTE broadband internet connection, 3D video streaming could soon be a promising option on mobile phones and tablets as well. Further areas of interest could be 3D live chats in social networks, as well as technical training and lecturing. In order to further optimize the efficiency of the setup, another direction of development is to intelligently leverage affordable infrastructure services from the growing cloud spot market.

Competing interests
The authors declare that they have no competing interests.

Authors' contributions
All the listed authors made substantive intellectual contributions to the research and manuscript. Specific details are as follows: MH designed the architecture and implemented solution. He evaluated the work and drafted the paper. MK is 3D-Live project lead. He was responsible for the overall technical approach and architecture and edited the paper. Both authors read and approved the final manuscript.

Acknowledgements
Part of the work presented in this paper has been funded by the KIT innovation management.

References
1. Invistra GmbH (2012) Invistra website. http://www.invistra.de/
2. Adobe Systems Inc (2012) Adobe flash media server. http://www.adobe.com/products/flash-media-server-family.html
3. BitTorrent Forum (2012) BitTorrent. http://www.bittorrent.org/
4. Schulzrinne E (2003) RTP: a transport protocol for real-time applications. http://tools.ietf.org/html/rfc3550
5. Parmar H, Thornburgh M (2009) Real time messaging protocol chunk stream. http://www.adobe.com/devnet/rtmp.html
6. Parmar H, Thornburgh M (2012) RTMPE description. http://www.adobe.com/devnet/rtmp.html
7. VideoLAN Organisation (2012) Video LAN website. http://www.videolan.org/
8. FlowPlayer Ltd (2012) FlowPlayer website. http://flowplayer.org/
9. Wowza Media Systems (2012) Wowza media systems home page. http://www.wowza.com/
10. Amazon Web Services (2012) Amazon web services homepage. http://aws.amazon.com
11. Webservices A (2012) Amazon EC2 home page. http://aws.amazon.com/de/ec2/
12. Google Inc (2012) Google App engine billing. https://developers.google.com/appengine/kb/billing
13. Profitbricks (2012) Profitbricks. https://www.profitbricks.com/
14. Microsoft Inc (2012) Microsoft silverlight. http://www.microsoft.com/silverlight/
15. Nvidia Inc (2012) NVIDIA 3D vision. http://www.nvidia.com/object/3d-vision-main.html
16. The Flazr Project (2012) The Flazr project website. http://flazr.com/
17. Webservices A (2012) Amazon EC2 instance types. http://aws.amazon.com/de/ec2/instance-types/
18. YouTube Inc (2011) YouTube. http://www.youtube.com/
19. KUK Filmproduktion (2012) KUK Homepage. http://www.kuk-film.de/en/stereoskopie.php
20. TV-Studios Leonberg (2012) Audiovisuelle medien. http://www.tvstudios.de/filmproduktionstechniken/3d-produktionen.html
21. Miroll GH (2011) Service compatible efficient 3D-HDTV Delivery. In: 14th ITG Conference on Electronic Media Technology
22. Sweha R, Ishakian V, Bestavros A (2012) AngelCast: Cloud-based peer-assisted live streaming using optimized multi-tree construction. In: Proceedings of the 3rd Multimedia Systems Conference. ACM, New York, pp 191–202
23. Feng J, Wen P, Liu J, Li H (2010) Elastic stream cloud (ESC): A stream-oriented cloud computing platform for Rich Internet Application In: High Performance Computing and Simulation (HPCS), 2010 International Conference on, pp 203–208. doi:10.1109/HPCS.2010.5547135
24. Ranjan R, Mitra K, Georgakopoulos D (2013) MediaWise cloud content orchestrator. J Internet Serv Appl 4: 1–14
25. Vakali A, Pallis G (2003) Content delivery networks: status and trends. Internet Comput, IEEE 7(6): 68–74
26. Mulerikkal J, Khalil I (2007) An architecture for distributed content delivery network In: Networks, 2007. ICON 2007. 15th IEEE International Conference on, pp 359–364
27. Alhamazani K, Ranjan R, Rabhi F, Wang L, Mitra K (2012) Cloud monitoring for optimizing the QoS of hosted applications. In: Cloud Computing Technology and Science (CloudCom), 2012 IEEE 4th International Conference on, pp 765–770
28. Invistra GmbH (2012) Trivido Website. http://www.trivido.com/

## 12

MapReduce for parallel trace validation of LTL properties

Sylvain Hallé* and Maxime Soucy-Boivin

Abstract

We present an algorithm for the automated verification of Linear Temporal Logic formulæ on event traces using an increasingly popular cloud computing framework called MapReduce. The algorithm can process multiple, arbitrary fragments of the trace in parallel, and compute its final result through a cycle of runs of MapReduce instances. Experimentation on a variety of cloud-based MapReduce frameworks, including Apache Hadoop, show how complex LTL properties can be validated in reasonable time in a completely distributed fashion. Compared to the classical LTL evaluation algorithm, results show how the use of a MapReduce framework can provide an interesting alternative to existing trace analysis techniques, performance-wise, under favourable conditions.

Introduction

Over the recent years, the volume and complexity of interactions between information systems has been steadily increasing. Large amounts of data are gathered about these interactions, forming a trace of events, also called a *log*, that can be stored, mined, and audited. Web servers, operating systems, database engines and business processes of various kinds all produce event logs, crash reports, test traces or dumps in some format or another.

One possible use of such a log is to perform *trace validation*: given a specification of the expected or agreed-upon interaction (or inversely, of invalid behaviour), the trace of actions recorded at runtime can then be searched automatically for patterns satisfying or violating that specification. The specification generally relates events to some sequence of actions, method calls or events: the validity of each event cannot be assessed individually, but must rather be evaluated according to the event's position with respect to surrounding events, both before and after. As we shall see in Section 'Trace validation use cases', there exists a variety of scenarios where event traces are subject to sequencing constraints, and the use of a language such as Linear Temporal Logic represents a reasonable mean of expressing these constraints formally.

Various solutions have been proposed in the past to automate the task of trace validation [1-6], either based on temporal logic or other kinds of formal specifications. While these solutions allow the expression of intricate relationships between events in a log, the scalability of many of them is jeopardized by the growing amount of data generated by today's systems. Recently, the advent of *cloud computing* has been put forward as a potential remedy to this problem, in particular for the tasks of process discovery and conformance checking [7]. By allowing the distributed processing of data spread across a network of commodity hardware, cloud computing opens the way to dramatic improvements in the performance of many applications.

Given the growing amount of collected trace data and the observed move towards distributed computing infrastructures, it is crucial that existing trace validation methodologies be ported to the cloud paradigm. However, the prospect of parallel processing of temporal constraints in general, and LTL formulæ in particular, is held back precisely because of the sequential nature of the properties to verify: since the validity of an event may depend on past and future events, the handling of parts of the trace in parallel and independent processes seems to be disqualified at the onset. A review of available solutions in Section 'Related work' observes, perhaps unsurprisingly, that most existing trace validation tools are based on algorithms that do not take advantage of parallelism, while those that do offer very limited specification

*Correspondence: shalle@acm.org
Laboratoire d'informatique formelle, Département d'informatique et de mathématique, Université du Québec à Chicoutimi, Chicoutimi (Québec) G7H 2B1, Canada

languages where sequential relationships between events are excluded.

The present paper addresses this issue by presenting a *parallelizable* algorithm for the automated validation of LTL properties in event traces. The algorithm uses a recent and popular execution framework, called MapReduce [8], which is described in Section 'An overview of MapReduce'. MapReduce provides an environment particularly suitable to the breaking up of a task into small, independent processes that can be distributed across multiple nodes in a network, and is currently being used in large-scale applications such as the Google search engine for the computation of the PageRank index [9]. The algorithm, detailed in Section 'LTL trace validation with MapReduce', exploits this framework by splitting the original property into subformulæ that can be evaluated separately through cycles of MapReduce jobs.

The algorithm has been implemented in two distinct MapReduce environments: MrSim and Apache Hadoop. Experiments were conducted on evaluating sample LTL properties on traces of up to 10 million events, and compare their running time with a state-of-the-art, classical trace analyzer for LTL. Results from these experiments, described in Section 'Experimental results', show that the algorithm offers similar or better performance when mappers and reducers are executed in a purely sequential fashion. This first result confirms that the proposed algorithm is not intrinsically penalizing a user over existing solutions.

However, our experiments also reveal that, with parallelism turned on, the same batch of MapReduce jobs offers lesser performance, slowing down the process by as much as two orders of magnitude. This seems to suggest that LTL trace analysis is indeed a fundamentally linear process, and that attempts at distributing its computation are offset by the cost of parallel management (threads, inter-process communication, etc.).

To the best of our knowledge, the present work is the first application and analysis of MapReduce for the verification of temporal logic properties on event traces. The approach presents an interesting alternative to existing tools when the formula to verify is below a certain complexity threshold, in cases where LTL with past operators is required, or when the trace to analyze is fragmented across multiple computing nodes.

Trace validation use cases

We shall first recall basic concepts related to the validation of event traces in various contexts. For the needs of this paper, an *event trace* $m_0 m_1 \ldots$, noted $\overline{m}$, represents a sequence of events over a period of time. Each event is an individual entity, made of one or more parameter-value pairs of arbitrary names and types. The schema (that is, the number and names of each parameter in each event) is not assumed to be known in advance, or even to be consistent across all events.

Constraints on event sequences: linear temporal logic

Given an event trace, one is then interested in expressing properties or *constraints* that must be fulfilled either by individual events or sequences thereof. Given an event trace $\overline{m}$ and some constraint φ, we denote by $\overline{m} \models \varphi$ the fact that the trace satisfies the constraint. A variety of formal languages are available to describe constraints of different kinds; one of them is a logical formalism called Linear Temporal Logic (LTL), whose syntax is described in Figure 1. The basic building blocks of LTL formulæ are *propositional variables* p, q, ..., expressing Boolean conditions on particular messages of the trace. In the present context, each propositional variable is an assertion of the form parameter = value, which evaluates to true if the equality holds for the current message, and to false otherwise.

The complete semantics of LTL is given in Figure 2. One can evaluate when a trace $\overline{m}$ satisfies a given formula φ, written as $\overline{m} \models \varphi$, by giving conditions to be evaluated recursively on the structure of the formula. On top of propositional variables, LTL allows *Boolean connectives* $\vee$ (or), $\wedge$ (and), $\neg$ (not), bearing their usual meaning and *temporal operators* to express constraints on the sequence of events. The temporal operator $\mathbf{G}$ means "globally"; the formula $\mathbf{G}\,\varphi$ means that formula φ is true in every event of the trace, starting from the current event. The operator $\mathbf{F}$ means "eventually"; the formula $\mathbf{F}\,\varphi$ is true if φ holds for some future event of the trace. The operator $\mathbf{X}$ means "next"; it is true whenever φ holds in the next event of the trace. Finally, the $\mathbf{U}$ operator means "until"; the formula $\varphi\,\mathbf{U}\,\psi$ is true if φ holds for all events until some event satisfies ψ. We also define $\varphi\,\mathbf{V}\,\psi$ as $\neg(\neg\varphi\,\mathbf{U}\,\neg\psi)$ and $\varphi\,\mathbf{W}\,\psi$ as $(\varphi\,\mathbf{U}\,\psi) \vee \mathbf{G}\,\varphi$. [a]

Two concepts bear particular importance in this paper. Given some operator $\star$ and a formula φ of the form $\star\varphi'$ or $\varphi' \star \psi$, expressions φ' and ψ are called the *direct subformulæ* of φ. Subformulæ form a partial ordering; we will denote as $\varphi' \prec \varphi$ the fact that φ' is a direct subformula of φ. The *depth* of a formula φ, noted $\delta(\varphi)$, is then defined as the maximum number of nested subformulæ it contains. For example, the expression $\mathbf{G}\,(p \wedge \mathbf{F}\,q)$ is of depth

---

$$\varphi := p \mid \neg\varphi \mid \varphi \vee \varphi \mid \varphi \wedge \varphi \mid \varphi \rightarrow \varphi \mid \mathbf{G}\,\varphi \mid \mathbf{F}\,\varphi \mid \mathbf{X}\,\varphi \mid \varphi\,\mathbf{U}\,\varphi$$

Figure 1 The syntax of linear temporal logic.

$$\overline{m} \models \neg\varphi \quad \equiv \quad \overline{m} \not\models \varphi$$

$$\overline{m} \models \varphi \wedge \psi \quad \equiv \quad \overline{m} \models \varphi \text{ and } \overline{m} \models \psi$$

$$\overline{m} \models \varphi \vee \psi \quad \equiv \quad \overline{m} \models \varphi \text{ or } \overline{m} \models \psi$$

$$\overline{m} \models \varphi \rightarrow \psi \quad \equiv \quad \overline{m} \not\models \varphi \text{ or } \overline{m} \models \psi$$

$$\overline{m} \models \mathbf{X}\,\varphi \quad \equiv \quad \overline{m}^1 \models \varphi$$

$$\overline{m} \models \mathbf{G}\,\varphi \quad \equiv \quad m_0 \models \varphi \text{ and } \overline{m}^1 \models \mathbf{G}\,\varphi$$

$$\overline{m} \models \mathbf{F}\,\varphi \quad \equiv \quad m_0 \models \varphi \text{ or } \overline{m}^1 \models \mathbf{F}\,\varphi$$

$$\overline{m} \models \varphi\,\mathbf{U}\,\psi \quad \equiv \quad m_0 \models \psi \text{ or both}$$
$$m_0 \models \varphi \text{ and } \overline{m}^1 \models \varphi\,\mathbf{U}\,\psi$$

$$\overline{m} \models \forall_\pi x : \varphi \quad \equiv \quad \text{for all } c \in Dom(\pi, m_0), \overline{m} \models \varphi[x/c]$$

$$\overline{m} \models \exists_\pi x : \varphi \quad \equiv \quad \text{for some } c \in Dom(\pi, m_0), \overline{m} \models \varphi[x/c]$$

Figure 2 The semantics of LTL operators, where φ and ψ are LTL formulæ, $\overline{m}$ is an event trace $m_0, m_1, m_2, \ldots$ and $\overline{m}^i$ designates its suffix $m_i, m_{i+1}, \ldots$.

3, and its set of proper subformulæ is $\{p \wedge \mathbf{F}\,q, p, \mathbf{F}\,q, q\}$. For a set of subformulæ S, we will say that φ is a (direct) *superformula* of ψ if $\varphi, \psi \in S$ and $\psi \prec \varphi$.

A use-case scenario

There exists a variety of scenarios where constraints on event traces can be modelled as LTL properties. This issue has gained considerable importance in the past decade with the advent of anti-fraud regulation such as the Sarbanes-Oxley Act (SOX) [10] or the Payment Card Industry Data Security Standard (PCI) [11], which require some form of storage and analysis of log files, such as database transaction history. We shall describe in the following a number of such scenarios described in past literature.

As a simple example, we recall an earlier work where a bookstore business process was modelled as a set of constraints in a language called DecSerFlow [12], [p.34]. The workflow is initiated by a customer placing an order (event place_c_order). This customer order is sent to and handled by the bookstore (event handle_order). The bookstore then transfers the order of the desired book to a publisher. If the bookstore receives a negative answer, it decides to either search for an alternative publisher or to reject the customer order (event c_reject). If the bookstore searches for an alternative publisher, a new bookstore order is sent to another publisher, etc. If the customer receives a negative answer (event rec_decl), then the workflow terminates. If the bookstore receives a positive answer (activity c_accept), the customer is informed (event rec_acc) and the bookstore continues processing the customer order.

From this workflow, the authors identify sequencing relationships between the various events that must be enforced for a valid transaction to take place. For example:

1. A customer order must eventually be acknowledged by the bookstore
2. Event rec_acc cannot occur unless some place_c_order has been seen previously

These relationships, expressed in a graphical notation called DecSerFlow, can be translated into equivalent LTL formulæ.

LTL can then be used to formalize the these properties. For example, the first property above becomes

$$\mathbf{G}\,(\text{place\_c\_order} \rightarrow \mathbf{F}\,(\text{rec\_acc}))$$

Similarly, the second can be expressed as:

$$(\neg\text{rec\_acc})\,\mathbf{U}\,\text{place\_c\_order}$$

We also mention that the same techniques used for LTL business process compliance can be reused for the verification of web service interface contracts [13], the detection of network intrusions in web server logs [14], and the analysis of system events produced by spacecraft hardware during testing [5].

Related work

Existing solutions for the validation of event traces can be split into two categories. On one side are formal trace validation tools, mostly experimental or academic, offering a rich input language but for which no parallel processing algorithms are available; on the other side lie distributed log analysis products whose input language and validation capabilities are relatively limited.

Formal trace analysis

A first category of tools is made of so-called "formal" trace analyzers. Complex sequential patterns of events are expressed using a rich, mathematically-based notation such as finite-state machines, temporal logic or Petri nets. Algorithms are then developed to process these specifications and automatically check that some trace satisfies the given pattern.

In this realm, a wide variety of techniques have been developed for different purposes. When the specifications are written as temporal logic formulæ, algorithms can manipulate the expressions symbolically, and progressively rewrite the original specification as the trace is being read; the pattern is violated when this rewriting process transforms the specification into a contradiction. This idea has been implemented in two independent tools, respectively based on the Maude engine [15] and the Java programming language [13].

An alternate approach consists of storing the events into a database, and to transform the sequential patterns into an equivalent database query. This has been experimented with traditional relational databases and SQL [1], and more recently using XML databases and the XQuery language [2]. The database approach has also been followed, to some degree, by the Monpoly tool [3], which associates to each event in the trace a set of conditions on its values.

ProM [4] is an open-source environment aimed at the mining of patterns in large sets of log data. Among the many plugins developed for ProM, one can find a tool for the automated verification of LTL formulæ on process logs. Also worthy of mention are Logscope [5] and RuleR [6], which use their own input language loosely based on logic and finite-state machines.

However, none of the aforementioned tools is reported to offer parallel processing capabilities, and in particular the leveraging of cloud-based infrastructures, such as MapReduce, to that end. On the contrary, [16] uses parallelism by sharing the truth values of common atomic propositions of a past-time LTL (ptLTL) among multiple, low-hardware footprint micro-CPU cores. The evaluation of LTL properties has been offloaded to multiple GPUs in [17,18], in the latter case by first reducing the LTL properties to Büchi automata. The term "parallelism" has also been used in [19] in the limited context of executing the monitor of a temporal logic specification in a separate thread from the program being observed. However, these approaches are CPU or GPU-based, and do not attempt to leverage the MapReduce framework.

Distributed trace analysis

The second category of related work comprises so-called "log analysis" solutions. Most products in that category are commercial software aimed at the filtering of event data (such as database or server logs) to search for the presence of specific patterns. Notable examples include Snare [20], ManageEngine [21] or Splunk [22]; even operating systems such as Windows provide viewing and filtering capabilities for internal events. These tools can be seen as refined variants of the well-known "Grep" function, which performs pattern matching over an input file and returns lines corresponding to some regular expression. It can be seen as a (somehow limited) form of log analysis that can be used to return parts of an event trace corresponding to a filter expression. Indeed, such mechanism has also been proposed as the basis of trace validation tools in the past [23].

"Distributed Grep" [24] is the name given to the parallel version of this procedure, where the input file is split into chunks that can be processed independently. For each line ℓ read from an input file chunk, the Map function emits a tuple $\langle \ell, \emptyset \rangle$ if it matches a given pattern; the Reduce function just copies the supplied intermediate data to the output. As a matter of fact, most log analysis tools that leverage cloud infrastructures speed up their data processing using essentially this procedure. Of these aforementioned solutions, some offer the possibility to distribute the processing of filtering functions across multiple nodes in a network. This includes a log analysis tool called that p3 has been developed to analyze packet traces in the cloud using Apache's Hadoop distributed computing environment [25].

A problem arises, however, when one wants to query an event trace using a more articulate query language than single-line regular expressions. Linear Temporal Logic is a prime illustration of this problem: if p and q define single event patterns, a temporal expression like $\mathbf{G}\,(p \rightarrow \mathbf{X}\,q)$ validates whether an event that satisfies p is always immediately followed by an event that satisfies q. Events (or lines) are no longer compared individually, but rather with respect to their sequential relationship. The main hypothesis of the aforementioned techniques, namely that event processing can be done individually, no longer holds. If the two lines of some temporal pattern are stored on different chunks of the trace, and processed by independent parallel threads, the sequential relationship will be missed.

Therefore, in all the aforementioned solutions, the filtering process is generally limited to single events taken in isolation. For example, it is possible to obtain the list of all events satisfying some criterion on the event's attributes or to compute aggregate numerical statistics on events collected (such as total throughput, average delay, etc.), but not to fetch events in relation with other events, or satisfying some sequence or temporal pattern. Similarly, p3 can only be used to perform simple filtering on individual instances, or to compute aggregate numerical statistics on events collected (such as total throughput, average delay, etc.).

A close cousin to the approach presented in this paper has been exposed by Bauer and Falcone [26]. In this setting, multiple components in a system each observe a subset of some global event trace. Given an LTL property φ, their goal is to create sound formulæ derived from φ that can be monitored on each local trace, while minimizing inter-component communication. However, this work assumes that the projection of the global trace upon each component is well-defined and known in advance. Moreover, all components consume events from the trace synchronously, such that the distribution of monitoring does not result in a speed-up of the whole process.

An overview of MapReduce

Since the emergence of the concept of cloud computing a few years ago, a variety of distributed computing environments have been released. One notable proponent is MapReduce, a framework introduced by Google in 2004 for the processing of large amounts of data [8]. It is one of the forerunners of the so-called "NoSQL" trend, which has seen the development and rising popularity of alternative data processing schemes steering away from mainstream relational databases.

Figure 3 summarizes the schematics of MapReduce. Data processing starts by the reading of some piece of data (typically an input file) by an Input Reader, whose task is to convert the input stream into a set of tuples. Each tuple is a key-value pair, denoted $\langle q_i, v \rangle$, where both keys and values can be of arbitrary types.

As Figure 3 shows, multiple instances of the Input Reader can run in parallel, and typically process separate fragments of the input data simultaneously. The tuples produced by the Input Reader are then sent one by one to a Mapper, whose task is to convert each input tuple $\langle q_i, v \rangle$ into some output tuple $\langle k_i, v' \rangle$. The processing is stateless —that is, each tuple must be transformed independently of any previously-seen tuple, and regardless of the order in which tuples are received. For an input tuple, the Mapper may as well decide not to produce any output tuple.

The pool of tuples from all Mapper instances then goes through a shuffling step; all tuples with the same key are grouped and dispatched to the same instance of Reducer. Therefore, a Reducer that receives a tuple $\langle k_i, v \rangle$ is guaranteed to receive all other tuples $\langle k_i, v' \rangle$ for that same key k_i. For the sake of clarity, we can safely assume that each Reducer instance receives the tuples for exactly one key; we can hence parameterize each such instance with the key it has been assigned.

Contrarily to the Mapper, the Reducer receives its input tuples at once, and is hence allowed to iterate through and

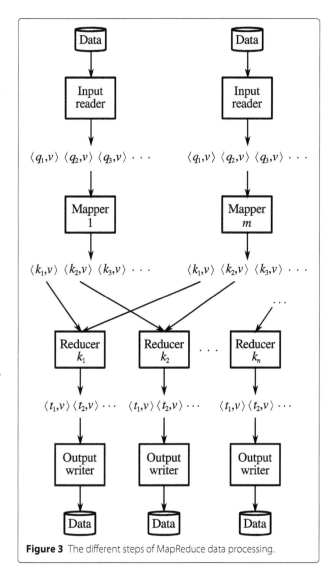

Figure 3 The different steps of MapReduce data processing.

retain information about previously seen tuples. Again, the Reducer's task is to read the input tuples, and produce as output one final set of tuples of the form $\langle t_i, v \rangle$. This set of tuples can then be read, and formatted back to some output format by an Output Writer.

In some cases, the Input Reader and Mapper may be fusioned into a single processing step, as is the case for the Reducer and Output Writer. Moreover, some definitions of MapReduce also imply that tuples are sorted according to their value before being fed to the Reducer, although we do not assume such sorting in the present paper.

Popular frameworks such as Google's or Apache's Hadoop [27] provide an environment and code libraries allowing one to write data processing tasks as MapReduce jobs. It generally suffices to write the (Java or Python) code for the Map and Reduce phases of the processing, compile it and send it to the nodes of the cloud infrastructure.

One can see from this simple description that the keys and values produced by a processing step need not be (and generally are not) the same for input and output. In the same way, there is no fixed relationship between the number of tuples read and the number of tuples sent out; a Mapper or Reducer processing some tuple may return zero, one, or even more than one tuple as output.

Moreover, it is possible to chain multiple MapReduce phases. It suffices to take the output of the Reducers as input for a subsequent cycle of Mappers. Google's PageRank algorithm is computed through three MapReduce phases, the second of which is repeated until convergence of some numerical value is reached [9]. The algorithm for Mappers and Reducers differs from phase to phase.

Although the MapReduce scheme is arguably less natural than a classical, linear program to an inexperienced developer, its architecture presents one key advantage: once a problem has been correctly split into Map and Reduce jobs, scaling up the processing to multiple nodes in the cloud becomes straightforward. Indeed, multiple Input Readers can simultaneously take care of a separate chunk of the input data. Then, since the Map step processes each tuple regardless of any past or future tuple, an arbitrary number of Mappers can process the tuples generated by the Input Readers in parallel. Similarly, the processing done by each Reducer only requires access to tuples of the same key, which entails that up to one Reducer per key can run in parallel. All in all, the whole processing chain greatly decreases the number of steps that require to be done in sequence. A good review of MapReduce's pros and cons can be found in Lee et al. [28].

LTL trace validation with MapReduce

Despite the potential parallelism brought about by the use of the MapReduce paradigm, the fundamental question of whether LTL trace validation is parallelizable remained open until very recently. We have already shown that, if one is to leverage distributed cloud frameworks for LTL querying of event traces, simple mechanisms such as Distributed Grep and their derivatives cannot be used directly.

Kuhtz and Finkbeiner showed in 2009 that LTL path checking belongs to the complexity class $AC^1(logDCFL)$ [29]; this result entails that the process can be efficiently split by evaluating entire blocks of events in parallel. Rather than sequentially traversing the trace, their work considers the circuit that results from "unrolling" the formula over the trace. However, while the evaluation of this unrolling can be done in parallel, a specific type of Boolean circuit requires to be built in advance, which depends on the length of the trace to evaluate. Moreover, the formal demonstration of the result shows that, while a fixed number of gates of this circuit can be contracted in parallel at each step of the process, the algorithm itself

requires a shared and global access to the trace from every parallel process. As such, it does not lend itself directly to distributed computing frameworks.

We take an alternate approach, and describe in this section an algorithm that performs LTL trace validation on event traces directly using the MapReduce computing paradigm. The algorithm evaluates an LTL formula in an iterative fashion. At the first iteration, all the states where ground terms are true are evaluated. In the next iteration, these results are used to evaluate all subformulæ directly using one of those ground terms. More generally, at the end of iteration i of the process, the events where all subformulæ of depth i hold are computed. It follows that, in order to evaluate an LTL formula of depth n, the algorithm will require exactly n MapReduce cycles. Each MapReduce cycle effectively acts as a form of temporal tester [30] processing a trace made of the evaluation of lower-level testers.

This does not mean, however, that the event trace must be read as many times. In fact, the input trace is entirely read only once, at the first iteration of the procedure. Afterwards, only sequential numbers referring to those events need to be passed between mappers and reducers. The contents of the original trace never need to be consulted ever again.

The system is described by providing details on each component of the MapReduce algorithm described in Figure 3. We suppose that every instance of the process (Input Reader, Mapper, Reducer, Output Writer) are parameterized by the formula to verify φ, and the length of the trace, ℓ.

We will illustrate the workings of this algorithm through a simple example, by considering the formula

$$\varphi \equiv \mathbf{G}\left(\neg c \vee \mathbf{F}\left(a \vee b\right)\right)$$

evaluated on the trace a,c,a,d,c,d,b.

Trace format and input reader

The Input Reader is responsible for the processing of a set of events from the trace to read and the generation of a first set of key-value tuples from that set. We assume that each event is sequentially numbered, or that its position in the whole trace can be easily computed otherwise. For some event e, we will refer by $\#(e)$ this event's sequential number.

The Input Reader, whose algorithm is given in Figure 4a, iterates through each event of the trace chunk, and evaluates on each event the ground terms present in φ. For each propositional variable a and each event e, it outputs a tuple $\langle a, (i, 0)\rangle$ where i is the event's sequential number in the trace. The ground terms of a formula φ are computed using the function atom(φ).

```
Procedure Input Reader_φ,ℓ(chunk)          Procedure Mapper_φ,ℓ(⟨ψ,(n,i)⟩)
    A[] := atoms(φ)                            If i ≤ δ(ψ)
    For each e in chunk do                         S[] := superformulæ(φ,ψ)
        i := #(e)                                  For each ξ in S do
        For each a in A do                             output ⟨ξ,(ψ,n,i+1)⟩
            If e ⊨ a then                          End If
                output ⟨a,(i,0)⟩                End
            End if                          End If
        End
    End
```

(a) Pseudo-code for the LTL Input Reader   (b) Pseudo-code for the LTL Mapper.

Figure 4 Pseudo-code for the LTL Input Reader **(a)** and Mapper **(b)**.

At the first iteration of the process on our sample formula, the InputR eader (or multiple input readers) process the trace and generates the first set of tuples:

$$\langle a,(0,0)\rangle, \langle a,(2,0)\rangle, \langle b,(6,0)\rangle, \langle \neg c,(0,0)\rangle,$$

$$\langle \neg c,(2,0)\rangle, \langle \neg c,(3,0)\rangle, \langle \neg c,(5,0)\rangle, \langle \neg c,(6,0)\rangle$$

One should remark that this initial processing step does not require that the trace be located on a single node, or even that each node's fragment consist of blocks of successive events. As long as each event can be placed in some total order (such as the value of a global, shared clock), any number of nodes can host any subset of the trace. This is particularly useful if event collection and storage is performed in a distributed fashion.

Mapper

The Mapper takes as input tuples of the form $\langle \psi,(n,i)\rangle$, either from the Input Reader or from the output of a previous MapReduce cycle. Each such tuple reads as "the process is at iteration i, and subformula ψ is true on event n". One can see, in particular, how the tuples returned by the Input Reader express this fact for ground terms of the formula to verify.

The Mapper, shown in Figure 4b, is responsible for lifting these results, computed for some ψ, up into every formulæ ψ' of which ψ is a *direct* subformula (these are obtained using the function superformulæ(φ,ψ)). For example, if the states where p is true have been computed, then these results can be used to determine the states where $\mathbf{F}p$ is true. To this end, the Mapper takes every tuple $\langle \psi,(n,i)\rangle$, and will output a tuple $\langle \psi',(\psi,n,i+1)\rangle$, where ψ is a subformula of ψ'. This tuple reads "the process is at iteration $i+1$, subformula ψ is true on event n, and this must be used to evaluate ψ'". In the definition of the reducer, ξ stands for whatever subformula the input tuple is build from.

On our example, the tuples produced by the Input Reader at the previous step are sent to mappers which produce the following output tuples:

$$\langle a \vee b,(a,0,1)\rangle, \langle a \vee b,(a,2,1)\rangle, \langle a \vee b,(b,6,1)\rangle, \langle \neg c \vee \mathbf{F}(a \vee b),(\neg c,0,1)\rangle,$$

$$\langle \neg c \vee \mathbf{F}(a \vee b),(\neg c,2,1)\rangle, \langle \neg c \vee \mathbf{F}(a \vee b),(\neg c,3,1)\rangle, \langle \neg c \vee \mathbf{F}(a \vee b),(\neg c,5,1)\rangle,$$

$$\langle \neg c \vee \mathbf{F}(a \vee b),(\neg c,6,1)\rangle$$

Reducer

The mappers are mostly used to prepare results from the last iteration to be used for the current iteration. In contrast, each instance of the reducer performs the actual evaluation of one more layer of the temporal formula to verify. After the shuffling step, each individual instance of the reducer receives all generated tuples of the form $\langle \psi',(\psi,n,i)\rangle$ for some formula ψ', and where ψ is a direct subformula of ψ'. Hence, the reducer is given information on all the event numbers for which ψ' holds, and is asked to compute the states where ψ holds based on this information. This task can then be decomposed depending on the top-level connective in ψ'. The algorithm for each reducer is shown in Figure 5.

When the top-level formula to evaluate is $\mathbf{X}\psi$, the events that satisfy the formula are exactly those immediately preceding an event where ψ holds. Consequently, the reducer iterates through its input tuples of $\langle \mathbf{X}\psi,(\psi,n,i)\rangle$ and produces for each one an output tuple $\langle \mathbf{X}\psi,(n-1,i)\rangle$.

When the top-level formula to evaluate is $\mathbf{F}\psi$, the events that satisfy the formula are exactly those for which some event in the future is such that ψ holds. The corresponding reducer iterates through the input tuples and computes the highest event number c for which ψ holds. All events preceding c satisfy $\mathbf{F}\psi$. Consequently, the reducer generates as output all tuples of the form $\langle \mathbf{F}\psi,(k,i)\rangle$, for each $k \in [0,c]$.

The reducer for $\neg\psi$ iterates through all tuples and stores in a Boolean array whether $e_i \models \psi$ for each event i in the trace. It then outputs a tuple $\langle \neg\psi,(k,i)\rangle$ for all event numbers k that were not seen in the input. The reducer for $\mathbf{G}\psi$ proceeds in reverse. It first iterates through all tuples in the same way. If we let c be the index of the last event for which ψ does not hold, the reducer will then output all tuples $\langle \mathbf{G}\psi,(k,i)\rangle$ for $k \in [c+1,\ell]$. This indeed corresponds to all events for which $\mathbf{G}\psi$ holds.

```
Procedure Reducer_{φ,ℓ}(F ψ, tuples[])                      Procedure Reducer_{φ,ℓ}(X ψ, tuples[])
    m := -1                                                     For each ⟨X ψ, (ξ, n, i)⟩ in tuples do
    For each ⟨F ψ, (ξ, n, i)⟩ in tuples do                          output ⟨X ψ, (n − 1, i)⟩
        If n > m then m := n                                    End
    End
    For k from 0 to m do                                    Procedure Reducer_{φ,ℓ}(ψ ∧ ψ', tuples[])
        output ⟨F ψ, (k, i)⟩                                    For each ⟨ψ ∧ ψ', (ξ, n, i)⟩ in tuples do
    End                                                            If δ(ψ ∧ ψ') ≠ i then
                                                                       output ⟨ξ, (n, i)⟩
Procedure Reducer_{φ,ℓ}(¬ψ, tuples[])                                   s_ξ[n] := ⊤
    For each ⟨¬ψ, (ξ, n, i)⟩ in tuples do                           End If
        s[n] := ⊤                                                   If s_ψ[n] := ⊤ and s_ψ'[n] := ⊤ then
    End                                                                output ⟨ψ ∧ ψ', (n, i)⟩
    For k from 0 to ℓ do                                            End If
        If s[k] ≠ ⊤ then                                        End
            output ⟨¬ψ, (k, i)⟩
        End If                                              Procedure Reducer_{φ,ℓ}(ψ U ψ', tuples[])
    End                                                         For each ⟨ψ U ψ', (ξ, n, i)⟩ in tuples do
                                                                   If δ(ψ U ψ') ≠ i then
Procedure Reducer_{φ,ℓ}(G ψ, tuples[])                                 output ⟨ξ, (n, i)⟩
    For each ⟨G ψ, (ξ, n, i)⟩ in tuples do                          End If
        s[n] := ⊤                                                   s_ξ[n] := ⊤
    End                                                         End
    For k from ℓ to 0 do                                        b := ⊥
        If s[k] ≠ ⊤ break                                       For k from ℓ to 0 do
        output ⟨G ψ, (k, i)⟩                                        If s_ψ'[n] = ⊤ then
    End                                                                output ⟨ψ U ψ', (k, i)⟩
                                                                       b := ⊤
Procedure Reducer_{φ,ℓ}(ψ ∨ ψ', tuples[])                           Else If s_ψ[n] := ⊤ and b = ⊤ then
    For each ⟨ψ ∨ ψ', (ξ, n, i)⟩ in tuples do                          output ⟨ψ U ψ', (k, i)⟩
        If δ(ψ ∨ ψ') ≠ i then                                      Else
            output ⟨ξ, (n, i)⟩                                         b := ⊥
        Else                                                       End If
            output ⟨ψ ∨ ψ', (n, i)⟩                              End
        End If
    End
```

Figure 5 Pseudo-code for the LTL Reducers.

The case of binary connectives $\vee$ and $\wedge$ is slightly more delicate. Special care must be taken to persist tuples whose result will be used in a later iteration. Consider the case of formula $(\mathbf{F}\,p) \wedge q$. The states where ground terms p and q hold will be computed by the Input Reader at iteration 0. However, although q is a direct subformula of $(\mathbf{F}\,p) \wedge q$, one has to wait until iteration 2 to combine it to $\mathbf{F}\,p$, evaluated at iteration 1. More precisely, a tuple $\langle \psi \star \psi', (\psi, n, i)\rangle$ can only be evaluated at iteration $\delta(\psi \star \psi')$; in all previous iterations, tuples $\langle \psi, (n, i)\rangle$ must be put back in circulation. The first condition in both reducers' algorithm takes care of this situation.

Otherwise, when the top-level formula to evaluate is $\psi \vee \psi'$, the reducer outputs a tuple $\langle \psi \vee \psi', (n, i)\rangle$ whenever it reads input tuples $\langle \psi \vee \psi', (\psi, n, i)\rangle$ or $\langle \psi \vee \psi', (\psi', n, i)\rangle$. When the top-level formula is $\psi \wedge \psi'$, the reducer must memorize event numbers n for which it has read tuples $\langle \psi \wedge \psi', (\psi, n, i)\rangle$ and $\langle \psi \wedge \psi', (\psi', n, i)\rangle$, and outputs $\langle \psi \wedge \psi', (n, i)\rangle$ as soon as it has seen both. The last case to consider is that of a formula of the form $\psi \mathbf{U} \psi'$. The reducer first iterates through all its input tuples and memorizes the event numbers for which ψ holds, and those for which ψ' holds. It then proceeds backwards from the last event of the trace, and outputs $\langle \psi \mathbf{U} \psi', (n, i)\rangle$ for some state n if ψ' holds for n, or if ψ holds for n and there exists an uninterrupted sequence of states leading to a state n' for which ψ' holds. This last information is handled through the Boolean variable b.

On our example formula, the reducer for $a \vee b$ will receive the first three tuples and output $\langle a \vee b, (0, 1)\rangle$, $\langle a \vee b, (2, 1)\rangle$, $\langle a \vee b, (6, 1)\rangle$. Since the iteration number is 1, and the depth of $\neg c \vee \mathbf{F}\,(a \vee b)$ is 3, the reducer for $\neg c \vee \mathbf{F}\,(a \vee b)$ will simply re-output the tuples

$$\langle \neg c, (0, 1)\rangle, \langle \neg c, (2, 1)\rangle, \langle \neg c, (3, 1)\rangle, \langle \neg c, (5, 1)\rangle, \langle \neg c, (6, 1)\rangle$$

As one can see, the tuples produced by each reducer is of the form $\langle \psi, (n, i)\rangle$, carrying the exact same meaning as those originally produced by the Input Reader, albeit for formulæ of greater depth. Therefore, the result of one MapReduce cycle can be fed back as input of a new cycle; as we have seen, it takes exactly $\delta(\varphi)$ such cycles to completely evaluate some LTL formula φ.

Output writer

At the end of the last MapReduce cycle, one is left with tuples $\langle \varphi, (n, \delta(\varphi))\rangle$. These represent all event numbers n such that $\overline{m}^n \models \varphi$. The output writer, shown in Figure 6, translates the last set of tuples into the truth value of the formula to evaluate. By the semantics of LTL, an event trace satisfies the formula φ if $\overline{m}^0 \models \varphi$. Hence the output

Procedure Output Writer$_{\varphi,\ell}(tuples[])$
  For each $\langle \varphi, (n,i) \rangle$ in *tuples* **do**
    If $n = 0$ **then**
      output "Formula is true"
      Break
    End if
  End
  output "Formula is false"

Figure 6 Pseudo-code for the LTL output writer.

writer simply writes "true" if $\langle \varphi, (0, \delta(\varphi)) \rangle$ is found, and false otherwise.

A complete example

For the sake of completeness, the remaining iterations of MapReduce processing on our example formula are given below.

Iteration 2

The tuples produced by the first round of Reducers are sent to mappers for a second cycle, producing:

$\langle F(a \vee b), (a \vee b, 0, 2) \rangle, \langle F(a \vee b), (a \vee b, 2, 2) \rangle, \langle F(a \vee b), (a \vee b, 6, 2) \rangle,$
$\langle \neg c \vee F(a \vee b), (\neg c, 0, 2) \rangle, \langle \neg c \vee F(a \vee b), (\neg c, 2, 2) \rangle, \langle \neg c \vee F(a \vee b), (\neg c, 3, 2) \rangle,$
$\langle \neg c \vee F(a \vee b), (\neg c, 5, 2) \rangle, \langle \neg c \vee F(a \vee b), (\neg c, 6, 2) \rangle.$

The reducer for $F(a \vee b)$ will produce:

$\langle F(a \vee b), (0, 2) \rangle, \langle F(a \vee b), (1, 2) \rangle, \langle F(a \vee b), (2, 2) \rangle, \langle F(a \vee b), (3, 2) \rangle,$
$\langle F(a \vee b), (4, 2) \rangle, \langle F(a \vee b), (5, 2) \rangle, \langle F(a \vee b), (6, 2) \rangle$

while the reducer for $\neg c \vee F(a \vee b)$ will again re-output:

$\langle \neg c, (0, 2) \rangle, \langle \neg c, (2, 2) \rangle, \langle \neg c, (3, 2) \rangle, \langle \neg c, (5, 2) \rangle, \langle \neg c, (6, 2) \rangle.$

Iteration 3

The tuples are sent into the penultimate cycle; the mappers will produce:

$\langle \neg c \vee F(a \vee b), (F(a \vee b), 0, 3) \rangle, \langle \neg c \vee F(a \vee b), (F(a \vee b), 1, 3) \rangle,$
$\langle \neg c \vee F(a \vee b), (F(a \vee b), 2, 3) \rangle, \langle \neg c \vee F(a \vee b), (F(a \vee b), 3, 3) \rangle,$
$\langle \neg c \vee F(a \vee b), (F(a \vee b), 4, 3) \rangle, \langle \neg c \vee F(a \vee b), (F(a \vee b), 5, 3) \rangle,$
$\langle \neg c \vee F(a \vee b), (F(a \vee b), 6, 3) \rangle, \langle \neg c \vee F(a \vee b), (\neg c, 0, 3) \rangle, \langle \neg c \vee F(a \vee b), (\neg c, 2, 3) \rangle,$
$\langle \neg c \vee F(a \vee b), (\neg c, 3, 3) \rangle, \langle \neg c \vee F(a \vee b), (\neg c, 5, 3) \rangle, \langle \neg c \vee F(a \vee b), (\neg c, 6, 3) \rangle.$

The reducer for $\neg c \vee F(a \vee b)$ will output:

$\langle \neg c \vee F(a \vee b), (0, 3) \rangle, \langle \neg c \vee F(a \vee b), (1, 3) \rangle, \langle \neg c \vee F(a \vee b), (2, 3) \rangle,$
$\langle \neg c \vee F(a \vee b), (3, 3) \rangle, \langle \neg c \vee F(a \vee b), (4, 3) \rangle, \langle \neg c \vee F(a \vee b), (5, 3) \rangle,$
$\langle \neg c \vee F(a \vee b), (6, 3) \rangle.$

Iteration 4

For the last iteration, the mappers produce

$\langle G(\neg c \vee F(a \vee b)), (\neg c \vee F(a \vee b), 0, 4) \rangle, \langle G(\neg c \vee F(a \vee b)), (\neg c \vee F(a \vee b), 1, 4) \rangle,$
$\langle G(\neg c \vee F(a \vee b)), (\neg c \vee F(a \vee b), 2, 4) \rangle, \langle G(\neg c \vee F(a \vee b)), (\neg c \vee F(a \vee b), 3, 4) \rangle,$
$\langle G(\neg c \vee F(a \vee b)), (\neg c \vee F(a \vee b), 4, 4) \rangle, \langle G(\neg c \vee F(a \vee b)), (\neg c \vee F(a \vee b), 5, 4) \rangle,$
$\langle G(\neg c \vee F(a \vee b)), (\neg c \vee F(a \vee b), 6, 4) \rangle$

The reducer for $G(\neg c \vee F(a \vee b))$ computes the output tuples

$\langle G(\neg c \vee F(a \vee b)), (0, 4) \rangle, \langle G(\neg c \vee F(a \vee b)), (1, 4) \rangle \langle G(\neg c \vee F(a \vee b)), (2, 4) \rangle$
$\langle G(\neg c \vee F(a \vee b)), (3, 4) \rangle \langle G(\neg c \vee F(a \vee b)), (4, 4) \rangle \langle G(\neg c \vee F(a \vee b)), (5, 4) \rangle$
$\langle G(\neg c \vee F(a \vee b)), (6, 4) \rangle$

Finally, since event number 0 is part of the tuple set, the output writer concludes that the formula is true for the trace considered.

From this simple example, one can see how multiple input readers can process separate chunks of the same event trace independently. As a matter of fact, each input reader does not even require that its chunk contains sets of consecutive events, as long as each event is properly numbered according to its sequential position. In addition, as a side effect of fitting the problem into the MapReduce framework, an arbitrary number of parallel Mapper instances can be used to process a set of input tuples at each cycle. Similarly, up to one Reducer per key (that is, one per subformula) can run in parallel in the Reduce phase of a cycle.

LTL with past

The use of the present algorithm for LTL validation provides a number of interesting side effects. The most notable one is that the evaluation of LTL *past* operators can be obtained mostly "for free". For instance the translation of operator Y (the past version of X) simply amounts to replacing $n-1$ by $n+1$ in the definition of the reducer for X. A similar reasoning can be applied for the remaining past temporal operators, like P (or F^{-1}), H (G^{-1}) or S (U^{-1}). Furthermore, unusual operators such as the C ("chop") modality [31] can also be defined easily with their custom reducer.

Experimental results

To illustrate the concept and evaluate its feasibility, we implemented the algorithm described earlier in two different MapReduce frameworks, and compared it to an existing trace analysis tool called BeepBeep, which uses a classical, non-parallel algorithm. Experiments were then conducted to compare their running time on the same set of traces; the point of the comparison is to get an intuition whether using MapReduce can provide an improvement over existing techniques, performance-wise.

Sample properties

To assess the running time of the MapReduce validation algorithm, we built a dataset consisting of traces of randomly-generated events, with each event being made of up to ten random parameters, labelled $p_0, \ldots p_9$, each carrying five possible values. Each trace has a length between 1 and 100,000 events, and 500 such traces were produced. In total, this dataset amounts to more than one gigabyte of randomly-generated event data.

Four properties, with increasing complexity, were verified on these traces. Property #1 is $\mathbf{G}\, p_0 \neq 0$, and simply asserts that in every event, parameter p_0, when present, is never equal to 0. Property #2 is $\mathbf{G}\,(p_0 = 0 \to \mathbf{X}\, p_1 = 0)$: it expresses the fact that whenever $p_0 = 0$ in some event, the next event is such that $p_1 = 0$. Property #3 is a generalization of Property #2:

$$\forall x \in [\,0,9\,] : \mathbf{G}\,(p_0 = x \to \mathbf{X}\, p_1 = x)$$

This property asserts that whatever value taken by p_0 will be taken by p_1 in the next event. The universal and existential quantifiers are meant as a shorthand notation; the actual LTL formula to be validated is the logical conjunction of the previous template for all possible values of x between 0 and 9, and reads

$$(\mathbf{G}\,(p_0 = 0 \to \mathbf{X}\, p_1 = 0)) \wedge (\mathbf{G}\,(p_0 = 1 \to \mathbf{X}\, p_1 = 1)) \ldots$$

Finally, Property #4 checks that *some* parameter p_m alternates between two possible values; this is true when the value of p_m in the current event is the same as the value two events from the current one, and is written:

$$\exists m \in [\,0,9\,] : \forall x \in [\,0,9\,] : \mathbf{G}\,(p_m = x \to \mathbf{X}\,\mathbf{X}\, p_m = x)$$

Again, the quantifiers are meant as a shorthand.

Execution environments

Our execution environment for the validation of properties consists of a virtual cluster inside a Solaris 11.1 server, equipped with 24 GB of RAM. One reason for the choice of Solaris is its possibility to create isolated environments, called *zones*, without the need for a full-fledged virtual machine. Each zone has its own resource controller, and communicates with the rest of the environment only through a connection using virtual network interfaces. This makes it easy to create and manage computing nodes.

The practice of using Solaris zones to create a Hadoop cluster is well known and documented [32]. Advantages of using such an architecture include fast provision of new cluster members using the zone cloning feature, very high network throughput between the zones for data node replication, optimized disk I/O utilization, and secure data at rest using ZFS encryption. In our setup, the cluster is made of five nodes: a master "name-node" whose task is to manage Hadoop jobs, three "data-nodes" that perform the actual Map and Reduce operations, and a backup of the name node that can resume its job should a failure occur. It is out of the scope of this paper to describe in detail the architecture of the cluster; we followed the basic setup steps contained in documentation from Oracle and available online [32].

We now proceed to describe the trace analysis tools that were run on the cluster. It shall be noted that only Hadoop requires a multi-node (and hence multi-zone) setup. The remaining tools were executed in the default, "global" zone of the system.

BeepBeep

The first tool included in our survey is a runtime monitor we developed in earlier work called BeepBeep [33].[b] BeepBeep receives a stream of events produced by some application or process, and constantly analyzes it against a specification given beforehand. When the stream of events deviates from what the specification stipulates, a signal is sent which can then be piped into another program for further processing. It can also work in offline mode and analyze a pre-recorded trace of events taken from a file.

Although BeepBeep accepts as input an LTL expression, its processing uses a completely different algorithm from the one described in this paper. This algorithm is *not* based on MapReduce: it is sequential, and requires a single process to analyze each event of the trace one by one in their proper order.

A recent benchmark has showed that BeepBeep provides performance in the average of a large number of other trace validation solutions [34]. It was included in our analysis as the baseline case, being representative of the kind of performance that classical solutions provide. It will hence be possible to compare the running time of our proposed MapReduce solution and measure any actual benefits in terms of performance.

MrSim

The second environment we used for the comparison is a hybrid between sequential trace processing and distributed MapReduce, called MrSim. MrSim [35] is a simple implementation of MapReduce in Java, intended for a pedagogical illustration of the programming model. It originates from frustrating experiences using other frameworks, which require a lengthy and cumbersome setup before running even the simplest example. In most cases those examples are entangled with technical considerations (distributed file system, network configuration) that distract from learning the MapReduce programming model itself.

MrSim aims at providing a simple framework to create and test MapReduce jobs with a minimal setup, using straightforward implementations of all necessary concepts. This entails some purposeful limitations to the system: for example, it is not optimized in any way. In counterpart, MrSim offers interesting features from a pedagogical point of view: it runs out of the box, and the centralized processing makes it easy to perform step-by-step debugging of a MapReduce job.

MrSim can run in two modes. In sequential mode, the actual coordination of Map and Reduce jobs is done locally on a single machine using a single-thread implementation of MapReduce: the data source is fed tuple by tuple to the mapper, the output tuples are collected, split according to their keys, and each list is sent to the reducer, again in a sequential fashion. As such, this sequential workflow reproduces exactly the processing done by MapReduce environments, without the distribution of computation. This was done on purpose, so that the running time of each mapper and reducer instance could be easily measured.

In multi-threaded mode, Map and Reduce jobs of the same iteration each run in a distinct thread provided by a thread dispatcher. The dispatcher is instantiated with a parameter n specifying the maximum number of concurrent threads. The first n Map and Reduce jobs that execute are immediately given a thread; remaining jobs in excess of n, if any, are put into a waiting queue for one of the existing threads to terminate. In terms of performance, the operation in sequential mode is equivalent to multi-threaded when $n = 1$ (barring some light thread management overhead), as was confirmed by a set of preliminary setup tests.

A first observation that can be made is that this execution environment is the simplest of all we tested: excluding the code for coordinating Mappers and Reducers (itself made of only 250 lines of code), the total implementation of the validator amounts to 1,000 lines of Java code. This should be put in contrast with BeepBeep, which is also implemented in Java and rather uses the classical, on-the-fly algorithm for the evaluation of LTL formulæ on traces [13]; BeepBeep is is made up of twice as many lines of Java code.

Hadoop

The third environment used in our experiments is Apache Hadoop version 1.2.1, already introduced earlier.

While Hadoop is regularly presented as the canonical example of a MapReduce implementation, it turns out that there are significant differences between the *theoretical* principle of MapReduce described in Section 'An overview of MapReduce', and the *real-life* implementation of MapReduce in Apache Hadoop.

Chaining MapReduce jobs In the theoretical MapReduce framework (and in MrSim), tuples output by reducers can be sent directly as input to mappers, making multiple iterations of MapReduce cycles possible. Hadoop does not support this: tuples produced by reducers must be sent serialized to an output collector, saved to a file, and then be re-read from an input collector and converted back into tuples. This makes the chaining of cycles of MapReduce jobs, necessary in our context for but the simplest LTL formulæ, very cumbersome, inefficient, and ultimately uncalled for, as the MrSim environment does not require such a mandatory serialization to chain cycles of MapReduce jobs.

Line input format A second limitation of the Hadoop implementation is the fact that input readers are line-based —that is, an input reader is fed one line at a time from the input source, and elements from which tuples are created cannot span multiple lines. While this behaviour is appropriate for simple log formats, it makes it hard to support rich data models such as, in our case, XML. We had to preprocess our input traces to remove line endings inside all events, so that each event occupies exactly one line. Again, input readers in MrSim do not present this limitation and can be fed arbitrary chunks of an input source.

Object inheritance An LTL expression is represented as a top-level LTL operator, which in turn may contain a number of children operators, hence creating a nested structure representing the contents of the formula. Every operator is a subclass of the general class LTLOperator; it is therefore natural to declare the key of tuples as an object of type LTLOperator, and this is precisely what is done in MrSim.

Yet, Hadoop does not support inheritance when manipulating tuples. This means that if a map or a reduce job is declared to accept tuples of type (K, V), Hadoop throws a runtime error when trying to process a tuple of type (K', V'), where K' and V' are descendants (in the object-oriented sense of the term) of K and V respectively. This poses a serious problem in our context, which necessitated rewriting our representation of LTL formulæ as a single object, using a member field whose value makes it behave like a conjunction, an operator **G**, etc. This unexplained limitation belongs to Hadoop, and is not an inherent limitation of the MapReduce principle, as MrSim does not present this problem. This arguably renders the validation code inelegant, and again, most assuredly affects its performance.

Results

To test and compare each validation solution, we randomly generated traces of XML events with abstract names p0, p1, etc., each containing a random integer value. The length of each trace varied from less than 10 events to more than 9 million; in this last case, the XML file weighed just short of 1 gigabyte. Each property P1–P4 was validated on each trace, and various statistics on the process were computed.

All tools operate in the same way: they accept as input a character string (the same for every tool) representing an LTL formula, and a filename pointing to an XML trace saved locally. Each tool then processes the formula and the trace using its own algorithm (the classical LTL evaluation algorithm for BeepBeep, and the MapReduce implementation described in this paper for the others).

It should be noted at the onset that all three MapReduce solutions (Hadoop and the two versions of MrSim) crashed when evaluating Property 4 on the two largest traces we generated (respectively 3.5 and 9 million events). Apart from these two events, every tool successfully completed each verification task and returned the same (correct) verdict.

Number of tuples

The first measurement is the number of tuples produced by the algorithm. This value is taken as the sum of T_i, the total number of tuples processed at the Map phase of each MapReduce cycle number i, for all cycles $i \in [1, \delta(\varphi)]$, as shown in Table 1. One can see that the number of tuples increases with the complexity of the formula: while Property #1 produces 180,000 tuples for a trace, the validation of Property #4 on the same trace generates more than 8 million such units.

For example, validating property P2 produces roughly twice as many tuples, in total, than there are events in the trace to analyze. From this ratio, it is possible to guess that the total number of tuples that would have been produced when evaluating property 4 on the largest trace is around 400 million.

The distribution of tuples across iterations is far from uniform, however. Table 2 shows the number of tuples produced by the reduce phase of each cycle for each property and two different traces.

We also computed the "sequential ratio" of the validation process. At each MapReduce cycle, we keep the largest number of tuples processed by a single instance of a reducer. This value, noted t_i, represents the minimum number of tuples that must be processed sequentially in

Table 1 The total number of tuples produced for the validation of each properties on traces of increasing sizes

Trace size	P1	P2	P3	P4
11	14	17	20	221
180,035	180,062	346,642	815,449	8,194,477
1,770,922	1,770,938	3,409,468	8,010,419	80,552,405
3,523,211	3,523,218	6,782,937	15,938,586	> 54 M
9,025,596	9,025,603	17,375,057	40,830,370	—
Ratio	1	1.9	4.5	45

Table 2 Number of tuples produced at each MapReduce iteration for the validation of properties P1–P4, for a trace of a few kilobytes (a) and a trace of around 100 megabytes (b)

(a)				
Iteration	P1	P2	P3	P4
1	8	8	9	11
2	3	3	4	43
3	3	3	4	42
4		3	3	59
5				34
6				24
7				8

(b)				
Iteration	P1	P2	P3	P4
1	132,392	132,392	662,013	856,275
2	1,638,530	1,638,530	3,674,133	26,563,830
3	16	1,638,530	3,674,133	26,563,830
4		16	47	26,564,584
5			31	1,508
6			31	1,022
7			31	750
8				336
9				28
10				28
11				54
12				80
13				80

that particular cycle. If all reducers for that cycle were allowed to run in parallel, and assuming similar processing time for each tuple, the ratio t_i/T_i is an indicator of the time the "parallel" cycle requires with respect to the "sequential" version. The global sequential ratio shown in Table 3 is taken as

$$ s = \frac{\sum_{i=1}^{\delta(\varphi)} t_i}{\sum_{i=1}^{\delta(\varphi)} T_i} $$

This sequential ratio shows one of the limits of the validation algorithm in its present incarnation: the potential for parallelism is bounded by the structure of the formula to validate, as there can be at most one instance of reducer for every possible subformula of the property to verify.

Table 3 Sequential ratio each of the four properties P1–P4

	Property #1	Property #2	Property #3	Property #4
Sequential ratio	100 %	92 %	19 %	3 %

Therefore, for simple formulæ such as Property #1 and #2, which have very few different subformulæ at each MapReduce cycle, almost all the work must be done sequentially (100% in the case of Property #1, and 92% in the case of Property #2). However, as soon as the property becomes more complex, as is the case for Properties #3 and #4, the situation is reversed, and each reducer handles a small fraction of the total number of tuples. Property #4 is most dramatic in that respect, since 97% of all tuples involved can be processed in parallel. The presence of quantifiers accounts for a large part of this phenomenon, as it rapidly blows up the size of the actual LTL formula passed to the trace validator: 50 copies of the same template are validated, with various combinations of values for m and x.

Running time

The second measurement is the total running time required to vaildate each property, on traces of increasing size. A summary of these results is given in Table 4, which shows, for each property, the average running time per event, which is the total processing time divided by the number of events in the trace; the value shown in the table is the average of these values over all traces.

From the sequential ratio s and the average sequential running time per event r obtained for each property, it is also possible to infer the theoretical validation time in the maximally-parallel case by computing $r \times s$; this inferred running time is also shown in Table 4, using the sequential run of MrSim as the baseline.

A first observation that can be made is that, for most properties, the BeepBeep runtime monitor is *many* orders of magnitude slower than any MapReduce implementation. Even the sequential MrSim setup provides runtime performance superior to BeepBeep, indicating that the use of a MapReduce algorithm in itself presents an intrinsic performance advantage.

Detailed results on the running time for every property, and trace are plotted, for each validation environment, in Figure 7. The figure reveals a running time that is roughly linear in terms of the length of the trace for all properties and all tools. The rate of growth, however, varies widely from one tool to the next, with BeepBeep faring the

worst. Surprisingly, the multi-thread versions of MrSim and the Hadoop cluster exhibit slower validation times than the sequential version of MrSim; depending on the properties, these tools are sometimes 40 times slower than the sequential version of MrSim. The running times estimated from the sequential ratio (last line of Table 4) are also sometimes orders of magnitude lower than the actual running times observed with the multi-thread version of MrSim. Since the sequential MrSim uses the same Map and Reduce jobs, the culprit cannot lie in the algorithm itself, but rather in the introduction of parallelism.

Worst-case bandwidth

Given that all three MapReduce approaches crashed for traces and formulæ producing the most tuples, we performed a theoretical analysis of the bandwidth required to evaluate a formula in the worst csae.

First, one can realize that a tuple can be reduced to at most four integers. Assuming 32-bit integers, a tuple can hence accommodate roughly 4 billion events (2^{32}), as many subformulæ and iteration cycles, and be serialized as a 12-byte string.

We can then estimate the maximum number of tuples that can be generated during the evaluation of a formula. There can be as many tuples as there are events in the trace to process, and one such tuple can be produced for each subformula of the formula to verify. If we let $|\varphi|$ be the length (i.e. number of symbols) of φ, one can conclude that there are at most $2|\varphi|$ subformulæ; indeed, each logical connective occurring in φ brings at most two proper subformulæ. Hence the cumulative tuple bandwidth B to be exchanged can be given by:

$$B = T \times \delta(\varphi) \times \ell \times 2|\sigma(\varphi)|$$

where T is the tuple size, $\delta(\varphi)$ is the depth of the formula to verify (and hence the number of MapReduce cycles), ℓ is the event trace length, and $2|\sigma(\varphi)|$ denotes the total number of subformulæ. The $\ell \times 2|\sigma(\varphi)|$ term is indeed a crude worst case bound, as it assumes that each event of the input trace generates one tuple for each subformula and at each cycle, that all subformulæ are present at each cycle (they obviously aren't), and that the formula is only composed of binary connectives (it generally isn't). It also assumes that every produced tuple must be transmitted to another site to be processed in the next step in the algorithm. For the properties given as an example in this paper, $|\sigma(\varphi)|$ is effectively bounded by 3.

One can see that, while this bound can amount to a large number of tuples, it nevertheless remains linear both in the length of the trace and the size of the LTL formula to evaluate. Therefore, the cheerless results we obtained with the parallel versions of the algorithm seem to be related to their implementation, and not to asymptotic complexity.

Table 4 Average running time in microseconds per event for each property and each tool

Tool	P1	P2	P3	P4
BeepBeep	15,788	6,332	0.2	31
MrSim (sequential)	1.9	3.6	10.4	335
Hadoop cluster	44	96	243	4,694
MrSim (multi-thread)	73	138	433	5,734
MrSim (predicted)	1.9	3.3	2.0	10

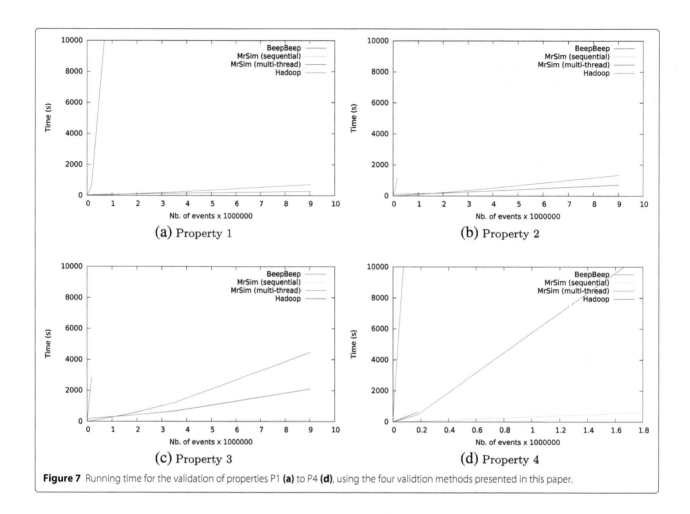

Figure 7 Running time for the validation of properties P1 **(a)** to P4 **(d)**, using the four validtion methods presented in this paper.

This is confirmed by the much better performance of the single-threaded MapReduce implementation.

To simplify the notation and reduce bandwidth, a simple modification can be made to the current method by computing all subformulæ of φ in advance and later on designate them with a single digit, as shown in Table 5 for the formula used as an example throughout the paper. This modification effectively reduces the amount of data

that needs to be exchanged between mappers and reducers, and emphasizes the fact that no manipulation of the formulæ is necessary during the validation process (apart from fetching formulæ from the table to determine which action to follow).

Discussion and conclusion

In this paper, we have presented an algorithm for the automated validation of Linear Temporal Logic properties on large traces of events using the MapReduce development framework. As far as we know, this work is the first published algorithm that leverages the MapReduce framework for the validation of temporal logic properties on large event traces. It opens the way to the use of cloud computing services for the efficient compliance checking of program traces and event logs of various kinds.

Summary

We have shown experimentally on a sample dataset how the algorithm presents reasonable running times when the MapReduce environment is restricted to a single thread. The breaking up of the algorithm into several phases of

Table 5 Shorthand symbols can be assigned to each subformula of the property to verify

Formula	Symbol
a	0
b	1
$\neg c$	2
$a \vee b$	3
$\mathbf{F}\,(a \vee b)$	4
$\neg c \vee (\mathbf{F}\,(a \vee b))$	5
$\mathbf{G}\,(\neg c \vee (\mathbf{F}\,(a \vee b)))$	6

independent mappers and reducers presents the potential of reducing the number of operations that must be performed linearly by executing these processes in parallel, yielding a *potential* speedup of 90% in some cases.

We were surprised to discover that among the three MapReduce implementations, the two that use parallelism (Hadoop and the multi-threaded MrSim) are *vastly* outperformed by the sequential, single-threaded implementation of MrSim –by more than two orders of magnitude in most cases. Since all three versions were given the same map and reduce jobs, the culprit cannot be put on the algorithm we propose and is therefore inherent in the actual environment used. We could not witness any of the potential execution time savings brought on by the use of parallel processing, as the sequential ratio of Table 3 led us to believe.

Strata and monotonic logic

This tends to indicate that verifying temporal properties on a trace of events is an essentially linear process, and that its breaking up into parallel steps requires a communication overhead that largely offsets the presence of parallelism. In some cases, we observed that the number of tuples produced (and hence the amount of data exchanged) amounts to more than 40 times the number of events in the trace to analyze. It might be tempting to explain the relatively poor runtime performance of the distributed tools by the volume of tuples that need to be produced and exchanged between nodes or threads; yet the reader shall be reminded that the sequential version of MrSim produces and manages the same tuples as well.

This sequential nature of the LTL validation process bears close resemblance to the concept of *stratification* in distributed Datalog [36]. In this context, the execution of a distributed database query is divided into "non-monotonic stratification boundaries": the evaluation of each strata can be split into multiple independent and distributed processes, but a global coordination of all process at strata N must be done before any process of strata $N+1$ can start. In the case of LTL property evaluation, the boundaries can clearly be equated to the levels of nesting of each subformula: evaluating subformulæ of a level of nesting $N-1$ can be done independently of each other, but the evaluation of a subformula of level of nesting N may require using the result of any subformula of level N, and hence a global coordination —materialized by the shuffling of tuples between reducers and mappers of the next iteration.

Potential uses

The results described in this paper are promising. They show how the use of a MapReduce framework can provide much better runtime performance than the classical LTL algorithm (sometimes by many orders of magnitude), especially for large traces. Despite the mild disappointment at the runtime performance of the Hadoop cluster, we conclude that the use of MapReduce to perform log analysis still is a viable solution that can analyze, in the worst case, hundreds if not thousands of events per second on very complex LTL formulæ. In addition to the performance argument, there also exist situations where the use of MapReduce is the *only* option; we list a few cases below.

- The property contains LTL past operators. Existing solutions (including BeepBeep) cannot handle LTL with past, while we have seen in Section 'LTL with past' that the MapReduce implementation provides these operators for free.
- The trace to analyze is fragmented across multiple locations. Existing trace validation tools all require the trace to be accessible sequentially from start to finish, which in general entails that the trace must be reconstructed and saved in a single location prior to analysis. In contrast, in the MapReduce implementation each single event can be located arbitrarily in any node, and each node needs not even to store contiguous sets of events. As a matter of fact, as long as the trace can be unambiguously ordered, events can be produced and recorded in multiple locations. This makes it particularly suited to verify, e.g. transaction processing systems [37].
- Using a professional MapReduce environment such as Hadoop provides side benefits, such as failure protection, generally absent from trace validators like BeepBeep or ProM.

Extensions and future work

The results obtained on the implementation discussed in this paper lead to a number of extensions and improvements over the current method. First, the algorithm presents an interest in that it can be reused as a basis for other temporal languages that intersect with LTL. This is the case, for example, of specifications written as finite-state machines, PSL [38] or DecSerFlow [12]. It is expected that similar techniques could also apply to to other logical formalisms, such as deontic logic [39]. Second, the technique itself could be expanded to take into account data parameters and quantification; the formulæ described in Section 'Sample properties' gave a foretaste of such quantification and initial results indicate that quantification is a fertile ground for parallelism. The proposed implementation is currently being ported as a free software suite for Apache Hadoop.

Finally, we have seen that the potential for parallelism is bounded by the structure of the formula to validate, as there can be at most one instance of reducer for every possible subformula of the property to verify. This entails that one cannot freely distribute the processing of the trace to an arbitrary number of parallel processes: for a simple formula, or one that contains few nested expressions, few reducers can be started in parallel. Therefore, a sought after refinement of the current method is currently being worked on, which will allow multiple Reducer instances for the same key to be merged in a later step.

Endnotes

[a] We implicitly assume a finite-trace semantics where $\epsilon \not\models \mathbf{X}\,\varphi$, $\epsilon \not\models \mathbf{F}\,\varphi$, and $\epsilon \models \mathbf{G}\,\varphi$, where ϵ represents the empty trace.

[b] http://beepbeep.sourceforge.net. The analysis in this paper has been done on version 1.7.6.

Competing interests
The authors declare that they have no competing interests.

Authors' contributions
SH was responsible for designing the MapReduce pseudo-code and providing the initial implementation of MrSim. MSB ported this work to the Hadoop framework and performed all the experiments and data analysis. Both authors read and approved the final manuscript.

References
1. Böhlen MH, Chomicki J, Snodgrass RT, Toman D (1996) Querying TSQL2 Databases with Temporal Logic. In: Apers PMG, Bouzeghoub M, Gardarin G (eds). EDBT Volume 1057 of Lecture Notes in Computer Science. Springer, Heidelberg. pp 325–341
2. Hallé S, Villemaire R (2008) XML Methods for Validation of Temporal Properties on Message Traces With Data. In: Meersman R, Tari Z (eds). CoopIS/DOA/ODBASE, Volume 5331 of Lecture Notes in Computer Science. Springer, Heidelberg. pp 337–353
3. Basin DA, Klaedtke F, Müller S (2010) Policy Monitoring in First-Order Temporal Logic. In: Touili T, Cook B, Jackson P (eds). CAV, Volume 6174 of Lecture Notes in Computer Science. Springer, Heidelberg. pp 1–18
4. Verbeek HMW, Buijs JCAM, van Dongen BF, van der Aalst WMP XES (2010) ESame, and ProM 6. In: Soffer P, Proper E (eds). CAiSE Forum, Volume 72 of Lecture Notes in Business Information Processing. Springer, Heidelberg. pp 60–75
5. Barringer H, Groce A, Havelund K, Smith M (2010) Formal Analysis of Log Files. J Aerospace Comput Inf Commun 7(11):365–390
6. Barringer H, Rydeheard D, Havelund K (2010) Rule Systems for Run-Time Monitoring: From Eagle to RuleR. J Logic Comput 20(3):675–706
7. van der Aalst WMP (2012) Distributed Process Discovery and Conformance Checking. In: de Lara J, Zisman A (eds). FASE, Volume 7212 of Lecture Notes in Computer Science. Springer, Heidelberg. pp 1–25
8. Dean J, Ghemawat S (2004) MapReduce: Simplified Data Processing on Large Clusters. In: OSDI. USENIX, Berkeley, CA. pp 137–150
9. Page L, Brin S, Motwani R, Winograd T (1999) The PageRank Citation Ranking Bringing Order to the Web. Technical Report 1999-66, Stanford InfoLab 1999, [http://ilpubs.stanford.edu:8090/422/]
10. An act to protect investors by improving the accuracy and reliability of corporate disclosures made pursuant to the securities laws, and for other purposes (2002). [U.S. Pub.L. 107-204, 116 Stat. 745]
11. Payment Card Industry Data Security Standard, version 2.0(2010). [https://www.pcisecuritystandards.org/security_standards/pci_dss.shtml]
12. van der Aalst WMP, Pesic M (2007) Specifying and Monitoring Service Flows: Making Web Services Process-Aware. In: Baresi L, Nitto ED (eds). Test and Analysis of Web Services. Springer, Heidelberg. pp 11–55
13. Hallé S, Villemaire R (2011) Runtime Enforcement of Web Service Message Contracts with Data. IEEE Trans Serv Comput 5(2):192–206. [doi:10.1109/TSC.2011.10]
14. Naldurg P, Sen K, Thati P (2004) A Temporal Logic Based Framework for Intrusion Detection. In: de Frutos-Escrig D, Núñez M (eds). FORTE, Volume 3235 of Lecture Notes in Computer Science. Springer, Heidelberg. pp 359–376
15. Rosu G, Havelund K (2005) Rewriting-Based Techniques for Runtime Verification. Autom Softw Eng 12(2):151–197
16. Reinbacher T, Geist J, Moosbrugger P, Horauer M, Steininger A (2012) Parallel runtime verification of temporal properties for embedded software. In: MESA. IEEE, New York, NY. pp 224–231
17. Medhat R, Joshi Y, Bonakdarpour B, Fischmeister S (2014) Parallelized Runtime Verification of First-order LTL Specifications. Tech. Rep. CS-2014-11, University of Waterloo
18. Berkovich S (2012) Parallel Run-Time Verification. Master's thesis, [https://uwspace.uwaterloo.ca/bitstream/handle/10012/7252/Berkovich_Shay.pdf]
19. Elmas T, Okur S, Tasiran S (2011) Rethinking Runtime Verification on Hundreds of Cores: Challenges and Opportunities. Tech. Rep. UCB/EECS-2011-74, EECS Department, University of California, Berkeley [http://www.eecs.berkeley.edu/Pubs/TechRpts/2011/EECS-2011-74.html]
20. Snare: gathering and filtering IT-event data (2014). http://www.intersectalliance.com/projects/index.html
21. ManageEngine: Network Management Software (2014). http://www.manageengine.com
22. Splunk: Operational Intelligence, Log Management, Application Management, Enterprise Security and Compliance (2014). http://www.splunk.com
23. Garavel H, Mateescu R (2004) SEQ.OPEN: A Tool for Efficient Trace-Based Verification. In: Graf S, Mounier L (eds). SPIN, Volume 2989 of Lecture Notes in Computer Science. Springer, Heidelberg. pp 151–157
24. Amazon Web Services (2008) Building GrepTheWeb in the Cloud, Part 1: Cloud Architectures. Tech. rep [http://aws.amazon.com/articles/1632]
25. Lee Y, Kang W, Lee Y (2011) A Hadoop-Based Packet Trace Processing Tool. In: Domingo-Pascual J, Shavitt Y, Uhlig S (eds). TMA, Volume 6613 of Lecture Notes in Computer Science. Springer, Heidelberg. pp 51–63
26. Bauer A, Falcone Y Decentralized LTL Monitoring. Tech. Rep arXiv:1111.5133v3 2011
27. Hadoop web site (2014). http://hadoop.apache.org
28. Lee KH, Lee YJ, Choi H, Chung YD, Moon B (2011) Parallel data processing with MapReduce: a survey. SIGMOD Record 40(4):11–20
29. Kuhtz L, Finkbeiner B (2009) LTL Path Checking Is Efficiently Parallelizable. In: Albers S, Marchetti-Spaccamela A, Matias Y, Nikoletseas SE, Thomas W (eds). ICALP (2), Volume 5556 of Lecture Notes in Computer Science. Springer, Heidelberg. pp 235–246
30. Pnueli A, Zaks A (2008) On the Merits of Temporal Testers. In: Grumberg O, Veith H (eds). 25 Years of Model Checking, Volume 5000 of Lecture Notes in Computer Science. Springer, Heidelberg. pp 172–195
31. Harel D, Kozen D, Parikh R (1980) Process Logic: Expressiveness, Decidability, Completeness. In: FOCS, IEEE Computer Society, Los Alamitos, CA. pp 129–142
32. Kimchi O (2013) How to Set Up a Hadoop Cluster Using Oracle Solaris Zones. [http://www.oracle.com/technetwork/articles/servers-storage-admin/howto-setup-hadoop-zones-1899993.html]
33. Hallé S, Villemaire R (2012) Runtime Enforcement of Web Service Message Contracts with Data. IEEE T Serv Comput 5(2):192–206
34. Vallet J, Mrad A, Hallé S (2013) The Relational Database Engine: an Efficient Validator of Temporal Properties on Event Traces. In: EDOCW. IEEE Computer Society, Los Alamitos, CA. pp 285–294
35. MrSim project page. (2014). http://github.com/sylvainhalle/MrSim
36. Hellerstein JM (2010) The declarative imperative: experiences and conjectures in distributed logic. SIGMOD Record 39:5–19
37. Su G, Iyengar A (2012) A highly available transaction processing system with non-disruptive failure handling. In: NOMS. IEEE, New York, NY. pp 409–416
38. Eisner C, Fisman D (2006) A Practical Introduction to PSL. Springer, Heidelberg
39. Åqvist L (1994) Deontic Logic, Kluwer, Alphen aan den Rijn

## 13

Cloud computing for the architecture, engineering & construction sector: requirements, prototype & experience

Thomas H Beach[1][*], Omer F Rana[2], Yacine Rezgui[1] and Manish Parashar[3]

Abstract

The Architecture, Engineering & Construction (AEC) sector is a highly fragmented, data intensive, project based industry, involving a number of very different professions and organisations. Projects carried out within this sector involve collaboration between various people, using a variety of different systems. This, along with the industry's strong data sharing and processing requirements, means that the management of building data is complex and challenging. This paper presents a solution to data sharing requirements of the AEC sector by utilising Cloud Computing. Our solution presents two key contributions, first a governance model for building data, based on extensive research and industry consultation. Second, a prototype implementation of this governance model, utilising the CometCloud autonomic Cloud Computing engine based on the Master/Worker paradigm. We have integrated our prototype with the 3D modelling software Google Sketchup. The approach and prototype presented has applicability in a number of other eScience related applications involving multi-disciplinary, collaborative working using Cloud Computing infrastructure.

Keywords: Cloud computing, Construction, Building information modelling, Governance

Introduction

The Architecture, Engineering & Construction (AEC) sector is a highly fragmented, data intensive, project-based industry depending on a large number of very different professions and firms, with strong data sharing and processing requirements across the lifecycle of its products (primarily buildings). The process of designing, repurposing, constructing and operating a building involves not only the traditional disciplines (Architecture, Structure, Mechanical & Electrical) but also many new professions in areas such as energy, environment and waste. All of these professions have large data sharing requirements.

In this context, data management within the industry can often be fragmented with a lack of an overall data management policy. Additionally, data sets relating to a particular project can often be stored in: (i) local computers of designers/architects - often with limited network connectivity, persistence and availability; (ii) independently managed, single company-owned archives – where access is dictated by a company specific policy or by a charging model; (iii) ad-hoc document archives, or (iv) Web-based document management systems in the context of a particular building project – based on an access policy associated with the project. Sharing data and supporting coordination between people involved is therefore often difficult – relying on the use of third party tools to support such capability. We believe that Cloud Computing platforms provide a more efficient and robust mechanism for individuals within the AEC industry to collaborate and share data. Work is already underway in the AEC sector for developing data and process models to enable greater interoperable working between project participants and, in recent years, this research has led to the development of the concept of Building Information Models (BIM). Currently, the UK AEC sector is working towards widespread BIM adoption, spurred on by the UK Government's requirement for BIM usage on certain publicly funded projects [1] by 2016.

*Correspondence: t.h.beach@cs.cf.ac.uk
[1] School of Engineering, Cardiff University, 5 The Parade, Roath, Cardiff, UK
Full list of author information is available at the end of the article

A key objective of our work has been to explore the potential of Cloud Computing in the AEC sector (with a particular focus on data management and collaborative working). We undertook various industry consultations with the assistance of the MBEKTN (Modern Build Environment Knowledge Transfer Network in the UK) [2] within two workshops (which attracted 72 industry representatives) and 4 focus group meetings (with a total of 20 participants) incorporating qualitative methods of inquiry over a duration of 5 months. It became clear that while Cloud Computing was clearly applicable in this sector, any data storage solutions supported using BIM must have appropriate governance in-place. Our consultation then moved onto a process of requirement elicitation to determine exactly what governance was necessary to allow the use of Cloud storage for BIM data and to enhance stakeholders' experience in adopting BIM across the lifecycle of a building.

In this paper we describe our experiences of utilising Cloud Computing and outline a governance model that could be supported for the storage and management of BIM. We first describe BIM and then show the data model that has been developed to enable the management of data in a BIM. We will then describe in detail our Cloud Computing prototype that has been developed in consultation with a number of industry partners, in particular the Building Research Establishment (BRE) in the UK. Our prototype makes use of the CometCloud platform [3] for supporting both data sharing and process execution (such as energy simulation).

Cloud computing in AEC

Our efforts in engaging with the industry have shown that Cloud Computing is still an emergent technology within the AEC sector. Technologies such as Google Drive and DropBox are often used informally and in an ad-hoc way between individuals - but concerns over security and the protection of intellectual property often dissuade major companies from adopting such services. There has, however, been moves towards adoption of virtual organisations for tasks such as E-procurement [4] and collaboration [5].

One of the key issues within the industry is the storage of building data during design/construction and over the entire life of the building. Several companies have developed servers for the storage of building data (represented using the Building Information Model) including the Onuma system (www.onuma.com), Revit Server (www.autodesk.com), ProjectWise and AssetWise (www.bentley.com), Graphisoft BIM Server (www.graphisoft.com) and EDMmodelServer (www.jotne.com). However, these servers often require local infrastructure and maintenance within the organisation that is using them - tending to utilise either central

(accessible to all team members over the WAN) or local (accessible to team members over the LAN) connectivity. However, recently many companies including software vendors such as Bentley Systems and Autodesk, have begun offering hosted solutions for building data. Additionally 4Projects (4Projects.com) offer a specific project collaboration service for the AEC sector including document and drawing management, contract management, and procurement management. Another issue with many of these products, is that they make use of their own proprietary file formats (especially in relation to 3D building models). While import/export functionality to standardised formats such as the Industry Foundation Classes (IFCs) [6] is possible, there are still issues with data interoperation surrounding this, i.e. complete mapping between different formats is not possible due to the use of proprietary extensions. There is however, currently, a drive to overcome these constraints and move towards a standardised format.

Data processing is also an important concern for the industry. During construction a large proportion of work takes place on construction sites where computing resources are limited. This is a use case of particular commercial importance, as ensuring the delivery and use of up to date and correct plans of construction sites is often a major challenge. Allowing users to make changes on a portable device on site - that can then be processed remotely leading to the plans on site being updated is extremely desirable.

Building information modelling

A Building Information Model(BIM) may be viewed as the complete collection of information about a building, offering a "phaseless" workflow [7]. In short this means a BIM should be a complete 4D virtual repository of all the data about the building from its conception through to its demolition. This includes not just 3D models of the building structure but also: (i) management information including work plans and schedules; (ii) product information (or links to product information data) about all items within the building - right down to the level of internal furnishings; (iii) building performance data collected by sensors within an operational building (i.e. heat, CO2 emissions, lighting levels).

Current research into BIM has also theorised that BIM data should be accessed and manipulated by utilising certain "tools of enquiry", such as "lenses" and "filters"; lenses highlight certain objects that meet a particular criteria whilst filters remove objects that do not meet the criteria [7].

The UK Government have defined an adoption process for BIM in the UK outlining three levels of adoption [1]:

- Level 0 - The use of hand drawn building plans.
- Level 1 - The use of Computer Aided Design Packages.
- Level 2 - The use of collaboration and document management.
- Level 3 - The use of a single data model encompassing all aspects of building data.

The UK is currently working towards compliance with Level 2 - however the are still key issues surrounding how the variety of document types, and different data formats can be managed - while preserving adherence to key industry requirements (many of which have a legal and contractual basis). In moving towards level three the Industry Foundation Classes (IFCs)[6] are a commonly used form for BIM which may well form the basis for level three compliance.

The IFCs are an open data model specification for defining building components geometry. They are intended to provide an authoritative semantic definition of all building elements, their properties and inter-relationships. Data associated with IFC can include: textual data, images (such as building schematics); structured documents, numerical models and designer/project manager annotations. The IFC specification is developed and maintained by BuildingSmart and has been included in several ISO standards.

Governance of BIM data

Following our consultation, it was felt that Cloud Computing capability would make most sense when utilized alongside a BIM data representation - in particular to support collaborative working between various participants involved in the lifecycle of a building. However, due to the complex project based nature of the AEC industry, any data stored in a cloud system would need to be heavily managed. This level of management is essential to ensure that the data is able to meet the legal and contractual requirements for each individual project and to also ensure that the intellectual property rights (e.g. not allowing unauthorised partners to view sensitive information) and professional accountability (e.g. not allow unqualified users to edit key documents) for all participants working together within the project is maintained. Additionally, the data stored would need to be structured to conform to the project management process that is being undertaken for the particular project(I.e. the RIBA Plan of work[8]). This process of ensuring all data is handled in compliance with the requirements of the industry and ensuring the data is structured in a way that meets the AEC sector's project management requirements we call "BIM Governance".

The first step in the creation of a BIM governance model to facilitate such collaboration was the identification of key characteristics of building information models,

their uses and the process used to support collaboration between users. To this end, four key areas have been identified [9,10], as discussed in the following subsections. These focus on how building data is represented, relationships between data sets generated at different stages of a building lifecycle, who can access such data (along the building lifecycle) and how access to the data is managed using access control policies.

Conceptualisation of building data

A Building Information Model (BIM) can be seen, conceptually, as a collection of data artefacts that arise during the lifecycle of a particular project. Hence, as a project matures, information is progressively added by participants who engage with the project [11]. Such information may consist of a 3D model of the building, or may include a schedule, spreadsheet, database, or text document [12]. The use of BIM artefacts as an abstraction for various types of content associated with a building is a key concept in this work and represents both previously recorded static data and dynamic output generated through a software package (such as a CAD program). Hence, an artefact can include structured, unstructured and graphical content, simulation output, scheduling and costing information and a project brief. In our governance model an artefact is treated as a view or a "lens" onto BIM data.

This idea of an artefact as "lens" can be illustrated by comparing the information needs of different disciplines within a building project. The architect will require detailed information about all physical aspects of the building, but not access to detailed structural analysis or scheduling information used by the project manager. Conversely, the structural engineer will often require detailed architectural models in order to perform their role, however (s)he may not require this information down to the level of internal furnishings and placement of individual electrical outlets.

However, rarely within such a model can any two artefacts be treated as completely separate entities and many artefacts will have relationships with others. Based on our focus group consultation, we identified three types of relationships: versioning, composition and derivation. Each of which have different implications about how data within the BIM as a whole is affected when new data is added. These are discussed below, with the variable B used to represent BIM:

> **No relationship**: A new artefact D_a is added to the BIM so that: $B = B + D_a$.
> **Versioning**: A new artefact D_b is created, based on an existing artefact D_a with changes made such that $D_b = D_a + X - Y$ where X is the addition and Y the removal of data from D_a.

Derivation: Given that a artefact D_b for use by discipline j is derived from artefact D_a which was created for discipline i then $D_b = f_j^i(D_a) + X$ where f_j^i is function to filter data and X is the new data added. **Composition**: New data is added to the BIM model forming part of an existing artefact. For example, if the top level artefact is D_a and each floor within a building is represented as a artefact layer $D_{f0}..D_{f3}$ then $D_a = D_{f0} + D_{f1} + D_{f2} + D_{f3}$. Each artefact in the composition may possess different access rights.

These relationships allow us to easily model three of the most common occurrences within an AEC project:

- When a user (e.g. a structural engineer) begins work on their design, they will require some of the information already present in the architects design. This is the *derived from* relationship and it allows a user to create an artefact that uses some or all of the information from another artefact.
- The *version of* relationship allows us to model the scenario when changes are made to an existing artefact leading to the creation of a new version. This allows the modelling of complex artefact structures that can occur within a construction project, where several parallel versions may be developed for experimentation by an architect before a final version is chosen for full development.
- The *composition* relationship allows the representation of an artefact as a collection i.e. when each floor of a structure is modelled separately and then aggregated into a single artefact.

The use of BIM enables better use of the above relationships, primarily due to the structured (model-based) and standardised nature of the underlying data. These relationships also provide the basis for allowing collaboration within the system. For instance, a structural engineer can add relevant information to a new artefact based on the work of the architect using the *derived from* relationship. Similarly, multiple architects working concurrently will be able to generate (for either later merging or for one version to be selected as the final version) multiple parallel versions of an artefact using the *version of* relationship.

The building life-cycle

BIM must also allow a building to be modelled across its entire life-cycle, from concept design through construction, operation and finally to decommissioning. This entire process would prove impossible to manage collectively, so our governance model divides this into stages. However, within the construction industry there are many "standard" approaches to managing a construction project. The most widely known of these in the UK is the RIBA plan of work [8], but many others exist. For this reason any model defined must be flexible enough to model all of these processes. Our approach to model this is illustrated in Figure 1.

In our approach we consider BIM to consist of a series of *stages*, at the end of which there is a *gate*, identifying a set of either mandatory or optional requirements such as the presence of data within the BIM, the accuracy of data, etc. For instance, in early stages of a building lifecycle, energy efficiency figures may be rough estimates which need to be refined in later stages (for instance, when results of detailed simulations become available). This division into stages allows the tracking of the BIM model throughout the project process. In essence each stage within the model can be viewed, once it has completed, as a snapshot of the BIM as it was at that time. This functionality will enable the use of the governance model as support for project managers, enabling the creation of reports that can be used to facilitate decision making and ensuring BIM compliance with standards, whether imposed by legislation, the client, or internally.

Multi user collaboration

Figure 2 describes the various components that make up a BIM artefact. This diagram shows that each BIM Artefact, which itself may be made up of one or more structured or unstructured data files or IFC objects, has a set of metadata attached to it allowing it to be properly managed.

Based on British Standard 1192:2007 [13], each artefact is given a suitability that allows the modelling of its lifecycle, illustrating the different ways in which an artefact can be used. Currently we define five artefact suitabilities (based on who can access them): (i) Private: document only for use of owner; (ii) Team: document only for use at a team level; (iii) Finalised: document is for use by other teams; (iv) Client - document is ready for release to client; or (v) Archived - document has reached end of its lifecycle and no further alterations will be made.

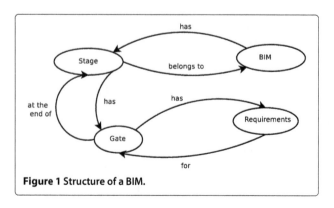

Figure 1 Structure of a BIM.

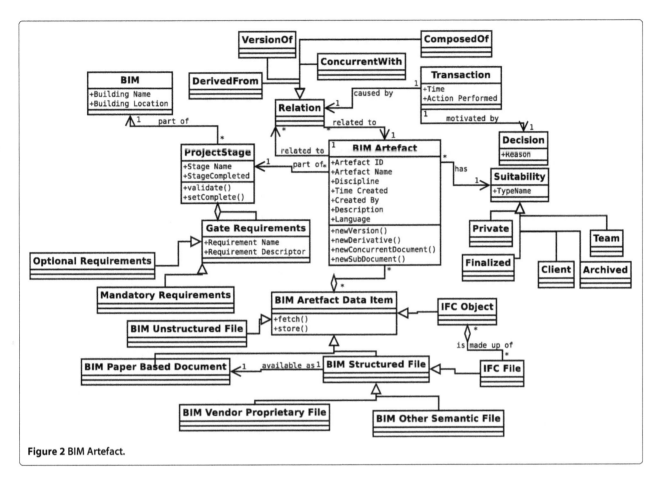

Figure 2 BIM Artefact.

Another important concept shown in Figure 2 is a BIM Artefact's relationships to other BIM Artefacts. Each Artefact is part of a specific stage of the project - but they can also be related to other individual BIM Artefacts using the relationships previously described. An important concept that is added to this is that of a transaction. A transaction occurs whenever a relationship between artefacts is created by a user [14]. The transaction entity is generated automatically, whereas the decision entity enables the user to make explicit the reasons for creating the relationship.

Figure 2 also shows all the metadata that is stored, using as a base-line, the Dublin Core metadata standard. This ensures that all elements defined in this standard are either provided explicitly within the Document object, or implicitly by its relation to data stored in other related objects within the data model.

Access rights, users, disciplines and roles

In order to enforce a fine grained access control over artefacts, we use the concepts of *users, disciplines, rights* and *roles* within the governance model – as shown in Figure 3:

- *Users* - A user is a single actor within the system.
- *Disciplines* - An industry recognised specialisation working on a specific aspect of a project.

- *Rights* - The conceptualisation of a permission to perform an operation on an artefact.
- *Roles* - A grouping of rights that can be applied to users or entire disciplines.

A detailed diagram of how these access rights will be implemented is shown in Figure 4. This figure illustrates the key concepts of Users, Disciplines, Roles and Rights and how they are connected. In this Figure, a right is made up of three components - i) the user/role being granted the right, ii) the operation that the right permits and iii) what artefacts the operation can be performed on.

For maximum flexibility we allow rights to be applied to an individual BIM Artefact, but also to all artefacts in the BIM, all artefacts within a stage of the project and all artefacts that belong to a particular discipline. Additionally, the functionality to allow role aggregation is present, allowing roles to be combined.

Development of a cloud computing prototype

With the consultation and initial design completed the next phase of the project involved the development of a Cloud Computing prototype. The decision was made to develop our prototype based on an existing Cloud Computing system, to this end it was decided to make use

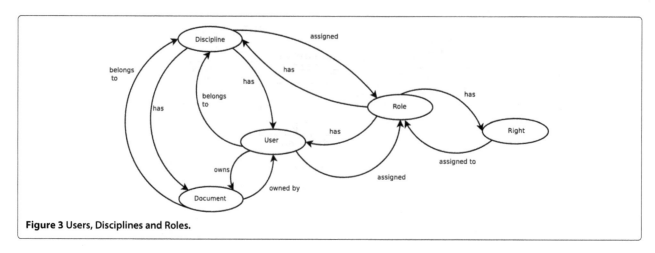

Figure 3 Users, Disciplines and Roles.

of CometCloud [15]. This section will firstly describe CometCloud, its features and why it was selected for use in this project. We will then outline the architecture of our Cloud Computing prototype named "CloudBIM".

CometCloud

The CometCloud system was utilised for this project due to its successful deployment in other data sharing scenarios within the computational finance area [15]. CometCloud uses a Linda-like tuple space referred to as "CometSpace" – which is implemented using a Peer-2-Peer overlay network. In this way, a virtual shared space for storing data can be implemented by aggregating the capability of a number of distributed storage and compute resources. CometCloud therefore provides a scalable backend deployment platform that can combine resources across a number of different providers dynamically – a key requirement for a project in the AEC sector.

The overarching goal of CometCloud is to realize a virtual computational cloud with resizable computing capability, which integrates local computational environments and public cloud services on-demand, and provides abstractions and mechanisms to support a range of programming paradigms and application requirements. Specifically, CometCloud enables policy-based autonomic *cloudbridging* and *cloudbursting*. Autonomic cloudbridging enables on-the-fly integration of local computational environments (datacenters, Grids) and public cloud services (such as Amazon EC2 and Eucalyptus), and autonomic cloudbursting enables dynamic application scale-out to address dynamic workloads and spikes in demand. Cloudbridging is useful when specialist capability available in-house needs to be integrated with high throughput computation that can be outsourced to an external cloud provider such as Amazon. Cloudbursting, on the other hand, enables scale-out of in-house computation and may not necessarily involve a change in capability between in-house and outsourced providers.

CometCloud is based on a decentralized coordination substrate, and supports highly heterogeneous and

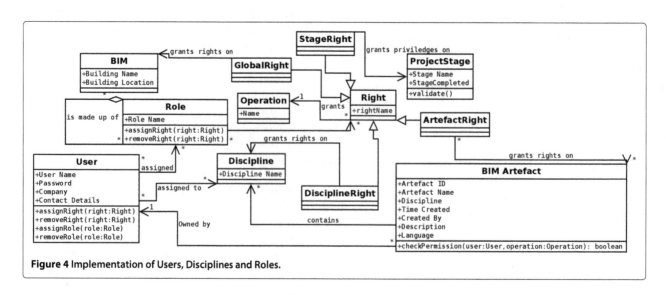

Figure 4 Implementation of Users, Disciplines and Roles.

dynamic cloud/Grid infrastructures, integration of public/private clouds and cloudbursts. The coordination substrate (based on a distributed Linda-based model) is also used to support a decentralized and scalable task space that coordinates the scheduling of tasks, submitted by a dynamic set of users, onto sets of dynamically provisioned workers on available private and/or public cloud resources based on their Quality of Service (QoS) constraints such as cost or performance. These QoS constraints along with policies, performance history and the state of resources are used to determine the appropriate size and mix of the public and private clouds that should be allocated to a specific application request. Additional details about CometCloud can be found at [3].

In this way, CometCloud differs from other Cloud computing environments currently available – as the focus in this system is specifically on bridging different distributed environment through the distributed tuple space implementation. Figure 5 illustrates the architecture of the CometCloud system – which consists of an: (i) infrastructure layer – enabling various data access and management capability to be supported (such as replication, routing, etc); (ii) a service layer – to enable a number of common services to be supported on the infrastructure, such as pub/sub, content/resource discovery, etc; and (iii) a programming layer – which enables the other two layers to be accessed in a number of ways using various programming models (such as map/reduce, master/worker, bag-of-tasks, etc). In practice, an application may not use all of these capabilities, as in our scenario which makes use of the master/worker paradigm. More details about the architecture, it use and source code downloads can be found in [3,16]. Various cloud bridging solutions are now available, such as IBM's Cast Iron Cloud Integration [17], part of the Web Sphere suite of tools for developing and deploying applications across different environments. Cast Iron enables integration, through plug-ins, with a number of IBM products (such as DB2) and systems from other vendors, such as SAP and Salesforces CRM – thereby enabling integration

between in-house systems and public & private Cloud environments. Many such systems remain proprietary to particular vendors however and are hard to customise to particular use scenarios.

As illustrated in Figure 5, at a lower level the Comet-Cloud system is made up of a set of computational resources each running the CometCloud overlay. When the CloudBIM system is initialised a set number of workers are initially launched on these resources, but additional workers can be started as required. The communication between these nodes is all done via the CometCloud communication space represented as a set of Linda-like tuples [15] which are placed into CometSpace using one of three concepts:

1. Adding a tuple - OUT;
2. Removing a tuple - IN;
3. Reading a tuple but not removing it - RD.

These nodes and their communication can be structured by CometCloud to enable support for multiple development models including: Map/Reduce, Master/Worker and the implementation of workflows (as described above).

The CloudBIM prototype

The CloudBIM prototype was constructed using Comet-Cloud's Master/Worker programming model and consists of three main components: A client and a set masters and workers. The architecture of the CloudBIM prototype is shown in Figure 6.

The flexibility of utilising CometCloud allows these components to be deployed in multiple configurations

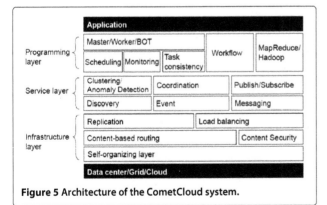

Figure 5 Architecture of the CometCloud system.

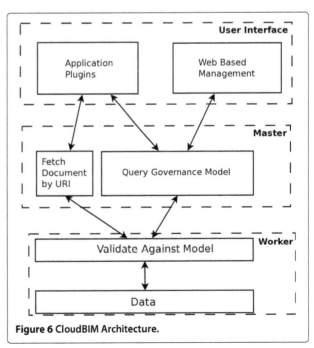

Figure 6 CloudBIM Architecture.

such as those shown in Figures 7 and 8. Figure 7 shows a configuration where a master node is deployed within each organisation working on the project but workers nodes are deployed externally - on a third party cloud services provider such as Amazon or Azure. An alternative configuration is shown in Figure 8 where masters and workers are deployed within organisations in addition to some worker nodes deployed externally.

The following sections will describe the implementation of the three main components, Masters, Workers and the two clients that have been developed; a web based interface, and plug-in for Google Sketchup.

Implementation of master and worker nodes
Masters

The CloudBIM master nodes do not store any data (other than temporarily caching for performance). These master nodes act only as gateways to the CloudBIM system. They are responsible to generating XML tasks that are inserted into the CometCloud coordination space. These XML tasks essentially wrap the queries that have been provided by the user (via the client) along with data needed internally by the cloud system. The format of these tasks is shown below:

```
<CloudBIMTask>
<TaskId> Unique ID of Query</TaskId>
<AuthToken> Authorisation
Token</AuthToken>
<MasterName> Name of Master that is
  Origin of Query</MasterName>
<DuplicationCount> Number of data is to
  be duplicated</DuplicationCount>
<InternalFlag> Flags whether this is
  an Internal Task to be ignored by all
  master nodes</InternalFlag>
<Query>User Query</Query>
</CloudBIMTask>
```

Workers

Each of the workers within the CloudBIM system hold a portion of the governance model and a subset of all the actual artefact data within the BIM. This ensures that all data is replicated allowing resilience if individual workers go off line. The workers, in addition to storing the data, are also responsible for validating each query they receive against the governance model to determine if they should execute the query, i.e. ensure that user A has authority to update artefact B before doing so.

The interaction between masters and workers is the key to how the CloudBIM system functions. This communication is done using CometCloud's distributed coordination space. Masters place XML tasks into this space and these are then read by the workers. Use of this distributed communication space allows for a variety of communication

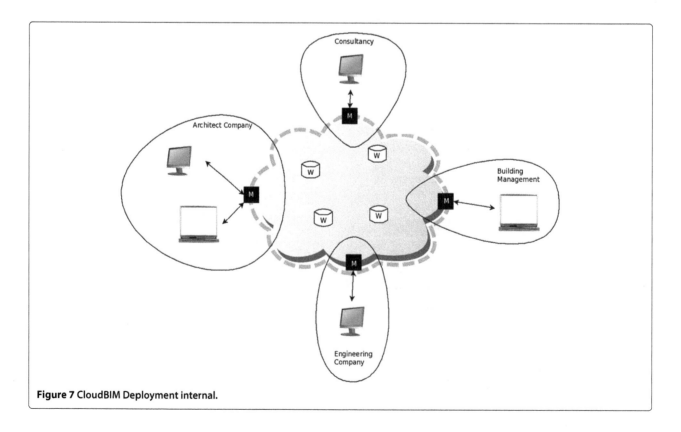

Figure 7 CloudBIM Deployment internal.

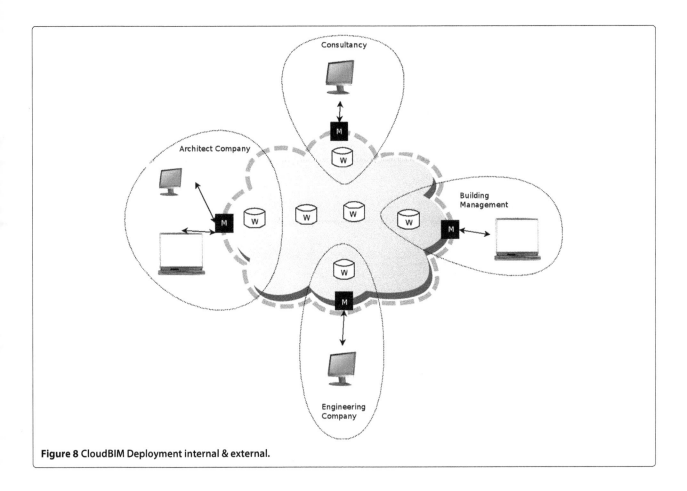

Figure 8 CloudBIM Deployment internal & external.

patterns to be utilised depending on the type of task being executed. These tasks can be broken down into one of four types: (i) tasks that read data; (ii) tasks that add data and (iii) tasks that remove data.

Figure 9 describes how data is retrieved from the system. Firstly a task containing an appropriate query is placed into the communication space by the master node. Each worker will read this task (using the non destructive RD function) and will determine if they have the capability to fulfil the query. If they have this ability - and the permissions of the user identified by the token contained within the query matches those enforced by the governance model, then the data will be returned to the master node. While this process is undertaken, the master node will monitor the data that is returned to it and, once it has recieved all the replies (or a timeout is exceeded) it will remove the query tasks from the communication space.

Figure 10 shows the similar process undertaken for adding new data for the system. When this type of query is executed the system must ensure that the data is duplicated across the cloud. So, when the Master receives the data from the user it will cache the data, so no delays occur for the user while duplication takes place. The query

is now inserted into the communication space. The first available worker will then remove the task, decrement the duplication count and then, as long as the duplication count is above zero, re-insert the task. On task re-insertion, the worker will then request the data from the Master. This process will then repeat until the duplication count reaches zero. As in the previous example, the authorization token is used to determine who can add data to the system.

The final scenario is where data is removed from the system. This process is similar to that outlined in Figure 9 - in this case a task is inserted into the communication space by the master and all worker nodes that are able to will remove the specified data (assuming the user requesting the deletion meets the requirements of the governance model). Each worker node will then send a confirmation to the master node which, once it has received all the acknowledgements (or a time-out has been exceed) will remove the task from the communication space.

Fault tolerance
The CloudBIM system also has mechanisms for fault tolerance and the ability to expand its pool of workers as required. This is an essential property to ensure

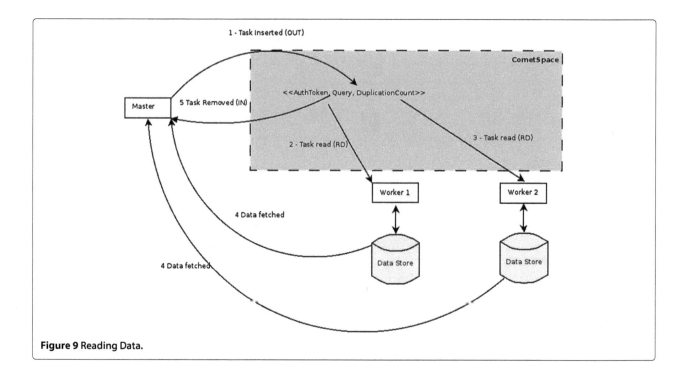

Figure 9 Reading Data.

availability of BIM data. As mentioned previously, the underlying CometCloud architecture consists of a pool of resources/machines running the CometCloud overlay. When the CloudBIM system is launched a set of workers, defined by IP addresses in a configuration file, are initialised using nodes from this pool. If a worker fails, the procedure outlined in Figure 11 is followed. When a query is issued, the Master node will count the number of workers that process the query and if a single worker repeatedly fails to respond within a certain time frame (the number of failures and the time-out value are configurable), then the worker is considered to have failed. While this is taking place user requests are still being processed because the BIM data will still be available from other workers in the

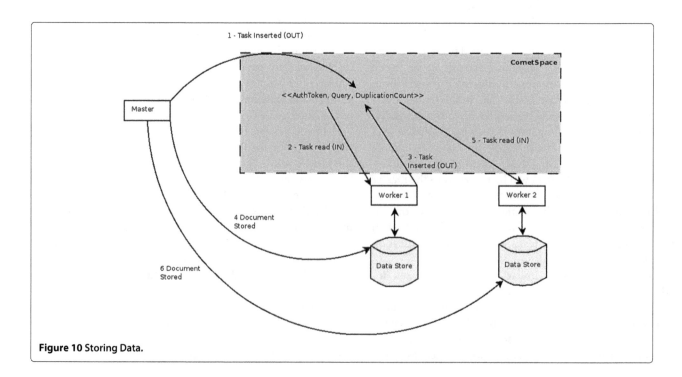

Figure 10 Storing Data.

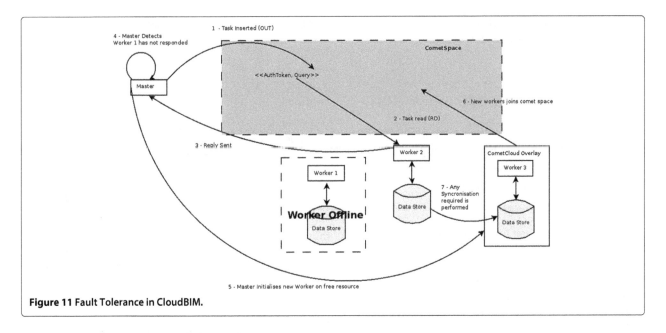

Figure 11 Fault Tolerance in CloudBIM.

system (due to data duplication). Only in the case of multiple simultaneous failures would users be unable to retrieve data. In cases where a worker (or set of workers) loses connection for a long period of time (a timeout value set by an administrator) the worker will be removed from the system.

Once a worker has permanently failed, it is removed from the current list of workers and a new worker is added from a pool of nodes that can be added to the cloud. This is done by communicating with the CometCloud overlay that will be running on the waiting node and instructing it to initialise itself as a CloudBIM worker. Once this is done, the CometCloud overlay must then be restarted to enable correct routing of messages to the new worker.

Finally, once the new worker has joined the communication space, synchronisation may be needed to ensure that

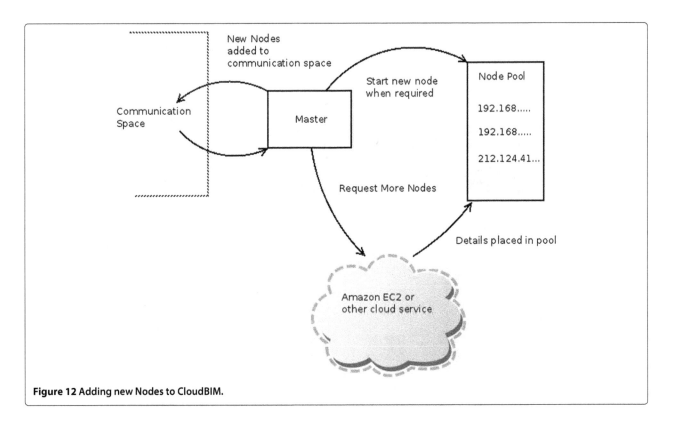

Figure 12 Adding new Nodes to CloudBIM.

there is sufficient duplication of BIM data. This entire process takes place transparently to the user and is done as follows:

- Each worker will send the new worker the IDs of the BIM artefacts that it holds (by placing an internal task into the communication space).
- The new worker will calculate which artefact Ids need additional duplication based on this data.
- The new worker will request the artefacts needed directly from the worker that holds them.

The same process is followed when a new worker needs to be added to the system from the pool to improve system throughput. This process is also followed when a worker that has been offline re-joins the system, this means that it can retrieve a new set of data from other workers in the CloudBIM system, removing the risk of any invalid (outdated or deleted) data from becoming available to users.

The key aspect of this fault tolerance process is that there are "spare" workers available for use in the pool.

This can be ensured in one of several ways as shown in Figure 12:

- By supplying the system with a list of IP addresses of nodes that have CometCloud installed and can be utilised.
- Utilising third party cloud providers to spawn additional virtual machines based on a defined policy. Currently this has been implemented by Rutgers using Amazon EC2 [3].

Integrating cloud computing and google sketchup

Within the CloudBIM system the client is responsible for providing the interface between users and the local master node. This is done by providing a user interface, which converts users' actions into a query which is then communicated to the master node in the form of a query language. We implemented two clients, a web based interface and a plug-in for Google Sketchup (A commonly used tool in the AEC industry). The Google Sketchup plugin is shown in Figure 13.

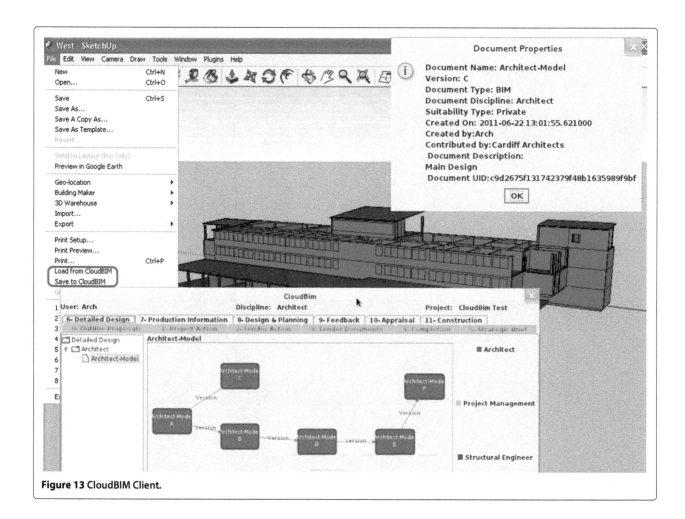

Figure 13 CloudBIM Client.

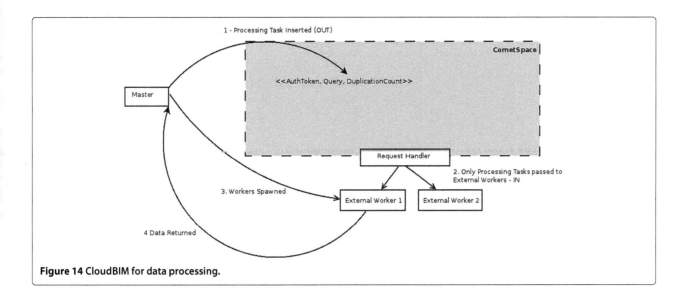

Figure 14 CloudBIM for data processing.

The decision to utilise a query language was to enable two possible usages of the system:

1. As a capability that could be integrated into a custom user interface implemented for a specific project.
2. As a capability integrated within existing software as a plug-in (such as existing CAD systems like Autodesk Revit [18] or Google sketchup [19]).

This allows third parties to leverage on the functionality provided by the CloudBIM system. An example of this would be a company that utilises their own proprietary software tools, this company could, using the CloudBIM query language, integrate their existing software tools with the CloudBIM system, possibly including development of a plug-in for their CAD software or integrating CloudBIM into an existing project management intranet system.

The prototype CloudBIM query language is specified below in EBNF (Extended Bachus Naur Form) notation.

```
CLOUDBIMQUERY=DOCUMENTUPPLOAD |
  DOCUMENTDOWNLOAD |GOVERNANCEQUERY
GOVERNANCEQUERY = UPDATEQUERY | OTHER QUERY
UPDATEQUERY = 'update',' ',OBJECT,'
  ',FIELDLIST,' ','set',' ',FIELDLIST
OTHERQUERY = ('get | 'add' | 'delete'),'
  ',OBJECT,' ',FIELDLIST
DOCUMENTDOWNLOAD='fetchdoc','
  ',FIELDLIST,[' ','all']
DOCUMENTUPLOAD = 'adddoc',' ',FIELDLIST,
  [' ','(',RELATION,',',RELATION,')']
```

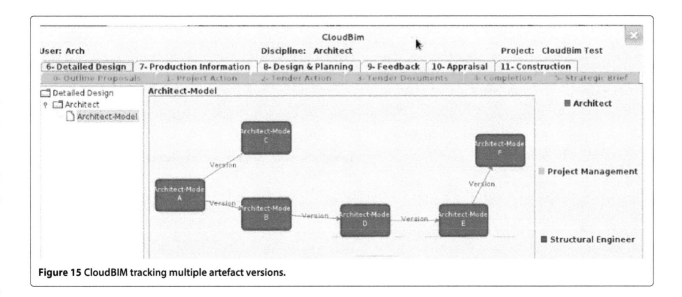

Figure 15 CloudBIM tracking multiple artefact versions.

```
OBJECT='ProjectStage'|'GateRequirement'
 |'DocumentSuitability'|'Discipline'
 |'Operation'|'Role'|'Right'|'User'
 |'Notification'|'Flag'|'NotificationType'
RELATION=RELTYPE,' ',<ID>
RELTYPE='ver'|'der'|'comp'|'conc'
FIELDLIST=FIELD,',',FIELD
FIELD=OBJECT,'=',FIELDVALUE
FIELDVALUE=VALUE|('(',VALUE,',',VALUE,')')
```

For the sake of brevity the terms ID (a unique ID) and VALUE (a string) are not defined, also omitted are commands used to authenticate a user. The Cloud-BIM query language defines six key commands: *get, add, delete, update, adddoc and fetchdoc*. These commands allow the manipulation of objects within the governance model, however it should be noted that not all objects are able to be directly manipulated by users, some are created/updated as a side effect of other queries i.e. specifying the relationship of a new document will lead to the automatic creation of Relationship and Transaction objects as necessary by using data supplied in the *adddoc* command. The *adddoc* and *fetchdoc* commands separate the uploading and downloading of documents from the CloudBIM system from the manipulation of the objects within the governance model. Additionally, it is worth noting that the fetchdoc command can be used to return either all matching documents (not always desirable) or just the first match.

CloudBIM for data processing

Workers within the CloudBIM system may also be used to launch external simulations (in batch mode), the results of which are also stored as artefacts. Access to these artefacts is then based on our governance model. This process enables the integration of third-party executable software, in addition to static artefacts that have been pre-generated and stored. The use of workers for processing operates in a similar way to that outlined previously, firstly a task is placed into the communication space that describes: (i) the program to be executed; or (ii) the artefacts that are needed as input to the program. These tasks will then only be read by workers that possess the application that the task is requesting. Once a worker has read the task it will place new internal tasks into the communication space to request any data it does not hold. Once the data has been received, the task will execute and a reply will be sent giving the artefact ID of the output data.

When utilising workers for data processing there are two different modes of operation that are supported:

- Utilising the processing of the existing workers that are used for data storage.

- Utilising CometCloud's CloudBursting capability to spawn workers solely for data processing.

The second type of execution we envisage as the most common mode of operation, especially in cases where the tasks being executed require either specialised software to be installed, or have large resource requirements. In these cases additional workers are spawned on a cloud service such as Amazon EC2, but, because they are temporary workers, are only permitted to access the communication space via a RequestHandler, this is shown in Figure 14. This restriction is imposed because we do not want external workers to process any data storage tasks as they are temporary workers with a lifespan of the length of a single computation task.

This ability to spawn extra "external" workers is highly useful and has the ability to be expanded to include a large number of common industry tasks:

- Energy Simulations
- Rendering of building models.
- Automatic Clash Detection.

Conclusion

The CloudBIM project was a feasibility study that aimed to explore the feasibility and potential for utilizing Cloud capability to address data storage and processing needs of stakeholders in the AEC sector. In the course of this project we have explored some of the technical and non-technical issues related to the outsourcing of BIM data into a Cloud Computing environment. Various other approaches currently exist to support collaborative working in the construction sector – most of these, however, are focused on the use of a centralised server that enable upload/download of BIM data – such as BIM server [20] and ProjectWise [21] from Bentley Systems. We believe such an approach limits the kinds of interactions that can be supported within the AEC sector and more effective approach would involve integration of data storage and processing capability across different industry partners involved a particular project.

We have found through a process of consultation that, unsurprising, the majority of the barriers to the adoption of Cloud-based BIM have been related to ensuring that the

Table 1 Performance of failure tolerance and addition of new workers

Activity	Time/s
Single Worker Failure	3.22
Adding 1 New Worker	3.59
Adding 2 New Workers	3.49
Adding 3 New Workers	3.94

Table 2 Performance overhead measurements

File size/mb	Download overhead/s	Download speed MByte/s	Upload overhead/s	Upload speed MByte/s
100	0.58	10.75	1.48	8.70
200	0.67	10.97	1.45	7.92
500	0.69	10.06	1.16	8.09
1000	0.84	9.94	1.53	5.80

design of a system is in compliance with complex industry requirements.

To this end a governance model and a prototype have been constructed and we have evaluated these in three ways. Firstly, the governance model has been validated using further industry review. Secondly, the governance model and the technical implementation has been evaluated by the utilising a number of use cases supplied by our construction project management industry partner. Finally, a technical performance analysis has been carried out of using the operations in our query language and CloudBIM's fault tolerance capability.

The results that we have so far are promising: The industry has reacted positively to the idea of the governance model and the functionality that it provides. The trials from the case study have shown the governance model is able to correctly model the scenarios presented to it. Figure 15 shows one example of this, where the CloudBIM system was able to successfully track a complex structure of versioning of the architects model.

The results of the performance analysis are also promising. In conducting this experiment we firstly timed several key operations - the dynamic addition of new workers to the system and the time to recover from worker failure. The results of this experiment is shown in Table 1. Secondly, we also measured the governance overhead - that is the extra time taken for upload/download of files to the CloudBIM system compared to standard file uploads to the same machine and the upload/download speeds when transferring BIM data to the CloudBIM system. These results are shown in Table 2.

In summary, both sets of results are promising and show that the CloudBIM System is able to:

- Recover from single worker failure.
- It is able to add multiple new workers in under 4 seconds.
- When transferring BIM data it can achieve an download speed of approximately 10MByte/s and an upload speed of 7.5MByte/s.
- The overhead of using the governance model to manage access to the BIM data is less than two seconds per query.

One of the interesting lessons learnt in this project, has been examining a number of other disciplines that are attempting to solve the problem of out-sourcing their data storage. It was interesting to find that many of these disciplines are facing different, but related problems and it is surprising that in many cases there were experiences from one discipline that can be carried over into another.

However, it has also become apparent that because the majority of buildings are unique, meaning each must be treated as a prototype, and that the lifetime of BIM data is far longer than the lifetime of many data-sets (the lifetime of the building), the problems faced in this industry are unique and challenging. Our future objective is to make CloudBIM more scalable and use it in a realistic end user system. This will involve integration of various backend systems that host BIM data using the Worker model used in CometCloud. These systems can range in complexity from a structured data base to a file system. Our current work is focused on developing suitable plugins to enable such integration to be supported.

Competing interests
The authors declare that they have no competing interests.

Authors' contributions
THB from Cardiff University School of Engineering developed the BIM Governance model and the CloudBIM prototype. OFR from the Cardiff University School of Computer Science and Informatics provided Cloud Computing expertise and supervised the development and testing of the prototype. YYR from Cardiff University School of Engineering conducted the industry consultation and provided domain specific expertise in the development of the BIM Governance Model. MP from RDI2/CAC at Rutgers University provided description of CometCloud and associated use of CometCloud in other scenarios. All authors read and approved the final manuscript.

Acknowledgements
The research was funded by the EPSRC under contract EP/I034270/1.

Author details
[1] School of Engineering, Cardiff University, 5 The Parade, Roath, Cardiff, UK. [2] School of Computer Science & Informatics, Cardiff University, 5 The Parade, Roath, Cardiff, UK. [3] RDI2/CAC/Dept. of Electrical & Computer Engineering, Rutgers University, Piscataway, NJ 08854-8058, USA.

References
1. UK Cabinet Office, Government Construction Strategy (2011) https://www.gov.uk/government/uploads/system/uploads/attachment_data/file/61152/Government-Construction-Strategy_0.pdf Accessed November 2012
2. https://connect.innovateuk.org/web/modernbuiltktn

3. Kim H, Parashar M (2011) CometCloud: An autonomic cloud engine, cloud computing: principles and paradigms. chap. 10. John Wiley & Sons, Inc., pp 275–297. http://onlinelibrary.wiley.com/doi/10.1002/9780470940105.ch10/summary

4. Grilo A, Jardim-Goncalves R (2011) Challenging electronic procurement in the AEC sector: A BIM-based integrated perspective. Automation in Construction 20: 107–114

5. Vorakulpipat C, Rezgui Y, Hopfe CJ (2010) Value creating construction virtual teams: A case study in the construction sector. Automation in Construction 19: 142–147

6. International Standard (ISO) 16739:2005 - Industry Foundation Classes

7. Succar B (2009) Automation in Construction 18: 357–375

8. Royal Institute of British Architects (RIBA) Plan of Work. Available at: http://www.ribaplanofwork.com/. [Last accessed: Jan 17, 2012]

9. Serror M (2007) Shared computer-aided structural design model for construction industry (infrastructure). Comput Aided Des 40: 778–788

10. Singh V (2010) A theoretical framework of a BIM-based multi-disciplinary platform. Automation in Construction 20: 131–144

11. Rezgui Y, Cooper G, Brandon P (1998) Information management in a collaborative multiactor environment: the COMMIT aApproach. J Comput Civil Eng 12: 136–145

12. Rezgui Y, Hopfe C, Vorakulpipat C (2010) Generations of knowledge management in the architecture, engineering and construction industry: an evolutionary perspective. Adv Eng Inform 24: 219–228

13. British Standards Institute (BSI): British Standard 1192:2007 – Collaborative production of architectural, engineering and construction information, Code of practice

14. Cooper G, Cerulli C, Lawson BR, Peng C, Rezgui Y (2010) Tracking decision-making during architectural design. Electron J Inf Technol Construction 10: 125–139

15. Kim H, Chaudhari S, Parashar M, Martyy C (2009) Online Risk Analytics on the Cloud International Workshop on Cloud Computing In: conjunction with the 9th IEEE International Symposium on Cluster Computing and the Grid, pp pp 484–489

16. CometCloud – available at: http://nsfcac.rutgers.edu/CometCloud/. [Last accessed: Jan 10, 2013]

17. IBM WebSphere Cast Iron Cloud Integration – available at: http://www-01.ibm.com/software/integration/cast-iron-cloud-integration/. [Last accessed: Jan 10, 2013]

18. Autodesk Revit Architecture – available at: http://www.autodesk.com/products/autodesk-revit-family/overview. [Last accessed: Jan 15, 2012]

19. 3D Modelling Software from Google (version 8) – available at: http://www.sketchup.com/. [Last accessed: Jan. 15, 2012]

20. bimserver.org

21. http://www.bentley.com/en-US/Products/projectwise+project+team+collaboration/

## 14

CMQ - A lightweight, asynchronous high-performance messaging queue for the cloud

Joerg Fritsch[1][*] and Coral Walker[2]

Abstract

In cloud computing environments guarantees, consistency mechanisms, (shared) state and transactions are frequently traded for robustness, scalability and performance. Based on this challenge we present CMQ, a UDP-based inherently asynchronous message queue to orchestrate messages, events and processes in the cloud. CMQ's inherently asynchronous design is shown to perform especially well in modern Layer 2 switches in data center networks, as well as in the presence of errors. CMQ's lightweight edge-to-edge design, which is somewhat similar to Unix Pipes, makes it very composable. By presenting our work, we hope to initiate discussion on how to implement lightweight messaging paradigms that are aligned with the overall architectures and goals of cloud computing.

Introduction

Cloud computing has two perspectives: first, an outward-looking perspective that embodies an elastic application executed in a secure container and accessible over the internet, as seen by developers and end users; Secondly, an inward-looking perspective that describes the large scale distributed cloud computing platform and its middleware as implemented and operated by the provider [1]. CMQ presents a message passing model (that is a middleware abstraction) implemented in Haskell that addresses the reality of both perspectives.

The inward-looking perspective

The physical cloud nodes in computing clouds are organized into "Points of Delivery"[a] and interconnected via equipment that either switches at line rate, or that uses lossless Ethernet fabric[b] technologies. In switched data center networks, all Ethernet (RFC 894) based networking protocols are switched without discrimination. Congestion and packet loss are extremely unlikely in such data center networks. The overhead of TCP/IP in 10Gbps data center fabrics has led to CPU performance issues ([2-4]) and has given rise to new connectionless Ethernet protocols, such as RDMA over converged Ethernet (RoCE)

and the Internet Wide Area RDMA Protocol (iWARP). However, both protocols require specialized hardware (network cards, switching gear) that is not in line with the trend to build clouds from commodity hardware [5], and accept occasional failures rather than preventing failure at any cost [6].

In CMQ, UDP is used as the transport protocol for the following reasons:

- It is connectionless.
- It is the protocol that adds the least overhead to the ethernet network: it adds only 28 bytes overhead to every packet (20 byte IPv4[c] header + 8 byte UDP header).
- It is accessible to guest systems on hypervisors and clouds and is readily available to (Haskell) developers via standard modules.

Above all, the design of the UDP protocol fits the above-mentioned notion of cloud computing well, that is, to accept occasional failure and manage it, rather than struggling to prevent it.

The outward-looking perspective

The guest systems in clouds often have to cope with the suboptimal network conditions caused by software devices, a problem that the VEPA[d] standard tried to solve in 2009. The software devices, such as vswitches and

*Correspondence: J.Fritsch@cs.cardiff.ac.uk
[1] NATO CI Agency, Den Haag, Netherlands
Full list of author information is available at the end of the article

vrouters, are responsible for regulating network traffic inside the cloud nodes and are guest systems themselves. Depending on the virtualization ratio, one virtual switch could be responsible for up to 64 guest systems. Guest systems frequently have to cope with packet loss [7] that, when using TCP/IP costs many CPU cycles on systems that are themselves billed according to the available CPU cycles. Packet loss in TCP/IP can easily cause guest systems to grind to a halt.

Furthermore, ubiquitous computing is becoming increasingly important and prevalent: according to [8], "7 trillion wireless devices [will be] serving 7 billion people by 2017". Considering that packet loss is very common in radio transmission wireless networks, reliable network transmission protocols such as TCP suffer undesirable performance reduction due to the congestion avoidance algorithm used in TCP, while protocols based on UDP and the like, with optimized data transmission and performance advantages, are becoming more attractive for mobile devices that experience significant packet loss. Therefore, it is reasonable to assume that future (cloud) services, most of which will be dependent on one of the 7 trillion wireless devices, require protocols that are significantly better than TCP in the presence of errors.

Related work
According to [1], "the cloud demands obedience to [its] overarching design goals", and "failing to keep the broader principles in mind" leads to a disconnection of cloud computing research from real world computing clouds. Furthermore, scientists "seem to be guilty of fine-tuning specific solutions without adequately thinking about the context in which they are used and the real needs to which they respond". One overarching design goal however is to avoid strong synchronization provided by locking services. Wherever possible, all building blocks of a computing cloud should be inherently asynchronous. CMQ, being designed to meet the real needs of cloud computing, is strictly asynchronous and is the combined research result from many different research fields, including network- and data- center design, network protocols, message oriented middleware and functional programming languages.

UDP Protocol
The increasingly wide adaptation of the UDP protocol indicates the suitability of the UDP protocol as an efficient transport protocol for supporting distributed applications. For example, UDP is used for data transportation in Network File System (NFS) and for state and event transportation in Massive Multiplayer Online Games (MMOGs) [9,10]. EverQuest, City of Heroes, Asheron's Call, Ultima Online, Final Fantasy XI, etc. are among many MMOGs that use UDP as its transport protocol. The fact that MMOG applications are by nature of large, but elastic scale make them ideal customers for IaaS and PaaS offerings. By using cloud computing and storage facilities, not only cost and risks, that are usually linked to building new MMOGs, reduced [11], but also over-provisioning MMOG hardware to be on standby for peak times will be avoided [12]. However, whether computing clouds can fulfil the stringent real-time requirements of MMOGs is still an open issue [13].

In contrast to MMOGs that are largely event driven where the size of individual messages is expected to be small [14], NFS is data driven with larger packet sizes and higher throughput. NFS, according to [15], the most successful distributed application ever, has been using UDP as underlying transport protocol for more than two decades and was a stateless protocol up to NFSv3^e. Compared with a large-scale cloud environment, NFS is arguably designed for a limited scale. The UDP based Data Transfer Protocol (UDT), described in [16], has showed the applicability of using the UDP-based UDT protocol for "cloud span applications" and won the bandwidth challenge at the International Conference for High Performance Computing, Networking, Storage, and Analysis 2009 (SC09). Furthermore, [17] also discovers that reliable transport protocols that outperform TCP transport protocols can be designed in the basis of UDP.

Message Oriented Middleware (MOM)
If we view computing clouds from the inward-looking perspective mentioned above, it can be seen that the cloud framework itself is a distributed application that in turn supports distributed guest applications, for the reasons listed below.

- Computing clouds have an inherent distributed character.
- The cloud framework enables elasticity, and parallelization (through distribution) of guest applications. The guest application should be distributable so that it has the flexibility to be distributed to other resources when the limits of the current available cloud resources are reached.

The relevance of message passing for computing clouds stems from the distributed programming model that is chosen to code either the cloud platform or the guest application. [18] sees the Actor concurrency model [19] as the foundation of cloud computing. The Actor model enables "asynchronous communication and control structures as patterns of passing messages" [20]. Two well-known implementations of the actor model are e.g. the functional programming language Erlang [21] and the Akka toolkit [22].

Whilst a UDP message queue for Actors is a new idea, UDP-based MOM (Message-Oriented Middleware) is not. The open source Light Weight Event System (LWES) [23] is a UDP-based MOM that is described as having a strong position in large scale, real-time systems that need to be non-blocking and is also described by Yahoo! as part of US Patent 2009/0094073 "Real Time Click (RTC) System and Methods". LWES is also described as being useful (for transporting large data to computing nodes) for parallel batch processing with Hadoop [24], which is an open source implementation of Google's Map Reduce [25]. In fact, MapReduce and Hadoop are posited, in [26], as the right cloud computing programming models.

Functional programming languages

The functional programming language Haskell is chosen as the programming language to implement CMQ because of the following reasons:

- It is independent from any third-party platform or runtime (e.g., Clojure and Scala are built on top of JVM, F# on top of the .NET platform).
- It is being actively researched and has an ever increasing large research community. According to the popularity tracking website langpop.com [27], in 2011, it was ranked fifth out of the 32 most talked-about programming languages on the internet.
- It supports a wide range of concurrency paradigms [28].
- It is very powerful in list manipulation. Lists are used in CMQ to provide lightweight data structure that holds messages in sequence. List manipulation is useful to implement selective receives of messages with defined characteristics (rather than accepting messages in FIFO sequence) in an Erlang-like fashion.

With regard to the question whether functional programming languages are at all the right tool for the implementation of CMQ, we share the opinion stated in [29] that it is best to start with a programming language "whose computational fabric is by-default parallel" and that in the future "parallel programming will increasingly mean functional programming". Notably, MapReduce and Hadoop are frameworks that are eventually based on the functions map and fold (aka reduce) of functional programming languages.

Cloud Haskell, proposed in [30], aimed to further develop Haskell as a programming language for developing distributed applications. It was influenced by Erlang, and was intended to provide support for the actor model, message passing, and the mobility (with limitations) of functions with co-located data (closures). Coutts states [31] that protocols, as the centre of distributed systems, are playing a main part in the future development of Cloud

Haskell. A proprietary protocol suite and protocol flexibility are among the considerations in the future of Cloud Haskell.

Although CMQ shares a similar goal to Cloud Haskell of providing a mechanism for distributed applications, it has adopted a different approach. Cloud Haskell, targeting language-level support for distributed applications, explores a lower, compiler-level implementation, while CMQ, is intented for a higher-level support. CMQ takes advantage of the current Haskell language to explore an implementation at the protocol level and above. The benefit of a higher-level implementation is the flexibility that the approach used in CMQ, since it is language-independent, can be easily adapted to other languages and environments, and thus serve the ultimate goal: finding appropriate communication approaches for cloud computing and the ubiquitous computing paradigm.

CMQ implementation

CMQ is a lightweight message queue implemented in Haskell. CMQ provides a polymorphic data type Cmq a where a is the content type of the queue. CMQ has currently three primitives: newRq (to initialize the queue and data structures), cwPush (to push a message into the queue), and cwPop (to pop a message from the queue). The code is published on github.com and available at https://github.com/viloocity/CMQ.

cwPush

Messages for remote processes are identified by a key tuple consisting of the IP address of the remote system and an integer which is reserved for future use, for example, it can be used to specify the PID of the remote process. When a message is pushed with cwPush two things happen:

- The key-tuple and the data are stored in a map, implemented using the Haskell library Data.Map (a dictionary that is implemented as a balanced binary tree).
- The key-tuple and the creation time are stored in a priority search queue (PSQ), implemented using the Haskell library Data.PSQueue [32] and used as a pointer to the corresponding binding in the map.

Figure 1 shows how CMQ works on the side of the sender. When cwPush is called to push a new message, a key-tuple k is built that consists of the IP address of the destination and a unique identifier (i.e. the PID). If the given key is not already a member of the PSQ, then a new binding (k, p) is inserted where the priority p is the creation-time of the binding. At the same time a new key-value pair (k, a) is inserted into the map, where a is a finite

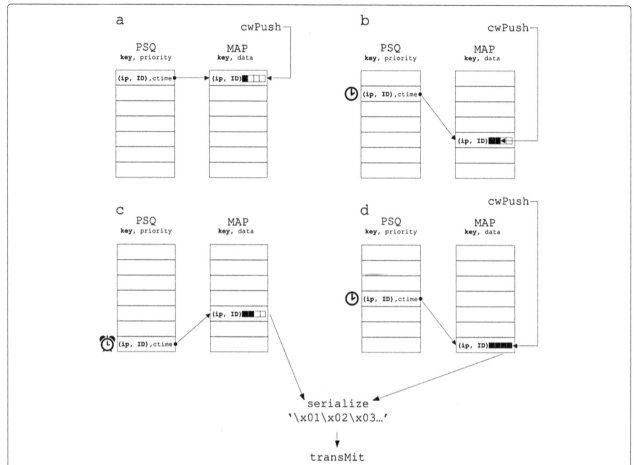

Figure 1 Map and PSQ pointer in CMQ. cwPush is called when the key for the recpient process is not present **(a)**, cwPush is called when the key for the recipient process is already present **(b)**, the timeout for a key has been reached **(c)**, cwPush is called when the key for the recipient process is present and the data length amounts to qthresh **(d)**.

list that contains the pushed messages (Figure 1(a)). Message queues are stored in the map structure and the map structure stores key-value pairs. The value of each key-value pair is a reference to a separate queue for a specific destination process.

If at the time when a new message is pushed its key k is already a member of the PSQ, the new message is appended to the end of the queue that corresponds to k (Figure 1(b)). When the total amount of messages in a queue (the gross length of all messages) for a specific key-tuple exceeds a set threshold (qthresh) then the whole queue will be serialized and transmitted to the recipient (Figure 1(d)). In order to ensure that messages only stay in the queue for a short time, a timeout threshold is used. No matter whether the data threshold qthresh is reached or not, once the timeout threshold is reached, all the messages in the queue will be serialized and sent once the timeout threshold is reached (Figure 1(c)). The function sendAllTo from the Haskell library Network.Socket.ByteString is used to bring the

UDP datagrams onto the wire. The function sendAllTo guarantees that all data is successfully brought onto the wire and that there were no errors on the local network interface.

Since CMQ is implemented in a pure functional programming language (Haskell), and pure functional data types are immutable, updating a node by writing directly to memory is not supported. The actual appending operation (++), which appends a new message to the end of a queue, does not update the tail node by changing its pointer so that it points to the new added message node, but recreates recursively each node in the queue, so that instead of writing a small node and a pointer to memory, the function returns, a complete new queue with the newly-added message returns [33,34]. This operation takes O(n) time.

It is observed that, while the appending operation has time complexity O(n), adding a new message to the head of a queue, by consing (cons :) the new message node directly to the head of queue, takes O(1) time. So an alternative method for the appending operation is to add a new message node to the head of a queue instead of the tail. The queue created using such a method maintains a reverse ordering of a FIFO queue. Before transmission of a particular queue, a reverse operation is performed on the queue to reverse the queue back to its normal FIFO form. The reverse operation takes $O(n)$ time.

cwPush is implemented using two parallel threads, where thread1 enqueues messages and checks the total amount of messages; thread2 surveys whether the timeout for a particular queue is reached. By using time profiling (see section on Messaging passing performance) it was discovered that thread2 was very costly and could use up 70% of the CPU time. As a result, a function called thread-Delay was introduced to control and limit the maximum number of times that the PSQ is checked.

From the above discussion, we see that CMQ can be tuned using two parameters: qthresh (the maximum amount of messages in bytes allowed in the queue) and the timeout (the maximum waiting time a message stays in the queue before it is sent).

All map queries that are used in CMQ, including insertion and deletion, have a complexity of $O(\log n)$. A function called findMin is used to check the PSQ for any queues that have exceeded the timeout threshold. The findMin function is implemented with a complexity of $O(1)$, which is an attractive feature, considering it is one of the most frequently used functions.

An alternative design solution is to use a more conventional method. Such a method, instead of using a map data structure with a PSQ as pointer, uses a sequence [35] of tuples (creationtime, message-queue) with each sequence data structure being responsible for a specific destination of messages. However, this method does not scale well. Although it is possible to examine the right (viewR) and left (viewL) end of a sequence with $O(1)$ complexity, all sequence data structures require identification and organization, which will increase the complexity of queries and insertions to up to $O(n)$ time. Thus, this method becomes inefficient when the number of sequences become very large, which unfortunately is a common case in cloud or large scale computing environments. Aiming for better scalability, CMQ is implemented in a way such that the identification information is maintained in the key k that associates queues with their creation time (in the PSQ) and recipients with their specific queues (in the map). Using the identification information, the system can quickly identify the queue for a newly pushed message. Since all map related queries take $O(\log n)$ time and all PSQ related queries take $O(1)$ time, comparing with a sequence based solution, CMQ demonstrates a clear advantage in terms of its efficiency and scalability.

cwPop

On the recipient the serialized data structure with all its messages is received, deserialized, and transferred onto a transactional channel (TChan). TChan is an unbounded FIFO channel implemented in Software Transactional Memory (STM, [36]). Once the messages are transferred into TChan, they are ready to be consumed. The function cwPop is used to pop an individual message from the queue. cwPop is a non-blocking function that examines the TChan to check whether there are messages before attempting to read messages from the TChan. If there are waiting messages they are returned having the type Maybe String whereas in a blocking implementation the returned messages would have the type String. The Maybe type in Haskell represents optional values making e.g. null pointers obsolete. In this case a String can be present in the queue or the queue can be empty.

Whilst in Erlang processes communicate with each other via mailboxes that are identified by the PID of the mailbox owner, in Haskell the preferred method for inter-process communication (IPC) are transactional channels TChan. TChan is created whenever it is needed. It has no dedicated owner and is not associated with any identifiers or addressing scheme. As a consequence, TChan is created by the developer and its identifier needs to be propagated. There have been some attempts to add additional layers of abstraction to TChan to make it work similar to Erlang mailboxes (e.g., Epass [37]) and more applicable to actor-based approaches. The majority of the attempts that are actually working and publicly available work only in local environment. Thus, they cannot send messages to a remote TChan. CMQ removes this limitation by allowing messages to be transmitted to a remote TChan via a CMQ queue.

The use of cwPush and cwPop

Figures 2 and 3 give a simple example that demonstrates how cwPush and cwPop are used in a real application. Figure 2 shows an example of a sender application which sends 10000 messages each of which contains a 4-byte string. The message type can be any Haskell data type that is a member of the Haskell serialize class. The application developer specifies the UPD port number (here UDP port 4711) to create the socket for UDP data transport. Figure 3 shows the example of the receiving application that uses cwPop to retrieve messages.

Where is the queue?

There are two queues involved for every recipient process: the queue stored in the map on the sender and the TChan, which is in fact a simple STM-based FIFO queue on the remote recipient host. However, the detailed implementation is completely hidden from the users, who can see the CMQ message queueing system as a single distributed

```
{-# LANGUAGE OverloadedStrings #-}

import System.CMQ
import Network . Socket hiding (send , sendTo , recv , recvFrom)
import Control . Monad

main = withSocketsDo $ do
        qs <- socket AFINET Datagram default Protocol
        hostAddr <- inetaddr "192.168.35.84"
        bindSocket qs (SockAddrInet 4711 hostAddr)
        (token) <- newRq qs 512 200—initializes the queue with the desired parameters
        —qlength = 512B and max delay time in the queue is 200ms (minimum is 40ms)
        —token is the queue identifier where messages are sent to or poped off
        forM_ [0..10000] $ \i -> do
              cwPush qs ("192.168.35.69" , 0) ("ping" :: String) token —send message "ping" to
              —ipv4 address 192.168.35.69 using the queue specified in token
```

Figure 2 Example of a sending application that uses cwPush.

queue with two functions cwPush and cwPop. The function cwPush is called when a message is needed to be sent to a recipient, and the function cwPop is called when the recipient process reads a message.

Zero Copy vs Functional Data Structures

TCP and UDP sockets need to copy received data from kernel space to the user space and vice versa. iWARP and RoCE address this and use zero copy implementations where the kernel shares buffers with the application rather than copying the data. Although this is not directly addressed in CMQ, there are two interesting aspects worth noticing: first, system calls are expensive and thus the number of send operations (which are systems calls) should be kept to a minimum; secondly, copying data, even in user space without involvement of system calls, is also far from optimal. Instead of invoking a send system call each time when a message is sent, CMQ reduces the number of send system calls by storing messages temporarily in a queue and sending the stored messages when either the total size of messages in the queue meets the size threshold, or the waiting time of the current oldest message in the queue meets the timeout limit. Accordingly, the number of receive system calls on the receiving end is also reduced.

However, functional data structures are by definition immutable. When bindings in a Map or PSQ are inserted, deleted or modified, strictly speaking, the returned data structure is not the original data structure but a data structure that is identical with the previous data structure but containing the alteration. The Map and PSQ data structures used in CMQ are pure functional data structures that are immutable, so their insert, update and delete operations involve some degree of copying as opposed to typical mutable data structures where changes are written directly to the memory. To be more precise, a Map or PSQ insertion involves the copy of $O(\log n)$ amount of data for a data structure with n elements [38] plus some additional logarithmic overhead [39]. It remains to be shown by future research whether or not a pure lazy language (e.g., Haskell) and its data types can retain the same asymptotic memory use as an impure strict one (e.g., Erlang) in all situations. However, in return functional data structures make it easier to keep multiple modified versions of the same data structure without storing whole copies.

By reducing the number of send and receive system calls, the data copying between kernel and user space is also reduced. Pure functional data structures may on the one hand be a slight drawback in terms of performance, but on the other hand give low cost access to data that needs to be replayed.

```
import System.CMQ
import Network.Socket hiding (send , sendTo , recv , recvFrom)
import Control.Monad
import Data.Maybe

main = withSocketsDo $ do
        qs <- socket AF_INET Datagram defaultProtocol
        hostAddr <- inet_addr "192.168.35.69"
        bindSocket qs (SockAddrInet 4711 hostAddr)
        token <- newRq qs 512 200
        forever $ do
            msg <- cwPop token :: IO (Maybe String)
            print msg
```

Figure 3 Example of a receiving application that uses cwPop.

UDP as a message passing paradigm

The Haskell benchmarking library Criterion [40] is used for all the tests and a garbage collection was performed after every test. The CMQ testbed was setup in a client-server model where at first the client and the server would alternately send and receive messages similar to the ping pong test of the INTEL MPI benchmarks (IMB) [41]. In order to investigate the benefits of asynchronous message exchange (fire-and-forget messaging) and queuing, CMQ itself was allowed to use asynchronous non-blocking send operations (which means CMQ was allowed to send the next message before a reply to the previous message had been received) similar to the IMB ping ping test.

The testbed consisted of a cloudstack [42] POD implemented on data centre grade hardware (listed in Table 1) analogous to commercial computing clouds. Figure 4 shows a logical diagram of two cloud computing nodes from our POD. The guest virtual machines (VMs) used for CMQ testing were resident on two separate computing nodes. Direct networking based on VLAN tagging is configured between the VMs and the physical networking gear. The VMs on our POD communicate via VLAN ID 2012, which is part of a VLAN trunk terminated on the computing nodes. The cloudstack (CS) virtual router is used to provide DHCP functionality and provide IP addressing to the VMs but, in this configuration, does not actually take part in routing and forwarding of packets.

The code that was used for benchmarking is published on github.com and is available at https://github.com/viloocity/Haskell-IPC-Benchmarks.

Message passing performance
MessagePack and 0MQ
Rather than doing strictly competitive benchmarks, it would be more beneficial to investigate and compare several paradigms. For this reason, MessagePack [43] and 0MQ [44] are chosen in the CMQ performance evaluation. MessagePack and 0MQ are two IPC systems that provide Haskell bindings. MessagePack is a library that is based on RPC and focuses on object serialization. 0MQ provides a framework that focuses solely on message passing and queuing.

MessagePack uses RPC to transfer messages which in fact are all serialized objects, and was initially described as IPC to "pass serialized objects across network connections" [45]. Although the most recent descriptions of MessagePack focus mainly on its outstanding object serialization capabilities, it serves also as a general message passing mechanism. Since every message has to be serialized before it is sent, providing an effective serialization method is one of the major concerns involving message passing.

In CMQ a message queue that consists of multiple messages is serialized before it is sent. The messages used in the tests are composed of only 8-bit ASCII characters and the Haskell library Data.Bytestring.Char8 is used

for the serialization. For messages or objects with other character encodings, the Haskell Data.Bytestring library or even MessagePack may be used for the serialization[f].

Mean performance
Figure 5 presents the mean performance of UDP Sockets, MessagePack, 0MQ and CMQ for exchanging 1000 messages with message sizes between 4 B and 16 KB. UDP Sockets are not included in Figure 6 for the reason that the benchmarking application used for UDP sockets supports only synchronous operations in lossless environments. The test results show that when message sizes are less than 1 KB UDP sockets perform comparable to TCP-based messaging queues; when message sizes are larger than 1 KB, UDP sockets outperform all tested TCP queuing methods. As for CMQ, it, in general, outperforms all other messaging queuing methods. CMQ demonstrates a clear advantage for small to medium sized messages up to 4KB. It shows a speed increase of up to 100 times for the transmission of small messages such as integers (e.g. error codes), flags or applications that need only a single request - response [46], since TCP messaging requires the establishment of a TCP connection which would incur a 60% overhead for a small sized message. From the tests it was discovered that CMQ achieves its best performance with a qthresh of 512 B (a value that is also used by the DNS protocol) and a queue timeout threshold of 200ms.

Performance in the presence of errors
TCP is a reliable protocol that provides reliable, connection-oriented delivery of data. It detects for example packet loss, delay, congestion and replays lost packets when required. However, the reliability causes a significant overhead, especially for messages of small sizes. This is one of the disadvantages of using TCP. More seriously, when delay or packet loss are detected, TCP assumes congestion and slows down the rate of outgoing data [46-48] propose formulae to calculate the effective bandwidth of TCP connections in the presence of errors where, for example, a 0.2% packet loss eventually slows down and limits the effective connection speed to 52.2 Mbps irrespective of the nominal bandwidth. In practice, retransmitting packets is very costly since it also involves queuing and reordering packets that arrive until the retransmit is complete, thus stopping time-sensitive data

Table 1 CMQ testbed setup

	Hardware	Software
2 Server	HP DL 580 G5 4 quad core Intel Xeon E5450 @ 3GHz 32GB RAM	Citrix XEN 5.6
2 Linux VMS on separate XEN Server	ARCH Linux 2011.8, Haskell GHC 7.0.4	2 vCPUs @ 2GHz 4GB RAM
2 Fabric extenders	Cisco Nexus 2248TP-E	
1 Core switch	Cisco Nexus 7000	NXOS 5.1(2)

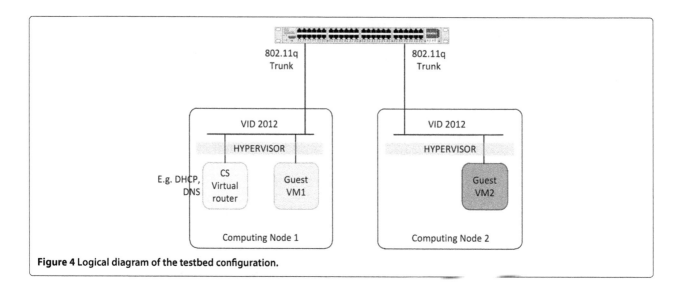

Figure 4 Logical diagram of the testbed configuration.

from going through in the meantime [49]. Furthermore CPU usage spikes when TCP retransmissions are needed and applications frequently become unresponsive.

In the CMQ testbed, where we test CMQ in the presence of data loss, in order to simulate packet data loss, iptables [50] (see command listed below) is used on one of the Linux VMs to drop incoming packets with 1.4% probability:

iptables -A INPUT -m statistic –mode random –probability 0.014 -j DROP

and it was found that CMQ is largely unaffected and produces the same performance results (within the standard deviations) as if there were no errors on the network. All other benchmarked queuing methods show an overall delay of approximately a factor of 4. It was also discovered that in the presence of errors the benchmark results

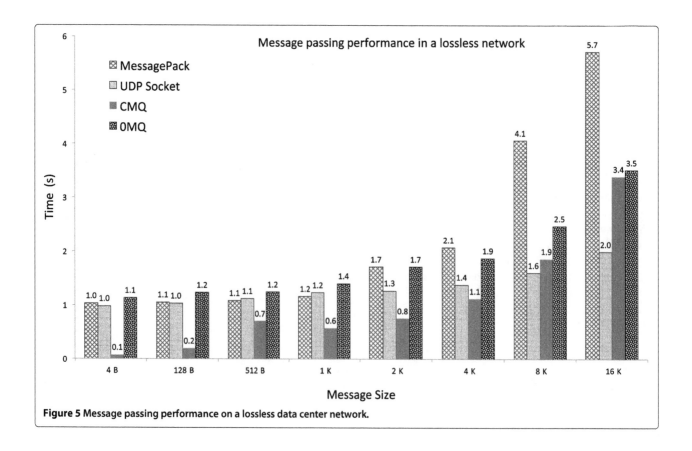

Figure 5 Message passing performance on a lossless data center network.

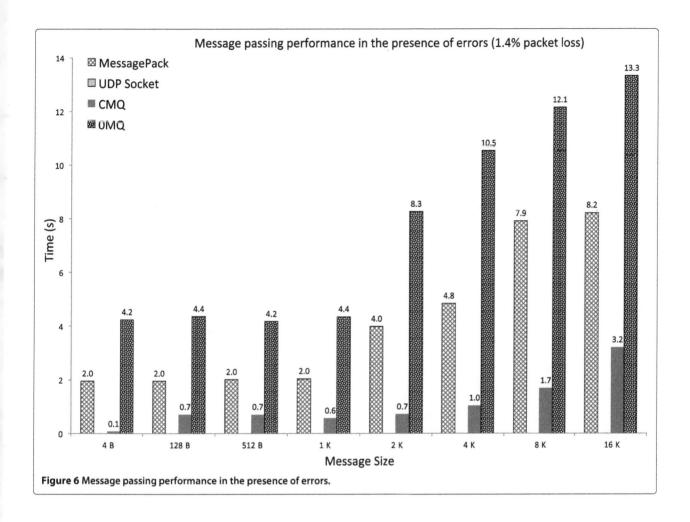

Figure 6 Message passing performance in the presence of errors.

of CMQ still show a narrow standard deviation. For example, for a message of 512 Bytes, the standard deviation of CMQ stayed at 52 ms whilst the standard deviation of MessagePack increased from 54 ms (with no simulated data loss) to 820 ms.

CMQ scalability at large

Birman and Chockler [1] state that currently "Not enough is known about stability of large-scale event notification platforms, management technologies, or other cloud computing solutions" and identifies the development of testing methods that can validate the relevance and demonstrate the scalability of any new solution "... without working at some company [e.g. Yahoo, Google, Amazon] that operates a massive but proprietary infrastructure" as an item on the cloud computing research agenda.

In the absence of established "cloud scale" testing methods, conventional tests and checks were used to examine CMQ and to demonstrate that nothing obvious is limiting its scalability:

- Haskell Program Coverage (HPC) [51] was used to determine which areas of the source code and boolean controls were actually exposed to testing.
- Space (Heap) Profiling was used to investigate whether any cost centre of the application may consume too much memory because of excessive laziness (also called "space leak"). Time profiling was used to identify functions that are possible CPU hogs.
- The criterion test suite was used to do the actual testing and produce additional data about the accuracy and repeatability of tests.

Although the areas of code that executed are dependent on the parameter settings for timeout and qthresh, overall all areas of code were exposed to the testing. The heap profile Figure 7 showed that the memory consumption of 80K is very moderate and we find that the memory consumption related to serialization cost (the band labelled as "PINNED") is the most prominent feature. Although for the performance tests we send messages composed of 8-bit ASCII characters, CMQ is internally built with poly-

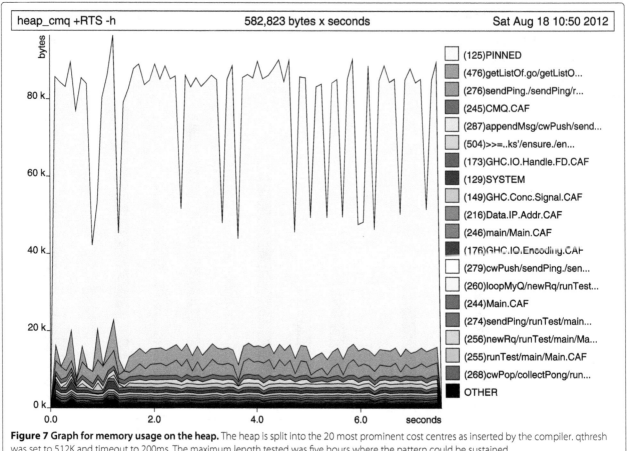

Figure 7 Graph for memory usage on the heap. The heap is split into the 20 most prominent cost centres as inserted by the compiler. qthresh was set to 512K and timeout to 200ms. The maximum length tested was five hours where the pattern could be sustained.

morphic functions and can transfer arbitrary Haskell Data Types under the condition that they can be serialized. In order to achieve polymorphism, CMQ must compare the queue length to qthresh when the queue is serialized, since functions that can determine the length of an ASCII based queue do not fire any more under these circumstances. Thus, more serialization activities are necessary compared to an implementation that would be limited to the data type String. Overall, there was no evidence of space leaks.

In the time profile we observe that half of the time is consumed in the benchmarking application that pops the ping messages from the queue after they have been received - this is a wrapper application for the non-blocking cwPop function. Having cwPop non-blocking, in the performance testing application amounts to using a continuous loop to pop incoming messages from the queue as they arrive. It seems natural to ask whether this overhead could be reduced. However, the key is that CMQ is architected in depth to retain "the core principle of [cloud]scale: decoupling" and avoid even minor blocking operations [1]. Whilst in our testing application this feature might not appear to be an advantage, we

are convinced that asynchronous operation is required in large scale computing clouds.

Based on the findings above, we conclude that nothing is hindering the scalability of CMQ.

Message passing strategies.
Replace vs Replay
Although message loss is very rare in switched data center networks (no message loss is detected in our testbed), the question of how to deal with message loss is always present. Although in switched data center networks it is unlikely that packets are lost in transit, there are still conditions existing where UDP packets will be discarded, for example, the exhaustion of the internal buffers or (un)-bounded message queues.

When using IPC that is based on UDP, the application needs to detect lost or partially ordered messages and, if required, will need to deal with it. One possibility is to replace lost messages rather than to replay them. This paradigm requires the application to replace a lost packet if necessary with either a message with the same data or with new data. The application would need to resubmit it to CMQ where it gets queued and delivered as every other new message without holding up any time critical messages that need to be sent at the same time.

Request - Response

(RR) message exchange patterns (MEP), for example as described in the OASIS SOAP over UDP standard [52], are an application-level means to detect packet loss and to act on it. Using this paradigm the application would maintain its own store to record sent requests and wait for a matching answer before a predefined timeout occurs. If a response is received the store is updated; if no response is received and the timeout is met, either the request is resent or the user is alerted of a failure. However, already the SOAP envelope that wraps the actual message is approximately 512 B in size, thus making SOAP envelopes less effective for smaller message sizes.

Multicast IPC

The publish/subscriber paradigm, where subscribers are notified when a message that is interesting to them has arrived, is a very popular means to achieve asynchronous message passing communication, although the underlying protocols (e.g. TCP or RPC) are strictly synchronous. Using conventional message queues, asynchronous communication is usually supported by a broker to decouple the sender and receiver and by maintaining publish/subscriber channels. However, because of the inherent asynchronous nature of CMQ, Multicast Messaging is easily supported without the need to maintain publish/subscriber channels and additional infrastructure for the broker.

Use cases for multicast IPC are connectionless servers that propagate information to the (local) network [53] e.g. simultaneous updates of databases (replication), the propagation of intermediate results in grids, multiplayer games or realtime news [54]. Multicast messaging has also been found applicable to Map Reduce where it can be used to propagate tasks and results [55].

To illustrate, conventional message queues are frequently deployed to enable parallelism by using a broker to decouple the sender and receiver. The publish/subscriber paradigm where subscribers are notified when a message that is interesting to them has arrived is a very popular means to achieve asynchronous message passing communication although the underlying protocols (e.g. TCP or RPC) are strictly synchronous. CMQ instead is inherently asynchronous and offers multicast Messaging without the need to maintain publish/subscriber channels.

Future type message passing

As described by [56], is a further message passing strategy that fits the nature of CMQ. Future Type Message Passing utilizes future objects that should behave like a queue similar to TChan. Analogue to concurrent programming with explicit futures [57], the future object is looked at by the time it is required. In case of CMQ, if cwPop returns Nothing by the time the result is required, the original message might be lost, and accordingly, the recipient process may have become unavailable or may have failed, and thus trigger some remedial action. The remedial action can be either replacing the missing message, re-sending it with a new future, or restarting the receiving process. A future object can be either a result of computation represented by an actor or as simple as a flag such as received? With CMQ, Future Type Message Passing can be easily implemented using the primitive newRq that creates a queue and a TChan where the TChan is subsequently used to represent the future message.

Conclusion and future work

CMQ is a lightweight message queue in Haskell. The concept to use UDP instead of TCP is motivated by our understanding that, in Cloud Computing, omnipresent off-the-shelf technologies (both in hard- and software) are encouraged, and if preventing errors from occurring becomes too costly, dealing with the errors may be a better solution. This paper has demonstrated the capability of using UDP for message queuing in the presence of errors, and has shown the stability of UDP messaging in such conditions. Methods that deal with packet loss at the application level are also discussed. The implementation of CMQ is a Haskell Module that utilizes pure functional data structures. The implementation of CMQ is available as module System.CMQ from the hackageDB at http://hackage.haskell.org/packages/hackage.html, and also it can be installed automatically via the Haskell package manager cabal on every Haskell Platform.

Although CMQ is a message queue oriented communication approach, CMQ is different than the conventional MOM approach because it challenges a number of assumptions under which conventional MOM is built. For instance, in conventional MOM, messages are "always" delivered, routed, queued and frequently follow the publish/subscriber paradigm. It is often accepted that this requires an additional layer of infrastructure and software where logic is split form the application and configured in the additional layer. On the contrary, CMQ does just enough. It does not offer guarantees, thus is very light weight with low overhead and fast speed. Although it does not offer guarantees, it appears to be stable in the presence of errors.

CMQ is a starting point for future research on distributed applications. It will serve as a message queuing mechanism for a lightweight cloud computing framework named CWMWL that we are currently developing. One of the main goals of CMQ is to make the use of pervasive asynchronous parallelism easy and with minimal effort. Furthermore, we are also interested in developing an optional reliability layer that supports reliable virtual connections, protocol-driven and/or application driven security mechanisms, and "persistent" templates for workloads that pre-distributes code and data to the target systems to enhance the performance and reduce the run-time distribution cost.

Endnotes

[a] physical unit of scale in a cloud, e.g. a standardized rack of interconnected servers

[b] e.g. IEEE 802.3 × PAUSE frames or vendor specific technologies

[c] IPv6 would be 40 bytes

[d] IEEE 802.1Qbg

[e] NFSv4 preserves state and is no longer built to deal with packet loss, thus requires the TCP protocol.

[f] An interesting detour would be to investigate whether MessagePack can better support
serialization of arbitrary functions and closures in order to transmit data, code and state over the wire.

Competing interests

The authors declare that they have no competing interests.

Author's contributions

JF had the initial vision of CMQ as part of an inherently asynchronous cloud computing framework that would follow the overall notion of remediating error rather than preventing it. Joerg Fritsch developed the Haskell code, carried out the laboratory experiments and wrote the first draft version of the paper. CW As the co-author of the paper, Dr. Walker contributed actively to the concept of the CMQ system, as well as providing guidance and support to the implementation of the system. She played a critical role in revising the draft manuscript and in ensuring a high standard of presentation. Both authors read and approved the final manuscript.

Author details

[1] NATO CI Agency, Den Haag, Netherlands. [2] School of Computer Science and Informatics, Cardiff University, Queen's Buildings, 5 The Parade, Roath, Cardiff CF24 3AA, UK.

References

1. Birman K, Chockler G, van Renesse R (2009) Toward a cloud computing research agenda. SIGACT News 40(2): 68–80. http://doi.acm.org/10.1145/1556154.1556172
2. Rashti M, Grant R, Afsahi A, Balaji P (2010) iwarp redefined: Scalable connectionless communication over high-speed ethernet. In: High Performance Computing (HiPC), 2010 International Conference on. pp 1–10
3. Feng W, Balaji P, Baron C, Bhuyan L, Panda D (2005) Performance characterization of a 10-gigabit ethernet toe. In: High Performance Interconnects, 2005. Proceedings. 13th Symposium on. pp 58–63
4. Regnier G, Makineni S, Illikkal I, Iyer R, Minturn D, Huggahalli R, Newell D, Cline L, Foong A (2004) TCP onloading for data center servers. Computer 37(11): 48–58
5. Barroso L, Dean J, Holzle U (2003) Web search for a planet: The Google cluster architecture. IEEE Micro 23(2): 22–28
6. Vogels W (2008) Keynote: Uncertainty, The Next Web Conference. https://vimeo.com/1386054. Accessed Oct 2012
7. Wang GWG, Ng T (2010) The Impact of Virtualization on Network Performance of Amazon EC2 Data Center. In: IEEE INFOCOM. Proceedings. pp 1–9, Mar. 2010
8. Uusitalo MA (2006) Global vision for the future wireless world from the wwrf. Vehicular Technol Mag, IEEE 1(2): 4–8
9. Wu C-C, Chen K-T, Chen C-M, Huang P, Lei C-L (2009) On the challenge and design of transport protocols for MMORPGs. Multimedia Tools and Appl 45(1-3): 7–32
10. Networking for Game Programmers. http://gafferongames.com/networking-for-game-programmers/. Accessed May 2012
11. Sung M (2010) From Cloud Computing To Cloud Computing. Network and Syst Support for Games (NetGames) 9th Annual Workshop: 1–48
12. Marzolla M, Ferretti S, D'Angelo G (2010) Dynamic scalability for next generation gaming infrastructures. Proc. 4th ACM/ICST Int Conference on Simul Tools and Techn (SIMUTools 2011): 1–8
13. Nae V, Prodan R, Fahringer T, Iosup A (2009) The impact of virtualization on the performance of Massively Multiplayer Online Games. Network and Systems Support for Games (NetGames), 2009 8th Annual Workshop on: 1–6
14. Henning M (2004) Massively multiplayer middleware. Queue 1(10): 38
15. Waldo J, Wyant G, Wollrath A, Kendall S (1997) A note on distributed computing. In: J. Vitek and C. Tschudin (eds) Mobile Object Systems Towards the Programmable Internet, ser. Lecture Notes in Computer Science. vol. 1222. Springer, Berlin / Heidelberg, pp 49–64
16. Gu Y, Grossman R (2007) UDT: UDP-based data transfer for high-speed wide area networks. Comput Networks 51(7): 1777–1799
17. Ren Y, Tang H, Li J, Qian H (2009) Performance comparison of UDP-based protocols over fast long distance network. Inf Technol J 8(4): 600–604
18. Hewitt C (2010) Actor model for discretionary, adaptive concurrency. CoRR abs/1008.1459
19. Agha G (1986) Actors: A Model of Concurrent Computation in Distributed Systems (Mit Press Series in Artificial Intelligence). The MIT Press, Cambridge, Massachusetts
20. Hewitt C (1977) Viewing control structures as patterns of passing messages. Artif Intelligence 8(3): 323–364. http://www.sciencedirect.com/science/article/pii/0004370277900339
21. Armstrong J, Virding R, Williams M (1993) Concurrent Programming in Erlang. Prentice Hall, Englewood Clics, N.J.
22. Akka (toolkit and runtime for building highly concurrent, distributed and fault tolerant event-driven applications on the jvm). http://akka.io Accessed May 2012
23. Light Weight Event System. http://www.lwes.org/ Accessed May 2012
24. Bialecki A, Cafarella M, Cutting D (2012) Hadoop: a framework for running applications on large clusters built of commodity hardware. http://wiki.apache.org/hadoop/. Accessed May 2012
25. Dean J, Ghemawat S (2008) Mapreduce: simplified data processing on large clusters. Commun ACM 51(1): 107–113. http://doi.acm.org/10.1145/1327452.1327492
26. Foster I, Zhao Y, Raicu I, Lu S (2008) Cloud computing and grid computing 360-degree compared. In: Grid Computing Environments Workshop, 2008. GCE '08. pp 1–10
27. Programming Language Popularity. http://www.langpop.com. Accessed May 2012
28. Marlow S (2012) Parallel and concurrent programming in haskell. In: Central European Functional Programming School, ser. Lecture Notes in Computer Science. vol. 7241. Springer, Berlin / Heidelberg, pp 339–401
29. Peyton-Jones S (2011) Parallel = Functional - The way of the future. http://research.microsoft.com/en-us/people/simonpj/. Accessed Oct 2012
30. Epstein J, Black AP, Peyton-Jones S (2011) Towards haskell in the cloud. In: Proceedings of the 4th ACM symposium on Haskell, ser. Haskell. ACM, New York, NY, USA, pp 118–129. http://doi.acm.org/10.1145/2034675.2034690
31. Coutts D (2012) Cloud Haskell. In: Fun in The Afternoon, FITA. Well-Typed LLP, Oxford
32. Hinze R (2001) A simple implementation technique for priority search queues. In: Proceedings of the sixth ACM SIGPLAN international conference on Functional programming, ser. ICFP '01. ACM, New York, NY, USA, pp 110–121. http://doi.acm.org/10.1145/507635.507650
33. Stackoverflow. http://stackoverflow.com/questions/1435359/why-can-you-only-prepend-to-lists-in-functional-languages. Accessed May 2012
34. Lipovača M (2011) Learn You a Haskell for Great Good!, ser. A Beginner's Guide. No Starch Pr, San Francisco
35. Data.Sequence. http://hackage.haskell.org/packages/archive/containers/0.4.2.1/doc/html/Data-Sequence.html. Accessed May 2012

36. Harris T, Marlow S, Jones SP, Herlihy M (2008) Composable memory transactions. Commun ACM 51(8): 91–100. http://doi.acm.org/10.1145/1378704.1378725
37. The epass package. http://hackage.haskell.org/package/epass. Accessed May 2012
38. Okasaki C (1999) Purely Functional Data Structures. Cambridge Univ Pr, Cambridge
39. Bird R, Jones G, De Moor O (1997) More haste, less speed: lazy versus eager evaluation. J Funct Programming 7(05): 541–547
40. O'Sullivan B The criterion package. http://hackage.haskell.org/package/criterion. Accessed May 2012
41. INTEL GmbH (2006) Intel® MPI Benchmarks, Users Guide and Methodology Description. Germany
42. cloudstack. http://cloudstack.org. Accessed May 2012
43. MessagePack. http://msgpack.org/ Accessed May 2012
44. 0MQ. http://www.zeromq.org/. Accessed May 2012
45. MessagePack Blog. http://msgpack.wordpress.com/. Accessed May 2012
46. Pessach Y (2006) UDP DELIVERS: take total control of your networking with .NET And UDP. Microsoft MSDN Mag: 56–65
47. Mathis M, Semke J, Mahdavi J, Ott T (1997) The macroscopic behavior of the TCP congestion avoidance algorithm. ACM SIGCOMM Comput Commun Rev 27(3): 67–82
48. Seveik P, Wetzel R (2008) Improving Effective WAN Throughput for Large Data Flows, NetForecast Report 5095. pp 1–8. http://www.netforecast.com/reports/
49. Fiedler G Reliability and Flow Control. http://gafferongames.com/networking-for-game-programmers/reliability-and-flow-control/. Accessed May 2012
50. The netfilter.org project. http://www.netfilter.org/. Accessed May 2012
51. Gill A, Runciman C (2007) Haskell program coverage. In: Proceedings of the ACM SIGPLAN workshop on Haskell workshop, ser. Haskell '07. ACM, New York, pp 1–12. http://doi.acm.org/10.1145/1291201.1291203
52. Jeyaraman R (2009) Soap-over-udp version 1.1. OASIS WS-DD TC
53. Leffler S, Fabry R, Joy W, Lapsley P, Miller S, Torek C (1986) An advanced 4.3 BSD interprocess communication tutorial. University of California, Berkeley, California
54. Larrabeiti D (2002) Multicast in IPv6, Global IPv6 Summit 2002. http://www.ipv6-es.com/02/docs/david_larrabeiti.pdf. Accessed May 2012
55. Lee K, Boykin DPO, Figueiredo DRJ (2009) Multicast Tree Map-Reduce: Self-organizing Resource Discovery and Monitoring using Structured P2P Systems. In: NSF CAC Semiannual Meeting. University of Florida
56. Romanovsky A, Xu J, Randell B (1998) Exception handling in object-oriented real-time distributed systems. Object-Oriented Real-time Distributed Computing, 1998.(ISORC 98) Proceedings. 1998 First International Symposium on. pp 32–42
57. Sabel D, Schmidt-Schauß M (2011) A contextual semantics for concurrent haskell with futures. In: Proceedings of the 13th international ACM SIGPLAN symposium on Principles and practices of declarative programming, ser. PPDP '11. ACM, New York, pp. 101–112. http://doi.acm.org/10.1145/2003476.2003492

Permissions

The contributors of this book come from diverse backgrounds, making this book a truly international effort. This book will bring forth new frontiers with its revolutionizing research information and detailed analysis of the nascent developments around the world.

We would like to thank all the contributing authors for lending their expertise to make the book truly unique. They have played a crucial role in the development of this book. Without their invaluable contributions this book wouldn't have been possible. They have made vital efforts to compile up to date information on the varied aspects of this subject to make this book a valuable addition to the collection of many professionals and students.

This book was conceptualized with the vision of imparting up-to-date information and advanced data in this field. To ensure the same, a matchless editorial board was set up. Every individual on the board went through rigorous rounds of assessment to prove their worth. After which they invested a large part of their time researching and compiling the most relevant data for our readers.

The editorial board has been involved in producing this book since its inception. They have spent rigorous hours researching and exploring the diverse topics which have resulted in the successful publishing of this book. They have passed on their knowledge of decades through this book. To expedite this challenging task, the publisher supported the team at every step. A small team of assistant editors was also appointed to further simplify the editing procedure and attain best results for the readers.

Apart from the editorial board, the designing team has also invested a significant amount of their time in understanding the subject and creating the most relevant covers. They scrutinized every image to scout for the most suitable representation of the subject and create an appropriate cover for the book.

The publishing team has been an ardent support to the editorial, designing and production team. Their endless efforts to recruit the best for this project, has resulted in the accomplishment of this book. They are a veteran in the field of academics and their pool of knowledge is as vast as their experience in printing. Their expertise and guidance has proved useful at every step. Their uncompromising quality standards have made this book an exceptional effort. Their encouragement from time to time has been an inspiration for everyone.

The publisher and the editorial board hope that this book will prove to be a valuable piece of knowledge for researchers, students, practitioners and scholars across the globe.

List of Contributors

Vassilis Glenis
School of Civil Engineering and Geosciences, Newcastle University, Newcastle upon Tyne, UK

Andrew Stephen McGough
School of Computing Science, Newcastle University, Newcastle upon Tyne, UK

Vedrana Kutija
School of Civil Engineering and Geosciences, Newcastle University, Newcastle upon Tyne, UK

Chris Kilsby
School of Civil Engineering and Geosciences, Newcastle University, Newcastle upon Tyne, UK

Simon Woodman
School of Computing Science, Newcastle University, Newcastle upon Tyne, UK

Simon Waddington
Centre for e-Research, King's College London, 26-29 Drury Lane, London WC2B 5RL, UK

Jun Zhang
Centre for e-Research, King's College London, 26-29 Drury Lane, London WC2B 5RL, UK

Gareth Knight
Centre for e-Research, King's College London, 26-29 Drury Lane, London WC2B 5RL, UK

Jens Jensen
Science and Technology Facilities Council, Harwell Oxford Campus, Oxon OX11 0QX, UK

Roger Downing
Science and Technology Facilities Council, Harwell Oxford Campus, Oxon OX11 0QX, UK

Cheney Ketley
Science and Technology Facilities Council, Harwell Oxford Campus, Oxon OX11 0QX, UK

Soguy Mak karé Gueye
ERODS Team - Bât. IMAG C, 220 rue de la Chimie, 38 400 St Martin d'Hères, France

Noël De Palma
ERODS Team - Bât. IMAG C, 220 rue de la Chimie, 38 400 St Martin d'Hères, France

Eric Rutten
INRIA Grenoble - Rhône-Alpes, 655, avenue de l'Europe, Montbonnot 38334 St-Ismier cedex, France

Alain Tchana
ERODS Team - Bât. IMAG C, 220 rue de la Chimie, 38 400 St Martin d'Hères, France

Daniel Hagimont
IRIT/ENSEEIHT, 2 rue Charles Camichel – BP 7122, 31071 Toulouse cedex 7, France

Thomas Ludescher
Fachhochschule Vorarlberg, University of Applied Sciences, Hochschulstrasse 1, 6850 Dornbirn, Austria

Thomas Feilhauer
Fachhochschule Vorarlberg, University of Applied Sciences, Hochschulstrasse 1, 6850 Dornbirn, Austria

Peter Brezany
Research Group Scientific Computing, Faculty of Computer Science, University of Vienna, Waehringer StraSSe 29, A-1090 Vienna, Austria

Lena Wiese
Institute of Computer Science, Georg-August-Universität Göttingen, Goldschmidtstraße 7, Göttingen, Germany

Ibrahim K Musa
School of Computer Science and Electronic Engineering, University of Essex, Wivenhoe Park, Colchester CO4 3SQ, Essex, UK

Stuart D Walker
School of Computer Science and Electronic Engineering, University of Essex, Wivenhoe Park, Colchester CO4 3SQ, Essex, UK

Anne M Owen
Department of Mathematical Sciences and Biological Sciences, University of Essex, Wivenhoe Park, Colchester CO4 3SQ, Essex, UK

Andrew P Harrison
Department of Mathematical Sciences and Biological Sciences, University of Essex, Wivenhoe Park, Colchester CO4 3SQ, Essex, UK

Gabriel Loewen
Department of Computer Science, The University of Alabama, Tuscaloosa, AL, USA

Jeffrey Galloway
Department of Computer Science, The University of Alabama, Tuscaloosa, AL, USA

Jeffrey Robinson
Department of Computer Science, The University of Alabama, Tuscaloosa, AL, USA

Xiaoyan Hong
Department of Computer Science, The University of Alabama, Tuscaloosa, AL, USA

Susan Vrbsky
Department of Computer Science, The University of Alabama, Tuscaloosa, AL, USA

Ran Jin
College of Information Science and Technology, Donghua University, Shanghai, P.R.C
School of Computer Science and Information Technology, Zhejiang Wanli University, Ningbo, P.R.C

Chunhai Kou
College of Information Science and Technology, Donghua University, Shanghai, P.R.C

Ruijuan Liu
College of Information Science and Technology, Donghua University, Shanghai, P.R.C

Yefeng Li
College of Information Science and Technology, Donghua University, Shanghai, P.R.C

Yoji Yamato
NTT Software Innovation Center, NTT Corporation, 3-9-11 Midori-cho, Musashino-shi 180-8585, Japan

Rustem Dautov
South-East European Research Centre, International Faculty of the University of Sheffield, City College, 24 Proxenou Koromila Street, 54646 Thessaloniki, Greece

Iraklis Paraskakis
South-East European Research Centre, International Faculty of the University of Sheffield, City College, 24 Proxenou Koromila Street, 54646 Thessaloniki, Greece

Mike Stannett
Department of Computer Science, University of Sheffield, Regent Court, 211 Portobello Street, S1 4DP Sheffield, UK

Maximilian Hoecker
Karlsruhe Institute of Technologie (KIT), Karlsruhe, Germany

Marcel Kunze
Karlsruhe Institute of Technologie (KIT), Karlsruhe, Germany

Sylvain Hallé
Laboratoire d'informatique formelle, Département d'informatique et de mathématique, Université du Québec à Chicoutimi, Chicoutimi (Québec) G7H 2B1, Canada

Maxime Soucy-Boivin
Laboratoire d'informatique formelle, Département d'informatique et de mathématique, Université du Québec à Chicoutimi, Chicoutimi (Québec) G7H 2B1, Canada

Thomas H Beach
School of Engineering, Cardiff University, 5 The Parade, Roath, Cardiff, UK

Omer F Rana
School of Computer Science & Informatics, Cardiff University, 5 The Parade, Roath, Cardiff, UK

Yacine Rezgui
School of Engineering, Cardiff University, 5 The Parade, Roath, Cardiff, UK

Manish Parashar
RDI2/CAC/Dept. of Electrical & Computer Engineering, Rutgers University, Piscataway, NJ 08854-8058, USA

Printed in the USA
CPSIA information can be obtained
at www.ICGtesting.com
JSHW051437221024
72173JS00006B/1499

9 781682 850992